third edition

CREATIVE DRAMA FOR THE CLASSROOM TEACHER

RUTH BEALL HEINIG
Western Michigan University

Prentice Hall, Englewood Cliffs, New Jersey 07632

Library of Congress Cataloging-in-Publication Data

Heinig, Ruth Beall.
   Creative drama for the classroom teacher.

   Bibliography.
   Includes index.
   1. Drama in education.   I. Title.
PN3171.H33 1988   372.6'6   87-7237
ISBN 0-13-189424-2

Editorial/production supervision and
   interior design: *Marjorie Borden Shustak*
Cover design: *Amy Scerbo*
Manufacturing buyer: *Ed O'Dougherty*

The first edition of this text was coauthored with Lyda Stillwell.

Printed in the United States of America

10 9 8 7 6 5 4 3 2 1

ISBN   0-13-189424-2   01

Prentice-Hall International (UK) Limited, *London*
Prentice-Hall of Australia Pty. Limited, *Sydney*
Prentice-Hall Canada Inc., *Toronto*
Prentice-Hall Hispanoamericana, S.A., *Mexico*
Prentice-Hall of India Private Limited, *New Delhi*
Prentice-Hall of Japan, Inc., *Tokyo*
Simon & Schuster Asia Pte. Ltd., *Singapore*
Editora Prentice-Hall do Brasil, Ltda., *Rio de Janeiro*

To my loving and understanding parents

and

to my dear husband, who is also my best friend.

Contents

Preface

Time passes, and we grow and change. As obvious as that statement is, it becomes even more graphic to me as I look at the picture of the child on page 33—who appeared in the two previous editions of this text—and on page 117 (bottom left), as she looked this past year as a college student in my drama class. "Recognizable and yet changed" is the way I hope readers of the past two editions will see this third edition. While it has grown and changed considerably, I trust that it is still recognizable and easy to be reacquainted with.

The text continues to grow out of our creative drama classes at Western Michigan University. For over 20 years, we have had demonstration classes from local elementary schools bused to our campus so that our college students can observe classes taught live. At the end of the semester course, students are placed in teaching pairs in classrooms or other settings for a practicum experience. Both pre-service and in-service teachers, as well as students from a variety of other fields, including special education, theatre, psychology, and recreation, are able to take the course. The practicum takes place in elementary classrooms of all types, including alternative, developmental, mainstreamed, special education, and bilingual. In addition, nursery schools, day care centers, libraries, churches, and recreational centers have also been utilized. My constant interaction with children, college students, and teachers in the field has encouraged me to continually develop and modify ideas and techniques, searching for better ways to introduce the art of creative drama to elementary-aged children.

This book is directed at the novice from any field who is interested in teaching creative drama and who needs practical advice on how to begin. Its aim is to guide students through a step-by-step explanation of a number of activities, ranging from the simple to the more complex. This does not mean that the reader must try each type of activity before proceeding to the next. One might wish, for example, to begin with the verbal activities in Chapter 8 or the circle stories in Chapter 10. This is possible with the cross references provided. Ultimately, leaders are encouraged to develop a personal approach and to create activities geared to meet the needs and interests of their own groups, no matter what the age or the setting.

I have continued to focus on materials and methods for teaching drama rather than on discussing various theories, other teaching approaches, history of the field, and so forth. Over the years, increasing numbers of teachers have become aware of creative drama from a variety of sources. Many have their own particular goals and objectives in mind and are usually eager to start with techniques and ideas that work. This purpose, which Lyda Stillwell and I had in mind with the first edition, I have continued to carry out.

Readers of the previous editions will note a number of changes. Many of these changes were first introduced in my two teacher resource books written for the state of Texas. (See *Creative Drama Resource Book Kindergarten Through Grade Three* and *Creative Drama Resource Book for Grades Four Through Six*, Prentice-Hall, 1987.) In this third edition, Chapter 2, "Creative Drama Instruction: Some Basics," is partially a new chapter. It introduces students to teaching goals and to a new way of determining level of difficulty in drama activities through an analysis of what I call "drama activity variables." Chapter 2 also includes a discussion of concentration and involvement, the substance of old Chapter 5. Chapter 3, now titled "Working in Groups," is a partial revision of old Chapter 13 and adds a discussion of children with special needs. Chapter 8, "Verbal Activities and Improvisation," incorporates and revises materials from old Chapters 9 and 10. Chapter 9, "Encouraging Creative Work," includes a reworking of old Chapters 6 and 7. Chapter 10, "Story Dramatization," discusses two methods I have developed, called "circle stories" and "segmented stories." Chapter 11, "Planning Drama Lessons and Units," is an expansion of old Chapter 12 with an added discussion of creative drama assessment. In addition, the entire book has been thoroughly rewritten, photos have been added, and bibliographies of children's literature have been completely revised and updated.

As before, I rely heavily on children's literature. This is not to suggest that teachers and children cannot have ideas of their own. Good literature, however, is an excellent stimulus for one's original ideas. Children's literature also provides a wealth and variety of materials to enhance many areas of the school curriculum, such as science and social studies. For these reasons, children's literature is particularly helpful to the beginning teacher and enriches any drama lesson. Therefore, I have included numerous annotated references to children's literature throughout the text. Although some of the books are out of print, they are still available in many educational and public libraries.

In thanking the many people who have helped make this book possible, I must begin with my mentor and former teacher, Dr. Barbara M.

McIntyre, whose friendship I still cherish. I also thank the many classroom teachers, college students, and children I have worked with over the years; their influence is evident on each page. A special thanks is also expressed to my user-friendly senior editor at Prentice-Hall, Steve Dalphin, production editor, Marjorie Shustak, whose encouragement and ready assistance make authorship an almost tolerable task. Thank you to Dr. Ted Solomon of Delta State University and Prof. Patricia M. Harlin of UCLA, who ably reviewed the manuscript.

Others who deserve recognition include: my opthalmologist, Dr. John Trittshuh, who knows why I am forever grateful to him; special friends Marilyn Heberling, Len Holmes, Duwain Hunt, Robin Nott, Gale Sharpe, Elaine Sievers, and Elizabeth Tinsley; and special children Andy, Anna, Ben, Brian, Brianna, Glenn, Melanie, Lee, Ravi, and Ryan. I deeply appreciate the many ways in which you have all aided my efforts.

TO LOOK AT ANY THING

To look at any thing,
If you would know that thing,
You must look at it long:
To look at this green and say
'I have seen spring in these
Woods,' will not do—you must
Be the thing you see:
You must be the dark snakes of
Stems and ferny plumes of leaves,
You must enter in
To the small silences between
The leaves,
You must take your time
And touch the very peace
They issue from.

John Moffitt

ONE

Introduction

We are looking in on three classrooms during creative drama sessions:

"The Three Little Pigs" is being dramatized in a first-grade classroom. The teacher has divided the class into groups of four. Each group has its specified area to work in. The teacher narrates the story, pausing for the children to act out the appropriate action.

In the background a recording of Henry Mancini's "Baby Elephant Walk" is being played softly. Its lilting beat obviously influences the movements of the children as they play the story.

After the first and second little pigs are eaten, they sit on the sidelines and become the sound effects for the rest of the story. They help the wolf huff and puff; they rumble for the butter churn rolling down the hill; and they make the noise of the crackling fire under the pot of boiling water.

There is spontaneous applause from everyone at the end. After a brief discussion of what they liked best about their playing, the children ask to repeat the story. Some decide they want to switch parts in their group, and the teacher helps them reorganize. A second playing begins.

We move to a third-grade classroom, where we learn that the teacher has been dealing with the subject of slavery and freedom. The children have been interested in the story of Harriet Tubman and her work with the Underground Railroad, so the teacher has decided to guide the children in exploring what it would be like to be a slave seeking freedom. Some of the activities the children have already experienced are writing secret messages of escape plans using code systems; learning the song "Follow the Drinking Gourd" and the significance of the gourd as a symbol of the Big Dipper or northward direction; discussions of situations encountered by slaves and the feelings they generate: separation from family, traveling by night under cover, and being assisted by sympathetic people. Today, the children will experience the trip to freedom.

> The classroom has been rearranged, and chairs have been pushed back against the walls. The children are sitting on the floor in the center of the room. The teacher specifies that one side of the room is a roadway, the adjacent side is designated as a marshland, the third is a forest, and the fourth side is a clearing and free territory. The window shades are pulled just enough to darken the room and to simulate night. A freedom song is being played softly on the record player. The children are just finishing group discussions about who they are planning to be in their drama and what they think will be their biggest difficulty on the trip. Some of the children are in groups of three and four; some are planning to work in pairs; and a few have preferred to make their freedom flight alone.
>
> The teacher asks the children to decide the order in which they will progress around the room, and they organize themselves accordingly. They begin the experience by pretending to be asleep, waiting until it is dark enough to start the journey. One child, who has suggested that a hooting owl should be the signal for the action to begin, hoots softly on a cue from the teacher. The children, still in the center of the room, silently make their preparations to depart. The first few children start along the "roadway."
>
> The teacher speaks softly as the action begins. She describes the surroundings and suggests the feelings that they might be having as they begin their adventure. She reminds them of the possible dangers. Suddenly she pops a blown-up paper bag, and there is no doubt that it is a gunshot. Everyone

"Little Pig, Little Pig, let me come in . . ."

huddles closer to the floor, and they proceed even more cautiously. Some appear to have been wounded and are assisted by others.

Now most of them have reached the "marshland" area, and again the teacher quietly describes this environment and suggests the problems it offers. As before, some of the children listen to her descriptions, while others are engrossed enough in their own ideas that they need no assistance.

As most of the children approach the end of the trip, the teacher turns up the music and reminds them that they have almost reached freedom; it is only a short way off—within grasp at any moment. The children's faces bear encouraged looks; the walking wounded who are being aided by friends smile faintly. As they pass by the record player, the teacher turns up the volume and begins to sing, encouraging the children to join in. They return to their original places on the floor, singing until everyone is seated and the teacher fades out the music.

The leader talks briefly with the children about their escape. As the discussion turns to the people who harbored the runaway slaves, she asks, "Would you like to try a short drama about those people?" The children agree. The leader stands, picks up a notebook from the desk, surveys the group slowly, and then addresses them authoritatively. "It has been reported to me that some runaway slaves are being harbored on these premises. I'm here to investigate. How do you answer to this charge?" She demands explanations of their recent whereabouts, the contents of their wagons, and the reports that they have been seen purchasing more supplies than their household needs. For several minutes, the children offer a variety of plausible explanations to the questions posed. The leader takes "notes," accepts the answers grudgingly and with some hesitation, and then ends by saying she will return the next day to investigate further. She returns the notebook to the desk, smiles at the children, and the session ends with the group exploring plans for the following day.

Our third and final visit is in a sixth-grade classroom, where we observe the following:

The children are listening to two records, "Alley-Oop"[1] and "I'm Bugged at My Ol' Man."[2] The teacher tells them that the records were favorites of his when he was their age. They discuss the songs for a few minutes, and he suggests that they create some skits based on the lyrics as a "fun experiment." The children seem eager to try this. They break up into small groups of their own choosing to prepare their skits. After about ten minutes of preparation, the following skits are enacted:

Four boys, standing in a row, are each a head taller than the one next in line. The tallest chants, in a deep voice, "I'm Alley-Oop and I'm the tallest and the strongest." The second repeats the chant in a somewhat deep voice. The third repeats on a higher pitch. The fourth, in the highest-pitched voice, chants, "I'm Alley-Oop and I'm the shortest and the weakest." Mock fighting for a few seconds between the boys is followed by the collpase of the three tallest. The little one remains, quietly smiling.

In another group three boys enact a scene from "I'm Bugged at My Ol'

---

[1]Words and music by Dallas Frazier. Recorded by The Hollywood Argyles, on a 45 (ERA Records).

[2]Words and music by Brian Wilson. Recorded by The Beach Boys on the album *Summer Days* (Capitol Records).

Improvising skits requires the concentration and cooperation of the whole group.

Man." One plays the father, one the son, and a third the police officer. The son talks for a long time on the phone. The irate father rips out the telephone. The son goes out to steal and is caught by the officer and taken to the police station. The officer calls the father (apparently the phone has been miraculously reconnected), and the father goes to the station and asks how much the bail is. He is told there is no bail allowed for adolescents, but that he must stay in jail in place of the son. The son leaves, and the father closes the scene with a "That's life!" gesture of hopelessness.

Four girls in another group pantomime to the accompaniment of the "Alley-Oop" record. The lead singer holds a ruler for a microphone. The backup singers have worked out a dance step they perform on the chorus of the song.

A fourth group chooses not to show its skit, even though their classmates encourage them. No reason is given, and the teacher accepts the group's decision.

Another group of boys also chooses to work on the record "I'm Bugged at My Ol' Man." They too select the reference to the father yanking the phone from the son. The boys engage in a verbal argument that seems to have no end. The teacher asks, "Are you finished?" They agree that they are and return to their seats.

After each of the skits the audience applauds appreciatively. As we leave, the teacher is about to play a record that he says will be "mushy" but that they might like. As the children listen to the first strains of romantic music, they begin to whisper excitedly to each other about their ideas.

WHAT IS CREATIVE DRAMA?

The preceding examples describe some of the many ways of working in *creative drama,* although other terms, such as *informal drama, creative play acting,* and *improvisational* (or *improvised*) *drama,* have sometimes been used interchangeably. In Britain and Canada the terms *developmental drama, educational drama,* and even *drama* are more widely used.

The American Alliance for Theatre and Education (AATE), a new national merger that includes creative drama educators and former members of Children's Theatre Association of America, uses the term "creative drama"[3] and defines it as "an improvisational, nonexhibitional, process-centered form of drama in which participants are guided by a leader to imagine, enact, and reflect upon human experiences."[4]

The definition further explains:

> The creative drama process is dynamic. The leader guides the group to explore, develop, express and communicate ideas, concepts, and feelings through dramatic enactment. In creative drama the group improvises action and dialogue appropriate to the content it is exploring, using elements of drama to give form and meaning to the experience.[5]

WHAT ACTIVITIES ARE INCLUDED IN CREATIVE DRAMA?

Because creative drama stresses improvisation and imagination as well as group process, a multitude of activities and approaches to those activities fall under its rubric. Among these activities are movement exercises and exploration, pantomime, theatre games, improvised story dramatization, and group improvisations. An activity might be as simple as a game of "Statues" or as sophisticated as improvised group dramatizations on the topic of nuclear energy.

Most drama leaders, particularly as they gain experience, develop their own activities and their own approaches to stimulating children's creative expression, taking into account their own personalities and styles of leadership. And although their materials and methods may differ, most leaders would subscribe to the use of the drama medium as one of the most effective ways of guiding children to grow and learn.

WHAT ARE THE GOALS OF CREATIVE DRAMA?

Referring again to AATE's definition of creative drama, "Participation in creative drama has the potential to develop language and communication abilities, problem solving skills, and creativity; to promote a positive self-concept, social awareness, empathy, a clarification of values and attitudes,

---

[3]"Creative drama" is preferred over "creative dramatics." Although the organization acknowledges some ambiguity in the term, it is considered the most frequently used and generally understood label.

[4]For a more complete discussion of this definition, see Jed H. Davis and Tom Behm, "Terminology of Drama/Theatre with and for Children: a Redefinition," *Children's Theatre Review*, 27, no. 1 (1978), 19–21.

[5]*Ibid.*, p. 10.

and an understanding of the art of theatre."[6] Although several of these areas overlap each other, an examination of each follows.

Language and Communication

In recent years oral language (speaking, listening, nonverbal communication) has received considerable attention from English educators, psycholinguists, and communication educators. Recognizing oral language as the precursor of reading and writing, they advocate its use as an underlying base for all language learning. Even more recently, the language-arts field has emphasized the "functions" of communication. We use language in all our daily encounters—whether in speaking, listening, reading, or writing—for five basic purposes or functions. These are information, persuasion, imagination, ritual (social conventions), and affective communication (the expression of emotions). Creative drama falls distinctly under imaginative communication, but the other communication functions are still dealt with in drama's many pretend situations.

McIntyre has specifically emphasized the language arts in her creative drama text.[7] A past president of the National Council of Teachers of English, John Stewig, emphasizes in numerous writings the importance of creative drama as a means to foster reading, the study of literature, oral language and vocabulary development, nonverbal communication, listening abilities, and creative writing.[8] English educator Betty Jane Wagner asserts that "drama is nothing less than the 'basic skill' that is the foundation of all language development."[9]

Several studies have demonstrated that creative drama is useful in language development. Tucker, for example, reported that creative drama sessions were important in developing reading readiness in kindergarten children.[10] Although population sample numbers were limited, Stewig and Young found positive relationships between the use of creative drama and oral language growth in fourth and fifth graders,[11] and Stewig and McKee noted significant growth in oral language with seventh graders who participated in creative drama.[12]

Creative drama also appears to be useful in remedial language development. One recent study, for example, demonstrated that creative drama

---

[6]*Ibid.*, p. 10.

[7]Barbara M. McIntyre, *Creative Drama in the Elementary School* (Itasca, Ill.: F. E. Peacock, 1974).

[8]See especially John W. Stewig, *Informal Drama in the Elementary Language Arts Program* (New York: Teachers College Press, 1983).

[9]Betty Jane Wagner, "Educational Drama and Language Development," in *Educational Drama for Today's Schools*, ed. R. Baird Shuman (Metuchen, N.J.: Scarecrow, 1978), p. 95.

[10]JoAnne Klineman Tucker, "The Use of Creative Dramatics as an Aid in Developing Readiness with Kindergarten Children" (Ph.D. dissertation, University of Wisconsin, 1971).

[11]John Warren Stewig and Linda Young, "An Exploration of the Relations Between Creative Drama and Language Growth," *Children's Theatre Review*, 27, no. 2 (1978), 10–12.

[12]John Warren Stewig and John A. McKee, "Drama and Language Growth: A Replication Study," *Children's Theatre Review*, 29, no. 3 (1980), 1.

is helpful in English as a Second Language (ESL) classrooms.[13] Another study demonstrated the usefulness of creative drama in improving the functional language of children identified as ineffective communicators.[14]

Creative drama offers a variety of communication experiences to children. By emphasizing self-expression, creative drama helps them to form their self-concepts and expand their self-confidence. Their increased abilities in self-expression lead to better interpersonal communication skills in informing and questioning, in organizing and sharing ideas, and in enjoying the companionship and group interaction process with others.

In fact, children use oral communication in creative drama constantly as they respond to and discuss ideas, share personal observations, and organize and plan their drama activities. Even in the characters they play, they communicate orally, working through the characters' dramatic situations and interacting with other characters. Enacting the dramatic scene or story itself encourages them to become more effective in their use of language.

When children improvise drama, language situations are enacted spontaneously—the way they occur in everyday life where there is no predetermined script. Children can experiment with alternatives, learning firsthand which ways are most effective without suffering any real-life consequences for mistakes they may make. As a result, they are able to increase their repertoire of communication options and to experience the self-confidence that comes from rehearsing life's situations before meeting them.

Problem-Solving Skills and Creativity

Drama can stimulate the development of problem-solving skills. When children are presented with problems to solve, with open-endedness that requires a filling in of gaps, with information and ideas to synthesize into new relationships, they are learning creatively, according to Torrance.[15] Although the degree of creativity may vary with each situation, in problem solving, children are encouraged to guess, hypothesize, test alternatives, and perhaps even redefine the problem.

Problem solving is frequently apparent in the stories the children enact. What solutions will they suggest for helping a princess learn to cry? How does one pretend not to understand in order to escape a villain's clutches? Or what does a mayor say to appease two opposing factions within the city council?

Children can experience group problem solving in other drama ac-

---

[13]Kathie Vitz, "The Effects of Creative Drama in English as a Second Language," *Children's Theatre Review*, 33, no. 2 (1984), 23–26.

[14]Snyder-Greco, Teresa, "The Effects of Creative Dramatic Techniques on Selected Language Functions of Language Disordered Children," *Children's Theatre Review*, 32, no. 2 (1983), 9–13.

[15]E. Paul Torrance, *Encouraging Creativity in the Classroom* (Dubuque, Iowa: William C. Brown, 1970), p. 1.

tivities as well. What machine will a group decide to create with their own bodies and how will they demonstrate its working parts? How will they choose to "stage" or present their drama, and how will they handle their simple props and costume pieces for maximum effect? For a group skit, how will they decide among themselves to demonstrate the meaning of a particular proverb?

In all of these experiences children are encouraged to seek answers, push for new ideas, generate and explore solutions, synthesize information, and exercise imagination. This is all a part of the problem-solving process which drama can stimulate.

Most researchers and writers on the subject of creativity believe that everyone has creative potential. In order to recognize the full development of each individual and to foster independent thinking in a free society, our educational system has come to include this aspect of learning in its curricula.

The characteristics of *creativity* have been identified by a number of writers. Creative people are innovators, problem solvers, alternative test-

Everyone has the potential to be creative.

ers, and adventurers. They are fearless, fluent, curious, unpredictable, constructively discontented, and sometimes even a bit "off center." But creative expression is necessary for the celebration of the individual, the one who will survive in a dehumanizing technological age and in a world that is so complex that its problems, let alone solutions, often elude us.

Although creative potential is present in each child, it needs to be released and given a nurturing environment in which to develop fully. Teachers can encourage creative thinking abilities by providing an accepting climate in which a child can try and fail—in which children are not afraid to take risks and explore. They can also help by sensitizing children to environmental stimuli and by encouraging the spirit of playing with ideas. They can stimulate creative thinking by presenting a variety of problems for children to explore.

Although studies of creative drama's effect on children's creativity are limited both in size and scope, at least three can be noted. Karioth's 1967 study showed that creative drama could aid in developing creative thinking abilities in disadvantaged fourth graders as measured by Thorndike tests of creative thinking.[16] In 1971 Prokes reported that creative drama was useful in promoting the imaginative capacities of 45 gifted junior high school students.[17] In an experimental study by Schmidt, Goforth, and Drew, 39 kindergarten students were exposed to 16 half-hour sessions of creative drama. The experimental group scored signficantly higher than the control group on two creativity tests, one verbal and one visual.[18] Although the need for more studies is apparent, the evidence seems to suggest that drama is an important vehicle for releasing and nurturing the creative potential of children.

Positive Self-concept

Within each individual is a distinct being ready to emerge. Being creative, according to Moustakas, means continually evolving into one's own unique self—growing forward, responding to life, fulfilling one's maximum potential.[19] To continue to grow we must value and have faith in ourselves. When we feel secure about ourselves, we are willing to explore, to experiment, and to take risks. This self-expression furthers the awareness and growth of the self.

In creative drama children's *positive self-concept* and self-expression are

[16]Emil Karioth, "Creative Dramatics as an Aid to Developing Creative Thinking Abilities" (Unpublished Ph.D. dissertation, University of Minnesota, 1967). Although problem-solving skills remained unchanged in this study, Torrance's work both with creative drama and with disadvantaged children may present additional insights. See Torrance, *Encouraging Creativity.*

[17]Sister Dorothy Prokes, F.S.P.A., "Exploring the Relationship Between Participation in Creative Dramatics and Development of the Imagination Capacities of Gifted Junior High School Students" (Unpublished Ph.D. dissertation, New York University, 1971).

[18]Toni Schmidt, Elissa Goforth, and Kathy Drew, "Creative Dramatics and Creativity: An Experimental Study," *Educational Theatre Journal,* 27 (March 1975), 111–14.

[19]Clark E. Moustakas, *Creative Life* (New York: Van Nostrand Reinhold, 1977). The theme of achieving a creative life pervades the entire book.

Drama can help develop a more positive self-concept.

fostered by the leader who believes in each child's personal worth and creative potential. The leader's attitude produces a climate of psychological security in the classroom, so that the children are not afraid to be themselves, growing and searching for new awareness. The teacher who uses an activity like creative drama is often one who already believes in children's need for self-expression and is sensitive to the kind of leadership that encourages it.

An early experimental study on the effect of creative drama on personal growth was done by Irwin.[20] She demonstrated that third graders, receiving 40 minutes of creative drama each week for 15 weeks, improved in personal and social adjustment when compared with a control group. A study reported in 1982 by Huntsman demonstrated that 30 university students from introductory psychology classes made significant gains in self-confidence, self-worth, and spontaneity after participating in improvisational drama activities.[21] In a third study, 150 economically disadvantaged fourth-, fifth-, and sixth-grade black and Hispanic schoolchildren participated in an improvisational dramatics program.[22] Results suggested that drama, in addition to improving reading achievement, also aided children's positive attitudes toward themselves and others. Students' attitudes and school performance were also rated more highly by their teachers after the program.

Among the kinds of anecdotal material most frequently shared by creative drama leaders are those which point to children's improved self-concept. Sometimes children feel better about themselves because of a certain role they have played which appealed to them: a king, a hero, a

[20]Eleanor Chima Irwin, "The Effects of a Program of Creative Dramatics Upon Personality as Measured by the California Test of Personality, Sociograms, Teacher Ratings, and Grades" (Unpublished Ph.D. dissertation, University of Pittsburgh, 1963).

[21]Karla Hendricks Huntsman, "Improvisational Dramatic Activities: Key to Self-Actualization?" *Children's Theatre Review*, 31, no. 2 (1982), 3–9.

[22]Annette F. Gourgey, Jason Bosseau and Judith Delgado, "The Impact of an Improvisational Dramatics Program on Student Attitudes and Achievement," *Children's Theatre Review*, 34, no. 3 (1985), 9–14.

brave person. Or because self-expression has been encouraged and positive guidance rather than criticism has been the leader's method, children who might otherwise feel incapable of success now feel that their ideas have importance. The self can stand taller.

Social Awareness

It has often been said that drama is a rehearsal for living.[23] Through creative drama children can pretend to be the people or things they find interesting and significant. They can relive the experiences of others, of the various people that inhabit their storybooks, their history and social-studies books, and their everyday life and fantasy world. They can experiment with societal roles and, in the process, identify and empathize with others, learning of their concerns, confronting their problems, and experiencing their successes as well as failures. Through drama children can begin to establish a tangible relationship with the human condition. What is it like to experience discrimination? What is it like to hold a particular political or religious view? What is it like to be a member of another culture or nation? Through drama children can discover the common bond of humanness that transcends time, age, and geographical boundaries.

Creative drama also provides learning experiences in social and group interaction. In many ways drama is a group art. Plays focus on social interaction; the theatre requires the talents and skills of numerous artists. So too, as children engage in drama, they must plan together, enact ideas together, organize their playing space, and experience a variety of human interactions in their dramatizations. Effective socialization becomes a high priority, and the rewards of cooperative group behaviors are often clearly demonstrated to even the youngest children.

Empathy

Empathy is the ability to see life from another's perspective and to feel with that person. This "as if" feeling is similar to the one the Russian theatre director Konstantin Stanislavsky attempted to encourage through what he called "emotional memory." Actors were urged to sense and understand the character they were playing by recalling similar situations in their own lives.

Children begin to develop empathy as their thinking matures and they move away from egocentricity. Two studies have specifically demonstrated the effectiveness of using creative drama as an aid to children's empathic or role-taking abilities. Wright, using sixth-grade students, discovered that children who had creative drama classes showed significant improvement in role-taking skills.[24] Lunz also found that training in cre-

[23]For a wide array of anecdotal observations of children involved in dramatic play, see Virginia Glasgow Koste, *Dramatic Play in Childhood: Rehearsal for Life* (Lanham, Md.: University Press of America, 1987).

[24]Mary Elin Sommers Wright, "The Effects of Creative Drama on Person Perception"

ative drama significantly increased seventh graders' communicative effectiveness by providing practice in role taking through dramatic role playing.[25]

Through creative drama children have the opportunity to see the world from another point of view and to respond as that person would respond. If the inner attitudes of another can be identified and understood through creative drama, if children can experience "walking in another's shoes," more tolerant understanding of others and more effective communication will result.

Values and Attitudes

An area of the curriculum that has received much attention in recent years is *values clarification*. Values clarification is the process of helping students find, test, and refine their own belief systems without imposing the specific religious or moral principles of any one group. Controversy occurred when it was felt that religious and moral principles were being sacrificed or ignored in the values-clarification process. Furthermore, many people believe that specific values should be taught in the home and church rather than in the schools. In many areas of the country values clarification has become such an unpopular term that many teachers have been afraid of approaching the subject of values at all.

But the tide is turning to a refocusing on values once again. With the many social problems we face as a nation, there is fear that we may become value*less*. Many professional organizations have turned their attention to a study of ethics and ethical practices within their fields. And there are certain values that are accepted without controversy. Honesty and truthfulness, for example, are almost universally upheld though not always practiced. So schools are once again being encouraged to foster the values and attitudes that make for a stronger society.

To deal with life's situations, children make decisions constantly, basing them on the values they hold. Yet if they are not sure what to believe, they may find it difficult to make the best decisions. In a world in which values are under constant scrutiny and appear to be changing at every turn, it is essential to help students develop the personal values that will affect their ways of behaving.

Creative drama deals with people in action—facing life, making decisions, and then living with the consequences of those decisions. In the dramatization of a story, for example, children are involved in a life situation in which events take a particular turn. Students experience firsthand

---

(Unpublished Ph.D. dissertation, University of Minnesota, 1972). See also Lin Wright, "Creative Dramatics and the Development of Role-Taking in the Elementary Classroom," *Elementary English*, 51 (January 1974), 89–93.

[25]Mary E. Lunz, "The Effects of Overt Dramatic Enactment on Communication Effectiveness and Role Taking Ability" (Unpublished Ph.D. dissertation, Northwestern University, 1974).

what it is like to be involved in those events. As Duke suggests, "When a person is required to act 'as if' he holds a certain belief, he is more likely to examine the application of that belief to his own life."[26]

In addition, with improvisational dramatizations alternative patterns of behavior can be explored. What happens when certain things are said or when a specific action is taken? Students can try out alternatives and see both the choices and the results of those choices that others make. Through this process children may be able to better understand the answers to universal questions.

An Understanding of the Art of Theatre

In creative drama children learn about the theatre in a way best suited to their developing talents and skills. Rather than focusing on the memorization of scripts and the elaborate production of a play, children are encouraged to improvise dramatic materials. Emphasis is placed on discussing and internalizing information and then playing it out, using self-expression rather than prescribed materials.

At the same time, children gain insights into the important elements of theatre, such as action, conflict, plot, mood, characterization, and spectacle. They will be exposed to plot structure and to the themes of stories. They will begin to understand characters—not only how they appear on the outside, but how they think and feel on the inside. They will be more attuned to the characters' motivations for their behaviors and attitudes. Their own interpretation of the characters will give them experiences in expression through movement and voice.

Children will also have the opportunity to experience the aspects of theatrical staging and, in modified forms, all the related spectacle of setting, props, lights, costumes, music, and dance. In bringing all the various art forms of the theatre together, students will learn the importance of working together to create a unified artistic whole.

The study of theatre, along with the other arts, too frequently has been neglected in our children's education. A significant panel report, *Coming to Our Senses: The Significance of the Arts for American Education,* documents how we, as a nation, have been remiss in acknowledging and appreciating the arts as an integral part of our cultural heritage.[27] The arts have traditionally provided a way for nations and cultures to develop, communicate, and preserve their identity. The report further documents the many interrelationships of the arts to the traditional disciplines of learning. Because the arts also develop intellectual and social skills, they are as basic to the curriculum as the three Rs.

---

[26]Charles R. Duke, "Educational Drama, Role-Taking, and Values Clarification," in *Educational Drama for Today's Schools,* ed. R. Baird Shuman (Metuchen, N.J.: Scarecrow Press, 1978), p. 95.

[27]David Rockefeller, Jr., Chairman, *Coming to Our Senses: The Significance of the Arts for American Education,* A Panel Report (New York: McGraw-Hill, 1977).

WHAT ARE SOME OF THE USES OF CREATIVE DRAMA?

Creative drama has been used in a variety of educational settings and with persons of all ages, including older adults. Many classroom teachers, who have either taken a preservice or an in-service introductory course in creative drama or read about it in texts or journals, have tried it out for themselves. Some school districts, on either a temporary or permanent basis, have the luxury of educational-drama specialists who work with children in addition to serving as consultants to teachers in providing drama experiences.[28] Some states, most notably Texas, have mandated the teaching of theatre arts at all grade levels, with regular classroom teachers serving as the instructors in the elementary grades.

Both recreational programs and library programs have long incorporated creative drama into their varied schedule of activities. Religious programs use creative drama as a more meaningful way to teach religious literature and ethical attitudes. In community theatre programs, creative drama is frequently offered to give children experience in informal drama and an understanding of the art of theatre.

Because of the therapeutic aspect of the arts in general, creative drama has been useful in a number of areas of special education. Even when the goals of creative drama are educational or aesthetic (stressing curricular information, encouraging imagination), the psychological well being of the participants can also be enhanced. Some educators and specialists have found creative drama useful in alleviating emotional tensions that contribute to reading problems, speech and language disorders, and socialization difficulties, to cite only a few examples.[29]

Thus the uses of creative drama continue to expand, reflecting the growing recognition of the power of the drama experience to enrich learning and enhance living for all persons.

HOW DOES THE TEACHER INCORPORATE CREATIVE DRAMA INTO AN ALREADY FULL CURRICULUM?

Many educators feel that creative drama provides an essential style of learning for children. Since children naturally dramatize, the teacher who uses creative drama is simply capitalizing on what the children already

[28]The School District of Evanston, Illinois, was for many years a notable center for drama specialists until severe budget cuts virtually wiped out the program in the 1970s. A new, though smaller, program is now successfully underway and expects continued growth.

[29]A distinction is made between "therapeutic" and "therapy." Generally, any activity in which participants feel better about themselves can be termed therapeutic. "Therapy" is a more restricted term and is the domain of the trained professional whose responsibility it is to bring about behavioral change in a client. For a more complete discussion of this point see Eleanor C. Irwin, "Drama Therapy with the Handicapped," in *Drama, Theatre, and the Handicapped,* ed. Ann M. Shaw and CJ Stevens (Washington, D.C.: American Theatre Association, 1979), pp. 21–30. For more information on drama, theatre, and the handicapped, see Linaya Leaf's excellent review of the literature and the annotated bibliography in Shaw and Stevens' text.

know how to do innately. Through dramatization they are provided an opportunity to use a wealth of information in a more concrete and meaningful way. When children play out an idea, they become an integral part of it. They become kinesthetically involved in experiences that might otherwise remain only words on a printed page.

Since it can incorporate so many desirable educational goals, creative drama is used in conjunction with many subject areas, such as language arts, science, social studies, or the fine arts. In history, for example, children might enact the conquests of Pizarro; in literature, the adventures of Alice in Wonderland. In music, children might dramatize the folk song "Frog Went A-Courtin'"; in science they might enact a day in the life of a kangaroo rat; and in an oral language activity they might be lobbyists advocating their causes.

Creative drama can focus on specific facts and concepts, as well as emphasizing broader goals such as problem solving and creative thinking. Children can pantomime various jobs in a logging camp or be members of two warring factions attempting to reach a compromise. They also may be encouraged to do further reading and research in order to play their ideas and roles with greater accuracy.

Drama experiences also provide a way of checking children's understandings of material covered. Suppose that after studying simple machines children pantomime some examples. As they play, it will be obvious what ideas are understood and what misconceptions need correcting. Or as older children take on roles of Northern and Southern sympathizers during the Civil War period, one can assess their understanding of events and attitudes which led to the conflict.

Learning experiences can be previewed or reviewed through creative drama. In preparation for a field trip to a fire department, a simulated field trip can be enacted. Afterward the experience can be replayed, utilizing the information gained.

Finally, creative drama is usually fun for all. Learning is made more enjoyable when it is dramatized. Often children who have difficulty with other classroom tasks find success and a place for themselves in drama, a discovery that gives them a renewed interest in learning. Enjoyment and success together lead to self-confidence, a prime requisite for becoming a thinking, feeling, and creative person able to face life's challenges.

WILL I BE ABLE TO DO IT?

For both the leader and the children, creative drama may be an adventure and an exploration into a new style of teaching and learning. It may take time to build the confidence needed to venture forth. But experimentation and the leeway to fail and try again are essential to the learning process. Just as we allow children to learn in this manner, we must allow it of ourselves, too. We must be as patient with ourselves as we are with the children.

This text is designed to make creative drama understandable, practical, meaningful, and enjoyable for everyone. Both the children's and the leader's needs have been kept in mind in order to insure maximum success. Some of the activities will seem easy; others will be highly challenging. Some you will love, but others may not interest you at all. The intent is to provide you with as many techniques, ideas, and materials as possible, so that you will have many choices and alternatives. It is hoped that this approach will help you to provide exciting learning experiences for both the children you teach and yourself. Welcome aboard!

FOR THE COLLEGE STUDENT

1. Using some of the material in Virginia Koste's *Dramatic Play in Childhood* (Lanham, Md.: University Press of America, 1987), discuss your own observations of children or your recollections from your own childhood. What do these experiences and observations teach you about the use of creative drama in the elementary classroom?

2. Using Richard DeMille's book *Put Your Mother on the Ceiling: Children's Imagination Games* (New York: Viking Penguin, 1973), begin to stretch your own imagination and recapture the play spirit you may have "misplaced" in the growing-up process. You might want to try these games with children also. Other useful books are *Left-Handed Teaching: Lessons in Affective Education,* 2nd ed. by Gloria A. Castillo (New York: Holt, Reinhart and Winston, 1978) and *One Hundred Ways to Enhance Self Concept in the Classroom: A Handbook for Teachers and Parents* by Jack Canfield and Harold C. Wells (Englewood Cliffs, N.J.: Prentice-Hall, 1976).

3. Discuss with your classmates your early experiences with drama in school or in other settings. What are your remembrances of them? Are there both pleasant and unpleasant memories? Identify them as specifically as you can. How might you increase the pleasant experiences and diminish the unpleasant ones for your students?

4. Read and report on one of the suggested readings in the bibliography at the end of this chapter.

5. Study the current curriculum goals and objectives in your state or local area. Is creative drama mentioned or implied in the teaching of basic skills, the fine arts, or other areas? What specific goals and objectives have been identified? Should others be added? What teacher resource materials in creative drama are made available from your state's department of education? Report on your findings in class.

SELECTED BIBLIOGRAPHY

BOLTON, GAVIN, *Towards a Theory of Drama in Education.* New York: Longman, 1979. Using classroom examples, a well-known British drama educator presents his theories and outlines a drama approach which combines children's play and elements of theatre.

————, *Drama as Education*. New York: Longman, 1984. Subtitled "an argument for placing drama at the centre of the curriculum," this text presents a British drama educator's theories as well as helpful analyses of a number of educational drama techniques.

COTTRELL, JUNE, *Creative Drama in the Classroom, Grades 1–3 and Grades 4–6*. Lincolnwood, Ill.: National Textbook Company, 1987. These companion texts are theatre arts resource guides for the elementary classroom teacher.

————, *Teaching with Creative Dramatics*. Lincolnwood, Ill.: National Textbook Company, 1975. The author presents a basic overview of creative drama, with chapters on play, sensory awareness, pantomime, dialogue, drama in curriculum, and storytelling.

COURTNEY, RICHARD, *The Dramatic Curriculum*. New York: Drama Book Publishers, 1980. The author, a well-known developmental drama educator and writer, develops his theory that the entire curriculum can be viewed in dramatic terms.

DAVIES, GEOFF, *Practical Primary Drama*. London: Heinemann Educational Books, 1983. As its title suggests, this slim volume is practical and highly readable. The author studied with Dorothy Heathcote and presents a simplified version of a number of her techniques.

GOODRIDGE, JANET, *Creative Drama and Improvised Movement*. Boston: Plays, 1971. This practical text presents many useful drama and movement activities for classroom use.

HEINIG, RUTH BEALL, *Creative Drama Resource Book for Kindergarten through Grade 3* and *Creative Drama Resource Book for Grades 4 through 6*. Englewood Cliffs, N.J.: Prentice-Hall, 1987. These two companion texts are theatre arts resource guides for elementary teachers.

JOHNSON, LIZ, AND CECILY O'NEILL, EDS., *Dorothy Heathcote*. London: Hutchinson & Co., 1984. These are the collected writings on education and drama by England's Dorothy Heathcote, perhaps the most widely-known drama educator in the world today.

MCCASLIN, NELLIE, *Creative Drama in the Classroom*, 4th ed. New York: Longman, 1984. This is a widely used introductory text on creative drama, presenting both theory and practical application. It includes exercises in sensory awareness, pantomime, and improvisation. Story dramatization and formal production are also covered.

————, *Creative Drama in the Primary Grades* and *Creative Drama in the Intermediate Grades*. New York: Longman, 1987. These companion texts are theatre arts resource guides for the elementary classroom teacher.

MCINTYRE, BARBARA M., *Creative Drama in the Elementary School*. Itasca, Ill.: F.E. Peacock Publishers, 1974. A rationale for using creative drama in a language-arts program is presented. Detailed activities are explained in two sections, one for kindergarten through grade 3 and another for grades 4 through 6.

O'NEILL, CECILY, AND ALAN LAMBERT, *Drama Structures*. London: Hutchinson & Co., 1982. This teaching handbook, developed by two British drama educators, is divided into four sections: theoretical basis, four drama structures, checklists for drama lessons, and encouragement for teachers to develop their own approaches to drama.

O'NEILL, CECILY, ALAN LAMBERT, ROSEMARY LINELL, AND JANET WARR-WOOD, *Drama Guidelines*. London: Heinemann Educational Books, 1977. This handbook is a statement of the aims of drama teaching with actual lesson descriptions and an examination of the leader's role and includes contributions from many practicing teachers.

POLSKY, MILTON, *Let's Improvise*. Englewood Cliffs, N.J.: Prentice-Hall, 1980. This book gives many useful ideas for leading improvisation activities with a variety of groups and settings.

ROSENBERG, HELANE S., *Creative Drama and Imagination: Transforming Ideas into Action*. New York: Holt, Rinehart and Winston, 1987. Beginning with a historical overview of creative drama and a theoretical foundation in imagination, this text introduces the Rutgers Imagination Method (RIM) of teaching creative drama. Activities and examples of this approach, developed by Rosenberg and her associates at Rutgers University, comprise the second half of the book.

SALISBURY, BARBARA T., *Theatre Arts in the Elementary Classroom Kindergarten through Grade 3* and *Theatre Arts in the Elementary Classroom Grade Four through Grade Six.* New Orleans: Anchorage Press, 1987. These two companion books are resource guides for the elementary classroom teacher. Emphasis is on creative drama.

SCHER, ANNA, AND CHARLES VERRALL, *One Hundred Plus Ideas for Drama.* London: Heinemann Educational Books, 1981. This book presents a practical listing of numerous activities, including games, pantomimes, improvisations, and verbal exercises. See also: *Another One Hundred Plus Ideas for Drama,* 1987.

SCHWARTZ, DOROTHY THAMES, AND DOROTHY ALDRICH, EDS., *Give Them Roots . . . and Wings!* New Orleans: Anchorage Press, 1985. This manual is the combined work of several creative drama leaders and is a useful source for the beginning teacher. It covers creative movement and pantomime, characterization, improvisation, dialogue, and story dramatization, with many sample lessons.

SHUMAN, R. BAIRD, ED., *Educational Drama for Today's Schools.* Metuchen, N.J.: Scarecrow Press, 1978. This book presents a variety of essays on some of the uses of drama—such as in language development and moral development—by several authors, including Dorothy Heathcote, Betty Jane Wagner, and Charles R. Duke. An extensive annotated bibliography is also included.

SIKS, GERALDINE BRAIN, *Children's Literature for Dramatization.* New York: Harper & Row, 1964. Many excellent stories and poems are presented in this anthology designed particularly for the creative drama leader. Each selection is introduced with suggestions for dramatization.

————, *Drama with Children,* 2nd ed. New York: Harper & Row, 1983. This is a presentation of the author's "process-centered drama" as a means of teaching theatre concepts to children. It includes numerous drama activities and lessons.

SPOLIN, VIOLA, *Improvisation for the Theater,* rev. ed. Evanston, Ill.: Northwestern University Press, 1983. This well-known text is considered a classic in its presentation of improvisation. A section is devoted to working with children.

————, *Theatre Games for the Classroom: A Teacher's Handbook, Grades 1–3* and *Grades 4–6.* Evanston, Ill.: Northwestern University Press, 1986. These companion texts are designed for a theatre arts curriculum.

STEWIG, JOHN W., *Informal Drama in the Elementary Language Arts Program.* New York: Teachers College Press, 1983. In this text the author, a past president of the National Council of Teachers of English, presents his rationale for the incorporation of creative drama into the language-arts curriculum. A number of language-arts activities and references to children's literature are made throughout.

WAGNER, BETTY JANE, *Dorothy Heathcote: Drama as a Learning Medium.* Washington, D.C.: National Education Association, 1976. This is an account of the procedures and techniques used in drama by British educator Dorothy Heathcote, whose work is well known in this country. Wagner carefully describes Heathcote's philosophy and practice with specific examples. Chapter headings focus on Heathcote's specific terminology, such as "edging in" and "dropping to the universal."

WARD, WINIFRED, *Playmaking with Children.* New York: Appleton-Century-Crofts, 1957. This text is the American classic in the field of creative drama written by "the first lady of child drama" in the United States. It discusses drama in elementary and junior high school as well as drama in recreation, religious education, and therapy. The emphasis is on story dramatization.

————, *Stories to Dramatize.* New Orleans: Anchorage Press, 1981. A collection of many excellent stories and poems suitable for dramatization with children from ages 5 to 14.

WAY, BRIAN, *Development Through Drama*. Atlantic Highlands, N.J.: Humanities Press, 1967. A well-known British drama educator presents his philosophy, focusing on development of the whole person. Included are a number of practical exercises and activities in sensory awareness, imagination, speech, and improvisation.

WILDER, ROSILYN, *A Space Where Anything Can Happen*. Rowayton, Conn.: New Plays, 1977. This guidebook is based on one leader's personal experience in a drama program in a middle school. Many techniques and ideas are presented in the author's description of her procedures.

Drama in Special Settings or with Special Populations

BARRAGAR, PAM, *Spiritual Understanding through Creative Drama*. Valley Forge: Judson Press, 1981. With a particular emphasis on Dorothy Heathcote's methods, the author shows how to use drama in religious education.

BURGER, ISABEL B., *Creative Drama and Religious Education*. Wilton, Conn.: Morehouse-Barlow, 1977. The author's many years of work in creative drama and children's theatre bring much insight and practicality to this useful text.

————, *Creative Drama for Senior Adults*. Wilton, Conn.: Morehouse-Barlow, 1980. In this text the author applies her many years of work with creative drama to a different, but equally receptive, population.

JENNINGS, SUE, *Remedial Drama: A Handbook for Teachers and Therapists*. New York: Theatre Arts Books, 1974. This text was one of the first to explore, in readable fashion, the use of drama in therapeutic settings.

NOBLEMAN, ROBERTA, *Using Creative Drama Outside the Classroom*. Rowayton, Conn.: New Plays, 1974. This practical guide explains how to teach creative drama in various community and recreational settings.

PEREIRA, NANCY, *Creative Dramatics in the Library*. Rowayton, Conn.: New Plays, 1974. Helpful tips are presented in this text for ways to begin, using time and space, handling groups of children, coordinating visual aids, and culminating activities in a library setting.

SCHATTNER, GURTRUD, AND RICHARD COURTNEY, EDS., *Drama in Therapy*, 2 vols. New York: Drama Book Publishers, 1981. This important collection presents the work of many practitioners and writers in the field of drama therapy.

TELANDER, MARCIE, FLORA QUINLAN, AND KAROL VERSON, *Acting Up!* Chicago: Coach House Press, 1982. Written by the founding directors of a performing company, this text explains the improvisational techniques used by older actors who write and perform their own work.

THURMAN, ANNE, AND CAROL ANNE PIGGINS, *Drama Activities with Older Adults: A Handbook for Leaders*. New York: Haworth Press, 1982. This highly practical text covers a multitude of activities for a special population.

WETHERED, AUDREY G., *Drama and Movement in Therapy*. London: Macdonald and Evans, 1973. This is a brief yet clear text on the therapeutic use of movement, pantomime, and drama. It provides a good introduction for the nonspecialist in this field.

TWO

Creative Drama Instruction: Some Basics

As has already been stated, the focus in creative drama is more on the creative process of drama than on some finished product such as a well-mounted play. How does drama instruction, in practice, differ from "putting on a play"? What is it that the drama leader does when guiding children in creative drama? This chapter will explore some of these basic questions.

CREATIVE DRAMA GOALS

In creative drama, as with many other curricular areas in the elementary school, there are multiple goals that can be identified. Generally these include

1. drama-theatre goals (for example, pantomime, dialogue improvisation)
2. personal development goals (for example, creativity, self-control, group work)
3. additional curricular or other subject-matter goals (for example, career education, health and safety)

Any one of these goals can be a justifiable reason for undertaking a creative drama activity. But to maximize limited teaching time in the classroom, teachers usually try to identify and emphasize several goals and objectives in every lesson. So although it is possible to focus mainly on one goal, you will often need to consider all three.

Notice also (again, as with other areas of the curriculum) that the goals and subgoals can easily, and often do, overlap and intertwine. For example, some leaders might list creativity under drama-theatre goals or under another subject-matter goal rather than under personal development goals, whereas others might place it under all three goals. We need not become overly concerned about our labeling of goals and subgoals and what gets placed where; all of them are important, and we will want to see that they are a part of the curriculum in whatever way they can be covered.

DRAMA-THEATRE GOALS

Many of the drama goals are derived from formal drama. You need to be familiar with them, as they will guide you in constructing drama activities and lessons.

Dramatic Structure

The basic components of a play are character, setting, and plot line. A plot develops with a beginning, which introduces the story with its characters and setting; a middle, which presents the problem of conflict the characters face; and an ending, which contains the resolution to the problem and brings the story to a close. In creative drama children should learn to recognize this dramatic structure. They should have opportunities to enact characters in a variety of situations and stories, experiencing their conflicts and their attempts to deal with them. They will also be creating and enacting their own plots.

Conflict

Conflict, or the struggle between opposing forces, is a necessary ingredient in dramatic structure. This struggle, whether comic or serious, arrests our attention and sustains our interest in the plot until it is resolved and the story ends. It is so essential to drama that it deserves special attention here.

Generally, there are five kinds of conflict. Characters may struggle *against nature,* as does the little spider in the simple action song "The Itsy Bitsy Spider," who is washed down the drain spout. A character may struggle *against another person*—as does Tom Sawyer, who has differences with both Aunt Polly and cousin Sid. An example of struggle *against society* would be Andersen's "Ugly Duckling," who is faced with the dilemma of living in a society that does not accept him. There are characters who struggle *against technology,* as Homer Price does when he cannot get the doughnut machine to stop. In the final and perhaps most abstract and complex type of conflict, characters may struggle *against themselves,* as does Pinocchio, whose goal to become human is thwarted by his own internal weakness.

Conflict is also needed to create suspense. Suspense keeps us in a state of anticipation over the outcome of the problem. It causes us to continually wonder what will happen next and keeps the drama interesting.

In creative drama you will find yourself considering conflict and suspense repeatedly, seeing ways to incorporate them into each activity and each lesson you teach. Children should learn to identify, enact, and see alternatives for various kinds of conflict and their resolutions. Younger children can identify conflict as a "problem" to be solved; they will also understand the four simpler types of conflict. Older children can use both the words "problem" and "conflict." To varying degrees, they should be able to understand the fifth (internal) type of conflict.

Movement and Pantomime

The plot of any dramatic story is carried out by the characters' actions. Movement and pantomime help to express that action. In drama children are encouraged to move rhythmically, freely, and creatively, but with attention to thought and discipline.

Pantomime is detailed movement which expresses specific ideas, emotions, characters, and situations. In drama children will communicate through pantomime for their own expressive satisfaction as well as to convey meaning to others.

Younger children, whose bodies are often in constant motion, need the frequent physical activity that drama provides. Older children, who have been trained to sit at school desks and to save physical movement for the gymnasium, may be somewhat self-conscious about movement and pantomime activities in the classroom. Eventually, both younger and older children should feel comfortable and successful with their expressive abilities in movement and pantomime.

Sensory Awareness

Sensory awareness is central to drama, as it is to all learning. Our basic knowledge of the world around us is derived from our sensory experiences with it. Through our senses we make observations, comparisons, and discriminations, and form our perceptions about the nature of things. We store our sensory experiences and retrieve them again and again as we express our inner thoughts in language and in movement and as we listen to or read the thoughts of others. Drama should expand children's sensory awareness and lead them to a greater understanding of themselves. It should strengthen their imaginative powers and increase their abilities to experience life with greater meaning.

Emotional Attitudes and Behaviors

In drama children have the opportunity to learn to identify, express, and interpret feelings and emotions. They should have experiences with a wide range of emotions and the opportunity to express them through various means, including facial expression, body movement and pantomime, vocal tone, and improvised dialogue. They will also need to play a variety of roles and characters, taking on their emotional attitudes and feelings and discovering the consequences of them. All this should progress toward a greater understanding of what motivates behaviors and why people behave as they do.

Characterization

Characters create and carry out the plot. They must be believable in order that we may identify with them and care about what happens to them. As children study about various characters and pretend to be them, they must pay attention to physical, mental, and emotional attitudes. Younger children should be able to portray successfully the actions and attitudes of simple characters, including animals, personified objects, and people. As they mature and grow in awareness of other points of view, children's interpretations and portrayals should demonstrate their more sophisticated understandings. And as all children play a variety of roles in varied situations, their insight into others' feelings, attitudes, and behaviors should also increase.

Verbal Skills and Dialogue

Characters express meaning through nonverbal communication, verbal expression, and interaction with others. In drama children should be encouraged to express their own ideas and to understand the messages of others, using both nonverbal and verbal communication and dialogue encounters. This wide range of experience will begin with activities that focus on vocal sound effects, vocal interpretation, and imitative speech, and progress through improvised speech and dialogue interaction.

GUIDING CREATIVE DRAMA

Working with children in creative drama requires the constant use of skills in group management. Many of the skills can be fairly easily acquired with practice, whereas others may take a lifetime to perfect. We will take a beginning look at the leader's role in the next section; a more thorough presentation will be given in Chapter 3.

The Leader's Role

Because creative drama is a planned learning experience, the leader has the responsibility of designing and organizing the lessons. Inexperienced leaders are often not sure they should plan, direct, or even incorporate disciplined attitudes into creative drama lessons for fear of stifling their own and the children's imagination. But groups need organization; people need limits; and creativity needs disciplined structure.

In addition, the leader must design and organize the lessons according to the group's abilities. The group's personality, age, needs, and interests must also be considered. To tax children beyond their capabilities frustrates them; to underestimate their abilities stifles their thinking and leads to boredom.

At the same time, leaders must consider their own personality, style of teaching, and feelings of confidence. They must continually assess their own progress as well as that of the group so that they can guide with the greatest sensitivity and flexibility.

Children's Participation

Children may participate in creative drama in several ways. They may participate as observers, discussants, analyzers, or players. Their participation will vary according to their interest in the topic, their mood, their confidence, and their awareness of their own needs.

Shy children.   Ideally, children should be invited rather than forced to participate. Some children will be relieved to hear the leader say "*If* you would like to play . . ." Extending an invitation encourages them to make their own decisions; feeling they are forced to play can cause anxiety. When they do join in, it is more likely to be because the activity looks like fun and they want to be a part of it.

Reticent children are often more comfortable "sitting out" during the first playing of an activity and entering in on replayings. Watching their peers lets them see how the activity is played. The leader's continual acceptance of children's efforts will eventually give reluctant ones the courage to try on their own. Forcing shy children to participate only increases their reluctance. For some, participation in itself is a significant achievement.

Forcing shy children to participate only increases their reluctance.

Outgoing children often want immediate and continuous involvement.

Outgoing children. On the other hand, many children want to be involved in as much of the playing as possible rather than watching their classmates. They often have difficulty waiting their turn. Although they can appreciate each other's contributions and can work cooperatively together, the fun of the activities is so compelling that they usually want immediate and continuous involvement.

These children may need frequent reminding of the limits and rules in playing. Sometimes they play superficially and need to be cajoled and pushed toward higher achievements. This can be done goodnaturedly, but then with quiet seriousness if the point is missed.

DRAMA ACTIVITY VARIABLES

This text is designed to help beginning drama leaders progress through the activities and related teaching skills step by step, from the easier to the more difficult. The activities that are easier for the children to play are usually the easier activities for you to teach; the same is also true for the more difficult activities. To help you see this progression, eight drama activity variables have been identified. They are listed in the chart below on a continuum of easier to more advanced, with the variables in the left-hand column *generally* being easier than the more advanced ones in the right-hand column.

The qualification "generally" is made since there can be exceptions. For example, older children who are highly verbal but self-conscious about their bodies' rapid changes may find it easier to undertake verbal activities before pantomime. Likewise, they may feel more comfortable playing in groups (rather than engaging in solo or individual playing in unison) because of their strong need to be with peers. A leader's own degree of skill or natural ability with any one of the variables may also affect the general continuum indicated in the chart. Some leaders, even if they are beginners, will have no trouble keeping groups organized in space; others will find it a real challenge. Nevertheless, it is helpful to use the chart as a general guideline.

Continuum of Drama Activity Variables

Easier	to more	Advanced
1. use of desk area		use of larger areas of space
2. teacher direction		creative or independent thinking
3. pantomime		verbal
4. solo or individual playing		pair and group work
5. unison playing for one's own satisfaction		playing to share or communicate with observers
6. run-through playing		in-depth playing for greater involvement
7. humorous or "light" material		highly dramatic or "serious" material
8. minimal information content		high data content

In the next section we will begin discussing these variables. They will also be referred to throughout the text and should become increasingly clear as you move through it.

The Use of Space (Variable 1)

One of the basic concerns in working with groups is keeping them organized physically. One of the simplest remedies is to limit the space they are allowed to work in. Contrary to many other texts on creative drama, this book does not encourage a beginning drama leader to use large areas of playing space. Teachers are frequently told to use gymnasiums or activity rooms for creative drama; in fact, if large rooms are not available, they naturally assume they will not be able to do creative drama at all.

But working in a gymnasium can be more of a curse than a blessing. The space is so open that voices constantly echo and meaningful communication is lost. Furthermore, children usually associate a gym with active sports and the chance to blow off steam and energy. Their anticipation of doing that rather than experiencing drama can be disconcerting and frustrating to them, which causes more problems for you. Large activity or all-purpose rooms create similar problems. More often than not, the classroom provides sufficient space for the beginning teacher, and even the use of that fairly well defined space requires a number of considerations.

In the beginning the children's desks are the most logical place to have them play drama. In fact, desks have important psychological advantages. First of all, the desk area is a convenient and concrete tactile boundary that defines the working space. It separates the children from each other and minimizes distractions. The desk is also a familiar territory and a home base to shy children; they may need the security it provides if they feel they are taking a risk in playing.

Using the desk area is important for initial teaching success. Most beginners would agree that it is difficult enough to concentrate on guiding the drama activities without additional worries about keeping 30 active children organized in space. In fact, using a desk activity as a warm-up before moving to larger areas of space will often be a helpful procedure in each drama lesson you teach—even after you become skilled.

Directed–Creative Activities (Variable 2)

The activities the leader uses for creative drama fall on a line that might be called a continuum of creativity. At one end of this continuum are the activities that tell children what to do and have strong structure built in. At the other end of the continuum are the activities the children create on their own with little help from the leader. They may even be able to organize them by themselves.

Eventually a leader is able to determine how much direction or creative latitude a group needs. Challenges are offered, but the leader also knows how to change to an easier activity if a creative one just will not work. The leader also learns how much independence a group can handle and how much organizational help it needs. Since creativity and imagination are so important to any art form, Chapter 9 will focus on these procedures specifically.

Pantomime–Verbal Activities (Variable 3)

For young children, movement is their natural means of exploring and discovering. They integrate themselves physically with whatever in-

Playing at the desk area provides control as well as psychological security.

terests them; rarely do they passively observe. Language development progresses rapidly, and the verbal skills of older elementary children are quite advanced compared with the younger ones. With this in mind we make a very general assumption that pantomime activities are easier than verbal activities.

This variable probably has more exceptions to it than any of the others. As was pointed out earlier, because of their verbal skills and possible concerns about their bodies' physical changes, older children may feel more comfortable with verbal activities than with pantomime. Furthermore, since they are given less opportunity for physical activity in the classroom than younger children, they may find it somewhat strange and foreign. Therefore, flexibility and caution are needed with this variable.

Solo or Individual–Pair and Group Playing (Variable 4)

As a general rule it is important to involve as many children in the playing as possible while still maintaining order and control. At times, the children will all work solo or individually without interacting with others. This procedure provides privacy to them and minimizes distractions. Both of these factors are essential for concentration. In addition, when children work alone they have the opportunity to focus on and savor their own ideas. For young children particularly, who want to do everything and are worried they may not get a turn, solo playing is very satisfying.

Children may also work in pairs and in small groups. Here they have the opportunity to engage in important social and educational interaction. They can stimulate each other's thinking, integrate ideas, lend support, and learn to compromise and cooperate. Although group process involves

Individual or solo playing lets students work by themselves and enjoy their own ideas.

trials in power struggles and personality conflicts, it also provides the opportunity to enmesh the creative thinking of several individuals. Individual efforts become part of the greater whole.

Unison–Shared Playing (Variable 5)

It is imporant, particularly in the beginning stages of creative drama, for children to play in unison. *Unison playing* means that several or all the children in the class are playing at the same time, whether by themselves, in pairs, or in groups. Each individual, pair, or group works privately, independently concentrating on their own ideas.

Unison playing lets children experience their own ideas for pure and simple enjoyment without worrying about audience evaluation. It gives them an opportunity to sort out their own thinking and to rehearse and polish their ideas in the event that they decide to share them with classmates.

Another benefit of unison playing is that it reduces the time spent waiting to take turns. For younger children and for older active ones who cannot bear to sit and wait, convinced that their turn will never come, unison playing is very satisfying.

Even though the purpose of creative drama is to promote the development of the players rather than entertain an audience, children do share their ideas in the classroom and serve as an audience for each other. For some children, the knowledge that they may eventually share something with others sparks their interest and motivates them to do their best work. They need an outlet for their creative expression, but they also want someone to view their work and to respond. There may also be times when the children have a collective desire to share a particular activity with other groups outside the classroom society. And if an activity has so captured the attention and interest of the children that they have spent a great deal of time on it, it may even appear to be as rehearsed and polished as a formal production.

Run-through Playing–In-depth Involvement (Variable 6)

In rehearsing a play, the term *run-through* is often used. As its name implies, the purpose is to get an overview or a total picture of an idea rather than to focus on a concentrated or intense study of it. An analogy might be made to the subject of reading. At times, we skim printed materials; at other times, we read for greater understanding.

Because the topic of involvement and the techniques for achieving it are so important, the second half of this chapter will be devoted entirely to it.

Humorous Material–Highly Dramatic Material (Variable 7)

It is usually easier to start off with materials that are humorous. Fun activities and situations relax everyone and help build group rapport. If the characters are funny, there is less pressure on the children to play the parts in a polished or formal way.

Yet, playing material rich in dramatic tension or conflict is often the most rewarding experience children can have. After all, life is not always a joke; there are many sad and hurtful times to balance the pleasant ones. There is no question that it is worth the time it takes to understand more serious material and to work at becoming involved in it. It is a surprise to find that the most unlikely children (for example, class clowns) are sometimes the ones who lead in the requests for challenging material once they have had a successful experience of being involved in it. (Special techniques for working with highly dramatic material are presented later in this chapter.)

Minimal Information Content–High Data Content (Variable 8)

The final variable, quite simply, refers to the amount of additional curricular information the leader wishes to incorporate into an activity. If children are asked to pantomime "something you like to do" as opposed to pantomiming "six exports from Chile," there is obviously a difference in the amount of information-recall involved. And obviously, the older the children, the more informational data they will have to draw from.

PLAYING FOR IN-DEPTH INVOLVEMENT (VARIABLE 6): ADDITIONAL CONSIDERATIONS

Generally speaking, the success of drama experiences, as measured by both the leader and the children, is dependent on the degree of the players' involvement in their work. The leader's encouragement of children's concentration and involvement in drama is crucial in helping them go beyond a superficial level of playing to more meaningful experiences. Since this variable is so important and will require many skills from the leader, this special section is devoted to a more complete exploration of it.

Identifying Involvement

According to one writer, there is an aesthetic dimension which distinguishes many play activities and is crucial to validating the claim that creative drama develops the whole person. "At the moment of doing," she states, "when nothing outside the situation matters, there emerges a sense of ultimate integration: a fusion of the person with his or her surroundings."[1] A distinguished researcher in developmental psychology comments on the "autotelic" (meaning that goals are self-contained in the activity) nature of drama, describing it this way:

---

[1]Maureen Mansell, "Dimensions of Play Experience," *Communication Education*, 29, no. 1 (1980), 48. The poem reprinted in the front of this text also describes this experience.

Involvement means believing what you are doing.

When everything is right—the challenges and skills are well meshed, the concentration deep, the goals clear, feedback sharp, distractions minimized, self-consciousness absent—actors and spectators achieve ecstasy. That is, they step outside accustomed reality, and feel with all possible concreteness another dimension of existence. For all they know at the moment, they are in a different reality. This feeling is what drama is about.[2]

It is this experience the leader constantly assesses in the children's playing and assists them in achieving.

Even the beginning teacher knows when children are engrossed in any classroom work. One can see the furrowed brow of concentration, the oblivious attitude to disruptions, and the look of pleasure and satisfaction that acknowledges a job well done. Similar moments in drama show children so absorbed and engrossed that they are unaware of anyone observing them. Perhaps they enjoy the material so much that they forget about everyone else, or perhaps they are able to block out distractions successfully.

When they are involved, children often demonstrate a detailed awareness of the experience they are enacting. For example, a child pretending to walk a tightrope may step very carefully, placing one foot exactly ahead of the other, balancing the body with outstretched arms. The child may stop momentarily, gently swaying, eyes fixed straight ahead, arms moving as if in an attempt to regain a temporary loss of balance, and then slowly move ahead. All these movements demonstrate that the pantomimer is very much aware of the narrow rope suspended high above the ground and of the skills required of one who performs on it.

[2]Mihaly Csikszentmihalyi, "What's Interesting in Children's Theatre," *Children's Theatre, Creative Drama and Learning,* ed. Judith Kase-Polisini (Lanham, Md.: University Press of America, 1986), p. 14.

Another clue to involved playing is the spontaneous addition of details that the activity has not specified. The child mentioned above might also pretend to hold an imaginary umbrella for balance while bowing and throwing kisses to an enthusiastic but imaginary audience. Involved players concentrate intently and are usually highly pleased with their work. They frequently ask to repeat the activity and seem to be revitalized with each playing.

When children are not absorbed, there may be showing-off behaviors. These, in reality, are the result of being embarrassed because others are watching, or simply being too concerned about what others think. Being shy or insecure can also stand in the way of concentration and involvement. These are the students who may giggle with embarrassment, crowd against others in an attempt to hide or disappear in the masses, or hesitantly look at other classmates to see what they are doing.

To complicate matters, there are times when the entire classroom responds as one person, all with the same depth of involvement or lack of it. At other times part of the class is involved, while some children are only superficially involved.

The leader can be instrumental in making an experience and the playing of it as meaningful as possible. From the time you select the material until the time the material is replayed for the third or fourth time, you have the opportunity to affect the involvement the children have in it. Those steps will be discussed along with some of the considerations that will help you assure involvement each step of the way.

Selecting Materials

The first consideration to be made is in the selection of appropriate, enjoyable, and meaningful material. Children work best when they are intrigued. No one can respond to or concentrate on an idea that seems to be a waste of time.

Obviously the material should also appeal to you as leader, since your own involvement is usually contagious. Select ideas to which you can be committed and with which you feel confident, since you may need to be enthusiastic about it in order to "sell" it to a group who need proof that the subject is worth their attention.

Materials that capture the children's attention may be subjects that thoroughly entertain, or they may be subjects that encourage intense discussions and stimulate sincere concerns. Leaders usually have to learn from their group what kinds of situations and materials they find most appealing. Many listings of materials will specify for which age groups they are suited; however, these are only guides and not sacred rules. You need to learn which material is most interesting and meaningful for a particular group, regardless of its age level.

Groups also vary in personality. Some groups are satisfied only when the material tickles their funny bones and contains a joke they can enjoy together. Others prefer to be involved in more serious situations. Some groups enjoy romantic themes; others will reject any hint of a love element. Some groups like anything and everything; others are finicky. Tastes and interests can be expanded, but that may take time and some careful planning.

Your choice of material will naturally reflect your personality and your values. For this reason, leaders should periodically examine the nature of their favorite materials to see if they are meeting the needs of the children. You may discover that children have other interests, values, and concerns. You may need to reach beyond a limited sphere of interest in order to keep alert to new materials, and to listen with a sensitive ear to both the spoken and implied interests of the children.

Presenting the Material

All material—whether it is music, props, pictures, literature, or simply an idea—is only as good a stimulus as your presentation makes it. As you tell a story, lead a discussion, or even give directions, your overall attitude can establish the appropriate atmosphere for the eventual playing.

Establishing mood. You can reinforce the mood of the material by reacting appropriately. One may smile and laugh along with a humorous story or tell it tongue-in-cheek. In playing recorded music the sensitive leader will carefully fade music in and out rather than dropping or lifting the needle abruptly. You can react to a curious prop by conveying some measure of surprise in your voice when you pose the question, "Who do you suppose owns this? Have you ever seen anything like it before?"

Vocal quality, pitch, timing, and intensity of voice are all tools you can use to contribute meaning and understanding. Your voice can become quiet and convey a soft quality when describing the feel of a kitten's fur. You can say the word "warm" and make the children feel it, or say "tangy, crisp apple" so that they almost taste it. A voice can creak like the door of a

A good story that is well-told will capture attention.

haunted house, moan like the wind, or boom like thunder. Emotions can be conveyed by drawing out the word "lonely"; sorrowful passages may need a lower voice; or anxiety can be conveyed when telling about someone trapped in a mine shaft.

Being familiar with the material. It is imperative that you be thoroughly familiar with the material you present. This is especially important in presenting literature. Even if the poem or story is well known or you have used it several times before, it should always be reviewed before it is presented again. Familiarity with the material eliminates the irritating tendency to omit crucial points, to mispronounce words, or to be halting and hesitant in delivery. It also allows you the opportunity to establish rapport with the children and to judge its effect on them.

It also helps children's concentration if you do not begin presenting the material until they are ready to listen. Some leaders are particularly adept at captivating children's attention with storytelling. They begin a story and allow the first sentence or two to calm down or to entice a wiggly or listless group. Most teachers have to establish the rule that the material will not be shared until the children show they are ready to listen. Then they wait a moment or two until the children settle down. Children might also be asked to put their heads on their desks or to close their eyes as aids to listening.

Finally, it is helpful if the children and the room are arranged to accommodate both the presentation of the material and the playing. For example, if the children are to play at the desk area, there is no need to have them listen to the story on the floor in the story corner and then return to the desks to play it. This can break the mood of the material and the children's concentration on it.

Understanding the Material

Children cannot play experiences they do not understand. There are several techniques you can use to aid understanding.

Stimulating Awareness

Understanding and involvement are reinforced when children are given materials they can touch, taste, smell, listen to, and carefully examine. Before playing an experience on scuba diving, for example, you may show some objects associated with the activity: fins, a mask, an oxygen tank, and perhaps some shells and a piece of dried seaweed. Children are allowed to handle them and talk about them; for some children these materials may be new ones that acquaint them with the subject for the first time. Or before children role-play young Helen Keller, you may ask them to close their eyes and examine various objects with their hands.

A film such as *Dream of the Wild Horses* (Contemporary Films, McGraw-Hill, 9 minutes, color) can illustrate the beauty of slowed movement. Or pictures from Edward Steichen's *Family of Man* (New York: Museum of Modern Art, 1955) can demonstrate the universality of human emotions. Such materials can create images and awareness that words alone cannot communicate.

Discussing Ideas

Discussion may also be needed to clarify language or perceptions and to bring experiences closer to the children's own. For example, in the poem "Foul Shot" (see bibliography on p. 109), the basketball player is said to be "squeezed by silence," and "measures the waiting net." Children may explain in their own words:

CHILD: "Squeezed by silence" means you feel cramped because it is so quiet and everyone's watching you.

CHILD: He "measures the waiting net" by sizing it up and aiming the ball really carefully.

Perhaps analogies are needed, especially with unfamiliar subjects. Before pretending to explore the moon's gravity-free environment, children might recall the floating sensation of wading in deep water. They can think of their own analogies also.

TEACHER: We already know some things about a desert, even though none of us has ever been there. Can you think of something you have seen or experienced that would be like something in the desert?

CHILD: It would be hotter than it was in here the day the heat was turned on too high and we almost suffocated.

CHILD: My grandpa says when it gets really hot you can fry an egg on the sidewalk.

CHILD: The chameleon the first grade has looks like the gila monster in our book about the desert.

Analyzing Characters

Discussions can also help children identify with characters by discovering similarities between their own thoughts and feelings and those of the characters. Some characters are very simply drawn and may even be stereotypes, such as "wily fox," "curious child," or "cruel king." Folktale characters are usually quite one-dimensional. A young man may be a "clever, handsome fellow"; a villain may be an "old witch." Because of their simple characters, folktales are usually the easiest stories to dramatize.

Generally, the more complex the literature, the more developed the characters. It may take the author the length of a book to show us the many facets of a character. Charlotte the spider in *Charlotte's Web* or Johnny in *Johnny Tremain* are characters we learn a great deal about and are not likely to forget.

In playing characters we look at how they are both similar to and different from us. Much of this information is revealed in the things that happen to them and how they feel and react to those events. We look at how we would react in the same instance or a similar one:

TEACHER: The story doesn't tell us, but I wonder how "Gertrude McFuzz" (see bibliography on p. 114) has her temper tantrum. What does she do, do you suppose?

TEACHER: How do you think Johnny Tremain (91) felt when Isannah screamed that his scarred hand was "dreadful"?

TEACHER: In *Shadow of a Bull* (112) there is one scene when all the boys merrily jump from a wagon of hay. All but Manolo; he's too afraid. What thoughts do you think are in Manolo's head when the boys suggest jumping? How do you think he feels? Have you ever been afraid of doing something the way Manolo is afraid of jumping?

Discussions are often important if an experience is a culturally different one for the children:

TEACHER: Before we dramatize some sections from *Call it Courage* (see bibliography in Chapter 6) let's talk about courage. What is courage to you? What are some things you think a courageous person might do?

TEACHER: James Huston vividly describes a very dramatic moment when the Eskimo Tiktaliktak (see bibliography in Chapter 6) gives up hope of surviving and builds himself a coffin. Why does he do that? What are his last thoughts as he carefully arranges his weapons by his side? Why does he want his relatives to understand the reason for his death?

You may find that children will be able to talk about feelings when you share yours also.

TEACHER: The "Star-Bellied Sneetches" (p. 123) don't play with the Sneetches that don't have stars. They don't invite them to their wiener roasts. I remember how I felt when a girl in my class at school didn't invite me to her party. I think I know how those Sneetches without stars must have felt.

Through discussion children have the opportunity to discover that others often share their ideas and their powerful feelings, and to realize that "I'm not the only person in the world who feels this way." Besides clarifying ideas, these discussions also help set the mood for the eventual enactment.

PLAYING THE MATERIAL

A frequently asked question is, "How do you keep the kids from acting silly?" Most of the time children act silly because they either do not know what to do or are being asked to do something too difficult or something they have not been fully prepared for. The silliness simply comes from embarrassment. Without understanding this, you may lose patience. And that adds to, rather than solves, the problem.

As was stated earlier, it is usually helpful to begin with humorous materials. In addition to its previously mentioned benefits, a little silliness or laughing in playing humorous material will not destroy the mood as easily as it does with dramatic material.

Playing Dramatic Material

Working with highly dramatic material does take additional and special considerations. Following are some suggestions.

1. Clarify the nature of the material and the expectations you have. Sometimes teachers assume that children will understand the material is of a serious nature and that they will automatically respond appropriately. Many times this is not the case. It may be helpful to simply alert them immediately to the fact that the material may be demanding.

TEACHER: We've been talking about the relocation of Indian tribes, and I thought we might be able to understand this idea a little better if we enact the march along the Trail of Tears. This may take some effort on our part.

2. At first, play briefly. For initial attempts at in-depth involvement with dramatic material, it is helpful to keep the playing fairly brief. If children know the experience will be short, they may be more apt to participate in it and may be less anxious. They can be assured that the experience will be over before they have time to be embarrassed by it.

Brief playings are also easier on leaders. They too will not have to work so long and hard at creating and sustaining the mood. An initial success will also bolster both the teacher's and the students' confidence for a longer playing another time.

3. Create the appropriate mood. Your voice can do a great deal in conveying the mood of dramatic material. The vocal quality you use to introduce, discuss, and side-coach the material will make a great difference in conveying and sustaining the appropriate mood.

As in the theatre, the use of music, lights, and sound effects can also affect the mood, create a wealth of pictorial images, and stimulate the imagination. Numerous selections of music—both classical and popular—can lend sadness, intrigue, and suspense and provide appropriate background for your voice. When the lights are off and the room dimmed, children can more easily imagine dark tunnels, mysterious underwater worlds, ancient ruins, or the Arctic. Quickly flashing classroom lights on and off can simulate lightning, neon lights, the glitter of an ice world, and the like.

Sound effects can have a similar influence. In some social studies books it is noted that the sound of fife and drum accompanied Nathan Hale to his place of execution. If children were to dramatize this moment, it might be intensified by the ominous sound of drumming on the desktops.

4. Create a working climate by limiting distractions. Separating students from each other can lessen distractions and aid concentration. Dimmed lights can, in addition to providing a mood, help students focus on their own work.

Another aid is having students close their eyes. (Particularly when they are playing individually and are in limited space, having their eyes closed will not pose a problem.) By closing their eyes the students are able to both block out distractions and to visualize their ideas. Some children adopt this aid on their own, judging for themselves when such a technique will make the playing more involving and hence more satisfying for them.

It is often helpful to discuss with the children what aids and what interferes with their concentration. Usually children know what distracts them. It may be other children just being near them, touching them, or purposely trying to distract them. Or they may be bothered by just being aware that others are nearby.

Keeping your eyes closed can help focus your thinking.

Distractions can keep a person from concentrating fully.

After playing, children can evaluate the conditions under which they were working and find ways to make them better. Particularly after children have given behavioral evidence that they were involved in the material, it is helpful to have them describe it.

CHILD: When I was being the bird with a broken wing, I remembered how hard it was to do anything with my right arm when it was in a cast all last summer.

CHILD: When I was being one of those explorers on the *Kon-Tiki* (see bibliography in Chapter 6), I remembered what it was like when my Dad and I were in a canoe and it capsized. If we had been closer to the rapids, we might not have made it. I wasn't scared then, but I was afterwards when I thought about it.

5. Select volunteers for initial playings. Although you will want to let as many students as possible play an activity, it is often a wise precaution for first playings to begin with just a few children who can be the most easily involved. Particularly when trying out new material and the group's response cannot be predicted, there is no point in taking chances with an entire class. The players can be a model for subsequent replayings and can set a mood for others to build on.

You might also ask for volunteers "who can really concentrate on the material and play it believably." Sometimes children who already have their hands raised for volunteering will think again about this requirement and sit out the first playing. This gives them the chance to self-select and avoid what they think they are not yet ready to handle. Surprisingly, many students do have an awareness of their own limitations and a willingness to approach a task with determined seriousness.

Side-coaching

Side-coaching is a technique in creative drama in which the leader gives suggestions or comments from the sidelines to heighten and advance as well as control the playing. It is literally "talking the children through" an experience and is an indispensable aid in encouraging concentration and involvement. Side-coaching can also fill in awkward silences, giving security to those who are unsure and guidance to those who might need calming down. Frequently a group's lukewarm response to an idea changes to excited involvement with expert side-coaching from an enthusiastic leader.

You should always be prepared to side-coach, although you will probably never know exactly how much and what kind of side-coaching will be necessary until the playing begins. Side-coaching is a skill that will grow with experience and with your own sensitivity to your students' needs.

The Leader's Participation

In many drama activities your own participation will be helpful and sometimes even necessary. You may simply pantomime along with the students as you side-coach. You may take your own turn at a sequence game or at playing a role in a story dramatization. You may play a role in discussions to give students a character or situation to respond to. This can set the scene, create the mood, and highlight the dramatic tension. By playing with the students you demonstrate a willingness to accept the challenge the activity presents. It can also be a lot of fun!

EVALUATION

When you and the students evaluate the playing together, you increase the possibility for further involvement in subsequent playings. When students say what they liked about their playing, they verbally reinforce themselves.

When you evaluate what the students have done, be as specific as possible. Saying "good," although it is nice to hear, does not really tell the students what you are referring to. However, if you say "Good ideas! I saw so many different animals," or "Good control. You stayed right with the music," students understand your judgment better and also know what to repeat in further playings.

Believability is also important: "Good pantomiming; I could really see some zoo animals that time" or "Your robots were so believable, I almost wondered for a minute if my fourth graders had disappeared!"—these comments place a premium on the look of reality, achieved only by controlled, imaginative thinking.

Without students' self-evaluation and the leader's evaluative guidance, drama work will probably only be superficial in the long run. Only when careful attention is given to all aspects of the playing will the best results occur.

REPLAYING

If a drama exercise or story is worth playing once, it is usually worth taking some time to replay it. Seldom does the best creative thinking and the deepest understanding emerge in a first playing, even if you and the students are experienced in drama work.

You may need to play an activity three times, even in one session. The first playing might be a run-through in order to get a total picture. A second playing gives the opportunity to add new ideas, drop out less effective ones, and do further refining and polishing. A third playing can become a final synthesis of ideas.

It is helpful to you and to the students to remember that the best work is not achieved immediately. Taking an experimental viewpoint is comforting to anxious students and will allay your own fears of not knowing what to expect. But not only is it important to remember, it is important to *verbalize*, for your own sake as well as the children's.

"We've never done this before. Let's just try it and see what happens."

"I thought we did well for our first time with this story. What did you think was particularly good—and where might we make some changes for the next time?"

All the techniques just discussed will play a great role in helping you lead children to greater involvement in their playing over time. Sometimes you will be amazed at how easily it happens; at other times you will be disappointed because you are not getting the response you expected immediately. But when students have once experienced in-depth involvement in drama work, they will often not be satisfied with superficial playing again. They may still need assistance in arriving at that goal. But with all working toward it, many more enriching experiences will be possible.

Example from *Venture for Freedom*

The following is an extended example of a 30-minute activity with a fifth-grade class during their fourth session of creative drama. It demonstrates many of the techniques for encouraging involvement.

Noteworthy is the fact that there was lengthy preparation in order to guide the understanding and to establish a strong, serious mood and a sense of deep involvement. The physical activity itself involved walking only about 6 feet. The drama event was focused literally on only about three sentences of text. But the understanding of the event, as well as the emotions involved, required much discussion and work.

The leader guided the children through three discussions and three playings. After 30 minutes of work, all the children had become involved in what developed into a very moving experience.

The children and the teacher grouped themselves on the floor at one end of the room. The teacher introduced the book *Venture for Freedom* (123), explaining that it was a true story based on the experience of a captured African tribe and of an African king's son whose English name was Venture Smith. She read short, specific episodes describing the fatal beating of Venture's father; the day Venture sneaked down to the ship's hold to find his mother; and the moment the Africans disembarked into the blinding Barbados sun and slavery.

Then the teacher and the children discussed the following questions:

What kind of people do you think they must have been to have a king who would die rather than betray his tribe?

The story gives us some idea of the grim condition in the ship's hold, but expanding on that with your imagination, what do you think the hold was like?

How must Venture have felt, knowing his mother was in that hold?

His mother told him to go back on deck and stay alive. How do you think she felt, saying that? How did Venture feel?

What do you think it was like to come out of the ship's hold, after so many weeks in the dark, into the blinding sun? What thoughts and feelings do you think they had?

How must Venture have felt, knowing that this would be the last time he would see his mother and his people?

After the discussion the leader played a recording of "Sometimes I Feel Like a Motherless Child." She explained that the song grew out of and reflected the sorrow of the slave-trading days.

The teacher asked the children to put themselves back into this time and into the lives of these Africans. The lights were turned off. They were to imagine that they were in the ship's hold and that the two chairs she had placed close together in the middle of the room represented the ship's disembarking plank. Slowly, one at a time or in pairs, they were to come out of the hold, walk the plank, and then sit and wait for their brothers and sisters.

She told them to think about who they were, their physical condition, their attitudes about seeing the earth again, about the slave seller who would bark his orders to them as they slowly emerged into the day, their feelings about each other, and their feelings about slavery.

To help establish a mood, the teacher asked the children to close their eyes and softly hum "Motherless Child" as they thought about their characters. After a few moments the teacher stood and in a rough and callous voice growled, "All right, look lively! Come on out!"

As the first children reached the plank, the teacher threw open the classroom window curtains to reveal the very bright sunlight. The children slowly walked between the chairs, some seriously involved in the activity, some snickering to their partners. After they had all assembled, the leader turned on the lights.

She talked to them for a few moments, commenting objectively. Quietly and in the mood of the material she said, "As we played this the first time, some of you were involved in the moment, and some of you found it difficult. It's not easy to play something as serious as this, but I think we can do it if we work at it some more. Let's try it again. Now that you know what it's about, let's have you decide if you think you can remain involved in it this next time. If you think you cannot, you may sit and watch."

Six children sat down. The activity was repeated. The involvement was stronger this time, but the leader noted that the children might be able to create an even more believable moment.

"What do you think? Shall we try it once again?" she asked.

They all agreed they wanted to try the experience again, and the leader offered them the choice again of playing or watching. All the children got up to play. This third playing was the most successful, and the children spontaneously expressed their satisfaction with it.

FOR THE COLLEGE STUDENT

1. Select some material suitable for dramatization. Have in mind a particular group of children who will play it. Consider the following questions:
    a. What are the drama-theatre, personal development, and additional curricular goals you would emphasize?
    b. How much emphasis on each drama activity variable will you aim for? Explain.
    c. What do you personally like about the material? What is your commitment to it?
    d. How will the material serve the interests, needs, and concerns of the group of children who are to play it?
    e. What will be important for you to consider in your presentation of the material to the children?
    f. What methods might you use to assist the children in understanding the material? Be specific.
    g. What considerations are necessary for the group or the material in playing it? Outline your plan for playing the material.
    h. What special effects might be used for the playing of the material?
2. Select some humorous material. Practice reading it aloud, using your voice to convey the mood. Select music appropriate for the material. Rehearse the music with your reading until you can smoothly operate the phonograph as you read. Share this with your classmates.
3. Select some material rich in dramatic conflict. Follow the same procedure as in exercise 2.
4. Using the *Venture for Freedom* example (pp. 41–43), enumerate all the techniques used by the leader to aid involvement. What other techniques might have been employed?

THREE

Working in Groups

In traditional classroom teaching, children are most frequently an *assembled* group, working individually on their own seatwork activities or projects. Generally, it takes considerable training and experience for classroom teachers to learn how to work with their students as an *interacting* group. As noted in Chapter 2, managing children in creative drama requires special skills. An important part of this management includes guiding children to be self-seeking, self-directed, authenticated individuals capable of integrating themselves into a democratic, cohesive group. In this chapter, some of the basic concepts regarding the nature of groups and group process, as applied to creative drama in the classroom setting, will be explored.

THE NATURE OF THE CLASSROOM GROUP

Every classroom is composed of a group, including the teacher, organized for the express purpose of education. To accomplish this most effectively, a high degree of cohesive interaction is required. It is the leader's responsibility to guide the group toward this goal.

The methods of achieving group interaction are not easily described because of the variables involved in the nature of groups themselves. No two children, leaders, or groups are alike. Neither do they remain consistent in their differences from day to day or even minute to minute. As every experienced teacher knows, variations in demeanor and attitude can be caused by such factors as weather, time of day and year, physical aspects of the environment, material presented, presence or absence of individual members, age, sex ratio, and size of the group. Furthermore, every indi-

Leadership in creative drama is an experience in group management.

vidual in the group, including the teacher, is a constantly growing and evolving human being—never static. Being aware of these variables is necessary to guide the group most effectively.

Likewise, each person in the group is unique because of different experiences and background. Yet each member is equally important, and each one's individuality makes its own special contribution. Leaders also play a role as a group member. Their backgrounds, with their unique experiences, have contributed to the persons they are. When leaders examine the source of their ideas, values, feelings, and behaviors, they will develop a greater awareness of why they favor certain curricular subjects, enjoy working on particular pet projects, like or dislike certain personalities, have a personality that can be labeled "jovial," "sensitive," or "demanding," or why they value certain ideas above others.

In all classroom learning, the leader's total personality will probably influence the children more than any subject matter taught. Especially in experiences dealing with human emotions and interpersonal relationships, the leader's own behaviors will serve as a strong example. Examining and understanding our own sensitivities as human beings will be required if we are to teach human interaction through creative drama to children with honesty and relevance.

POSITIVE CLASSROOM CLIMATE

The emotional climate in the classroom is determined by the overall feelings experienced by the group members. In a positive climate the students

The leader is responsible for establishing a secure climate in the classroom.

and the teacher have a mutual trust and respect for each other, an essential ingredient in facilitating the development of self-esteem and optimal learning. Individuals make their best contributions when they feel confident and possess a positive self-image. This attitude develops in a climate of *acceptance, psychological freedom,* and *open communication.*

Acceptance is the belief that all people are worthy individuals. Although certain behaviors and actions may be disapproved of, there is a recognition of a person's basic self. Acceptance forms the very foundation for successful group interaction which creative drama attempts to foster. The leader initiates acceptance and becomes the model for it by demonstrating acceptance of each child as a human being with important feelings and ideas. The leader's guidance also reflects an understanding of children's various stages of growth and development as well as their interests, needs, and concerns. The right of every child to be treated with equality is respected, and this attitude is taught to the group by example and practice.

Psychological freedom allows a person to be secure enough in the social, physical, and emotional environment to operate with relative ease. Everyone has known the feelings of fear and anxiety in uncomfortable and tense situations. At such times all the eyes of the world appear to be staring at us, making impossible demands. Our insecurity may cause us to become shy and withdrawn or hostile and aggressive, making it impossible for us to operate with maximum effectiveness.

The leader is responsible for establishing an atmosphere of psychological freedom and creating the secure climate in which children can express their thoughts freely, without fear of reprisal. Not only is this condition important for positive self-growth, it is crucial for encouraging the risk taking that creativity demands.

Creative drama is a natural medium for the free expression of ideas, feelings, and attitudes. Fostering open communication becomes fundamental and paramount in the leader's successful guidance of creative drama. Leaders must value and respect the sincere, open, and honest communication from children that creative drama can engender. Furthermore, they must be ready to communicate their own thoughts and feelings with equal sincerity.

Conveying Acceptance

Conveying acceptance to children is one of the most important factors in fostering their self-growth. We convey acceptance both openly and subtly by our general attitudes, our nonverbal behaviors, and our verbal comments.

Self-acceptance. The first step in being able to accept another person is to accept oneself. Essentially, when we recognize our own humanness, we are accepting of others. Leaders who expect perfection from themselves and from their students will continually be frustrated, a condition which builds more unacceptance. These accumulating, unaccepting behaviors are then translated into a negativism which can pervade the entire classroom.

When we are aware of our personal makeup and our feelings, we can more easily reflect them in our verbal comments. For example, the teacher who says "I get really upset when I hear so much chattering" rather than "You're the noisiest bunch of kids I've ever seen" has owned up to personal feelings and has taken responsibility for them. Since the same amount of noise might not be bothersome to another person, the feelings lie in the speaker. By speaking I-statements, we can get in touch with our personal feelings and values, making them clear to ourselves and to others. With I-statements we can also be more exact in expressing our needs: "This noise may not be bothering anyone else, but it's interrupting my thinking. Please hold it down."

Our You-messages, on the other hand, place blame and negative judgment on the other person, often causing guilt and resentment. Probably the last thing it will accomplish is the change of behavior we had hoped for. Saying "You're rude" seldom generates politeness.

Children sometimes have a difficult time accepting themselves. Often it is their own self-rejection statements we are most tempted to reject.

"That's a pretty sweater you have on, Mark," said the leader at the beginning of the session.

"I don't like it. I hate myself in it," said chubby Mark, who had not yet played with his classmates in creative drama, although he had been attending the sessions regularly.

The leader was tempted to say, "Well, I don't know why you don't like it. It really is a pretty sweater" or "You shouldn't hate anyone, not even yourself." But she knew that these statements would have rejected Mark's feelings. And because she also recognized that Mark's weight problem may have caused his concern over his appearance, she simply made no further comment. As it turned out, Mark played that day for the first time and continued to participate on succeeding days.

Accepting ideas and behaviors.   Students assess their worth as human beings by the verbal and nonverbal statements communicated to them. Most children flourish under accepting comments like flowers responding to a warm spring rain. In fact, we all appreciate acceptance demonstrated by a nod, a pat on the back, a smile, a kind word about our efforts and thoughts, and an understanding of feelings.

In verbally accepting children's ideas and behaviors, we might say

"That's a good idea."
"Nice work!"
"I think all this noise means you're excited."

By hearing accepting statements children will often begin to express acceptance and appreciation also.

"Mr. Burns, what music were you playing when we were pretending? It's super."
"I liked watching Jim when he pretended he was that stubborn donkey and rolled on his back."
"You were good, Annette."

Creative drama fosters the expression of ideas.

Although it is important to be accepting of ideas, there is no need to claim creative genius for a good but rather ordinary idea. Children have an awareness of what is pretty good and what is outstanding, and exaggerated praise is usually recognized as phony. One leader discovered this fact from the children themselves. She had the habit of being overly enthusiastic with everyone and everything. When a group of children spontaneously praised one child's ideas in playing a scene, the child expressed delight and was very pleased. The children reminded him that the teacher often praised his work, but his response was "Oh, she says everything's good." The child viewed his classmates' praise as more discerning and therefore more meaningful than the teacher's constant global praise.

Accepting statements may be particularly difficult to give when one appears to be under direct attack.

> One seven-year-old boy in an early session in creative drama said to the leader, "You're stupid." Although stunned, she probed, "Why do you think so, Rocky?" "Because you pretend and make up things. That's stupid," was his reply. The leader reflected his feelings: "It's true that I do like to pretend and make up things. You feel that pretending is stupid."

Possibly Rocky had heard a similar statement himself. Perhaps he did not want to risk pretending if someone might call *him* "stupid," so in defense he applied it to someone else before anyone had the chance to label him. In being allowed to express his concerns and in hearing that someone had understood them, Rocky's anxiety may have been relieved. Interestingly, he continued to attend the voluntary sessions and in time participated freely.

Understanding and accepting feelings. Every experienced teacher knows the importance of a learner's healthy emotional outlook. Without a feeling of well-being, learning is not possible. If for no other reason, emotions must be dealt with because of their effect on learning.

Throughout all drama experiences sincere and honest expression of ideas and feelings is encouraged. If they are rejected, the open channels of communication are at risk. Consider the following examples.

> A group of fourth graders were pretending to be robots. In the first playing they were robots working at their jobs, performing a variety of tasks. For the second playing, the leader suggested that they be robots entertaining themselves on a night off. In the discussion that followed the playing, one boy said, "I had a fight with my wife and went to the gasoline station and got oil and got drunk."

The child's answer was logical for the situation and, more important, was delivered sincerely. The answer was accepted with a simple nod of the head. If the leader had given a shocked look or rejected the answer as inappropriate, he would have given reproof to a child's honest expression.

From a pragmatic point of view, he could also have triggered other children into creating "drunken robots" too, if they thought it would get attention.

In another instance, a six-year-old, pretending to be a witch casting an evil spell, said fervently that he was "turning all the parents in the world into furniture." The leader, playing the "oldest and wisest" witch, merely cackled and said, "I see." If the leader had remarked "Are you sure that's what you'd like to do to parents?" or "You shouldn't say things like that," she would have rejected the child's strong feelings. Apparently he felt secure enough to express his thoughts in what he assumed to be a safe environment, and the leader verified his assumption by accepting his statement.

Creative drama, as an enjoyable, active experience, creates by itself a positive emotional atmosphere. The strong movement of marching around the room to a bouncy rhythm can help a child achieve a fresh and renewed outlook on the rest of the day; or pretending to be on a raft with Tom Sawyer floating down the Mississippi may help children forget, if only temporarily, their own struggles with life.

Creative drama leaders can deal even more directly with the subject of emotion. They can help children understand what emotions are, how they are expressed, why people behave as they do, and how emotional responses differ. Such topics are also a part of other curricular areas, such as social studies, literature, or health.

The subject of emotions is also dealt with every time the leader guides the children in a discussion of the characters in stories and the motivations behind their behaviors. Children readily identify with certain characters. These are often the ones they choose to play, and through these characters they have the opportunity to release important feelings. They feel safe under the guise of the character to express feelings that may not be allowed them otherwise.

Many creative drama leaders have noted shy students suddenly becoming assertive in a particular character role, or aggressive ones becoming subdued. One leader tells the following:

> I remember distinctly the overly feminine youngster who pleasantly surprised her classmates (who were usually put off by her phoniness) and me by playing Tom Sawyer with great honesty and believability. I also remember the rather aggressive boy who was a class clown but who asked to play a wish-granting sprite in a story we were dramatizing. I threw caution to the winds and allowed him to do it, and was amazed to find a caring and kind personality emerge in the playing. Both these students apparently felt safe in expressing their emotions through the characters they chose to play.

When students discuss people, situations and emotions, they often draw upon their own experiences. You need to be aware and accepting of these comments without showing judgments so that students realize that they, and the feelings they are experiencing, are normal.

STUDENT: I hate his guts!
TEACHER: You're really angry with him.

STUDENT: My sister's dumb.
TEACHER: You seem to be upset with something your sister did.

Said objectively, these statements reflect the emotions the students are expressing, letting the children know they have been heard. This is often all that is needed to assist them in handling their feelings.

Although we think of feelings as good (happy, excited, loving) and bad (angry, lonely, unhappy) because of the effect they have on us, having a particular feeling is neither good nor bad in itself. It used to be thought (and some people still think) that we should be able to keep ourselves from having "bad" feelings. That is why many people will say "Don't be unhappy" or "You shouldn't be afraid" or even "You must never hate anyone." But all feelings are normal and just *are*. We cannot keep ourselves from having them. What we *do* with our feelings is what makes a difference.

Often children have been denied normal emotions by such statements as "Big boys don't cry" or "It's silly to be afraid of the dark." But rejection of feelings only causes one to be defensive or to question one's perceptions of the world. Rather than rejecting feelings, it is more helpful if we acknowledge that they are normal, allowable, and have a reason for being. "Sometimes crying helps us feel better" or "We're sometimes afraid of the dark because we can't see what's there" are statements that encourage positive emotional growth.

We will want children to understand that people all over the world share emotions of fear, love, hate, and joy. When students hear someone expressing understanding of their emotions, they know their feelings are normal. For some children it can be particularly helpful for the teacher to identify with them in the experiencing of common human emotions with

Expressing emotions—fear and rage—with expressionless masks made from paper plates.

statements such as "I know how you feel," "I can understand how you must have felt," or "I felt the same way when I was in that situation."

We will want children to understand that even though feelings are neither good nor bad in themselves, some can be troublesome or painful:

"No one likes to be called names."

"Yes, you can feel hurt if someone won't let you walk with them to school."

Learning to cope with emotions may mean learning to understand that feelings are normal and have a reason for existing. Instead of rejecting them we try to understand why they occur and what causes them.

Differences of emotional expression are influenced by the concepts and values held by different cultures and subcultures. No doubt it is surprising for some children to learn that in some parts of the world men greet each other by kissing, or that fist fighting in some cultures is a shameful way to express anger. Even within the classroom community there may be some dissimilar practices or values. Children may be surprised to find that a classmate does not like ice cream—something they think is universally liked. Or they may find it curious that some children say they are not afraid of thunder and even like the sound of it. Understanding and appreciating these differences is a valuable learning experience that begins with the leader's interaction with the children.

A leader was guiding a class of third graders in creative drama. She noticed one boy's negative response to physical contact when she took his hand to form a circle and later when she unthinkingly gave him a friendly pat on the head. She made a mental note that Tom did not like contact and that she should not touch him.

But the very next time she met the children, she forgot her intentions. This time she was playing with the children, pretending to be smoke rising from the floor. The mood was quiet and mysterious, but it was quickly broken for Tom when her smoke movements accidentally touched him. The teacher stopped playing and said quietly, "Tom, I know you don't like for me to touch you. I'm sorry that I did just now. I've told myself not to do it, but I seem to be having a hard time making myself mind."

There was a moment of absolute silence. By now everyone was aware of what was happening. Tom's face changed from one of real disgust to one of surprise. Then the eight-year-old said, "That's all right, I understand." Tom obviously appreciated her concern for his feelings and, in turn, was able to understand hers. At that moment a bond of understanding and respect was formed between them.

Many children have difficulty dealing with emotions. Realistically the teacher will not be able to solve many of the child's problems; neither can one legitimately assume the role of a therapist or a counselor who diagnoses and treats specific emotional disorders. But simply in the number of waking hours spent together, perhaps the teacher, of all the people in the child's world, is in an ideal position to help the child understand and cope with human emotions.

Accepting creativity and imitation. Beginning leaders are often so concerned about evoking creativity in children that they expect immediate and outstanding results. But we all have rather ordinary ideas at first until we have had the chance to experiment further and probe deeper. Some leaders express their disappointment openly or with thinly disguised, forlorn facial expressions when students give initial responses. However, one needs to be accepting of these first attempts at creative thinking and to continue to be supportive to keep the flow of ideas coming.

In creative drama activities, children will often imitate each other or even repeat a previous response, particularly if the leader has praised it. This is normal and natural; imitation, after all, is a basic mode of learning. Yet some feel that imitating is similar to cheating and convey this attitude to children. As a result, children may express considerable concern about imitative behaviors in classmates:

"Mary's doing *my* idea!"
"Tom's copying!"

In response to these protestations, one can communicate an acceptance of imitation in a way that protects the child who is imitating yet reassures the child who has originated the idea.

"When people see an idea they like, they enjoy using it. Tom must have liked your idea. . . ."

Acceptance through leader participation. Acceptance can also be demonstrated when the leader participates and plays with the children. At first you may feel reluctant or even a little nervous (perhaps "vulnerable" is a better word) in playing. But in time and as experience is gained and you become more relaxed, participation usually becomes more comfortable. It is not important to be skilled in playing; in fact, one could intimidate some children by being too accomplished. Participation should therefore emphasize entering the spirit and enjoyment of play rather than skill. Many children will find your participation encouraging, and will more readily participate and relax and enjoy themselves also.

Whether leaders play a character role in a story or pantomime along with the children in a guessing game, the communication bond is stronger than if they simply observe from the sidelines. One thus becomes a contributing member of the group and establishes a meaningful working relationship with it. As a result, we learn to understand ourselves and the other members more clearly. This insight can be valuable in assisting effective classroom interrelationships in all learning activities.

Accepting mistakes. The process of learning involves experimenting, often accompanied by uncertainty and mistakes. But many adults and chil-

Acceptance is demonstrated when the leader plays with the children.

dren are trained to feel that mistakes indicate failure. And since, in their minds, failure cannot be tolerated, they become unduly distressed by mistakes.

One of the most effective ways for drama leaders to help children realize that mistakes are natural and normal for everyone is to acknowledge their own.

"Boy, I seemed to goof that time. Let me try another idea. . . ."

"I think I should have explained the directions differently. It was my fault we had a mixup."

And just as we can stop and acknowledge our own difficulties, we can guide children to do the same.

"I sensed that some of you had second thoughts about the way your scene went. Would you like to try again?"

"Some people seemed to forget the rules. Let's try it again, and remember this time that you are to use only the space at the side of your desk."

SETTING LIMITS

Even though we accept the children's ideas and feelings, limits must be set on negative behaviors. We obviously cannot allow them to fight with each other, hurt each other's feelings purposely, shout obscenities, or refuse to follow rules. Children need guidance in learning that the blatant expression of all feelings and actions can get them into trouble. A person who acts out aggression by kicking someone, for example, will certainly be avoided or possibly even kicked in return.

It is important to disapprove of behaviors and actions without rejecting the individual who expresses them. Children need to know that not *they* but their actions are being rejected. Notice how the following statements acknowledge the children's feelings but reject the behavior accompanying them.

> "I know that you're angry, but fighting is not allowed in the classroom."

> "All your talking lets me know you're excited. But you know the rules. We can't begin playing until everyone settled down. I'll know that you're ready when everything is quiet. . . ."

> "I know you're disappointed that you can't all play this first time. But in just a few moments we'll be repeating it, and everyone will have a chance."

There may be times when children's behaviors become disruptive to the rest of the class. When this happens, rules for participating should be reinforced as objectively as possible. It is also helpful to speak to children privately so they are able to "save face."

> "Please sit down. When you feel that you can follow the rules to remain by yourself and not disturb others, you may rejoin the group."

Children's behavior is sometimes such that they cannot be allowed to participate with the group at all for an entire session.

> "I'm sorry. I know you are disappointed. But I cannot allow you to poke and pinch other people who are trying to do their work. Perhaps it will be easier for you to follow the rules tomorrow. For the rest of today, just watch."

Although the other children will enjoy playing their activities in a quieter setting after disruptive children have been removed, it is important for the offenders to be returned to drama as soon as possible. It is within the framework of drama itself that children have one of their best opportunities to learn social interaction skills and to get along with one another.

A simple ignoring of unwanted behaviors will sometimes serve to diminish them. Consider the following:

> As an only child of career parents, David was often left on his own and craved attention. Although bright and likable, he was unusually outspoken and aggressive. He also had the annoying habit of contradicting the leader's remarks or pointedly doing the opposite of everything that was requested in order to draw attention to himself. The leader, who often gave in to his demands, decided to change tactics.

LEADER: I'll be the North Wind that blows all the Snow People inside the house. Here we go!
DAVID: *I'm* not going inside.
LEADER: OK. The rest of us will go inside and you can stay outside.
DAVID: I'm coming! I'm coming!

GROUP DYNAMICS

Learning to function in a democratic society is an educational priority. While we encourage each child to develop individual expression, we also emphasize the value of social interrelationships. Ultimately the leader guides the group to learn that it functions best when everyone contributes. Organization, cooperation, group problem solving and decision making thus become an integral part of the group experience.

The dynamics of group behavior are interesting. Although a group may be composed of a wide range of individuals, it has a personality all its own—as if it were one huge and unique individual embodying the separate members. A common saying among professional group leaders is "The group contains all the people in the group plus one more." Teachers note this phenomenon of group behavior when they make such statements as "My class is so rowdy this year!" or "My class would really like that," as if the class is a person by itself.

Creative drama encourages group interaction. When activities are carefully planned, when instructions are clearly given, and when the group knows what is expected of it, group work should pose few problems. If organization is not handled carefully, however, there can be problems, especially for the beginning leader. When the group is given too much independence before it is ready, it can develop a life of its own and may even get out of control. Beginning leaders who have not had much experience with group work may panic at seeing this unleashed power, particularly if they see their own contact and control diminishing. (Even experienced leaders can find such moments threatening and traumatic.) This panic may freeze leaders into inaction at a time when their leadership is most needed.

Fortunately, no group really wants to get out of control; in fact, group members can also feel panic at a group's uncontrolled power. It is much more comfortable to be a part of a group that is organized and on course. Strong direction, as well as support from the leader, is usually welcomed until children feel confident working in more independent ways.

Some children have an easy time cooperating and integrating themselves within almost any group. They obviously enjoy working together and demonstrate the maturity, as well as a readiness, to accept one another. For them group involvement is natural:

"Maria and I have an idea. Can we do it together?"

"John and I are going to be the ticket men and Alonzo and Mack are going to come and buy a ticket from us. What are you girls going to do?"

They have ideas for facilitating organization and interaction:

"I think we should put our hand up if we want to say something."

"I think each group should have a corner of the room to plan our skits so we can work in private."

"Oh, I know how we can do this story, Mrs. Hackett. You be the old lady and we'll be the rabbits."

They listen to each other with understanding and empathy:

LESLIE: I know how the boy in that story felt. The saddest time for me was when my dog died. He was run over by a car.
MICHAEL: That's sad.

They are interested in each other and spontaneously comment on, and question further, the ideas of their peers:

OWEN: I wanted a horse.
TEACHER: Did you get one?
OWEN: I'm too little. If I rode it, I'd fall off.
ERIC: Oh, you're crazy. You can't have a horse because you gotta have a ranch to have a horse and you gotta have a saddle and you gotta have a bridle and you gotta have horseshoes and you gotta have a lot of food to feed 'em.
OWEN: Oh, no. You don't have to have all that stuff for a horse.
ERIC: Well, maybe you're right.

DICK: If I could have my wish, I'd go to another planet and help start a new civilization there.
PAUL: Like the boy in our story.
CLINTON: You'd have to get used to living in pressurized buildings all your life.
PAUL: Yeah. And maybe you'd even save the spaceship like that kid did.

On the other hand, some children have difficulties in group interaction. Some are ignored by the group. Some choose to avoid any group, hesitating to participate or to contribute an idea or opinion. Still others with personal ego needs demand undivided attention from the group, refusing to listen to others, to compromise, or to cooperate. For these children and their leader, group work will take time and effort.

The seemingly simple act of dividing the larger group into pairs and smaller groups can be a particular problem for beginning leaders. Although children often work best when they are allowed to choose their co-workers, you will want to avoid the formation of cliques. Some children are mature enough to handle this on their own. They can pair and group themselves with few arguments and no hard feelings, rotating their choices of classmates.

Most children, however, will need your assistance in rotating group membership. Quickly counting off and placing 1s together, 2s together, and so on is a common way to mix the group. Not only does this system prevent petty squabbling over who plays with whom, it gets to the fun of the activity and the excitement of playing sooner. With some planning ahead, you can easily vary your grouping methods to keep interest high.

No matter what your procedures, some children are never satisifed. Yet if you allow the voicing of too many complaints, the playing is usually held up and little is solved. For this reason, many leaders say that if they keep the activities moving forward and act as if they assume the children can get along together, the children soon learn to live up to the expectation.

Leaders often find it helpful to formulate a list of rules for working in groups. One class collectively listed the following:

> Because I like to have people listen to me, I will listen to others
>
> Because I wouldn't want anyone to say my ideas are stupid or dumb, I won't say that about anyone else's.
>
> Because I don't want anyone to make fun of the way I feel, I won't make fun of anyone else's feelings.
>
> Because I don't like being disturbed when I act things out, I won't disturb others.
>
> Because I want people to be a good audience for me, I will be a good audience for them.
>
> Because I don't like being left out of a group, I will include others in my group.

General discussions about group cooperation and compromise can also help, stimulated by such questions as

> "When people cooperate, what do they have to do?"
>
> "How can a group decide what ideas it will use?"
>
> "How can a group make certain that everyone has a chance to speak and contribute?"
>
> "When only a few members in a group do all the talking, how do the other members feel? What can they do?"

The subject of group cooperation and compromise can even be the basis for drama experiences:

TEACHER: What examples can you think of to show why groups must compromise and cooperate?

CHILD: Every summer my family decides where we'll spend our vacation. My mom and dad tell us how much money we can spend and how far that will take us, and then we vote. Before we voted we used to argue a lot. My sister always screamed about going to the lake because she had a boyfriend there. I always vote for camping.

CHILD: Well, this isn't about compromise, just the opposite. My brother's in Mr. Bender's class, and when the art teacher wanted groups to make a mural, they couldn't do it. They couldn't agree on anything. One of the kids even ripped up the paper. My brother said Mr. Bender just flipped and really got mad at them.

CHILD: Our committee had a hard time planning the class Halloween party. Not to mention names, but *someone* wanted to bring in *real* eyeballs and guts for kids to touch when they had their blindfolds on. He was going to get them from a butcher. Some kids said they'd get sick, so we made him take a vote.

TEACHER: I can see you have lots of ideas. We'll divide into groups of five. Each group will act out a situation to show the importance of cooperation and compromise. Be sure everyone has a part to play, and be sure to have an ending so you know when to stop.

Group Decision Making

It is necessary to a democratic society and to the growth and development of children that they learn to handle their own problems and make their own decisions. The decisions they make may not always be the ones the leader would have made, but the process of thinking through an idea and experimenting with trial and error is an excellent learning experience.

Children can be granted the opportunity to be self-directed in many ways:

"Let's see, how can we do this? Does anyone have a suggestion?"

"We've been playing this story for quite a while. Are you still interested in it or should we go on to something else?"

"Do we need a preview playing this time?"

"Do you think everyone can play all at the same time, or should we start out with just a few people first?"

"How much space do you think we can handle today?"

Of course, whenever children make their own decisions they must also accept the consequences. If things don't work out, the playing will have to be stopped and the situation reanalyzed. Just as the leader can make mistakes and miscalculations about what a group is ready to do, so can the children in managing themselves. The more important point is that they have had a hand in the decision making.

The group may also deal with its own problems of personal interaction in everyday classroom living. In the example below, a teachable moment was used to help a group of second graders see alternatives in handling a particular behavior problem. The class had just begun a discussion when a rather constant and irritating problem reoccurred.

GEORGE:	Troy's hitting me again.
TEACHER:	Troy seems to be a problem for you, George. What are you going to do about it?
GEORGE:	What am *I* going to do about it?
TEACHER:	Yes. How are you going to solve your problem?
GEORGE:	Well—I'll—(shouts at Troy) STOP DOING THAT!!!!
TEACHER:	That's one way that might work. Is there anything else you could do?
GEORGE:	I'd hit him, too.
TEACHER:	That's another possibility. Do you think it will work?
ANGELA:	Troy would hit you back, wouldn't you, Troy? (Troy doesn't respond.)
CINDY:	Ask him nice to leave you alone.
TEACHER:	That's another idea. Any others?
JIMMY:	Just don't play with him anymore.
RUSTY:	Go sit by somebody else.
TEACHER:	Let's take a few minutes to have you work together in pairs. Decide on a way to show how you would handle a problem like George's. But we don't do any real hitting in drama, so you'll have to pretend everything you show us. (After rehearsing and playing, the group returns to a discussion of the most workable ideas they saw.)

Democratic living is not easy! Cooperative interaction takes time, and social maturation is not necessarily correlated with chronological age. Furthermore, the group's personality and behavior will fluctuate and change. There will invariably be days when both the leader and the children wonder how they will ever be able to work together or why in the world they would even want to! These seemingly backward steps are a natural part of the group process and the group's growth toward cohesiveness. The children are constantly growing in awareness of themselves as individuals and as a part of the group.

The need to belong to a group is strong.

Yet, the group is powerful, and the need to belong to a group is strong. Usually you can count on this need to motivate children to continue to make attempts at integrating themselves. For children who do have difficulties, you will need to give emotional support; and for those trying times, you may need an extra dose of patience and understanding to survive.

CREATIVE DRAMA FOR ALL CHILDREN: CONSIDERATIONS FOR CHILDREN WITH SPECIAL NEEDS

A child in a wheelchair participates in a story dramatization; he is aided in moving about the room by a classmate who is double-cast in the same character role. A drama leader tells a story, making sure that her lips and face can be seen by a child wearing a hearing aid. A child with special talents has written a story that a small group of her classmates are dramatizing. And a child with behavior difficulties is making a noticeable effort to restrain his outbursts in order to play a drama activity with his classmates and be a part of the group. Today's elementary classroom has students with a multitude of different needs, and individual children may have multiple handicaps or needs. Addressing these needs is mandatory if we are going to provide equal opportunities for all.

In conducting drama activities we consider, without overreacting to, children's special needs in order to help them participate as fully as possible. Although there may seem to be certain aspects of drama some handicapped children cannot participate in fully, the children themselves will frequently see ways to solve the problem creatively on their own. Focusing on the children's abilities rather than on their inabilities will encourage these attempts.

It is generally assumed that the leader is the one responsible for implementing compensatory learning experiences. However, the classroom can also become a community of learners who willingly assist each other and help each other succeed. Many goals can be achieved by establishing a "buddy" or support system. A child who speaks a different language, for example, can be aided by the child who is bilingual. The academically gifted, in addition to pursuing their own interests, may be able to assist those who need special tutoring. Children can assist handicapped classmates; in fact, some handicapped children can assist others whose handicaps are different from theirs. All these experiences can give children a needed sense of responsibility and importance in serving the classroom community.

Although each child is special in some way, many children come to school with preconceived notions of their abilities. A child with a minor handicap may come from an overprotective environment; a gifted child may have been told that he or she is superior to his or her classmates and should not pay attention to them. Such conditions will obviously complicate matters. It also means that there will never be just one answer to a problem or just one way to deal with it. The following general guidelines are presented for consideration.

General Drama Techniques to Consider

A basic axiom to remember is that drama is most often a group art. Unlike the musician who can perform solo or the artist who paints pictures alone, the actor generally must work with other actors as well as with "behind the scenes" artists. The same is true of creative drama: it is a shared art. Therefore, attention is not, and should not be, placed on single individuals. Furthermore, there is an obligation to work together as a group to make the most successful dramatization. This philosophy leads to some specific techniques employed throughout the text that will be particularly beneficial in working with children who have special needs.

One of these techniques is *simultaneous or unison playing*. When all children are playing an idea at the same time, they are automatically part of the group. They can also see other children participating and learn from this modeling and demonstrating. Yet, there is no undue attention on the children themselves, and they can participate and blend into the activity at their own pace.

A second technique is *multiple casting of roles*. Almost any role in a story can be double-cast, allowing two children to work together, each supporting the other. Some character parts can be played by even more than two players. This technique allows any child to play virtually any part because of the assistance from a partner.

Multiple casting is also used with other drama activities. Consider, for

Drama is a group art.

example, the simple debate (p. 193). The class is divided into two character roles. Yet, even if children choose not to say anything, they are still included in the playing experience. For many children, this is as much participation as they want or can handle. And, again, they can increase that participation at their own pace.

There is one final point in the overall consideration of children with special needs. Drama encourages participants to get *outside themselves*. Much of the stress we feel in our lives is the result of inward focus, and children who have been made aware of their special differences undoubtedly carry an extra burden. By extending ourselves into the world around us and "losing ourselves" in activities like drama, we can experience a therapeutic release. This release can help us put life back into its proper perspective and render us healthier for future tasks.

Additional Suggestions for Specific Special Needs

Following are some additional suggestions for working in creative drama with children of varying needs and abilities. They are not all-inclusive but merely intended to encourage your thinking. Eventually you will discover many more options yourself that will fit your own and your classroom's particular needs.

Bilingual-bicultural.

1. Many drama activities in this text are based on folk literature, a universal literary form. Some folktale plot lines (for example, "Cinderella") have been found to exist in almost every language and culture. Take special note to include stories from your classroom's language and cultural heritage. Encourage the children to bring such stories to your attention for drama activities.
2. Movement, pantomime, and nonverbal communication are also universal languages. They can take over when words fail or are inadequate to express needs. Bilingual children will particularly enjoy the focus on pantomime activities.
3. Another universal activity is puppetry. Crafting a puppet, making it move, and giving it a personality can all be done without verbal language. Some children may have knowledge of special kinds of puppets from their country or culture that they can share with the class.
4. Incorporate references to special cultural holidays, customs, and experiences in drama activities, from simple sensory activities to more elaborate story dramatizations. Utilize the rich multiethnic resources your students can provide for you and for each other.
5. Many story dramatizations can be a good vehicle for learning vocabulary. Headbands or name tags can be made for characters (for example, dog, king, and man) using both the English words and native language words.

Mentally handicapped.

1. These children will need to have as many concrete experiences as possible. Pictures, props, character headbands, and other similar aids will be necessary for them to understand information and concepts.

2. Pantomime is also valuable for the slow learner, whose verbal skills may not be advanced enough to engage fully in the dialogue and improvisational activities. Include plenty of pantomime activities in each drama lesson.

3. The graded materials in this text should assist in finding literature these children can handle successfully.

4. The roles these children play in drama activities should not tax them beyond their academic skills; and at the same time, they can often surprise us with their concentration and involvement, their careful observation of classmates, and their contentment in participating with their peers in a group activity. Be sure to reinforce the things they can do well.

Academically gifted and talented.   Academically gifted children, those who have high IQ scores, are ahead of their classmates mainly in the use of language. However, there are other talents that children can be gifted in, such as music, athletics, or even interpersonal skills. Therefore, children can be gifted or talented in some areas but not in others.

Enriching experiences are usually required for gifted and talented youngsters, who can bypass the kind of drill work other children may need.

1. In drama some gifted children will excel in dialogue and improvisation. They will particularly enjoy verbal encounters and debates. And it may be easy for them to invent all manner of dialogue in story dramatization.

2. Some gifted and talented children may be interested in creating drama materials. They may even wish to develop some of the activities discussed in this text, from narrative pantomimes to sequence games to segmented story activities. Encourage these activities, perhaps letting them work with the many bibliographic references in this text.

3. Gifted children may also want to try their hand at leading drama activities. They may wish to narrate a narrative pantomime story for the class or for a small group to perform. They may show directorial skills by visualizing interesting ways for their classmates to interpret stories.

4. Gifted children may also be encouraged to try their hand at playwriting, creating puppet shows, or even leading a small group to perform dramas for other classrooms in their school.

5. Other avenues of enrichment for these children may include working with film, television, or appropriate community theatre activities. They may be interested in reading further about theatre and sharing their findings with the rest of the class.

6. Because they have often pursued their interests as lone individuals, some academically gifted children may have difficulty integrating themselves into a group. Drama as a group art should make this easier, but be alert to the uncomfortableness they may feel at first.

Physically disabled.

1. Limited space activities will be easier to manage. However, a partner can assist in moving a wheelchair or in making an area accessible to children with limited mobility.

2. These children may be partial to verbal and dialogue activities if they are

limited in bodily movement. Give plenty of opportunity for such activities in each lesson.

3. Remember that nonverbal communication (pantomime) is conveyed by all parts of the body—from body posture to facial expression and from hand gestures to the way we move out feet. Depending on the impairment, focus on pantomime activities that can be done with the children's most mobile parts of their body. Facial expression can be focused on for those whose arms and legs are impaired. Or gestures can be focused on if the hands and arms are mobile.

4. People in wheelchairs tend not to receive as much supportive touch as other children, probably because the chair itself acts as a barrier. Be alert to this fact and give reassurance and emotional tactile support to these children as often as you do to the rest of the class.

Visually impaired.

1. Limited space activities will be easier for these children. However, with a sighted partner they can explore expanded areas of space gradually.

2. Try to paint word pictures and clear details of what you are talking about. Describe pictures, props, and tell stories with great detail to create mental pictures for the visually impaired.

3. Recorded music is valuable in aiding the mood or environment you are trying to create.

4. Let visually impaired children explore through touch as much and as often as possible. If you are using props, for example, they will want and need to touch and handle them.

5. Abstract concepts and ideas may not be easily understood by these children. Consider this as you plan a lesson to make sure you cover all points clearly.

6. Touch, if carefully monitored, can assist in calming, directing, or assisting the child and can give moral support and encouragement.

7. Use a "buddy system." A partner can help explain quietly any points that may be missed.

Hearing impaired.

1. Be sure these children can see your face and particularly your lips if they are trying to lip read. There is no need to exaggerate your speech; in fact, that will distort the sounds they have been trained to observe. Also try not to stand with a window behind you, as this will cast a shadow over your face.

2. Repeat comments made by children whose voices are too soft to be heard easily.

3. Visual cues, pictures, props, gestures, and directions on cards are very helpful for these children. Use them generously.

4. In general, these children particularly enjoy, and are successful with, pantomime activities.

5. A partner can repeat directions or explanations quietly whenever the child needs additional assistance.

Speech impaired.
Speech impairments generally include articulation disorders, stuttering, phonation problems, and delayed or limited speech.

1. Generally the classroom teacher can assist with speech difficulties by providing an open and relaxed atmosphere that encourages, rather than inhibits, these children in their speech. Since children usually consider drama fun, they tend to forget about their speech difficulties during drama class.
2. Pantomime experiences will be particularly enjoyable for these children.
3. Being able to play with oral activities is useful for the speech impaired youngster. They need opportunities to speak and to hear others engaging in language.
4. Engaging in rhythmic activities, choral-type speaking in unison, and character role-playing often lessens stuttering behaviors.

Emotionally handicapped. Emotionally handicapped children may have difficulty controlling themselves, but some may be very quiet and withdrawn.

1. Because these children often have short attention spans, they will need to move frequently from one task to another. Be alert to their responses and to the fact that you may need to cut an activity short and go to another for variety's sake.
2. At the same time, extending their periods of concentration on a task is also desirable. Move by slow increments in this goal for maximum success.
3. Movements of larger muscles are often successful. Body-movement activities and pantomime should be particularly useful for them.
4. A secure, consistent, and supportive environment is important for these children. They also need to experience success and to feel good about themselves. Initially, using a series of short activities that they can feel competent in doing should provide a good foundation to build on.

As a final word, remember that there are more similarities than differences between children with "special" needs and their classmates. We are all human, and we all have the needs to love and be loved, to communicate, to learn, and to feel successful.

The subject of drama is the subject of life. And because it provides a variety of avenues for all to express their specific talents in unique ways, drama has often been called a great leveler of persons. No one is considered any greater or lesser than anyone else in drama. And this is also as it should be in life itself.

Throughout all experiences in creative drama, the goal is to help children understand and empathize with others—to learn to put themselves into other people's shoes. We want them to discover the common bond of feelings with people they know, people they read about, historical or famous personalities, and people of other countries and cultures. We want them to know each other better and to appreciate themselves as viable human beings. This understanding and awareness is the essence of drama. And it is this understanding that frees us from alienation in a world where the quality of life depends on the quality of human relationships.

FOR THE COLLEGE STUDENT

1. After reading this chapter, consider your own individual uniqueness. What are some of the values, feelings, likes, dislikes, and so on that are predominant in your personality? Discuss and share ideas with a small group of your classmates.

2. Discuss with your classmates those specific incidents during your elementary years when a teacher demonstrated acceptance of you. Recall specific incidents when you felt rejected. What conclusions can you draw?

3. Brainstorm with a group of your classmates some situations involving children's expression of ideas and feelings in the elementary classroom. What specific verbal statements can you think of to demonstrate acceptance of children's ideas and feelings in these situations?

4. Consider situations in which children demonstrate negative behaviors. Practice giving statements that reject the behavior without rejecting the child. Take turns giving your statements and have classmates listen as if they were the children receiving them. What reactions and emotions do the listeners feel?

5. Make a list of situations that involve groups working together. Which ones might be suitable material to use for drama enactment in the classroom?

6. Read Chapter 9 of Elizabeth George Speare's *The Witch of Blackbird Pond* (128), in which Kit leads children in a dramatization of the parable of the good Samaritan; or read the episode in Chapter 7 of Louise Fitzhugh's *Harriet the Spy* (83) in which the gym teacher attempts an enactment of Christmas dinner. Analyze the problems each teacher faces. What suggestions can you offer?

7. Examine some of the many books that deal with emotional situations in the classroom. Share one or two of your favorites in a classroom discussion. How might the material be suitable for a creative drama activity?

SELECTED RESOURCES TO USE WITH CHILDREN

The following materials are a selection of the many that are available dealing with interactions. You will find them interesting just for children to read on their own or to use for reading and discussion with the entire class. Many will also provide material for creative drama lessons.

ADOFF, ARNOLD, Outside/Inside Poems. New York: Lothrop, Lee & Shepard Books, 1981. This collection of poems sensitively describes feelings we have on the inside that do not often appear on the outside.

ALIKI, *Feelings*. New York: Greenwillow Books, 1984. These are brief stories and sketches of childhood feelings.

BERGER, TERRY, *I Have Feelings*. New York: Behavioral Publications, 1971. This useful text presents black-and-white photos covering seventeen different feelings, giving a situation for each followed by an explanation. See also *I Have Feelings, Too* (1979).

BROOKS, GWENDOLYN, *Bronzeville Boys and Girls*. New York: Harper & Row, 1956. Black children express their feelings in this sensitive poet's classic work.

BUSCAGLIA, LEO, *Because I Am Human*. Thorofare, N.J.: Slack, 1982 (distributed by Holt, Rinehart and Winston). Black-and-white photos illustrate this simple text which describes all the things children can do because they are human—from rolling down a hill to chewing five sticks of bubble gum all at once. Younger children will love doing this one as a narrative pantomime (see Chapter 5) or as a count-and-freeze pantomime (see Chapter 7).

CHAPMAN, CAROL, *Herbie's Troubles*. New York: E. P. Dutton, 1981. Herbie does not want to go to school because of a bully. Upon advice from other children, Herbie becomes assertive, then shares, and then hits, but nothing works. Finally he ignores the bully, who then claims Herbie's no fun anymore and walks away with Herbie as the winner.

ESTES, ELEANOR, *The Hundred Dresses*. San Diego: Harcourt Brace Jovanovich, 1944, 1974. Wanda, the daughter of a poor immigrant family, is rejected by her classmates. Her escape is to talk about her many dresses, which turn out to be beautiful drawings. In spite of its age, this book has stood the test of time in evoking readers' concern for Wanda's plight.

FEELINGS, TOM, AND NIKKI GRIMES, *Something on My Mind*. New York: Dial Press, 1978. This book presents descriptions of many inner emotions not often expressed.

ROSENBAUM, JEAN, AND LUTIE MCAULIFFE, *What Is Fear: An Introduction to Feelings*. Englewood Cliffs, N.J.: Prentice-Hall, 1972. A basic emotion that is often difficult to discuss is covered in this helpful book.

SCHULTZ, CHARLES, *Love Is . . . Walking Hand in Hand*. San Francisco: Determined Productions, 1983. This "typically Peanuts" collection has many pantomime possibilities for twos and threes to play.

SHOWERS, PAUL, *A Book of Scary Things*. New York: Doubleday, 1977. A child tells of all the things that can be scary—from spiders to monsters at night. It is one good example of how to get fears out in the open in a constructive way.

TESTER, SYLVIA, *Moods and Emotions*. Elgin, Ill.: David C. Cook, 1970. Sixteen poster-size photos, some in color and some in black and white, are accompanied by a booklet discussing various ways to teach the subject of emotions in the classroom.

VIORST, JUDITH, *Alexander and the Terrible, Horrible, No Good, Very Bad Day*. New York: Atheneum, 1972. Everything goes wrong for Alexander from the moment he wakes up till the end of the day. He thinks he will go off to Australia, until his mother tells him there are bad days there too. Children will be glad to know they are not the only ones who have bad days. This story can be played as a solo narrative pantomime (See Chapter 5) with a little editing.

YASHIMA, TARO, *Crow Boy*. New York: Viking Penguin, 1955. In this classic book, a young Japanese boy is rewarded for six years of perfect attendance in school. Yet he is an outsider to the other children in the classroom until a sensitive teacher finds a way to give him the recognition he deserves.

SELECTED TEACHER RESOURCE MATERIALS

AMIDON, EDMUND, AND ELIZABETH HUNTER, *Improving Teaching*. New York: Holt, Rinehart and Winston, 1966. This valuable text was one of the first ever devoted to helping teachers be aware of their specific verbal behaviors and the consequences of them in seven teaching categories: motivating, planning, informing, discussing, disciplining, counseling, and evaluating.

CANTER, L., AND M. CANTER, *Assertive Discipline*. Los Angeles: Canter and Associates, 1976. The authors emphasize the teacher's need !o be assertive—rather than passive or aggressive—in establishing an orderly classroom environment, and give many practical suggestions for accomplishing this end.

EVERTSON, CAROLYN M., EDMUND T. EMMER, BARBARA S. CLEMENTS, JULIE P. SANFORD, AND MURRAY E. WORSHAM, *Classroom Management for Elementary Teachers.* Englewood Cliffs, N.J.: Prentice-Hall, 1984. This practical guide to effective classroom management covers a variety of topics from classroom organization to managing special groups.

GINOTT, HAIM G., *Between Teacher and Child.* New York: Macmillan, 1972. Here is a classic, highly readable book for strengthening interpersonal relationships in the classroom.

GORDON, THOMAS, *T.E.T. Teacher Effectiveness Training.* New York: Peter H. Wyden, Publisher, 1974. A psychotherapist applies his knowledge to the classroom setting and discusses such topics as communication, active listening, and conflict resolution.

FOUR

Simple Drama Activities and Games

When both the leader and the children are new to creative drama, it is helpful to use some simple activities first, such as drama games, action songs, and brief pantomimes. These activities can also be used as warmups for longer drama periods. They often involve some skill building or "rehearsing" that is useful before playing more challenging material. Simple activities are also good for ending a drama period, particularly if they have a calming effect on the group.

THE GOALS OF BEGINNING ACTIVITIES

One goal of beginning activities is to create the approximate climate for psychological security. They can relax the class, generate good feelings, and promote a sense of group cohesiveness. They can often unite the children in a common effort, which becomes strong enough that individuals forget themselves and participate freely.

Another important aspect of these beginning materials is that they encourage movement, focus and concentration, imagination, social cooperation, and self-control of the players, necessary skills in other areas of learning as well as in further drama work. Although not all the activities presented in this chapter will achieve each of these goals equally, consider for example the intense concentration little children exhibit in mastering and coordinating the movements in a simple finger play, the imagination required in inventing different ways to move about the room to a musical stimulus, or the discipline required to mirror the movements of a partner.

Another value of these materials is that they almost organize themselves. When the children learn the rules of a game or learn how an activity is to be played, they help keep each other "in line." The student teacher who has not had much experience working with groups of children will usually find it easier to begin with these activities.

Giving directions, rearranging the classroom, and keeping order and control are tasks that require some thinking ahead and planning. Just one experience with unorganized and chaotic "running around" is enough to discourage any future attempts with creative drama. The beginning leader must recognize and accept the responsibility for guiding and controlling even the simplest activity. It does not happen magically or automatically. This chapter is designed to help the inexperienced teacher learn some initial skills in planning simple activities.

DIRECTED ACTIVITIES

The kind of activity that keeps the most control, is the easiest to organize, and is the simplest for the children to play is one in which a leader tells or shows the children what to do. Another value of such activities is that the children can play many of them seated or standing in one location while still being actively involved in a movement experience. Following is a discussion of several kinds of leader-directed activities.

Finger Plays

Finger plays—little rhymes, songs, or chants that the children act out as they recite them—are very popular with young children. Some classic examples are "The Itsy Bitsy Spider" and "I'm a Little Teapot." Traditional finger plays are readily available in numerous sources. Many can be created from favorite nursery rhymes.

Single-Action Poetry

Some poems suggest single rhythmic movements—such as running, hopping, or galloping—that are fun to act out. While the leader reads the poem, the children simply perform the actions seated at their desks or standing at the side of them. Actions are done *in place*. Following are some examples.

"A Farmer Went Trotting upon His Grey Mare," Mother Goose (4).[1] Trotting can be done standing or sitting at the desk. The "bumps" and "lumps" can be acted out in various ways of your choice.

"The Grand Old Duke of York," Mother Goose (4). With this rhyme, you can march in place. Then, at the same time, stand for "up," crouch for "down," and half crouch for "half way up."

[1]Throughout this text, numbers in parentheses correspond to the numbered anthologies and books in the final bibliography at the back.

Fingerplays are a good warmup for
more challenging activities.

"Hoppity," A. A. Milne (4). A little boy hops everywhere he goes. Children
can "hop" this one on their bottoms at the desk. For variety, on the line
beginning "If he stopped hopping," slow down your reading like a record
player running out of electricity. Let your voice get slower and slower until
you and the hoppers come to a "sitstill" on "couldn't go anywhere." Then pick
up the tempo again at "That's why he always goes . . ." One class decided to
add "Pop!" at the very end.

"Jump—jump—jump," Kate Greenaway (4). Children can jump three times
on the first line of each stanza. Do this *in place.* Children hold crouched
position while you read the next three lines. On the last two lines they sit.

"Merry-Go-Round," Dorothy Baruch (4). Children can go up and down like
the horses on a merry-go-round. As you read, the lines (and the horses)
gradually go faster and then slow down to a final half. Try adding music such
as "Carousel Waltz" from Rodgers and Hammerstein's Broadway musical
Carousel.

"Rocking Chair," John Travers Moore (9). Children can rock back and forth
in this poem as the poet tells what fun it is to rock.

"The Swing," Robert Louis Stevenson (4) (35). Swinging can be acted by
leaning forward and backward in seated position or by taking four small steps
forward and back for each two lines.

"Trot Along, Pony," Marion Edey and Dorothy Grider (4). Children can
trot, clapping thighs in rhythm to this poem. The last line takes the pony
home to supper, so you can finish off by feeding the pony and bedding him
for the night. (The children can pretend they are feeding an imaginary pony,
or they can be the pony that *you* feed.)

Action Songs

Action songs are also fun to sing and act out. Many are traditional, such
as the following: "Did You Ever See a Lassie?" "Here We Go 'Round the
Mulberry Bush" (or "This Is the Way We Wash Our Clothes"), "If You're
Happy and You Know It," "She'll Be Comin' 'Round the Mountain," and
"This Old Man, He Played One."

There are also some songs that can easily be made into action songs.
For example, the traditional African folk song "Kum Bay Yah" has a very

strong, steady, and slow rhythm. The words are constantly repeated in the different verses with little variation. Simple gestures of singing, crying, and praying can be added to the song in addition to the clapping and swaying that is usually inevitable when a group sings such a song. *Very simple* dance movements are also easily added when the group is strongly moved by the song.

Another example might be a song such as "Michael, Row the Boat Ashore." One teacher discussed with the children all the activities that sailors must do on a ship. Verses were added that included the children's names and various tasks that everyone acted out: "Sally, help to swab the deck," "Andy, pull up the anchor slow," and so on.

Additional songs that lend themselves to acting out are traditional ones such as "Frog Went A-Courtin'," "I Know an Old Lady Who Swallowed a Fly," "Old MacDonald Had a Farm," "Sing a Song of Sixpence," "Twelve Days of Christmas," and "Waltzing Matilda."

Action Stories

Action stories are well known in recreational circles, and many are taught by word of mouth. They are narrated by a leader, with children performing specified actions or sounds or both. You may already be familiar with such traditional stories as "Lion Hunt" or "Bear Hunt" or "Brave Little Indian."

You can easily make up similar kinds of action stories by narrating a brief version of a folktale. Young children will enjoy a story like "The

An action song is a good warmup.

Three Billy Goats Gruff," with actions for each of the billy goats, the troll, and even the bridge. Older children enjoy stories with more "sophisticated" subject matter, such as melodramas (complete with moustached villains and swooning lasses), spy and detective stories, or cowboy and rustler adventures.

You can assign parts and have small groups play the various roles. Or for greater challenge to listening skills, the entire class can perform them all. Here is one example with a folktale.

JACK AND THE BEANSTALK

JACK:	Hey, nonny nonny! (snap fingers)
JACK'S MOTHER:	Who, me? (point to self)
BEANSTALK:	Flutter, flutter. (wiggle fingers at side of body for leaves)
GIANT:	Fee, fi, fo, fum! (stamp feet)
GIANT'S WIFE:	Oh, dear! (hand to forehead)
HEN:	Cackle, cackle! (flap wings)
HARP:	Twang, twang! (pluck nose to make nasal sound)
BAGS OF GOLD:	Clink, clink! (assume shape of lumpy bag)

Story: Once upon a time a poor boy named *Jack,* who lived with his *mother,* traded a cow for a handful of so-called magic beans. His *mother,* angered with his stupidity, threw the beans out the window. That night a huge *beanstalk* grew up into the sky. The next morning *Jack* climbed the *beanstalk* and found a castle belonging to a *giant. Jack* asked the *giant's wife* to let him in, and she did. But when the *giant's wife* heard the *giant* approaching, she hid *Jack* in the oven. The *giant* ate his breakfast and asked for his *hen* that laid the golden eggs. "Lay an egg, *Hen!*" growled the *giant.* Then he called for his *harp.* "Play a tune, *Harp!*" growled the *giant.* Then he called for his *bags of gold.* The *giant* counted the *bags of gold* until he grew sleepy. As the *giant* slept, *Jack* crept out of the oven and grabbed the *hen,* the *harp,* and the *bags of gold* and climbed down the *beanstalk.* But the *hen,* the *harp,* and the *bags of gold* made so much noise that the *giant* woke up. The *giant* and the *giant's wife* chased *Jack* down the *beanstalk.* When *Jack* reached the bottom, he called to his *mother* to bring an ax. With the ax he chopped down the *beanstalk,* and the *giant* and the *giant's wife* fell to their death. And *Jack* and his *mother* lived happily ever after.

The End—Everyone takes a bow!

Children can even make up their own stories. After a third grade class had tried the preceding story, two children wrote the following stories:[2]

---

[2]Elizabeth Tinsley, substitute teacher in Mattawan Elementary School, Mattawan, Michigan, shared these stories.

SLEEPING BEAUTY

by Camille Thompson

PRINCESS:	girls stand and turn around once, sit down
FAIRY:	flutter, flutter (use hand motions)
BEAUTY:	Oh! she's so beautiful (say higher pitch)
WITCH:	cackle, cackle (laugh)
DIE:	Boo hoo hoo! (say sadly)
SLEEP:	make snoring sounds
PRINCE:	boys stand and turn around once, sit down
KISSING:	long, loud kissing sound
POKE:	Ouch! (say as if in pain)

Story: Once long ago there was a King and a Queen. They wished for a *Princess*. Then their wish came true. But, one day the castle had a big party. The three good *fairies* were there. The first good *fairy* gave the *Princess* the gift of *beauty*. The second good *fairy* gave her friendship with all living creatures. But all of a sudden a *witch* appeared. Everybody gasped. She cackled that when the *Princess* was sixteen, she would *poke* her finger on a spindle and she would *die*. The guards tried to grab the *witch*, but she disappeared. The third good *fairy* said the *Princess* would *poke* her finger when she was sixteen, but she would instead fall into a deep *sleep*. To break the spell, she would have to be *kissed* by a *Prince*. But, on her sixteenth birthday, the King burned all of the spindles. The *Princess* was so curious, though, that she went to a small room way up high in the castle. She *poked* her finger and the *Princess* fell into a deep *sleep*. But soon enough, a *Prince* came and broke the spell by *kissing* the *Princess*. And they got married and lived happily ever after.

CINDERELLA

by Corby T. DeBoer

CINDERELLA:	Work! Work! Work! (say with hand motions for type of work)
STEPMOTHER:	Cinderella! (say gruffly)
STEPSISTERS:	We're so beautiful! (say slowly and higher pitch)
BALL:	La! La! La! La! La! (sing this)
FAIRY GODMOTHER:	Bibbety, boppety, boo! (pretend to have magic wand)
PRINCE:	Charming! Charming! Charming! (bow as this is said)
GLASS SLIPPER:	Ting Ting! (say in high voice)

Story: *Cinderella* lived with her *stepmother* and her *stepsisters*. One day when *Cinderella* was washing the floor, the doorbell rang. She opened the door and saw a messenger from the *Prince*. He said, "There shall be a *ball!*" When the day of the *ball* came, *Cinderella* was too busy getting her *stepsisters* ready. She could not get herself ready, and besides, she had nothing to wear and no way to get to the *ball*. When her *stepmother* and *stepsisters* left, *Cinderella* began to cry. "Oh, how I wish I could go to the *ball!*" she cried. Suddenly an old lady appeared! *Cinderella* asked, "Who are you?"

"I'm your *fairy godmother*. I've come to see you off to the *ball!*" When *Cinderella* was about to leave, her *fairy godmother* said, "You must leave before the clock strikes twelve for everything will turn back as it was!"

The *Prince* was dazzled. He said, "Please dance with me!" And she did, but the clock struck its first strike—DONG!

"I must leave!!" When she was leaving, her *glass slipper* fell on the steps.

The *Prince* found it and said, "Whoever has the foot that fits this small *slipper*, I will marry."

Finally, the *slipper* came to *Cinderella's* house. Her *stepsisters* said, "OOH AHHH!" Then, *Cinderella* tried it on. It's a perfect fit! And that very day, she married the *Prince*. And they lived happily ever after!

SIMPLE PANTOMIMES

Simple pantomimes are brief vignettes you create for children to act out at their desks. They are not to be guessed but are intended to give the children a chance to explore pantomime action without being evaluated.[3] Particular learning benefits are that they require the children to concentrate on remembering past experiences, to recall information they have read or heard about, and to form mental pictures. These skills are necessary for most learning tasks and can be sharpened through exercises that simple pantomime activities provide.

Variety of action in pantomimes is important. You can create action to involve the entire body:

TEACHER: Wonderperson! There isn't a thing you can't do! You can leap tall buildings . . . run faster than a speeding bullet . . . break chains with a snap . . . hang by your teeth . . . twirl a rope on the end of your little finger . . . now with both hands . . . and rotate a hula hoop around your neck at the same time!

Movements can involve levels and directions: up and down, back and forth, left and right, bending over, turning around, going in reverse, and so forth. The following example uses directions in movement while the children pretend to be a power shovel in operation:

TEACHER: . . . you drive over to your job. Now swing the cab around to the left and lower the dipper (outstretched arms) to that mound of dirt.

---

[3]Extensive discussion of techniques for developing pantomime material can be found in Chapter 6. Pantomimes for audience guessing will be discussed in Chapter 7.

Slowly, now . . . scoop up the dirt. Now raise the dipper and swing back to the right. . . . That's it. . . . Now very slowly and carefully swing the dipper over the dump truck. . . . Now open the dipper and drop the dirt in. . . .

Try changes of tempo. Actions can be done in double time or even triple time, speeded up like an old-fashioned movie. Or they can be done in "slow-motion time," as if one were in space or performing in a television replay. Note these techniques in the following example:

TEACHER: Pretend you are a bow-legged cowboy walking down a frontier town's dusty main road. . . . Now do that same walk a little faster. . . . a little faster . . . Now stop! In slow motion take your pistol out of the holster. . . . Now reverse that action. . . . Take out the gun even slower. . . . Now reverse that action just as slowly. . . . Practice taking the gun out in double time . . . triple time. . . .

In addition to focusing on a variety of actions, pantomimes can involve a variety of characters and topics.

A. Community Helpers

TEACHER: First let's pretend to be a doctor giving children shots to help their bodies fight disease. . . . Now let's pretend to be a mail carrier, driving a truck and stopping to deliver some mail. . . . The foresters who trim the city trees are important. Now you're a forester carefully sawing limbs from a tall tree. . . .

B. Storybook Characters

TEACHER: Let's first pretend to be the wolf, sneaking through the woods, looking for Little Red Riding Hood. . . . Now you're the giant in "Jack and the Beanstalk" coming home for dinner and sitting down to eat a mountain of food. . . . How about Pecos Bill lassoing a cyclone to ride. . . .

The Senses

Pantomimes can focus on sensory awareness. Following are some examples:

TEACHER: Pretend that you are

(tasting)   Taking a dose of bitter medicine.
Biting into a piece of your favorite cake.
Eating a dill pickle.

(touching)   Threading a needle.
Shuffling cards.
Playing a musical instrument.

(hearing)   A bird listening for a worm.

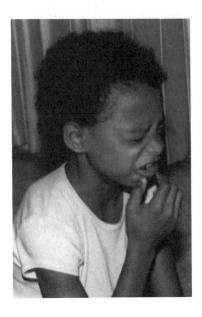

Pretend to eat a sour pickle.

	Asleep and the alarm rings and wakens you.
	Hearing a small voice inside your pocket.
(seeing)	Observing the actions of a small insect on your desk.
	Peeking through a knothole in a board fence.
	Flipping through a magazine looking at food ads.
(smelling)	Opening a carton of milk and finding it sour.
	Peeling onions.
	Smelling smoke coming from inside your desk.

Emotions

Pantomimes may also emphasize emotions. For example:

TEACHER: Pretend that

You are watching a scary television show all alone.

You are a cautious rabbit. You never take chances. You are eating a carrot for the very first time.

You are a mean witch mixing a powerful brew in your cauldron.

You are a very shy person at a party drinking a cup of punch.

Conflict

Many of the previous pantomimes have had conflict in them to heighten their dramatic impact. Notice how the addition of conflict to the following pantomimes makes them more intriguing and involving:

Expressing emotions: surprise and disgust.

Pantomime Activity	**Pantomime Conflict**
Eat an ice cream cone.	Eat an ice cream cone; the temperature is 100°.
Pretend to read a book.	Pretend to read a book; a pesky fly keeps bothering you.
Pretend to be listening to a very boring speech.	Pretend to be listening to a very boring speech; your boss is giving the speech and will be upset if you don't act interested.

As you gain practice in developing pantomime activities, it will become easier to create original ideas or to modify an activity to make it fit particular needs. In the following example, a student leader used an idea he called a "Time Circle Machine." He wanted to give his class a lot of controlled action and to cover some historical events in chronological order. The children played the activity standing at the sides of their desks.

TEACHER: We're going to take a quick historical tour through time in a Time Circle Machine. For each period of time we change to, we'll have to go through certain actions in order to make the machine work for us.

To go all the way back in time, turn in a circle once. Now you are back in prehistoric time. . . . You are a cave dweller, looking about, hunting for food. . . . Look all around . . . up and down. . . . Search. . . .

Now stop. Turn around in the smallest circle you can. Crouch down. Stand up. Now we are in another time period. You are on the *Mayflower,* traveling to the New World. The boat is rocking back and forth . . . back and forth. . . . You've been on the ship for many days. . . . Oh, boy, we'd better go to another time period before we get seasick. . . .

Now stop. Stand perfectly still. Close your eyes. Turn around once to the right, and once to the left. Wiggle your nose. Snap your fingers once—only once. Now open your eyes. You are Paul Revere riding your horse, galloping faster and faster, carrying the message that the British are coming. Hurry, make your horse go faster. Halt! Whoa! The Time Machine moves on.

The activity continued through the Wright brothers flying their plane at Kitty Hawk and Neil Armstrong landing on the moon. Almost any type of information, however, can be included in such a format.

GAMES

Games are also useful for beginning drama work. In fact, games have been used extensively in the work of Viola Spolin. (See bibliography at the end of Chapter 1.) In addition to Spolin's games, many traditional games are also usable. However, the games selected for drama work should involve action or the development of some skill needed for further dramatization. Many games can also serve double duty in the classroom with the incorporation of additional curricular concepts.

There are some cautions about traditional games. Those that eliminate players do not give children a chance to practice the skills they need to master. Eliminated players understandably become bored watching classmates excel where they have failed. Games that encourage competition cause children to be more concerned about winning, gaining points, or teasing those who lose than about mastering the game's skills. In some games, winners get to become the next leader or get to choose the next player; but many children will never be the winner or may never be chosen by their classmates. Games with such rules should be avoided or redesigned.

Miming Games

Traditional games that encourage imitative actions are Follow the Leader and Simon Says. Both can be played at the desk area. Instead of eliminating players in Simon Says, you can simply note that "ah, a few were caught that time," and continue the game. Older children can take turns being leaders for these games.

These games can be varied to incorporate other curricular concepts. One teacher used the game to review sizes and shapes: "Simon says: make yourself shaped like a box; walk in place taking giant steps; shape yourself like a piece of pie; become as small as a mouse"; and so forth. Another used it to review foreign language words: "blink your *yeux;* clap your *mains;* stamp your *pieds.*" Still another used it for the names of bones: "shake your cranium"; "wiggle your ilium"; "rotate your clavicle"; and so on.

Sensory Games

Games that emphasize the development of sensory awareness are useful in drama work as well as in many areas of the curriculum, such as science and language arts. Following are some examples.

Seeing

Who Started the Motion? Players form a circle. One (more are possible) child is "it." A leader in the circle performs a series of actions that the other players must imitate. Imitators must try to stay with the leader without directly looking at the person. "It" must guess who is the initiator.

Scavenger Hunt. The children are given a list of articles to collect within a given time limit. The articles may be a green pencil, a paper clip, a book with a picture of a Toltec temple, a paragraph with the word "magnet" in it, or a picture of a scientist conducting an experiment. The children may work on their own, in pairs, or in groups. After, discuss which method worked best and why.

Concentration. (a) Arrange a variety of items on a tray and allow the children to study them for a minute. Then have them recall the items from memory. (b) For variation, remove one or two items while the children close their eyes and see if they can guess which have been removed. (c) Rearrange the sequence of items after children have observed them and see if they can replace them in the original order. (d) For a variation of this game, have children face a partner whom they observe carefully. While observers' backs are turned, partners change one thing about themselves (for example, untie a shoe or take off piece of jewelry). Observers must identify partner's change.

Hearing

Guess the Sound. The leader (and the children) can tape record a number of familiar sounds. Or the sounds could be made behind a screen. Examples of sounds might be tearing a piece of paper, snapping fingers, the sound of a vacuum cleaner, or a running faucet. As the children listen to the sounds, they are to guess the source. The fun of the game is in the variety of identifications that can be made of one sound.

Who's My Partner? The leader distributes to each child a slip of paper with directions for a specific sound, such as "mew like a cat" or "whistle a bobwhite call." Each sound has two (or more) children performing it. On a signal everyone begins making the sound softly, repeating it until the partner is found. When the partner is located, the sounds stop, and the pairs wait where they are until all partners are discovered. Papers may be redistributed for repeated playing.

Touching

Guess the Object. Have the children try to identify numerous items by their shape and texture. The objects might be in paper bags, the children might be blindfolded, or they might sit in a circle and have the objects passed behind their backs. Objects might be a fingernail file, a toy truck, a key chain, and so forth.

Leading the Blind. Have children work in pairs, one with eyes closed and the other as leader. They explore the classroom, discovering that what is usually taken for granted is different when "viewed" in this way. Usually it is best not to allow any talking during this activity in order to aid concentration.

Tasting

Discuss the differences in tasting and smelling with such items as onion, chocolate, peppermint, and potato. We taste only sweet, sour, salt, and bitter.

We smell rather than taste foods we eat. By holding the nose when tasting, it it difficult to guess a number of foods and flavors.

Smelling

Put a variety of items with distinctive odors in small containers. Have the children guess the items by sniffing *gently*. Items might be vinegar, ammonia, turpentine, coke, banana oil, vanilla, cedar wood, and onion.

Imagination Games

Many drama leaders speak of imagination as a muscle that needs frequent exercising. Games which focus on stimulating children's imagination may be played.

Pass the object I.   Children sit in a circle. Pass a simple object such as a ball or a pencil and suggest that it is "a bird with a broken wing," "a very sharp knife," or another significant item. Silence is required so that the children can concentrate on the object, handle it, and respond to it before passing it on.

Pass the object II.   Without using a prop the children pass an "object" of their own choosing. After the first child responds to the teacher's suggestion, (ice cube) he or she gives a new suggestion (sticky taffy) to which the next child must respond, and so on. The suggestions should remain an appropriate size for passing hand to hand.

Mystery box.   Bring an imaginary box of any size into the center of the circle. For a very large box, several children may help carry it in. Volunteers, singly or in pairs, may open the box, which might become a packing carton, an elaborately wrapped gift, a cage, and so forth. Children take the item out of the box, handle or use it in some way, and then return it. The item should be appropriate to the size of the box.

What could it be?   Show children objects which they are to imagine might be something else. For example, a pair of scissors might become a dancing puppet, a spear for catching a fish, or a lorgnette. An interesting piece of driftwood might take on a variety of shapes as it is turned in different ways and examined. A conch shell might become a large rosebud, a horn, or a fairy's palace.

Communication Games

Some games help children increase their communication skills, both in speaking and in listening. Such games are designed to help children realize the importance of sending and receiving messages as accurately as possible.

What's this?   One person describes an object—such as a safety pin, a paper clip, a light bulb, or an article of clothing—without naming what the item is. The listeners must draw each part of the object as they listen to the description. They cannot ask questions. Whenever listeners think they know what the object is, they may guess.

Giving directions.   This game is similar to the previous one. Two children stand back to back with a desk or table in front of each of them. Several items, such as a pencil, an eraser, and a book, are on each desk. Children take turns arranging the objects and then telling the partner how to arrange his or her items in the same pattern. Again, the listener cannot ask questions.

Variation: To help children see the importance of questioning for clarity, one partner—or both children—may be allowed to ask questions as the game is played.

Character voices.   Different types of people speak with different voices. Even an inanimate object might have a voice that is affected by the material it is made of: tin produces a metallic sound, whereas cotton has a muffled quality. Place a number of simple sentences ("Good morning," "Hello," "How are you?" "Why me?") on cards and distribute them. On another set of cards a variety of characters (Papa Bear, Paul Bunyan, a grandfather clock, a tin soldier, a weeping willow, or a wooden spoon) are listed. Children say the sentence as the character might sound.

The olde junke shoppe.   Children pretend to be items in an old junk shop. They create sounds for each item to make as it moves. Children may choose to be a squeaking old rocking chair, a scratchy gramophone, an out-of-tune music box, and so on.

Movement Games

The following games encourage a variety of movements. The goal is to work toward relaxed and free movements, but with attention to the specifications of the games. They can all be played at the desk, although as you and the students become more accustomed to using more space, these games can expand.

Move to the beat.   The children sit at their desks. The leader beats a drum, while the children move in as many different ways as possible. They may move *only* when the drum beats, so you should vary the beats, halt suddenly, and the like, so that the children are encouraged to listen closely.

Balance movement game.   While standing by the sides of their desks, the children can perform a variety of movements that you call out. For example, they can stand on tiptoes, crouch and touch both knees, or take one step forward and one step back. The challenge: all the actions are to be done while they balance a book on their heads!

Painting. Children pretend to paint with a small brush that grows into a larger and larger brush until it is the size of a broom. Then it shrinks again. Children move from painting on their desk top to painting in the air and then at the side of the desk. They return to a seated position as the brush shrinks back to its original size. Encourage children to think of themselves as famous artists painting with great skill. Leroy Anderson's "Waltzing Cat" record is a useful accompaniment.

Activities with a ball. Children pretend to bounce different-sized balls: a basketball, a volleyball, a tennis ball, and so forth. Change the weights of the balls: the ball is heavy, and then it is light. The Harlem Globetrotters' theme, "Sweet Georgia Brown," is wonderful background music for this one.

GROUP MANAGEMENT IN LARGER AREAS OF SPACE

Foresight and preparation are needed in managing any group. Interestingly, when operating as a group, adults actually behave very much like a classroom of children. If you have gained experience leading a group of your own classmates in an activity, you will probably have fewer difficulties with a classroom of children. Following are some tips to keep in mind.

We pretend to paint a very big picture.

Giving Directions

Word directions explicitly and carefully. Children will usually do what is asked of them if it is clearly and firmly stated. Unfortunately, they usually cannot tell you when they do not understand. They simply go ahead and do something—even if it leads to chaos. That is your clue that your directions were unclear, and that you need to intervene before it is too late to rectify the situation.

As much as possible, give directions while children are seated and you have their attention. Once any group gets up and begins moving, you will have difficulty getting their attention again without reseating them—and that's not easy for you or them. (It's a little like the old song "How ya gonna keep 'em down on the farm, after they've seen Paree?")

How to manage rearranging the room. Always make sure you really need more space and that changing the classroom arrangement is really necessary before you go ahead and do it. If more space is needed, the desks can be moved to the edges of the room.

In many classrooms, a usual procedure in expanding space is to move the furniture against the walls. Experienced teachers can make it look ridiculously easy, but for a beginner it can be an awesome experience. Frequently a novice will tell an entire class to "quietly push your desks against the wall" and then expect that it will be done in absolute silence. The sound of 30 desks scraping and 30 pairs of feet scuffling, added to spontaneous whispering and chattering, may be enough to convince the neophyte that experienced teachers possess supernatural powers. Furthermore, if one's voice lacks assurance, the verbal directions can sound more like a question than a command. This, in itself, can cause perfectly normal children to take advantage and "cut loose." They never hear the pandemonium they create with zestful abandon, but the rest of the school probably will!

What the casual observer often does not realize is that the seasoned teacher usually has previously set up an efficient procedure for moving desks which the children have followed many times. It only *seems* spontaneously organized. Until a beginning teacher has set up a similar procedure, there is no substitute for caution. It is much wiser to take a little more time and proceed step by step.

TEACHER: Row one, pick up your desks and place them here. (When they have finished and are seated, continue.) Row two, over here (and so on).

Avoid sugarcoating directions in fantasy. Inexperienced teachers are often afraid to make rules and give directions because they think it will alienate them from the children or that the children will not like them as much. As a coverup they sugarcoat directions in fantasy. For example, some leaders try to make a game out of moving desks, suggesting that the desks are "explosives" which the children have to move carefully so they do not blow up. However, such directions are too tempting for some children. "Exploding" one's desk may be even more interesting than the planned activity! It is usually best to be straightforward about getting the furniture arranged.

As another example, suppose you want the children to remain in a designated area, yet you warn:

TEACHER: You're like sticky gum, so don't touch anyone or you may stick together.

For most children this statement is like a Wet Paint sign; it becomes an interesting possibility and announces itself as a challenge to be tested. Ironically, they are then beguiled into doing exactly what you are trying to avoid. Not only do they touch each other; they clump in a huge mass before you ever figure out what happened! Being straightforward is usually safer.

TEACHER: During this activity you are to remain in your own space. Give yourself enough room that you do not touch anyone.

It is always best to be explicit about no talking. You may be tempted to downplay directions. For example, you are doing a poem about snowflakes, and you say (quite creatively, you think):

TEACHER: Remember now, snowflakes don't talk.

But if children can imagine being a snowflake, they can also imagine that their snowflake is capable of speech. (In fact, you just might ask for this kind of imagination on another occasion.) So they begin chattering, rationalizing in their own minds that they are using "snowflake voices," and your good intentions have backfired. It is generally best to just say simply and directly:

TEACHER: For this activity I want you to move as silently as possible. There should be no talking at all. When everyone is quiet, we shall begin.

Repeating directions.   Do not assume that once you give directions children will automatically understand and remember them. It may be difficult, for example, for children to stay in their area once the playing begins. Usually they mean well, but it is natural to gravitate toward friends, and soon social and sometimes physical interaction completely overshadows the activity. Of course, concentration is usually lost.

It may take practice for children to learn to stay in separate playing areas, particularly for young ones, whose bodies are constantly in motion. You may need to repeat your directions and your reasons for your rules—patiently—several times before children can follow through successfully.

When children see how your rules help their concentration and make the playing more interesting, they will be able to follow them more readily.

Staying in control with nonverbal directions. Look for ways to maintain control without constantly scolding and nagging children about their behavior. Much of this control can be done nonverbally. Experienced teachers can do much with a glance, a definite shake of the head, or other simple tactics that convey as strong a message as a verbally stated one—such as waiting with folded hands or a finger to the lips for a group to settle down before trying to talk above their chattering. Many of these gestures will take time to learn and perfect, but you will do well to think of some possibilities for yourself.

One student teacher who was having a difficult time getting the children's attention because of her soft voice drew a large, colorful sign saying Cool It! in bold letters. Whenever she wanted the group to be quiet and listen for further directions, she simply held up the sign and waited for a few seconds until everyone saw it. Then she proceeded with the activity. For her it worked.

You can often stop negative behaviors, such as disturbing chattering or minor horseplay, if you simply move in the direction of the offenders. The close proximity of the authority figure speaks for itself. If needed, a hand on the shoulder can be an additional nonverbal reminder of the rules.

Getting the group's attention. When any group moves out into larger areas of space, they make some noise just in their moving about. They also pay more attention to each other than to you, and may even begin to talk. If you try to shout above the group's noise to get their attention, it only adds to the din and confusion. The children often are too engrossed in their activities to be aware that you are talking at all. Furthermore, when you raise your voice's volume, your pitch usually rises too. As the situation escalates, you begin to sound like a screaming banshee. This obviously contributes to cacophony, to say nothing of causing one a loss of dignity!

Visual and auditory cues are usually more effective. They may be auditory, such as the ring of a small bell or a beat on a drum; they may be visual, such as the flicking of lights or the raising of a hand.

Some commands can be fun, challenging, and effective. For example, children usually like the word "freeze" to call them to attention. It seems to them more of a game rule than a command. Other signals might be "Cut!" "Lights, camera, action!" "Quiet on the set!" "Roll tape!" or other commands from theatre, film, or television that children are familiar with. It makes them feel more professional and adult.

Be careful, however, of overusing any one signal; signals are more effective when used judiciously and sparingly. As you become more skilled and develop a rapport with the group, and as they become sensitive to your procedures and expectations, you may need only say

Attention-getting devices are useful.

TEACHER: Groups, go to your areas. When you're settled, I'll give you some further directions.

Taking action.   When things go wrong, it is best to take direct action. Inexperienced teachers are often hesitant to do this, trying instead to muddle through or to look the other way rather than face a problem. This usually makes an already bad situation even worse. Although there are many minor situations that can be overlooked and will diminish on their own, a whole session can deteriorate quickly if problems are allowed to continue.

You may even need to stop the activity to sort out what has happened and find a way to remedy it. Even the children are aware that this procedure can be helpful. Once some kindergarten children were pretending to be baby animals and suddenly turned into ferocious tigers and lions, fighting one another. The student teacher stood in a near daze until, "out of the mouths of babes," a five-year-old, while tugging on her skirt, suggested, "Teacher, I think we need to sit down in a circle."

Understanding Problems

Children often get excited as they get ready to participate in drama. Excitement leads to whispered talking. Suddenly they are moving about, and disorganization sets in. It is not necessary to scold children for something that is a natural response. Just say good-naturedly,

TEACHER: Whoops, I can see we've got a problem. Let's work on it.

Problems may also occur in spite of your best planning and intentions. You may get excited and rush the children before they are ready, thus contributing to their hyperactivity. Or you may do too much discussing of an idea, and the children begin to get restless.

Recognizing and admitting one's own mistakes is important so that children know that the difficulties may not have been their fault:

TEACHER: I think I've kept you sitting a long time while we've discussed this. . . .

TEACHER: Sometimes I get so excited about what we're doing that I rush you too fast. I think that may be what happened just now. We were really getting ahead of ourselves.

For your own emotional health, verbally acknowledging the problem is usually more helpful than silently blaming yourself or the children. Once, in trying to organize a group the author became exasperated with one child who was talking with a friend. Accusingly she asked, pointing a finger at him, "Can you do this?" He, puzzled but cooperative, nodded his head and pointed his finger also! At a time like this, a sense of humor is the best antidote.

These hints, though not all-inclusive, should help keep order and control, so that everyone can focus on the drama activities rather than on discipline problems.

GAMES FOR SELF-CONTROL

Although games in themselves have a built-in control, there are several games which particularly focus on building self-control and self-discipline.

Problems can occur despite your best planning.

Children need to learn that artistic discipline is necessary for artists to perform at their best—just as sound minds and bodies are important to athletes.

Eventually you want to guide older groups to let their physical needs and their ideas determine the use of space. They may move wherever they feel they need to and wherever their ideas take them, provided they can remain absorbed in their work and can be aware of the others in the group. Such an experience in democratic responsibility is extremely valuable but usually needs to be approached systematically.

The student leader will find these games helpful in enticing children to work at developing these important skills. The repeated playings of the exercises should result in increased skills. Many similar games are practiced continuously by professional actors, so the games can provide constant practice material.

The solo materials will be the easiest for younger children, though a few of the paired activities are also possible. Group activities are reserved for older or more advanced players.

Solo Work in Self-Control

Parades. Young children love parades. They are fun, but they are also controlled and precise. Children can be assigned parts or may decide who they want to be. Begin marching in a circle with a few children, and then add on in ones, twos, threes, or more.

Parade ideas can come from music, literature, or other sources of stimulus. Following are a few ideas.

1. Music

"Parade of the Wooden Soldiers," Leon Jessel. Stiff, wooden movements are encouraged. This music is good also for a parade of marionettes, robots, and windup or mechanical toys.

"March Past of the Kitchen Utensils," Vaughan Williams. This is fun for physical characterization of various cooking tools.

"Baby Elephant Walk," Henry Mancini. Other animals, in addition to the elephants, can take part in this parade.

"Circus Music," from *The Red Pony,* Aaron Copland. A circus parade is always good fun.

2. Literature

And to Think that I Saw It on Mulberry Street, Dr. Seuss. New York: Vanguard Press, 1937. Marco makes up a story about what he sees after being asked daily "What did you see today?"

The Snow Parade, Barbara Brenner. New York: Crown Publishers, 1984. Young Andrew Barclay creates a parade with animals, people, and "hundreds more." Try using Leroy Anderson's "Sleigh Ride" for accompaniment.

The Wedding Procession of the Rag Doll and the Broom Handle and Who Was in It,

Carl Sandburg. San Diego: Harcourt Brace Jovanovich, 1922. An unusual procession is made up of many unlikely characters—such as Spoon Lickers, Easy Ticklers, and Musical Soup Eaters—that offer ideas for different movements. Try Nacio Herb Brown's "Wedding of the Painted Doll" for this one.

Walking game. Establish the point that space must be used responsibly. Play "walking" music, such as "Walking to Missouri," "There's a Kind of Walk you Walk," Henry Mancini's "March of the Cue Balls," or lively ¾ beat selections from a Mitch Miller record. Children simply walk about the room sharing space. There can be no bumping into anyone. Begin with a few children, and then add on more. A group discussion with the children might be helpful at some point, asking children to share their observations on "What do people do in order to share space with each other?" (They watch each other; they have to vary their speed or even stop in order not to bump into anyone; sometimes you pass around them, moving sideways.)

Slow-motion activities. Slow motion is a good way to control movement. It is also an excellent exercise in disciplined, thoughtful movement, focusing concentration and involvement on an idea as well as on bodily awareness. And when slow motion is mastered, it can be as fascinating to watch as it is to perform. Since almost any activity can be played in slow motion, this technique will be mentioned frequently throughout the text.

Children will first need to learn the concept. Compare slow motion to moving underwater or through heavy syrup, to the television replays of sports events, or to time-lapse photography.

Moving in slow motion is not always easy and requires the guidance of

We pretend to go shopping as fast as we can without bumping into anyone.

the leader. Children have to be reminded to keep the movement slow; in the excitement of moving, the tendency is to speed up.

TEACHER: That's it. Keep it slow. Freeze. Now this time go even slower—three times as slow as you just did. (Give these directions in a slow-motion voice, like a record playing on slow speed.)

Music can be helpful. Try selections such as Debussy's "Clair de Lune" or "Afternoon of a Faun." With a variable-speed record player, a slow-motion effect can be gained by playing almost any slow selection at a slower speed.

Freeze game.   This game establishes the fact that space must be used responsibly. Children may move about the room quickly in any way they wish (without bumping into each other), but on signal (drum beat, ringing bell) they must freeze. Specify certain movements, such as hopping or skipping. They may also be directed to freeze into a position or an expression, such as looking funny or becoming an animal.

Be sure to give a definite signal for freezing and test it out first with just a few children. It is also better to begin with only a few children at a time and gradually add on more. The goal is to have the entire class playing the game at the same time, but this will probably not happen the first time you try it.

Variation: Children move only when you beat a drum or while the music plays. They must stop when you do.

"Freeze" game encourages physical control and self-discipline.

Circle game. Two concentric circles are formed. They rotate in opposite directions. Players are to remain equally spaced as they march around the circle to lively music. When the leader calls "Change," the players must reverse directions.

After this much of the game is mastered another challenge can be added: the leader moves around the circles and taps players on the shoulder. The tapped person moves into the opposite circle and changes directions while still marching. Other players must adjust the spacing so that the space is still equidistant between players. The leader can continue to call "Change" at any time.

Caught in the act. In this game children move in any way they wish while their feet are "glued" to the floor. A signal is given to freeze into position. Another signal is given and they move about the room *in the position they were frozen in*. Another signal stops them, roots them to the spot, and the game repeats.

Be careful! Pantomime walking over stepping stones, on a tightrope, or on a fence top, retaining balance. Do this at the side of the desks or have small groups go from one end of the room to the other.

Conduct an orchestra. All the children are orchestra leaders and must keep with the beat of a particular record. "Sabre Dance" by Khachaturian or the *Star Wars* theme is useful.

Burglars. In groups (one group at a time), be burglars sneaking through a museum guarded by electronic eyes. Children must move as rapidly as possible from one side of the room to another but must go down to the floor whenever they hear the sound cue which indicates activation of the electronic eye. (An alarm-clock bell or buzzer works well for this.) The objective is to move quickly *and* quietly. Groups can work to improve their speed.

I won't laugh. Several students at a time sit facing the class. They cannot close their eyes or plug their ears. The rest of the class volunteers to tell jokes, make faces, or whatever else they can think of (without touching the contestants) to make them laugh. Again, groups or individuals could work to increase the length of time they can hold out.

Interrogation. In each group, one child is the questioner. He or she focuses on one person, but it is the person on the right of the questioned person who must answer, and with a straight face. The questioned person must maintain eye contact with the questioner and not laugh. Whoever in the group cannot remain solemn throughout the proceedings becomes the next interrogator. For an added challenge, if the questioner points a finger at a subject, the person on the left must answer. Try going fast.

Student tries to break classmates' concentration in the game "I Won't Laugh."

Falling. Children love to fall. Suggest that anyone can fall, but that it takes real skill to do it with control. Caution them not to fall on unprotected parts of their bodies like elbows, knees, and heads. Think of different kinds of objects that fall: a leaf, a balloon losing air. Fall in slow motion. No one can reach the ground before you count to a slow 10. Have them close their eyes so they concentrate only on their own work.

To tire out an overactive group, make them fall in a variety of ways very quickly: "Up again. This time fall quickly like a falling star. Now! (They fall.) Up. This time you're a feather. Fall on the count of five. (They fall.) Up again. . . ."

Making noiseless sounds. Children pantomime making a vocal sound by using their face and body but not their voice. Try it in slow motion. Cough, sneeze, gulp, gasp, sigh, and shout.

Pair and Group Work in Self-Control

Many groups of children need assistance and motivation in order to work together. The games in this section are useful in achieving this goal.

Sound pantomime. One child pantomimes while another creates the sound effects. At first, the sound effects should fit the timing of the pantomime. Then let the pantomimer fit movements to the sound effects. Use simple ideas at first: someone sneaking across a creaky floor trying not to be heard; sawing a piece of lumber; cutting down a tree with an ax; trying to start an old, junky car; a robot moving with creaking joints.

In-service teachers practice moving in slow motion.

Two-person jobs. Select a task which requires two people to perform. Pretend to fold a flag or tablecloth; saw wood with a lumberjack's saw; play seesaw. Pairs must concentrate on the pantomimed object and cooperate to make the object appear real.

Mirroring. Two people face each other. One is the mirror, and the other the person using the mirror. The mirror must follow the leader in putting on makeup, face washing, shaving, and so on. Consider possibilities with a full-length mirror also, as in practicing a dance step. Switch parts. Try this in slow motion to keep the actions carefully "mirrored."

Sculpturing. One person is the sculptor, and the other a piece of clay. The sculptor molds clay into a statue, giving it a particular stance or emotional attitude. The status must allow itself to be moved about. Nontouchers and the ticklish will find this a real challenge.

Group jobs. Five people are carrying a large piece of glass from one side of the room to the other. The five people must coordinate their movements so that the imaginary piece of glass really seems to exist. As the group walks, the pane of glass must stay in one piece! As an added challenge have the group walk as fast as possible, "upstairs," "downstairs," and the like. Other group jobs might be firefighters carrying an extension ladder, pirates carrying a large treasure chest, or police moving a very tall murder victim.

Kindergarteners play the "Mirror Game."

Tug-of-war.   Two teams of three or more pretend to pull on an imaginary rope. The rope must seem to exist. The leader needs to side-coach the game: "Team 1 is ahead. . . . Now it's team 2. . . ." On the leader's signal the rope breaks and the players fall in slow motion. Players cannot reach the floor until the leader, who is counting slowly, reaches the count of 10.

Conducting an orchestra.   This time the children are in groups pantomiming to a record. One is the conductor, while the others are playing specific instruments. Drums, cymbals, violins, and trombones are particularly good because they require large movements. March music (Sousa) is easiest to begin on. For further self-discipline stop the record periodically so players have to freeze.

Mirroring in groups.   After experiencing pair mirroring, the children can try pairs mirroring pairs. For example, a person at a beauty or barber shop is mirrored; then the hairdresser or barber is mirrored. A manicurist and shoe shiner, both mirrored, may even be added.

One at a time.   Several players pretend to be in a given setting, perhaps a living room. They are seated randomly. They may move about the room as they like, but they do not interact. However, only one person may move at a time. The action of the next person moving freezes the first mover in place until that player decides to initiate movement again. For example, person 1 gets out of a chair and turns on an imaginary TV set. Person 2 picks up a newspaper from a table, which freezes person 1 at the TV. Perhaps person 3 crosses her legs and freezes person 2. Then person 1

"Tug of War" encourages concentration and focus.

might decide to return to his seat, and so forth. Children must become very sensitive to each other's movements or the game fails. They must also be assertive if they want to move. The leader monitors and coaches: "Only one person can move at a time. . . ."

To help children learn the game, it is useful to give players a number. You call the numbers at random to indicate when the children may move. Once the children understand how the game is played, they initiate their own actions.

A variation of the game is to have children sit in a circle and not move from their seats. All initiated action must be in a seated position. Work toward using smaller and smaller actions. Groups of five to ten work best, but more than one group may play at a time. (Note: The spontaneity of this game makes it fun for the rest of the children to watch.)

QUIETING ACTIVITIES

A creative drama period should come to a quieting end. There will probably have been a lot of action, concentration, and hard work. It is usually essential to calm the children down rather than let them go on to their next work at a high pitch.

One technique is to narrate a quieting selection. There are several

Kindergarteners rest in a quieting activity.

poems suitable for this purpose. The characters in the poems are relaxed or tired; thus, the actions are subdued. Some examples are

"Fatigue," Peggy Bacon (34). The subway ride at night features tired workers.
"Keep a Poem in Your Pocket," Beatrice Schenk de Regniers (35, 36). A poem will sing to you at night when you are in bed.
"Lullaby," Robert Hillyer (37). We are in a rowboat, drifting along peacefully.
"Slowly," James Reeves (57). Everything moves very slowly in this poem.
"Snow Toward Evening," Melville Crane (4, 35). A calm, peaceful snowy night is described.
"Sunning," James S. Tippett (4, 36). An old dog sleeps lazily on a porch.
"Tired Tim," Walter De la Mare (4, 36). Poor Tim is just too tired to move.
"Who Has Seen the Wind?" Christina Rossetti (35, 36, 57). Leaves hang trembling and bow their heads when wind passes by.

It is usually helpful to have the children close their eyes as they enact the poem. Try to capture the quieting mood in your voice, or perhaps use a quiet record for accompaniment.

Leaders may also create their own simple quieting activities. You can narrate a few sentences about a candle burning and slowly melting away or have the children pretend to be a leaf floating on calm waters.

The importance of the quieting experience is to relax the group and to calm down any hyperactivity. Perhaps more important than that, however, it helps the children to absorb the concepts, experiences, and feelings covered during the drama period.

The snow sculpture melts slowly in a quieting activity to close the drama session.

FOR THE COLLEGE STUDENT

1. Collect or design each of the following:
   a. a finger play
   b. a single-action poem
   c. an action song
   d. an action game
   e. an action story
   f. a quieting activity
2. Find a game or design one of your own that has action in it but can be played at the desk.
3. Select a game to lead your classmates in. Give the directions for playing the activity. Organize the group for playing the game. Bring the playing to a close. Afterward discuss with your classmates what your strengths and weaknesses were. Brainstorm ways to improve the activity.
4. Select or design a game that illustrates the use of controls.
5. Find or create a game to develop children's imagination.
6. Select or design five sensory games, one for each of the senses.
7. Select or design a communication game, emphasizing either speaking or listening skills.
8. Write a pantomime, of at least fifty words, which emphasizes a variety of actions.
9. Write five sensory pantomimes, one for each of the five major senses.
10. Write a pantomime emphasizing emotions.

11. Make a list of three brief pantomimes; then in a second list add conflict to each.
12. As a class, play some of the games for self-control. Afterward discuss your reactions. Were you able to improve your skills as a result of the playing? How do you think this was accomplished?
13. Discuss various physical features of the classroom environment. Consider such factors as fixed desks, rows of desks on runners, large rooms with movable furniture, small rooms with tables and chairs, carpeting, thin classroom partitions and walls, skylights, and shades. Consider ways to accommodate any of these physical features. Include selection of material, planning and organizing space, and giving directions.

FIVE

Stories and Poems for Narrative Pantomime: From Solo Desk Activities to Improvised Plays

A number of years ago, while searching for an easy way to help teachers get started in creative drama, we discovered that many excellent pieces of children's literature centered primarily on action. We found that if such pieces were narrated, children could play along, pantomiming the actions. We called both the materials and the technique of playing them narrative pantomime.[1] Some of the most familiar pieces include Paul Galdone's version of *The Three Bears*, Beatrix Potter's *The Tale of Peter Rabbit*, and Dr. Seuss's *How the Grinch Stole Christmas*.[2]

THE VALUE OF NARRATIVE MATERIALS

Narrative pantomime provides an expedient, efficient, and enjoyable way to dramatize excellent literature. It is a useful activity regardless of the amount of experience you and the children have had in creative drama. Since pantomime materials are usually easier to enact than dialogue materials, narrative pantomimes are useful for beginning groups as well as for warm-ups with experienced groups.

Narrative materials also provide a foundation for further creative work. There are a variety of ways to elaborate on them, as you will see. Children are also introduced to basic dramatic structure: a plot with a conflict and a beginning, middle, and ending.

[1]See earlier editions of this text, *Creative Drama for the Classroom Teacher*, by Ruth Beall Heinig and Lyda Stillwell (Englewood Cliffs, N.J.: Prentice-Hall, 1974 and 1981).

[2]All materials referred to in this chapter are listed in the bibliographies in this chapter.

A popular school superintendent takes time to read stories to children. (Supt. James Weeldreyer, Mattawan, Michigan.)

The Value to Children

Narrative pantomimes provide a way for children to experience excellent literature, trying on favorite characters and joining them in their adventures. Through this process they interpret the literature and increase their understanding of it. Particularly with the stories, children feel a sense of accomplishment and satisfaction in being able to enact completed little dramas early on.

Children are able to be successful in narrative activities, since they need only follow the actions the literature prescribes. This gives children security and self-confidence to try more challenging drama work later. At the same time, they must also listen carefully to know what to do and when to do it. This helps them focus their concentration and develops listening skills.

The Value to the Leader

Because children must follow the literature's directions in narrative pantomime, there is built-in organization, an important aid to the beginning leader. By narrating the action, you give the cues for playing and have control of the dramatization.

As you become proficient in narrative pantomime, you will quickly learn what literature works best and will soon find yourself being able to edit material easily and even to write some of your own materials. (This will be discussed further in the next chapter.) Narrative pantomime will also help you in developing descriptive commentary, useful in the technique of side-coaching in other activities.

THE TYPES OF NARRATIVE PANTOMIME MATERIAL

Narrative pantomime literature may have one character (solo or individual playing), two characters (paired playing), or even several (group playing).

Material for Solo or Individual Playing

In solo material the character may live alone, as in *The Man Who Didn't Wash His Dishes*, the story of a lazy fellow's problem with housework. Or the character may be alone on an adventure, as is Harold on his many purple crayon adventures. (See *Harold and the Purple Crayon, Harold's Circus, Harold's Fairy Tale,* and *Harold's Trip to the Sky.*) Some material has two or more characters who act independently of each other. In such material the child can play all the parts, changing from one to the other with relative ease. *The Pond,* for example describes the movements of several characters, one at a time: the water, a dragonfly, shadows, and so forth. Or in the poem "Foul Shot" by Edwin A. Hoey, the students can first be the ball-player, then the basketball, and finally the crowd watching the basketball game.

Material for Paired Playing

Stories or poems with two fairly equal characters are played in pairs. Such a story might be Beatrix Potter's *The Tale of Two Bad Mice.* Paired playing can be used with stories in which one character goes on an adventure and meets different people along the way. One child plays the adventurer, and the partner plays all the people who are met. Or in a story like "Gertrude McFuzz," the same child who plays Lolla-Lee-Lou can also play Uncle Dake.

Material for Group Playing

Material which has several characters (or has the potential for adding characters) can be played in groups. Group stories resemble a popular theatre form called story theatre.

Some of the characters in group stories have small parts, but if they are interesting ones, the children will want to include them all. For example, in *Ittki Pittki* there are, in addition to the title role, the prince, the wife, four sons, the prince's messenger, the doctor, the funeral director, and all the customers and mourners. Although some appear only briefly, they are all important to the plot.

As you become more familiar with narrative pantomime, you will want to try many varieties. This chapter will cover techniques for playing narrative pantomime. Within the chapter there are extensive bibliographies, listed in three groups according to the playing that the literature is most suited for: solo, pair, and group playing. Let us first look at the general considerations you will need to make in playing narrative pantomimes.

GENERAL CONSIDERATIONS FOR PREPARING NARRATIVE PANTOMIMES

Selecting and Editing the Material

Material used for narrative pantomime must have enough continuous action to keep children actively involved from beginning to end. The selections in the bibliographies in this chapter are some of the easiest to use. But since most authors and poets have not written their materials for narrative pantomime purposes, almost any selection can benefit from minor editing. Some material benefits from tightening the physical action, even to the extent of omitting some words or even sentences, as long as the plot is not destroyed.

The most dramatic materials build to a climax and have a quieting ending. Many stories and poems even have the character in a settled position at the end. This is a welcome aid in getting the students back in their seats or in a stationary position after playing. In some cases you will want to add this feature with an added line or two or a simple rewording. For example, even though you read the entire story *The Snowy Day* to children, you might end their *playing* of it with Peter going to bed and dreaming of tomorrow and another day in the snow. This way the children are seated and sleeping at the end, rather than waking and going outdoors again as the book's ending does.

You will sometimes find that additional action is helpful, particularly in picture books, where much of the story is told through the artwork. Adding descriptive detail to action can also enrich the drama experience. For example, a line may read, "The farmer worked in the field all day long." You might add the words "cutting and stacking the hay." Or if you want to give them something to do without being too active, you might narrate "The bears became tired and sat down under a tree to rest and enjoy the scenery."

Editing Dialogue

Some stories have brief lines of dialogue. If they are short, the children will enjoy repeating them. It is almost crucial, for example, to let children say "Gwot, I ate it!" the final line of George Mendoza's "The Hairy Toe." Or in Russell Hoban's *The Little Brute Family,* the lines "How nice" or "May we keep it?" are fun to repeat. Longer lines can be dropped.

Some dialogue is easily pantomimed (for example, "No," "I don't know," or "Here"), but generally the mouthing of words is distracting.

Therefore, if you see the children doing this as you narrate, it probably means that there is too much dialogue and it should be cut (or that children are ready to add dialogue, which will be discussed later in this chapter).

Presenting the Material

There is no one way to present the material before enacting it. You might want to read the story first and discuss it to make sure the children understand it and know what they are to do. Other times you might want to read a story "cold" and have them improvise on the spot. In any event, you will always want to be sure they know what they are to do, have ideas for doing it, understand how to use space, and can handle any physical action safely. It is sometimes helpful to have competent students demonstrate to the others how to play difficult or problem situations.

Creative Interpretation of Movement

Although narrative materials have many actions to perform, there is no one way to interpret a particular action. Children may interpret their ideas in whatever way they choose. Even with a fairly explicit line such as "frogs hop," there is room for creativity. Some children may choose to enact their frog in an upright position, hopping on hind legs. Others may want to be on all fours, perhaps even crooking their arms to represent the frog's bowed front legs.

Some actions are more challenging. For example, in Carl Sandburg's "Lines Written for Gene Kelly to Dance to," the children are asked if they can dance a question mark. This could be interpreted in a variety of ways: the feet might draw a question mark on the floor; the hands might inscribe one in the air; or the whole body might form one, dissolving and reforming in a rhythmic dance.

You will want to encourage students to find their own ways of performing an action. The ideas can be discussed prior to the playing and perhaps tried out and demonstrated before the entire selection is played.

Limiting Space

As discussed earlier, it is most useful to keep the students working at their desks or in a designated place on the floor. The desks can often become part of the drama if you refer to them as a bed, a car, a table, or whatever the material calls for.

For pair and group playing, be sure the children understand the limits of their space. In some cases it may also be necessary to let only half the class play while the other half observes. (Observers might help with the sound effects or other technical aspects.)

Narrating the Material

Much of the artistic burden of narrative pantomime lies on the narrator's reading abilities. You need to practice giving a good oral reading interpretation. You also need to know the story well enough to be able to keep an eye on the class's performance and to time the pauses for playing.

One student teacher learned the value of good narrating most graphically. She began by selecting a short poem that was too difficult for her kindergartners to understand. Then she read the poem, haltingly and without once glancing up. The children stood patiently, listening, but had no idea what to do. At the end of the poem and after a moment's silence, one little voice piped up, "Is that it?" Although the student had made an error in selecting inappropriate material, she should have realized the children were doing nothing. A couple of glances up from the page would have made this clear.

You will probably need to experiment to determine your vocal capabilities. Even when children are pantomiming, they are moving about and making some noise in the process. If you have a soft voice, it may be necessary to allow only half the class to play at a time in order that your voice may be heard.

Your timing and vocal intensity can also control the action and the noise level. Although you should not rush your narrating, it is generally better to use shorter pauses rather than longer ones until you are sure the children are filling in the time with meaningful actions. Also, if the students should get a bit too noisy, just pause. As they quiet down to hear the next cue, you can speak in a softer voice. This should help calm their playing down.

It is usually best not to let the students be the narrators, particularly at first. Later, when they become familiar with narrative pantomime, you may

A small group rehearses its play with a student narrator.

find superior readers volunteering to narrate and doing an excellent job. (One of our best narrators was a second grader who read *Seven Skinny Goats* for his classmates to play. His only problem was keeping from laughing at the antics of the players!)

If you have several talented readers, you might want to let them all be narrators for one selection. Just divide the material at logical intervals. This technique is then very similar to "reader's theatre."

It should be added that when children see the importance of the narrator's role and have a desire to try it, they are often motivated to perfect their reading skills. The narrator's role then becomes as significant to them as the "lead" part in the story.

Using Music

Some materials benefit from musical background, which lends atmosphere, sustains involvement, and encourages ideas. Some suggestions are indicated in the bibliographies in this chapter. At first you will probably need to rehearse the narration with the music before trying it with the class to be sure you are enhancing the playing.

Evaluating

Both you and the students will be evaluating the playing throughout. Acknowledge the good work you see them doing, although it is best not to praise one idea over another. Your acknowledgment can pertain both to the playing and to the students' management of themselves:

"You had so many interesting and different ways of being a cat. I saw some washing themselves; some were sitting on their haunches; and I think I even heard some quiet purring."

"I liked the way you were able to stay in your own space and not interfere with someone else's work."

Self evaluation is also important and can be encouraged by asking

"What's one thing you did that you liked the best?"

"What do you think you might do differently the next time we play it?"

Some may like to share their ideas for interpretation, both in telling about it as well as in demonstrating.

Replaying

If students have enjoyed the material and their own expression of it, they may ask to repeat it. In repeated playings they can perfect their ideas with your encouragement and guidance. New goals may also be established.

"This time you may want to try some new ideas."

"I'll slow down this time in the part where you thought I read a little too fast for you to act out all the ideas you had."

In replaying, children might wish to add new characters, creating a group story. In *The Little Auto,* for example, children might like to create the auto itself for Mr. Small. Four children on their hands and knees can create the car, bouncing along in place, with one, as one of the tires, going flat and being pumped up again. They can also be the engine humming and the horn beeping. A sixth person could act out the minor characters of the police officer, the gas station attendant, and even a person who sells the newspaper to Mr. Small.

A BIBLIOGRAPHY OF NARRATIVE PANTOMIMES FOR SOLO PLAYING

At first, young children generally prefer narratives that are solo or individual. Since each child can be the "star" in his or her own little drama, it is a very satisfying experience. But they will eventually find paired and group playing fun to try, as long as they can take turns and play every part.

Older students, on the other hand, may at first prefer enacting the narrative pantomimes that have two or more characters, because these materials resemble a skit or a play. But as they begin to understand what narrative pantomime is and become more comfortable in their pantomiming abilities, they will also enjoy the materials that feature one character.

The following stories and poems are suitable for solo playing. They are arranged alphabetically by title. Numbers in parentheses refer to anthologies listed in the final bibliography. The following symbols are used to indicate the age level the material might be best suited for:

Y   young children in kindergarten, first, and second grades

M   middle-grade children in third and fourth grades

O   older children in fifth and sixth grades

Y *The Adventures of Albert the Running Bear,* BARBARA ISENBERG and SUSAN WOLF. New York: Clarion Books, 1982. Albert, a zoo bear, gets too fat eating all the snacks people throw to him. When his food is restricted, he escapes and, after finding a jogging suit, winds up in a marathon race. Edit for solo playing. You may also wish to shorten the story. This makes a good health lesson.

M–O "Base Stealer," ROBERT FRANCIS (36, 37). In this poem, a baseball player's actions are described as he hesitates and then decides to steal a base. Experiment with slow motion on this one, as in televised sports replays. Let students run in place on the last line. You call "Safe!" to end the playing.

Y *Beady Bear,* DON FREEMAN. New York: Viking Penguin, 1954. A stuffed toy bear thinks he should live in a cave. You can easily edit this for solo playing.

Y *Bearymore,* DON FREEMAN. New York: Viking Penguin, 1976. A circus bear must think of a new act to perform, even though it is time for him to hibernate for winter. It is easy to edit for solo playing so that everyone can play Bearymore.

Y–M *"Could Be Worse!"* JAMES STEVENSON. New York: William Morrow, 1977. Grandpa tells an incredibly tall tale about what happened to him one night. Everyone can play Grandpa when his adventure begins.

Y–M *Do You Move As I Move?* HELEN BORTEN. New York: Abelard-Schuman, 1963. There are many wonderful ideas for movement in this book. You can select excerpts from sections focusing on slow and fast movement, upwards and downwards movement, and so forth. A good ending is with the line "a flower closing its petals against the frosty night air."

M *Fortunately,* REMY CHARLIP. New York: Parents' Magazine Press, 1964. Good fortune and bad fortune go hand in hand in this adventure.

M–O *"Foul Shot,"* EDWIN A. HOEY (36, 37, 57). This careful poetic description gives all the minute details of a basketball shot. In solo playing, students can be the player and then the ball. For a final touch, they can be a person in the crowd giving a *silent slow-motion* "roarup," and then freeze.

Y–M *Frances Face-Maker,* WILLIAM COLE and TOMI UNGERER. New York: Collins, 1963. Frances does not like to go to bed at night, so Daddy plays a game of face making with her. After each face is described, the book instructs "You do it!" This is a good seat activity for a study of emotions.

Y–M *Giant John,* ARNOLD LOBEL. New York: Harper & Row, 1964. Everyone can play Giant John, who gets a job working for a very tiny king and queen in a very tiny castle. When fairies tempt him to dance, he accidentally destroys the castle. But he rebuilds it, and all is forgiven. The little characters can just be imagined.

Y *Good Hunting, Little Indian,* PEGGY PARISH. Reading, Mass.: Addison-Wesley, 1962. A little Indian gets more than he bargained for in his hunting adventure.

M–O *"The Hairy Toe,"* GEORGE MENDOZA (18). This deliciously weird tale is similar to the tale of "Teeny Tiny" (43). Everyone will want to say the line "Gwot, I ate it!" at the end.

Y–M *Harold and the Purple Crayon,* CROCKETT JOHNSON. New York: Harper & Row, 1955. A little boy has many adventures to draw with the help of a purple crayon. In all the Harold stories, be sure to specify with each detail that Harold is drawing it.

Y–M *Harold's Circus,* CROCKETT JOHNSON. New York: Harper & Row, 1959. Harold creates a circus with his purple crayon and saves the day by getting the lion back into his cage.

Y–M *Harold's Fairy Tale,* CROCKETT JOHNSON. New York: Harper & Row, 1956. Harold has an adventure with a king and a castle.

Y–M *Harold's Trip to the Sky,* CROCKETT JOHNSON. New York: Harper & Row, 1957. Harold goes off on a rocket in this adventure.

Y–M *Harry the Dirty Dog,* GENE ZION. New York: Harper & Row, 1956. Harry refuses to take a bath. But when he gets so dirty that his family does not recognize him, he realizes the importance of cleanliness.

Y–M *Hildilid's Night,* CHELI DURAN RYAN. New York: Macmillan, 1971. A woman tries everything she can think of to get rid of the night, until she becomes so exhausted she falls asleep just as day returns. Check out the line "She even spat at the night" before playing.

Y–M *If You Were an Eel, How Would You Feel?* MINA and HOWARD SIMON. Chicago: Follett, 1963. Various animals are described according to their characteristic actions. Children can play all the animals solo.

Y *Indian Two Feet and His Horse,* MARGARET FRISKEY. New York: Scholastic Book Services, 1964. A little Indian wishes for a horse and finally gets one.

Y *I Was a Second Grade Werewolf,* DANIEL PINKWATER. New York: E. P. Dutton, 1983. A second grader's imagination turns him into a werewolf, but no one seems to notice. Edit for solo playing. Extra characters can just be imagined. Halloween-type music might be fun to add.

Y–M *I Will Not Go to Market Today,* HARRY ALLARD. New York: Dial Press, 1979. Day after day, Fenimore B. Buttercrunch attempts to go to market for strawberry jam. But there is always a problem: a dam breaks, a dinosaur is in his front yard, and he even breaks his leg and is laid up for six months. Finally his persistence pays off.

Y–M *Just Suppose,* MAY GARELICK. New York: Scholastic Book Services, 1969. Suppose you were a number of animals, doing what they do. There is plenty of opportunity to explore animal movement and habits in this experience.

M–O "Lines Written for Gene Kelly to Dance to," CARL SANDBURG (55). This poem asks the famous dancer to dance such ideas as the alphabet and the wind. The first section is the easiest to do, but the entire poem offers wonderful possibilities. Try it with a musical background such as Leroy Anderson's "Sandpaper Ballet." (Say a line, turn up the volume of the record for a few seconds so that the students can act it, fade down and say the next line, and so on. Maintain a rhythm as you do this.)

Y *The Little Auto,* LOIS LENSKI. Silver Spring, Md.: Henry Z. Walck, 1934, 1962. See also (25). Mr. Small has a little auto which he takes care of and drives around town on errands. Young children will love beeping the horn and having a flat tire.

Y *The Little Sailboat,* LOIS LENSKI. Silver Spring, Md.: Henry Z. Walck, 1937, 1966. See also (25). Captain Small has an adventure with his sailboat.

"See how the world looks upside down . . ." (Carl Sandburg's "Lines Written for Gene Kelly to Dance to.")

M *The Man Who Didn't Wash His Dishes,* PHYLLIS KRASILOVSKY. New York: Doubleday, 1950. A lazy man's neglect poses housekeeping problems. Children's desks can be the man's easy chair, kitchen chair, and truck.

M *The Man Who Entered a Contest,* PHYLLIS KRASILOVSKY. New York: Doubleday, 1980. A man decides to enter a baking contest. But when the cat knocks over the baking powder, unnoticed, the batter bakes all over the furniture. The man wins the contest, of course. Students can play in pairs if you want to add the cat; other characters are easily omitted.

Y *Martin's Hats,* JOAN W. BLOS. New York: William Morrow, 1984. Martin experiences a variety of occupations by trying on different hats while playing in his room.

Y *Monday I Was an Alligator,* SUSAN PEARSON. Philadelphia: J. B. Lippincott, 1979. A little girl pretends to be something different for each day of the week.

Y–M "On Our Way," EVE MERRIAM (6). In this poem children experiment with the walks of various animals.

M–O "The Passer," GEORGE ABBE (42). This is a brief description of a football pass. Try it in slow motion. A college football fight song playing in the background, perhaps at slow speed, will lend good atmosphere.

M–O *The Pond,* CAROL AND DONALD CARRICK. New York: Macmillan, 1970. This sensitive poem describes movements of water, insects, and all life near and in a pond. Students can switch from one character to another. Try Debussy's "La Mer" or something similar as background music. Try it also as a shadow dance behind a backlit sheet.

M–O "Rodeo," EDWARD LUEDERS (37). This poem describes a cowboy readying to mount and ride a Brahma bull and is another good possibility for slow motion playing.

M *Salt Boy,* MARY PERRINE. Boston: Houghton Mifflin, 1968. A young boy rescues a lamb in a storm and gets his wish: to learn to rope a horse. Edit for solo playing so that everyone can be the boy.

Y *The Snowy Day,* EZRA JACK KEATS. New York: Viking Penguin, 1962. Young Peter plays in the snow and finds out that snowballs melt indoors. End with Peter in bed at the desk, dreaming of more snow.

M *Sometimes I Dance Mountains,* BYRD BAYLOR. New York: Charles Scribner's Sons, 1973. Ideas for dance pantomime are presented in this long poetic work that you can select excerpts from. Photographs of a girl dancing illustrate movement ideas. Simple instruments (wooden xylophone, tambourine, drum, and so forth) can provide background effects. Try it as a shadow dance behind a backlit sheet.

M–O "The Sorcerer's Apprentice," Richard Roston. (43). A young apprentice remembers only part of a magic spell and finds himself in much trouble. Begin the action where the sorcerer leaves. Try the music of Paul Dukas written for this story for background. It can also be played in groups. (See other versions by Lesi Well [Boston: Little, Brown, 1962] and Wanda Gag [New York: Coward-McCann, 1979]).

Y–M *The Story About Ping,* MARJORIE FLACK. New York: Viking Penguin, 1961. This is the adventure of a little duck on the Yangtze River in China. Edit to shorten and to focus on Ping's experiences.

M *Theodore Turtle,* ELLEN MACGREGOR. New York: McGraw-Hill, 1955. Forgetful Theodore first loses one of his rubber boots and then misplaces almost everything else he touches.

Y *Today Was a Terrible Day,* PATRICIA REILLY GIFF. New York: Penguin Books, 1980. Poor Ronald, a second grader, has a series of problems during his school day. But his sympathetic teacher helps him to feel better about himself with a thoughtful note. With some editing this can be played solo. Children will be glad to know others have bad days too.

M–O "Trinity Place," PHYLLIS McGINLEY (34). This poem describes the actions of pigeons in a city park to the actions of humans. Although brief, it has wonderful possibilities for sophisticated movement.

M *We Were Tired of Living in a House*, LIESEL MOAK SKORPEN. New York: Coward-McCann, 1969. Some children decide to investigate other places to live and find that their house is not so bad after all. Fill in narrative detail from the pictures.

Y—M *What Will You Do Today, Little Russell?* ROBERT WAHL. New York: Putnam Publishing Group, 1972. In this story, a little boy explores a farm.

Y *Whistle for Willie*, EZRA JACK KEATS. New York: Viking Penguin, 1964. Peter finally learns how to whistle for his dog, Willie.

NARRATIVE PANTOMIMES FOR PAIRED PLAYING

Unless they are very little or socially immature, young children can also successfully play stories that have two characters. (Most children want equal stage time!) A good example of such a story is Margaret Wise Brown's *The Golden Egg Book*, which features a bunny and a duck.

As stated earlier, older elementary students will particularly enjoy playing stories that have two or more characters, since these stories resemble a skit or a play. (An example might be George Mendoza's "The Crack in the Wall," the story of a hermit whose house falls apart, beginning with a crack that will not stop spreading.) They feel a sense of accomplishment in creating their own dramas quickly and easily without having to memorize a script. Older students also prefer interacting with classmates and do not feel as isolated as they might with solo stories.

Other paired playing can be done with stories that have several characters. For example, in some stories one character meets several other characters during an adventure. One student can play the major character, while the second one plays each of the other characters. This procedure is often preferred by the students, as it gives them more opportunity to enact more roles.

In paired playing, the entire class (or as many as you can handle) are paired and the pairs play simultaneously. This procedure allows more students the opportunity to play.

Physical Contact in Paired and Group Playing

You will quickly note that when a story has two or more characters, the characters frequently interact socially and even physically. For example, in *The Golden Egg Book*, the bunny rolls the duck (who is still inside the unhatched egg) down a hill. "The Crack in the Wall" is fun to play with one student being the hermit and one being the expanding crack. But the hermit pounds and kicks the wall. (Obviously you will want to make sure the children can perform such actions appropriately and safely before you let an entire class enact the story. A preview demonstration with a pair of trustworthy and competent children will probably be required.) The actions in "The Crack in the Wall" can be done *close* to the "wall" without actually touching it. This means the players will have to use caution in judging their distance from each other, and the "hermits" will have to control their actions. Such physical contact has to be pretended or faked, as

Stories with two or more characters often have physical interaction and conflict
as part of the plot.

is done in movies and on television. (See Chapter 9 for more detailed
instruction on stage combat.)

A BIBLIOGRAPHY OF NARRATIVE PANTOMIMES FOR PAIRED PLAYING

The following stories and poems are arranged alphabetically according to
title. Numbers in parentheses refer to anthologies listed in the final bibliography. Suggested grade levels are listed in the left margin.

M *Andy and the Lion,* JAMES DAUGHERTY. New York: Viking Penguin, 1966. A young boy
   reads about lions and imagines himself in an adventure similar to that of the fabled
   Androcles. You may prefer to begin with Part II.

Y *Beady Bear,* DON FREEMAN. New York: Viking Penguin, 1954. A stuffed toy bear thinks he
   should live in a cave. Thayer's part is important enough to make this story fun to play in
   pairs. Also listed for solo playing with just Beady.

M–O "The Bear in the Pear Tree," ALICE GEER KELSEY (39). The Hodja meets a bear and
   hides from him in a pear tree. Note the subtle humor in this one.

M–O *The Boy Who Would Be a Hero,* MARJORIE LEWIS. New York: Coward-McCann, 1982. A
   lad who sets off on an adventure to become a hero meets a witch who wants him for a
   hero *sandwich* to celebrate her birthday. Try this first with pairs—the boy and witch
   who can also play minor characters. Since the witch's body appears in parts and later
   becomes disassembled, you might want to do this story in groups. Edit out the simple
   dialogue for initial playings.

Y–M *Caps for Sale,* ESPHYR SLOBODKINA. New York: Scholastic Book Services, 1947. Thieving
   monkeys take a peddler's caps. This version is easiest to use for narrative pantomime. It
   can be played in pairs, using one monkey to one peddler.

M–O "The Crack in the Wall," GEORGE MENDOZA (10). A hermit loses his house to a crack in the wall that will not stop spreading. Pairs include the hermit and a crack that starts out "knife-thin, the length of the hermit's hand" and keeps reappearing on different walls until the whole place collapses. Plan carefully the hermit's examination of the crack. Let everyone fall at the end, but in slow motion to a count of 3.

M "Gertrude McFuzz," DR. SEUSS (58). Gertrude finds that growing a big beautiful tail may not be what she really wants after all. The same child who plays Lolla-Lee-Lou can also play Uncle Dake.

Y *Gilberto and the Wind*, MARIE HALL ETS. New York: Viking Penguin, 1963. A young boy encounters all the things the wind can do—and cannot do. You will want to discuss and perhaps try out some of the more abstract ideas in this story with the children before playing the entire selection.

Y *The Golden Egg Book*, MARGARET WISE BROWN. New York: Simon & Schuster, 1947. A bunny and a newly hatched duck discover each other. Plan the interaction carefully.

M–O *Gone is Gone*, WANDA GÁG. New York: Coward-McCann, 1935. This is the old tale of the man who swaps chores with his wife only to discover that her work is not as simple as he had thought. Another version is "The Husband Who Was to Mind the House" (4, 39). You can combine the best features of both stories.

Y–M *The Gunniwolf*, WILHELMINA HARPER. New York: E. P. Dutton, 1967. See also (52). A little girl goes into the woods and meets the Gunniwolf, whom she charms with her "guten sweeten song." Children will probably want to say the phrases that repeat: the song "Kum kwa, khi wa," the running "pit pat," the Gunniwolf's question "Why for you move?" and the little girl's answer, "I no move." The running should be done in a small circle of space or may be done by tapping hands on thighs in rhythm.

M *How the Grinch Stole Christmas!* DR. SEUSS. New York: Random House, 1957. A modern classic of a spiteful character who learns the true meaning of Christmas giving. While one child plays the Grinch, another child can be Max the dog and the Who child.

M *How the Rhinoceros Got His Skin*, RUDYARD KIPLING. New York: Walker, 1974. A Parsi gets revenge on a rhinoceros who keeps stealing cakes. You may prefer to edit out the fact that the Parsi wears no clothes, even though this beautifully illustrated version by Leonard Weisgard is tastefully done. See also (22).

M–O *The Knight and the Dragon*, TOMIE DE PAOLA. New York: Putnam Publishing Group, 1980. A knight and a dragon fight each other unsuccessfully. In the end the knight opens a barbecue restaurant with the dragon providing the fire for the cooking. There is little text, but you and the students will have fun creating your own. You can make this a drama for three, should you want to add the princess. Good practice for mock battling; see Chapter 9 for additional techniques.

Y *The Little Man in Winter*, WALBURGA ATTENBERGER. New York: Random House, 1972. The little man goes sledding in winter. When his friend Katrina falls through the ice, he rescues her and they end sipping hot soup. This has a simple text for paired playing; Katrina appears halfway through the story.

M *Lizard Lying in the Sun*, BERNICE FRESCHET. New York: Charles Scribner's Sons, 1975. A lizard has a peaceful day in the sun until an eagle flies by. Play this in pairs with one child as the lizard and the second child as each of the other animals.

O "The Mouse and the Flea," CHARLES E. GILLHAM (5). In this funny Alaskan Eskimo tale, two friends get tired of each other and begin to play tricks on one another.

M *Mrs. Gaddy and the Ghost*, WILSON GAGE. New York: Greenwillow Books, 1979. Mrs. Gaddy lives in an old farmhouse with a ghost. When all efforts to get rid of him fail, she decides to move; but when she sees how dejected the ghost is, she decides to remain. Mrs. Gaddy talks to herself, but the dialogue can be kept in if the children just mime it.

Y *The Tale of Peter Rabbit,* BEATRIX POTTER. New York: Frederick Warne, 1901. The timeless story of a misbehaving bunny who finds adventure in Mr. McGregor's garden. You can also play this solo, but most children will want to have Mr. McGregor on hand. The same child who plays Mr. McGregor can also play some of the other minor characters. You may want to simplify and shorten the text a bit for the playing, but children should hear the inimitable Beatrix Potter language the rest of the time.

Y–M *The Tale of Two Bad Mice,* BEATRIX POTTER. New York: Frederick Warne, 1932. Two mice find a doll house and create havoc when they discover the play food is not edible. Edit for just the two mice, Hunca-Munca and Tom Thumb.

O "Wait Till Martin Comes," MARIA LEACH (47). A man has a scary adventure in a haunted house with four cats. A second actor can play all the cats. The man can be "rocking" in a rocking chair while he observes all the goings-on. This is a good story for Halloween.

M "What Was I Scared Of?" DR. SEUSS (41). A typical Seuss character is frightened of a pair of pants with nobody in them until it finds the pants are afraid of it! This one is also appropriate for Halloween.

GROUP STORIES INTO PLAYS

Some narrative pantomime stories have three characters, and some have an unlimited number of characters. Younger children can play short stories with three to five characters fairly easily. From second grade up, students will want to make these stories into skits or informal plays.

Some stories have only a few characters. Oliver Herford's "The Elf and the Dormouse" has the two title characters and a mushroom. *The Little Brute Family,* by Russell Hoban, has a mother, and father, and three children. By dividing the class into small groups, it is possible to let several casts play the story simultaneously. Young children are often quite happy doing this. At first it may seem a little like a three-ring circus, but it does give more children a chance to play. The remainder of the class who are watching can see different interpretations of characters and lines. Older students are especially interested in this latter feature.

Some stories have entire villages or crowd scenes included in the cast of characters. In this case, an entire class can often play in one of these group stories. For example, in *The Beast of Monsieur Racine,* by Tomi Ungerer, there are crowds in both the railway scene and in the auditorium at the Paris Academy of Science. The picture book shows numerous interesting characters which the students can develop in greater detail. The same is true of Tomie de Paola's *Strega Nona,* which features an entire town inundated with spaghetti from a magic pasta pot.

With older children you may prefer to divide the class into small groups and let each group act out a different play, working out their own portrayals. The working groups should probably not be larger than five to seven students, including the narrator, to keep the decision-making tasks easier. Students may draw lots to see who plays which part. If there are several minor parts in a story, they can often be played by one person. (Some students are especially adept at changing characters quickly and love the idea of having several parts to play in one story.) An informal drama "festival," with each group sharing its performance with the rest of the class, can be the end result of this more elaborate procedure.

Adding Dialogue

If a class enjoys a group story and likes replaying it, they may begin to perfect it much as they might in rehearsing a play. They may even begin to add dialogue in repeated playings. This happens because these stories develop so easily into a play format.

Consider for a moment that when you put on a play, the first step you take is to select a script. And what is a script but the dialogue or speeches of the characters? Actors must memorize the speeches (or script) and then add the action or stage directions so that the plot unfolds.

However, in the process being recommended here, we begin with the pantomimed action first, organizing and rehearsing it. As the students work with the story they may see opportunities for dialogue. All you need do is pause in the appropriate places and allow them to improvise their dialogue. In some cases and with some stories, the students may carry the story along so completely that narrating will be needed only sporadically. It may even be eliminated in time.

Adding Technical Aspects

Students will enjoy adding technical aspects to their plays, particularly if they are planning to share them with classmates. It is best to keep these additions simple and not clutter or overpower the most important part of the drama: the actors and the story.

Costumes can be simple pieces of material draped or tied around any child of any size. Cast-off curtains, blankets, tablecloths, and fabric remnants do nicely. Hats and scarves are also useful. Some of the stories are particularly suited to the use of masks, which can be made of paper bags, paper plates, or other simple materials.

Props should be made of simple materials. Many can still be pantomimed. And indeed, this procedure is sometimes more aesthetically pleasing than using real objects. Children have played the pasta pot (three on their knees with arms encircled) and also the pasta (bubbling up and over the pot and even slithering on the floor) in *Strega Nona*.

You and the students can also find ways to use objects creatively. Some fourth graders once played a version of "Jack and the Beanstalk" and for the beanstalk used a broom and a chair. Jack stood on the chair and held the broom high. Then as he "climbed the beanstalk," he went hand over hand along the broomstick. As the broom lowered to the floor, the illusion of climbing was cleverly, yet simply, executed.

Scenery is usually never required. Students can get very literal about what is needed and should instead be encouraged to use their imaginations. Again, simplicity is the key: children have often created their own

College students enact "The Sneetches" in garbage bag costumes.

scenery by physically being doors that open and close, trees waving in the breeze, machines, vehicles, or whatever their imagination has inspired.

Some of the stories in the bibliography can be played as *shadow dramas*. For this you need a darkened room and a spotlight (or the light from an

Paper bag masks can be added to group plays. (*Who's in Rabbit's House?* by Verna Aardema.)

overhead projector) behind an old sheet. The actors move behind the sheet in front of the light, and interesting shadows are the result.

Music and sound effects, if they aid the interpretation of the story, can also be added.

Finally, some students will enjoy working on the technical aspects of the production more than performing the story itself. Some may even show abilities in managing, designing, and executing these simple technical aspects. Encourage this and give as much attention to these technical artists as to the actors. You may even find some students exhibiting excellent directing and overall management skills.

Sharing with an Audience

As students gain more confidence in themselves and in their work, they may ask to share it with an audience. However, sharing should be the collective desire of the group rather than being imposed by you.

Students often have more success sharing these narrated materials than they would a scripted play. Fear of forgetting lines, usually the biggest worry in performing a play, can be eliminated, since the dialogue is not essential to these stories. There is less pressure than with a scripted play, since these plays go on as long as the narrating and pantomiming continue. If some students are hesitant with dialogue, they can still participate in the playing, and those who are ready for improvising can add it.

Older elementary students may find it a rewarding experience to perform their stories for students in the lower grades. Of course, they should perform the stories that are most appealing to that age group and ones younger children will understand.

When sharing the play with classmates, you have an excellent opportunity to emphasize what an audience is and how it shows its appreciation of theatrical events. An audience watches to learn and enjoy; it is polite and shows respect for the actors. Those students who form the audience should be as courteous to their classmates as they will want their classmates to be when their roles are reversed.

Example from "Urashima Taro and the Princess of the Sea"

The following is a description of the development of a group story into a classroom play with a fourth-grade class. The narrative was condensed from the Japanese folktale "Urashima Taro and the Princess of the Sea," which the students had read in their basal reader. In this story, a young man who saves a turtle is rewarded with a trip under the sea. While enjoying himself there for what he thinks are three days, many years pass on earth. One day he asks to return to visit his parents. He is given a box which he is told not to open so that he may use it to return to the sea again. When he finds that he is in another time period on earth, he opens the box and is transformed into an old man.

A narrative pantomime was developed from this story for the entire class to play. The story was shortened, the action tightened, and all but the simplest of dialogue was edited out. The major characters in the story were Urashima Taro, the princess of the sea, and the turtle. Other characters were added by focusing on the underwater sea life (crabs, fish, octopuses, and so on) which Urashima would pass on his ride to and from the sea on the turtle's back. Then when the princess showed Urashima the seasons, several children pantomimed actions appropriate to each—swimming in summer, skiing in winter, and so forth. Other characters were a group of children who taunted the turtle in the opening scene, courtiers under the sea, and a couple who greeted Urashima at the end of the story.

The action of the play began at the front of the room, moved around the side, and then to the back of the room for the princess's palace. The return trip was made on the other side of the room, and the story ended in the front of the classroom again.

For the costumes, pieces of sheer pastel fabric were used, mainly of green and blue shades, to represent the underwater world. The only scenery was crepe-paper streamers of various colors which were twisted slightly. With one child at each end of a streamer, several streamers were alternately raised up and down. The effect was of sea waves, so that as Urashima and the turtle moved in between the two streamers, they appeared to be swimming in the sea. At the back of the room the same technique was used with various colored streamers depicting the seasons— red and orange for fall, blue and white for winter, and so on. The pantomimes of the seasons were enacted between the streamers. A small jewelry box, serving as the princess's gift to Urashima, was the only prop used.

The actions under the sea, as well as Urashima's turning into an old man at the end of the story, were done in slow motion to add to the mood. For background music, a recording of Orff instruments was used because of its somewhat oriental sound.[3] With more time, the children could have played the instrumental music themselves.

The entire lesson took only about forty minutes to complete. At the end, the children expressed pleasure with their work and thought that the story was a beautiful one.

The major objective was to enhance a reading lesson, not to prepare a play for performance. However, if the children had wished to share it, this could easily have been done.

A BIBLIOGRAPHY OF NARRATIVE PANTOMIMES FOR GROUP PLAYING

M–O *Abiyoyo*, PETE SEEGER. New York: Macmillan, 1986. The author has adapted this story from a South African lullaby and folk story. It is a simple tale of a boy with a ukulele and his magician father who are banished from a town. But they are welcomed back when they are able to make the giant Abiyoyo disappear. With a little imagination this

---

[3]Carl Orff and Gunhild Keetman. English version by Margaret Murray, *Music for Children* (Angel Records, 1959).

can easily be developed into a group story. Musical notation for the song is included and would be effective.

M *Alistair's Elephant,* MARILYN SADLER. Englewood Cliffs, N.J.: Prentice-Hall, 1983. Alistair Grittle, a busy little boy, is followed home from the zoo by an elephant. All week he tries to cope, but it is a big problem. The elephant is returned to the zoo, and a giraffe follows him this time. Fun to play this as two actors, but with perhaps three children hooked together for the elephant.

Y–M *The Bears Who Stayed Indoors,* SUSANNA GRETZ. Chicago: Follett, 1970. Five bears and a dog named Fred spend a rainy day playing spaceship. The bears' actions are so cleverly written and fun to play that even older students should enjoy this one.

M–O *The Beast of Monsieur Racine,* TOMI UNGERER. New York: Farrar, Straus & Giroux, 1971. A retired French tax collector discovers a rare beast, befriends it, and takes it to the Academy of Sciences. The surprise ending will delight all. It may be played in threes (two are the "beast") or with the added crowd scenes. Try a series of frozen pictures (see Chapter 7) for the line "Unspeakable acts were performed."

M–O *The Big Yellow Balloon,* EDWARD FENTON. New York: Doubleday, 1967. With his yellow balloon, Roger manages to lure an unlikely parade of a cat, a dog, a dog catcher, a lady, a thief, and a police officer. Organize this one carefully. Precise timing is required for maximum effect.

M *Blueberries for Sal,* ROBERT MCCLOSKEY. New York: Viking Penguin, 1948. Little Sal and her mother get separated on a blueberry hunt, as does the bear cub from its mother. Sal and the bear cub mix mothers for a very amusing story. Four players.

Y–M *Brownies—Hush!* GLADYS L. ADSHEAD. Silver Spring, Md.: Henry Z. Walck, 1938. This version of "The Elves and the Shoemaker" story has fourteen separate elves, but the story can be reworded so that all elves perform all the tasks.

M *Caps for Sale,* ESPHYR SLOBODKINA. New York: Scholastic Book Services, 1947. Thieving monkeys take a peddler's caps. Although this story is popular with younger children, older students often like playing the monkey's antics. This version of an oft-told tale is the easiest to use for narrative pantomime. Try groups of five, or two peddlers and the rest monkeys.

M–O *Casey at the Bat,* ERNEST LAWRENCE THAYER. Englewood Cliffs, N.J.: Prentice-Hall, 1964. The well-known poem of the ball player who strikes out and causes Mudville to lose the baseball game. This edition has wonderful gay-nineties pictures. The poem should not be edited, so action needs to be created in several sections. Another effective way to do it is through a series of frozen pictures (see Chapter 7). The frozen pictures might also be done as a shadow play. Two other picture-book versions of this poem are by Wallace Tripp (New York: Coward-McCann, 1978), which has animal characters, and Ken Bachaus (Milwaukee: Raintree, 1985).

Y–M *Chipmunk Stew,* BETH WEINER WOLDIN. New York: Frederick Warne, 1980. This is a fun story for three. Two chipmunks want to open a restaurant and hire a chipmunk chef, Pierre La Chippe. Dialogue can be mimed or easily edited out. Extra characters can be imagined or perhaps added in replayings.

Y–M *Curious George,* H.A. REY. Boston: Houghton Mifflin, 1941. The original story of the curious little monkey who cannot stay out of trouble. Edit for solo playing at least once to give everyone a chance to be George. Again, this is a story for the young, but many older children find monkey behaviors fascinating to play. Check the sequels for more adventures of this famous character; most of the stories have a number of additional characters of George to interact with.

M–O *Drummer Hoff,* BARBARA EMBERLEY. Englewood-Cliffs, N.J.: Prentice-Hall, 1967. This is a simple cumulative story of a cannon being loaded and fired off. Older students will like the challenge of mechanical movement in this one. You might like to watch the Weston Woods film company's animated version of this award-winning picture book for movement ideas. Be sure to add flowers growing at the end, as shown in the final scene. Many background musical or sound-effects possibilities exist, but do not overpower the simplicity of the text. You might also try this as a shadow play.

Y–M *The Duchess Bakes a Cake*, VIRGINIA KAHL. New York: Charles Scribner's Sons, 1955. A bored duchess tries her hand at baking and winds up on top of a huge cake. There are numerous characters in this rhyming tale. The dialogue can be pantomimed. Some children can play more than one part if desired.

Y "The Elf and the Dormouse," OLIVER HERFORD (36, 43). In this brief poem an elf takes a Dormouse's mushroom shelter on a rainy day and invents umbrellas. One child can be the mushroom. You will need to clarify the poem's language.

M–O *The Funny Little Woman*, ARLENE MOSEL. New York: E.P. Dutton, 1972. A giggling little woman in Japan chases a rolling rice dumpling underground. When the statues of the gods are unable to protect her, she is captured by the wicked Oni, who force her to make rice dumplings for them. She escapes with a magic wooden paddle that brings her great wealth. There is some dialogue, but it can easily be mimed. It is a good story for simple paper bag masks.

Y–M *The Goblin Under the Stairs*, MARY CALHOUN. New York: William Morrow, 1967. A boy and his parents each have a special way of viewing the goblin who lives in their house. And the goblin lives up to each one's expectations. The narrator can also play the part of the neighbor.

Y *The Great Big Enormous Turnip*, ALEXEI TOLSTOY. New York: Franklin Watts, 1968. Grandfather, grandmother, granddaughter, dog, cat, and mouse finally succeed in pulling up a stubborn turnip. One child (or more) can be the turnip. The text is simple and short. Encourage physical differences in the various characters.

Y–M *Gregory*, ROBERT BRIGHT. New York: Doubleday, 1969. Proud Gregory is fast, can jump high, and holler loud, but he has a problem listening. Use caution with the mule and bear riding. Encourage children to find ways to create the illusion of riding rather than simply sitting on one another's backs.

M–O *Harriet and the Promised Land*, JACOB LAWRENCE. New York: Windmill Books, 1968. This story of Harriet Tubman can be done in frozen pictures (see Chapter 7) or as a shadow play. The text is illustrated in beautiful, stark woodcuts.

Y–O *Horton Hatches the Egg*, DR. SEUSS. New York: Random House, 1940, 1968. Horton, the elephant who is "faithful, 100 percent," hatches an egg for the lazy Maizie bird.

M *Inspector Aardvark and the Perfect Cake*, KATHY CAPLE. New York: Windmill Books, 1980. Aardvark, with his two rat friends, searches for the perfect cake. Try this in threes. Although the rats do not have a lot of action, more can be added. Or those who play the rats can also play the waiter, the police, and other minor characters.

O *It Could Always Be Worse*, MARGOT ZEMACH. New York: Farrar, Straus & Giroux, 1976. A rabbi advises a crowded, irritable family to keep taking animals into their house. Then when he advises taking the animals out, the house seems spacious and quiet. Freeze the mayhem in the house each time the father visits the rabbi.

M–O *Ittki Pittki*, MIRIAM CHAIKIN. New York: Parent's Magazine Press, 1971. Ittki Pittki, a Mideastern cloth merchant, fears he has been accidentally poisoned at the prince's palace and returns home to wait for death. This funny tale has a moral as well: that life is precious and should be enjoyed.

Y–M *The King, the Mice, and the Cheese*, NANCY AND ERIC GURNEY. New York: Random House, 1965. To get rid of mice, cats are brought into the palace. Dogs replace cats, followed by lions, elephants, and then a return to mice. There are numerous characters. Try slow motion for the chasing, with music or sound-effects background. (Compare with *The Mouse and Mrs. Proudfoot*.)

O *Lentil*, ROBERT MCCLOSKEY. New York: Viking Penguin, 1940, 1968. In a small town in

Ohio, villainous old man Sneep sucks a lemon to keep the band from playing welcoming music for the town's benefactor who is being greeted at the train. A boy saves the day with his harmonica playing of "She'll Be Comin' 'Round the Mountain." There are plenty of characters. Although it features minimum dialogue, there is plenty of opportunity to improvise.

Y–M *Little Bear's Sunday Breakfast,* JANICE. New York: Lothrop, Lee & Shepard Books, 1958. The Three Bears story is told in reverse. Little Bear visits *her* house this time. You may want to edit the dialogue. Four characters are required.

Y *The Little Brute Family,* RUSSELL HOBAN. New York: Macmillan, 1966. Papa, Mama, Brother, Sister, and Baby Brute consistently have grumpy and unpleasant days until a little lost feeling enters their lives. A child can play the little lost feeling, or music can be played to represent it.

M *Meal One,* IVOR CUTLER. New York: Franklin Watts, 1971. In Helbert's dream, Helbert and Mum plant a plum tree. It grows into the bed and down into the kitchen. Mum gets rid of it by setting the clock back an hour. Try this in groups of five: Helbert, Mum, and three to grow into the top of the tree and then to play the roots at the bottom.

M–O *Ming Lo Moves the Mountain,* ARNOLD LOBEL. New York: Greenwillow Books, 1982. This is a good narrative pantomime for three: the man, his wife, and the wise man who sits in varying positions.

M *The Mouse and Mrs. Proudfoot,* ALBERT RUSLING. Englewood Cliffs, N.J.: Prentice-Hall, 1985. Mrs. Proudfoot and Miranda try to get rid of a little mouse in their cottage. Owls, cats, foxes, dogs, boars, hunters, bears, lions, and elephants follow, the last to be frightened off by the original mouse. (Compare this with *The King, the Mice, and the Cheese.*)

M–O *Mrs. Beggs and the Wizard,* MERCER MAYER. New York: Parent's Magazine Press, 1973. Mrs. Beggs owns a boarding house. A strange renter seems to be the source of many unusual happenings, and Mrs. Beggs is forced to use her witchery kit to get rid of him. Several interesting boarding house characters are presented. The ending can use a quick blackout.

M–O *My Grandpa is a Pirate,* JAN LÖÖF (English translation by Else Holmelund Minarik). New York: Harper & Row, 1968. A young boy and his grandfather go off on a pirate adventure one summer afternoon while Grandma takes a nap. There are lots of characters and exciting action in this one.

M–O *Oté,* PURA BELPRÉ. New York: Pantheon Books, 1969. This is a funny Puerto Rican folktale about a man and his family who are plagued by an unwanted, nearsighted little devil.

Y *Papa Small,* LOIS LENSKI. Silver Spring, Md.: Henry Z. Walck, 1951. This is the story of the Small family, who all work together. Papa even hangs out clothes on the clothesline.

M–O *The Pond,* CAROL AND DONALD CARRICK. New York: Macmillan, 1970. Sensitive poetic descriptions of movements of water, insects, and all life near and in a pond are presented. For group playing, you might want to try some simple choreography with shadow dancing. As with solo playing, try Debussy's "La Mer" or something similar as background music.

Y *Roll Over!* MORDECAI GERSTEIN. New York: Crown Publishers, 1984. Ten various animals are in bed and roll out one by one. This is another version of *Ten Bears in My Bed.*

M *Seven Skinny Goats,* VICTOR G. AMBRUS. San Diego: Harcourt Brace Jovanovich, 1969. Jano, a young goat herder, does not realize that his flute playing, which causes the goats and everyone else to dance, is not appreciated. Children will love the scenes of frenzied dancing. The control is that they must stop immediately whenever the music stops. And you (or a trusted designee) are in charge of the record player. You might let them all dance with one foot "glued" to the floor, as in the game "caught in the act" in Chapter

In-service teachers act out *My Grandpa is a Pirate* by Jan Lööf.

4. Playing a recording of Sid Lawrence's "Swinging Shepherd Blues" at fast speed can also add to the fun.

M–O *Silly Goose*, JACK KENT. Englewood Cliffs, N.J.: Prentice-Hall, 1983, 1986. When a silly goose goes on a jogging adventure in the woods with a fox, he turns out not to be the silly one after all. Play in threes, with the third person being all the characters who are met. Although this story has quite a bit of dialogue, it can all be mimed, with the jogging action continuing throughout.

M *The Sneetches*, DR. SEUSS. New York: Random House, 1961. Sneetches with stars on their bellies feel superior to those without. An enterprising salesperson, Sylvester McMonkey McBean, takes advantage of the situation. It is fun for children to become the machine. As many as ten children can play the various parts of the machine successfully if you plan with them their exact movements. (What part of the machine are they, and what does that part do? See "Mechanical Movement," Chapter 9). Because the story is Seuss and in rhyme, you will want to keep it just as it is, including the dialogue. Encourage the children to fill in appropriate mimed action during the speeches rather than mouth the words. Seuss is easy to memorize for those who might want to add dialogue to the playing. The children may already be familiar with the story and the television production.

M–O *The Sorcerer's Apprentice*, RICHARD ROSTRON (43). The young apprentice to a magician remembers only part of a magic spell and finds himself in much trouble with brooms that fetch water but will not stop. When the apprentice tries to stop the brooms with an ax, his troubles keep doubling. It is fun to add people enacting bottles, books, and other sorcery items that float about as the water rises in the sorcerer's workshop. Try adding the famous music of the same title by composer Paul Dukas. (See other versions by Lesi Well [Boston: Little, Brown, 1962] and Wanda Gag [New York: Coward-McCann, 1979].)

M–O *The Stonecutter*, GERALD MCDERMOTT. New York: Viking Penguin, 1975. This is a well-known Japanese folktale simply told with numerous characters and no dialogue. McDermott's illustrations give many ideas for a shadow play also.

M–O *The Story of Ferdinand,* MUNRO LEAF. New York: Viking Penguin, 1936, 1977. This classic story of Ferdinand, the bull who would rather smell flowers than fight in the bullring, gives children the opportunity to learn about bullfighting customs. A parade of bulls, matadors, picadors, and others is always fun to add before the bullfighting scene. Try using classical bullfighting music or Herb Alpert's "The Lonely Bull."

M–O *Strega Nona,* TOMIE DE PAOLA. Englewood Cliffs, N.J.: Prentice-Hall, 1975. Strega Nona, or "Grandma Witch," has a magic pasta pot which Big Anthony misuses, and the town is flooded with pasta. There are numerous characters. Children also like to pretend to be the pasta pot, joining hands in a circle and jiggling to show the boiling. They also might like to become the spaghetti that boils up and over the pot and covers the town.

Y *Ten Bears in My Bed,* STAN MACK. New York: Pantheon Books, 1974. This is a counting story with each bear going out the window in a different way. Line up ten "bears" and let all the children sing out the "Roll over" lines. Even the littlest children can do this fun rhyme. (Compare with *Roll Over!*)

Y *The Three Bears,* PAUL GALDONE. New York: Seabury Press, 1972. This classic tale of a little girl who invites herself to the bears' house works nicely for a narrative pantomime. It can also be played solo with everyone being Goldilocks, but most children will want all four of the famous and familiar characters present.

M–O *The Three Poor Tailors,* VICTOR G. AMBRUS. New York: Harcourt Brace Jovanovich, 1965. Three tailors go off on the back of a goat to see the city and find fun, adventure, and trouble. It requires groups of four: three tailors, with a fourth to play soldier, innkeeper, and guards. It is more fun just to imagine the goat.

M–O "Urashima Taro and the Princess of the Sea," YOSHIKO UCHIDA (4, 11). Urashima is enticed to live in the sea and spends much more time there than he imagines. On returning home, he finds out just how much time has elapsed. The dialogue can easily be edited out. It is effective as a shadow play.

Sister Roberta plays Ferdinand, the bull who would rather smell flowers than fight in the bull ring.

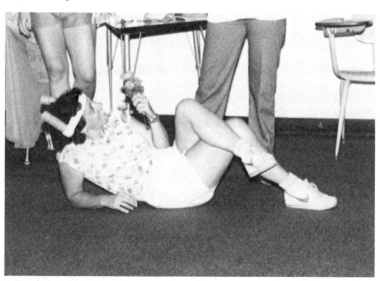

Three Poor Tailors (by Victor Ambrus) ride off on a goat to seek adventure in the city.

M–O *The Way the Tiger Walked,* Doris J. Chaconas. New York: Simon & Schuster, 1970. Porcupine, zebra, and elephant try unsuccessfully to imitate tiger's regal walk while monkeys watch the show. When tiger imitates *their* walks, they return to their natural movement. Subtle humor underlies this story that can be done quite simply or perfected into a finely tuned precision piece, perhaps with rhythm instruments for sound effects.

M–O *Who's in Rabbit's House?* Verna Aardema. New York: Dial Press, 1977. In this African Masai tale, Caterpillar is hiding in Rabbit's house and scares all the animals away. The pictures show the folktale presented as a play performed by villagers wearing masks. Although there is dialogue, the narrator can still read while actors mime in masks.

M–O *Yeh-Shen,* Ai-Ling Louie. New York: Philomel Books, 1982. This is a Chinese retelling of the Cinderella story with a fish taking the place of the fairy godmother. The tale is told mainly in action, and the dialogue can easily be mimed. The illustrations are free flowing and suggest stylized pantomime, aided by flowing scarves and masks. A shadow play is also possible.

FOR THE COLLEGE STUDENT

1. Select a story and a poem suitable for a narrated activity. Prepare it to read aloud to your classmates. Practice and experiment with pauses, timing, and

vocal pitch and quality to make the selection as interesting as possible. Find some background music suitable to the mood of the selection and play it as you read.

2. Select a narrative poem or story suitable for individual playing. Lead your classmates through a playing of the material you have selected. Consider whether or not a discussion will be necessary and whether demonstration playing is required. Give all the necessary instructions for organizing the playing. Consider the possibility of special lighting effects, sound effects, and so forth. Evaluate the playing.

3. Select a narrative poem or story to be played in pairs or groups, following the format in exercise 2.

4. Divide into groups. Select several group stories for each of the groups to prepare. Rehearse and arrange the story as a play, perhaps adding simple costumes and props. Share your stories with the class.

5. Find as many other suitable materials for narration as you can. Keep a file of these materials. Select from reading books and trade books used in the classroom.

SIX

Further Uses of Narrative Pantomime: Adapting Literature and Writing Original Material

Once you have become familiar with narrative pantomime, you will quickly see that there are many other uses for it. You have probably already discovered a number of your own favorite stories and poems suitable for narrative pantomime.

In addition, many action episodes from longer books can easily be adapted or spliced together for narrative pantomime. For example, Michael Bond's Paddington (63)* stories for younger children have many wonderful episodes useful for solo pantomime. This popular little bear is frequently undertaking an adventure, such as wallpapering a room or cleaning out a chimney, and, of course, running into all sorts of difficulties along the way. For older children, there are numerous episodes in Armstrong Sperry's *Call it Courage* or Scott O'Dell's *Island of the Blue Dolphins*—two books about young people who face a lone existence—that can easily be excerpted or spliced together for excellent narrative pantomime experiences.

Narrative pantomime is also useful in additional curricular areas of study. The topics are almost limitless. Science stories about animals or experiments, biographical data on historical or modern-day figures, information on various occupations, and stories about people in other times and geographical and cultural settings are just some of the many possibilities. By enacting these materials and the facts and concepts presented in them, the children should be able to internalize the information more completely than if they simply read about it.

*Unless otherwise indicated, literature mentioned in this chapter can be found in the bibliography at the end of this chapter. Numbers in parentheses correspond to the numbered anthologies in the final bibliography at the back of this text.

A number of excellent curricular stories already exist. At the end of this chapter is a bibliography of stories covering animal life cycles, career education, biography, history, and so forth. You can use these materials as they are, with editing in some cases, or as a stimulus for your own writing.

In this chapter you will also get some tips for writing your own original materials. Although the length of narrative pantomimes can vary from a brief paragraph to a story of several hundred words, the techniques remain the same. It is good practice at first for you to write out your materials before using them with a group of children. As you become more experienced, an outline for handy reference may be all that is needed.

This chapter will examine and consider the dramatic principles in narrative pantomimes. Understanding and applying these principles should help you in selecting and adapting, as well as in writing your own materials.

FOCUSING ON ACTION

Although action is always the central focus of narrative pantomime, several cautions and considerations are in order.

Action in Poetry

Although there are some excellent poems you can use for narrative pantomime, such as Edwin A. Hoey's "Foul Shot" (p. 109) or Byrd Baylor's *Sometimes I Dance Mountains* (p. 111), they are not as readily available as prose selections. By its very nature the language of poetry often does not focus on a continuous, forward-moving action that can be performed logically. Sentences may be incomplete, and wording may be convoluted. The rhythm and rhyme may be so exact that even minor editing is difficult, if not impossible. Therefore, use caution in selecting poetry and become comfortable with prose first. As you become more skilled, you will discover ways to adapt poetry to narrative pantomime. Of course, poetry has many other uses in drama, as you will see throughout this text.

Inanimate Objects

Inanimate objects must have enough action to make them interesting for children to play. Virginia Lee Burton's charming story, *The Little House* (Boston: Houghton Mifflin, 1942), tells of the many emotional reactions of a deserted house to its lonely situation, but there is very little, if any, action the house can perform. A similar book is Rachel Field's *Hitty* (New York: Macmillan, 1959), the fascinating story of a doll to whom many things happen. But since she cannot move by herself, the experiences are all passive ones.

Generally, it is easier to play an inanimate object going through a process of some sort. Sam Rosenfeld's *A Drop of Water* takes us through a waterdrop's many changes, at times being part of the ocean or fog or rain.

As another example, a tree may be cut down and the log sent to a paper mill, where the bark is removed and the log chipped, blown, soaked, cooked, beaten, and finally rolled into paper. The children can react to these various processes and can pantomime the various shapes the wood is put through. Additional topics with inanimate objects might be the journey of an egg from an egg ranch through a modern-day processing plant, the recycling of glass or cans, the adventure of a tomato from vine to soup can, or the steps a letter goes through getting mailed.

Editing Dialogue

Because the emphasis in narrative pantomime is on action, dialogue should be nonexistent, or almost so. In stories, when people talk to each other at great length, they often stop performing actions. If children play such material, they will have to stand for long periods of time looking at one another and probably feeling foolish. Obviously, they will quickly lose interest and involvement in the material.

In searching for narrative materials, a helpful first clue is the absence of quotation marks. Keeping this in mind, you can flip through the pages of books rather rapidly, eliminating unlikely candidates.

Stories with several characters will probably have some dialogue in them and are often a poor choice. However, if the plot of the story is action centered, it is possible to edit out the dialogue. Or dialogue can sometimes be changed from direct to indirect. Note this change in the following two sentences:

> *(direct dialogue)* "Isn't this a fine piece of cloth?" said the peddler to the old woman.

> *(indirect dialogue)* The peddler proudly held up a piece of cloth for the old woman to see and asked if she agreed.

Condensing Action

As a general rule, action should be condensed in time. When spread out over a period of time, action tends to lose its dramatic impact. Note this in the following passage:

> The men worked, eagerly packing their gear for the adventure. After two weeks they were ready to start off. They left full of energy and with high hopes that they would be successful. Three months later they were weary and disappointed. Almost everyone in the exploring party was ready to turn back.

Continuous Action

The action of narrative pantomime should be as continuous as possible. Flashbacks, reflective thinking, or additional information interrupt the flow of action and usually require the players to wait before they can continue the action. For example, a passage may read

His hand touched the doorknob, and in that moment his mind raced back to a thousand memories. *Like the time he opened the door to Old Man Henry's place on that stormy Halloween night. The guys had run off just as he was about to open the door. They had all decided to go in together, and then everybody chickened out and left him standing there to hear Old Man Henry's voice bellow out at him.* He shook the thought from his mind, opened the door, and stepped into the darkened interior.

By going back in time, the italicized passage keeps the players poised at the doorknob without moving. The action can be tightened by eliminating or shortening such interruptions.

Be careful also of narrative that bounces back and forth in time. For example:

That day he decided to go for a swim. The following day it rained. By the end of the summer, he had enjoyed boating, waterskiing, and swimming—but it was the swimming he enjoyed the most.

Although there is plenty of action suggested in this passage, it is too disjointed to perform meaningfully.

Chronological Word Order

The cues for action should always follow chronologically. If they do not, players may be misled. For example:

She left the apartment and went down to the first floor. When she got off the elevator and entered the lobby, she . . .

Players following this narration might *walk down steps* rather than riding an elevator, since this information is not specified until the second sentence.

Immediacy of Action

A sense of immediacy in narrative and side-coaching is indicated by the use of the present tense and the wording "you." "You" may also be implied.

Now (you) run your hand along the bark of the old tree. (You) Lean forward and smell the mossy dampness. . . .

Robert McCloskey has incorporated this wording in his award-winning book *Time of Wonder*. A few other books—such as Roger Caras' *Skunk for a Day*, which begins "Today you are a skunk . . ."—also use this technique. But it is not a style of writing you will see frequently.

Although it is not necessary to change all narrative pantomime literature into this wording style, your side-coaching will be more effective in present tense and "you" wording. Children often respond more naturally

You get up in the morning and wash your face . . .

to this direct wording, feeling that the action is happening right now and to them.

Because you are not used to reading stories in the present tense and with "you" wording, it may be difficult to write your stories in this fashion. It is a good practice experience to try it, even though other styles will also work. Note the following examples.

> *(third person, present tense)* As the sun shines, the Athenian citizen gets out of bed and folds a piece of wool cloth around himself, pins it at the shoulder, and ties a sash around his waist. Then he sits down to breakfast and drinks a cup of wine mixed with hot water and honey and eats a dry barley cake.

. . . and brush your teeth.

(first person plural, present tense)   We begin cleaning out the horse's stall, shoveling the old hay into a wheelbarrow and wheeling it carefully outside the barn. We empty it into a large pile. The pitchfork is used to bring fresh hay to the horse's stall and spread it evenly over the floor.

(third person, past tense)   To build his wigwam, Running Bear first had to find a level surface. He marked a groove in the ground with a sharp stick. Then he made an oval shape about twice as long as it was wide. . . .

But whatever person and tense you do use in your story, it is important that you remain consistent throughout and not shift back and forth.

Descriptive Language

Language that is descriptive paints the mental images of sensory and emotional detail. It artfully compels the children to be aware of the setting and environment and invites their involvement. In the story of Goldilocks and the Three Bears, for example, the scene of eating the porridge might be narrated as follows:

"You see three bowls of porridge, and you are so very hungry . . . so you taste the porridge in Papa Bear's bowl. Oh! That's too hot! It burns your tongue!! Oh dear, well, you are still hungry. . . . Maybe the porridge in the middle-sized bowl will be better. Scoop up a big spoonful from Mama Bear's bowl. Take a big bite and . . . oh, no! That one is too cold. And LUMPY! . . . Well, there's one bowl left. This time you take a tiny spoonful of porridge and carefully taste it. Ahhh, this is perfect. What good porridge; not too hot, not too cold. The cream in the porridge is sweet . . . and you think you detect the flavor of butter and just the tiniest pinch of salt. And you eat . . . and eat . . . and eat . . . until there is just one spoonful left . . . and you eat that one slowly and savor the last bite . . . ummmmmmm, good!"

The Amount of Action and Description

The amount of action and descriptive language you use in narrative pantomime and in side-coaching depends on the children's needs. Some children will be able to elaborate on ideas more easily than others. For example, a line may read,

They prepared their equipment for the camping trip.

Some children may be observed packing numerous items and making considerable preparations, whereas other children quickly finish only one idea. Detailed, descriptive, and compelling narration may be needed to involve some children in playing it. On the other hand, too much narration can interrupt or hold up the inventive children's own ideas. Therefore, it is best to be flexible with any narrative or side-coaching material and let the needs of the *majority* dictate the amount of action you include. With practice and by knowing your material so that you can observe the class carefully, you should quite readily become skilled.

THE STORY FRAMEWORK

The overall outline of a narrative activity or side-coaching, no matter what its length, should have a beginning, middle, and end for a sense of completeness. One clue is the sense of progression or chronological order in wording such as "First . . . and then . . . finally . . ."

> "All the marionettes' strings are breaking one by one. First to go is the string on the right arm. . . . Now on the left. . . . Now the right leg. . . . Then the left. . . . And finally their heads droop. Now they are as limp as the rag dolls on the shelf above them."

Longer narratives are generally built around such story frameworks as the performance of a task, the setting of a goal and its accomplishment, or starting out on a journey and returning home. There is one episode in Scott O'Dell's *Island of the Blue Dolphins* in which Karana builds a house for herself. The process of a day's work is covered in Wanda Gág's *Gone is Gone* (p. 114), and part of a mole cricket's life cycle is experienced in Jean George's *All Upon a Stone.* These "rounded out" experiences are generally the most satisfying to play.

Suspense and Conflict

Many narrative pantomime activities are based simply on an interesting experience. It may be a mainly pleasant one, as in Donald Hall's *Ox Cart Man,* or a funny one, as in Peggy Parish's *Amelia Bedelia* stories. Most dramatic stories, however, have some conflict in them, so you should be familiar with the various ways to include it in your side-coaching and your writing.

Children usually enjoy and want plenty of exciting action and conflict in their activities. They will sometimes even add it if you do not. A line says to smell a flower; they do, and a bee stings them. Or a line says, "He walked carefully so he would not slip"; they walk carefully but slip too! For some children there can never be too much excitement in their stories.

There are many kinds of conflict. Strong conflict is obvious in fights, chases, or the meeting of an enemy face to face. Conflict is also present in nature. A threatening storm begins slowly. Then the winds blow and waves billow, while thunder crashes and lightning strikes, until a dramatic climax is reached. When the storm subsides, the conflict of nature is resolved. George Maxim Ross's *The Pine Tree* demonstrates the drama in nature most graphically.

Conflict can be present in the daily struggle of life. Even if a task is a rather ordinary and methodical one, its importance is increased if it is crucial to continued survival. Karana in *Island of the Blue Dolphins* faces such a crisis in building a house to protect herself from the wild dogs.

Conflict and suspense can sometimes be additionally implied in the language. If an action is "carefully" done or if a line reads "He held his breath as he lifted the cargo," an imminent problem is suggested.

"Don't forget to put suntan lotion on your nose." Getting ready for the beach.

"At the fair you eat some salt water taffy—and it gets stuck in your teeth. . . ."

Conflict in a narrative or in side-coaching not only makes it more dramatic and suspenseful; it usually also creates a physical intensity in the players. The physical movements may become larger and stronger or more energized and hurried as the players exert themselves to solve the conflict. Perhaps one must swim rapidly to escape a shark. Meeting some sort of deadline also creates hurried action. Cleaning house before company comes, shopping before a store closes, getting the game ended or the picnic dinner eaten before it rains, or getting to work on time are all examples. This physical exertion then more logically leads to the restful conclusion of the story.

Beginnings and Endings

The beginning of a narrative should be like the warm-up of an airplane for takeoff. The ending should be like the plane's smooth three-point landing. Considered another way, the children begin in a quiet position and are calmed down again at the end. This structure is invaluable in helping you to keep a classroom full of children controlled in their playing.

Many stories and experiences include calm beginnings and endings. For example, an animal may be lying in quiet wait for a prey. After hunting and eating it often rests. There is often an awakening from sleep, a working at a daily task, and then a returning to rest again. In writing your own materials, you will want to model this structure for maximum effectiveness.

WRITING ORIGINAL MATERIALS

Creating original materials need not be a difficult experience. Many ideas are readily available in literature or in resource materials such as those in the bibliography at the end of this chapter.

Let us consider a simple example. We are told in one sentence of A. A. Milne's *Winnie-the-Pooh* (127) that this famous teddy bear does "Stoutness Exercises." All we are told is that he reaches up and then down to try to touch his toes. This suggests an interesting pantomime activity. A simple conflict is implied if we remember that Winnie has a protruding tummy that probably makes bending over a bit of a problem.

Elaborating on this idea, you might decide to write an activity taking Pooh through an entire fitness program, doing all sorts of bodybuilding exercises. There might be some jogging, weightlifting, pushups, and hitting of a punching bag. The sense of completeness is the exercise program itself. The beginning might be a slow warm-up, exercising with just the paws. (After all, Pooh would not want to overexert himself!) As the activities progress in intensity and difficulty, Pooh Bear will no doubt become tired and eventually need a rest—with the reward of a bit of honey perhaps.

Playing Space

As in all previous work, you must consider the use of playing space. The desk, for example may be the box for a jack-in-the-box, which pops up on specific words in a brief story. Or it may be the frying pan or popper in which kernels of corn heat up and puff out into popcorn. Or as in the following example, the desk may become several things.

> "Let's pretend you're going shopping. First, drive your car—that's your desk. Put your key in the ignition, give it some gas, and you're off. Back out of the driveway . . . carefully. . . . Look to be sure you're not going to hit anything. . . . Now stop, put it in "drive," and head for town. (Here one could include detail about traffic, safety rules, or the sights.) Now you're at the department store. Get out of the car (at the side of the desk). Go through the revolving door. Now up the escalator. Up to the second floor where you're going to shop for a bicycle. Ah, there's a nice-looking one. Try that one out (some may prefer to sit back at the desk). Now you see a snowmobile. Try one of those out (sit at desk). . . ."

The Leader in a Character Role

Often it adds to the fun as well as to the meaning of the playing if you play a character role in narrating. Generally, this character is an authority figure or one who can legitimately direct and guide the actions of the children.

For example, in the Winnie-the-Pooh exercise activity mentioned earlier, you might play Christopher Robin, the teddy bear's owner. The wording of the narration can reflect this role as follows:

> "Now Pooh Bear, I know you have good intentions, but sometimes you need a little help. It's time for your exercises, and I shall watch to see that you do them. In fact, I'll even count for you. We'll begin with the first one. . . ."

The children often get more enjoyment out of following a character-narrator's rules and comply with them more willingly. Being Pooh following Christopher Robin's directions is usually more fun than simply doing what the teacher says.

Other roles might be Zeus, who gives the cues for the thunderstorms; an inventor who designs and tests out robots; the captain of an expedition; the oldest and wisest member of a tribe; or a tour guide. Because the role is that of an authority figure, it can bring with it control and discipline. If necessary, you can use the role to make and enforce rules when they are needed along the way.

> "As your guide, I must ask you not to touch any of the stalactites or stalagmites in this cave. They have been growing for centuries, and one careless move from a tourist could cause inestimable damage. From this point on, you must walk through the passageways with extreme caution. Anyone who cannot abide by the rules will be asked to return to the entrance—with no refund of admission charge, I might add. Are we ready?"

It is usually helpful in playing a role if you subtly change your voice or manner in order to separate the role from your everyday self. If this is difficult, perhaps a small prop can help. A tourist guide, for example, might have a special hat or a badge. A clipboard to hold your story and a pencil for "taking notes" can help make you look like a supervisor or manager. A pretend microphone can be suggested by a chalkboard eraser, a small vase turned upside down, or even a stapler.

A Story about an Inanimate Object

As mentioned earlier, it is possible to create a story with inanimate objects if they are given enough action and involvement to make them interesting to play. In the following example, children pretend to be a chair. But note that a recliner chair has been chosen because it has more possibility of movement. The chair has also been personified, or given human qualities, so that it can react with senses and emotion to its experiences.

TEACHER: Here you are, all ready for the day to begin. You can hear the family getting up for the day. Here comes Mom to open up the curtains and let in the morning sunshine. Swish! . . . Yikes, that sun's bright. . . . It makes your button eyes blink! Now she goes out in the kitchen to fix breakfast, and here comes the kids and the dog. You hope they don't jump on you this morning . . . but they do! Zingo! All of them at once. . . . They stretch you out flat in your reclining position. Ooh, for so early in the morning that's hard to take! Now Mom is calling them to breakfast. . . . Good. . . . Zingo! . . . You flip back into your upright position and now you ache all over. You just weren't built for this sort of thing. . . .

Now breakfast's over and the older kids and Dad have gone, and here comes Mom to sit down for the extra cup of coffee and the newspaper. Oh, you really love to read the newspaper. Mom gets all comfy and reclines you and opens up the paper. You have to read over her shoulder. . . . There's your favorite comic, *"Peanuts."* Oh, darn, she turned the page . . . and there's a furniture sale. Oh, boy, if there's anything that makes you nervous it's an ad for a furniture sale. Your stuffing gets tight and your nap stands right on end. Good, now she's turned the page again . . . and that's the end of the morning paper. She gets up and you pop upright again.

Now Mom's getting ready to clean. Here comes the vacuum cleaner and she's . . . oh, no! . . . she's going to clean you today. Oh, gosh, it tickles so . . . up at the top . . . and then your back . . . your face . . . arms . . . footrest . . . oh, oh, oh, it makes you giggle so. . . . Ah, now she stops and goes on with the rest of the cleaning. . . . Now here comes Bobby the four-year-old to watch his favorite TV shows. Hey, Mom, look at that jelly all over him. . . . He's coming toward you and Mom doesn't even see him. . . . Yuck, jelly all over your arms . . . how uncomfortable. . . . Now Bobby turns on the TV set and watches a cartoon of a cat chasing a mouse. . . . Bobby starts to jump up and down on you. . . . He pounds your arms and kicks at your legs . . . ouch . . . ouch. . . .

> Oh, boy, here comes Mom to chase him off you. There he goes and here she comes with some cleaner for you. She sprays the foam where Bobby put the jelly. . . . It makes you want to cough or sneeze or something . . . and you do, and again. . . . Oh, boy, that's all you need. . . . Now Mom finishes cleaning up the jelly. She takes Bobby upstairs with her, and you are left for a little peace and quiet, so you try to catch a little shut-eye while you can. Ah . . . how nice. . . . Sleep tight.

Sources for Materials

One of the best sources for curricular narrative pantomimes is your own personal experiences. Various occupations experienced by you or people you know offer curricular stories for career education. Grocery checkout cashier, construction worker, camp counselor, table waiter, dental assistant, truck driver, and tour guide at a cereal factory are just some of the many jobs students have written about.

Sports have been another popular topic for narratives, including skiing, sky diving, scuba diving, and hiking for physical education emphasis. Pets such as hamsters, turtles, and guinea pigs have also had stories told about them that children have enjoyed playing. In the process they have learned about how the animals must be cared for, an important part of nature study.

Geographical areas and various settings lend possibilities. Stories have been written about maple sugaring in Vermont, selecting and cutting down a Christmas tree in Washington, being taken on a personal tour of the family's dairy farm, and even visiting a local junkyard to discover items to recycle or going through army basic training.

The detail and realism you can bring to these activities are a direct result of your own involvement in them. You usually also feel comfortable with and enthusiastic about these topics, which, of course, adds to the children's enjoyment in playing them.

Finding Material through Research

Through research you can also find information suitable for narrative pantomime. Trade books, encyclopedias, and information magazines supply us with a wealth of subjects to draw from. Many of the sources in the bibliography at the end of this chapter will give you a sampling of the numerous trade-book materials that exist.

You might write with a story framework such as "A Day in the Life of————" and then select an occupation, a child in another country, historical figure, animal, or insect to base the story on. You might consider "The Process of Making————" and select a product, food, shelter, or clothing to write about. For "Journey to————," you can select a particular building, historical sight, city, country, or even another planet to build the story around.

In the following story an unusual species of spider called *Argyoneta aquatica* lives underwater by building air-filled bubbles. It must struggle to keep the captured air bubbles anchored and to pull itself with guidelines. It is alert to the vibrations in the water and aware of its need to secure food. The story ends with the satisfying completion of a project and a deserved rest.

TEACHER: You're in the process of building your web for the air bubbles you will soon capture. You move from one plant stem to another, throwing from your spinnerets silken web strands. . . . Deftly your legs secure the threads to the plants . . . and you carefully move back and forth from stem to stem until you have a finely meshed web. This web will become your summer bell home; later you'll build another for winter.

Now for the air bubbles. . . . You swim to the top of the water. . . . Once there, you turn over and with your back legs you grab a bubble of air, pulling it gently toward you so that it covers the breathing pores around your abdomen. . . . Now your legs search for the silken guidelines you set earlier . . . there you are! . . . and holding securely to the line, you begin to pull yourself down to the new web. It's a difficult feat . . . for the air bubble is heavy and would rise to the surface if you didn't pull. . . . At the web you release your air bubble . . . and it rises into the web—captured!

You take more trips to the surface for air . . . and soon your home contains several bubbles and is completed. Now it is time for a rest. . . . You carefully enter your air-filled home . . . and hang head downward. . . . As you rest, the water house sways to the rhythm of the moving water . . . its vibrations can communicate that danger or a potential meal is near. . . . It's vibrating!

Your eight eyes signal food. . . . You emerge from your bell, carefully carrying an air supply with you. . . . A tiny fish swims near . . . you lunge . . . grab . . . sting with your poison . . . and carry the dead fish into your new home. You'll eat it in a while . . . but now you'll rest. The spider's day has been a busy one.

Fantasy and Reality in Science Topics

For curricular subjects such as science, topics must be handled realistically, as in the preceding story. Animals and plants have often been personified in literature and given human senses, feelings, and cognitive ability. Although there can be humor in a story about a crayfish who needs a squirt from an oil can to unstick a stubborn antenna, this is fantasy that is more appropriate as cartoon material and cannot be considered a science lesson. As much as possible you should have faith in the information itself to create the drama.

Compare the following two passages and note that even a few words can make a difference in writing that leans toward fantasy and writing that is more scientifically stated. The excerpt is based on the life cycle of a dragonfly.

You spy a crack in your old skin and struggle to squirm through it. It's hard work and you're glad this is the last time you'll have to shed it. You push and push until you get rid of the clumsy thing. Now you admire your slim, new body. But it's still stiff, and your joints creak as you slowly try it out. The sun feels warm and you decide to unfold your wings. . . .

Note that the words "glad," "clumsy," "admire," and "decide" all attribute human understanding and emotional feeling to an insect and therefore make the material less scientifically accurate than the following:

You wiggle and squirm through the crack in your old skin. It's hard work, but this will be the last time you will have to shed it. You push and push until you are freed. Your slim, new body is still stiff, and your old shell clings to the stalk below you. The sun is warm and your four wings start to unfold slowly. . . .

There are writers of excellent literature who are also knowledgeable about scientific information. Jean George (see *All Upon a Stone, Moon of the Winter Bird,* and *Vulpes, the Red Fox,* for example) and Miska Miles (*Fox and the Fire, Wharf Rat*) have created nature stories that are accurate in their information and dramatically captivating as well. You would do well to select such literature for narrative pantomime and to use it as a model for your original narrative writing.

Science Fiction

The combination of accurate information and a fictional setting is, however, a valid kind of writing and extremely useful for a number of curricular topics. Children frequently enjoy, for example, the idea of being made small in order to make explorations of various environments, such as a beehive, the workings of a watch, the inside of a tree, or the human eye. One leader took her class on an exploration of the ear, which they had been studying. Not only were they delighted to experience such events as bouncing trampoline fashion on the tympanic membrane, they also found it difficult to forget such an adventure and all the related information.

The following is an excerpt from an exploration of the parts of a flower:

TEACHER: Today we're going to look at the construction of a flower, but we're going to pretend that it is the year 3001 and scientists have developed some new ways to conduct scientific explorations. You are a special consultant who has been called in for this mission. But it is a secret mission, so you will be given your instructions at special points along the way. Let me know when you're ready for your mission by sitting at attention, saluting, and reporting for duty. (The children respond.)

Good. (The leader now speaks in an impersonal voice, as if over an intercom.) *Good morning, scientists. Please check your equipment.* You notice that you've been issued a very tiny notepad, a very small pencil, and very tiny (handle them carefully!) special pollen-resistant goggles. There is also a capsule, but it is unmarked. Everything is encased in plastic to keep it clean.

Now enter the greenhouse. Inside you will be given additional equipment. As soon as you open the door you sense the cool, damp atmosphere. *In front of you there is a small box on the table. Add it to your equipment. In a moment you are to drink the contents of the vial, which will make you small enough to explore the flower from the inside. Now drink the special formula.*

You do and notice that it is a tasteless clear liquid. Very quickly and painlessly your body shrinks. Your clothing shrinks with you. Your head swims and you feel the slightest bit of nausea. You look around and calculate that you must be about one inch high, the perfect size for this assignment.

Now open the box. Inside you find a laboratory coat, just your new size. *Remove any jewelry and anything that protrudes sharply or has a rough texture. You must leave the scientific environment exactly as you have found it: no marks, no telltale signs of human intrusion.* Inside the box you also find a pair of soft cloth slippers. *Put on the laboratory coat. Remove your shoes and put the slippers on. Now the goggles. Check that you have the notepad and pencil and you are now ready to begin. . . .*

Stories for Pairs and Groups

Although it can present an additional challenge, you may want to try writing activities for pairs and groups. Each character in the narrative, of course, must have action to perform. The activity of Winnie-the-Pooh exercising (p. 135), for example, could easily be played in pairs, since Pooh does his exercises before a mirror. A partner could thus play the mirror image.

Other topics that lend themselves to paired playing are tasks that require more than one person, such as dentist and technician, pilot and flight attendant, or disc jockey and radio engineer. A scientist building and testing a robot, a plant competing with a weed, or red and white corpuscles working together in the blood stream are other possible ideas.

The following is a narrative for paired playing:

A PLANE RIDE

TEACHER: Today we're going to pretend to be Amelia Earhart or Charles Lindbergh flying our planes. The desks will be the airplanes. You'll be playing with partners. One partner will be the pilot; the other will be a student who is learning to fly. We'll play twice so each person will have the chance to play both parts. Choose a partner and decide between you who will be the pilot first. (Pause for organization.)

Now, in our plane, the Stearman biplane, the pilot sits behind the passenger-student. So arrange yourselves accordingly. (Pause again.)

You're going to take a ride across the mountains and land on the other side. This is going to be a dangerous trip because of the bad weather through the mountains, and the landing will be very difficult, owing to the rugged mountains surrounding the landing field. Because this is a dangerous trip, you will have to listen to directions carefully.

The Stearman biplane needs its propeller twirled to help the pilot start the engine. Student, you need to learn this, so you stand at the side of the plane by the propeller. Now, pilot, fasten your seat belt and shoulder harness. Make sure they're on tight. You'll have to take your signal from the control tower. I'm operating the control tower, and you will get your signal from me. Put on your earphones so you can make contact with the control tower and make sure everything is all set for takeoff. (The children pantomime earphones. The teacher holds hand to mouth to make a rather muffled sound as if speaking over the radio transmitter.) *Biplane NC 211, cleared for takeoff.*

OK, pilot, adjust your engine controls. Student, spin the prop to start the engine. Whoops. Guess the old plane will need several spins to get started. You'll have to try again. (pause) There! The engine throbs to life. Pilot, apply the brakes. Student, pull out the wheel chocks. Now climb aboard. Fasten your seat belt and harness.

Students, listen carefully. In front of you is a stick that controls the plane's direction. It is connected to the pilot's control stick. By placing your hands lightly—I repeat, lightly—around it, you will be able to follow the pilot's sensitive control. In this way, you can get the "feel" of controlling the plane.

Both of you be sure your goggles are in place. Now let up on the brake and taxi down to the end of the runway. You'll have to zigzag so that you can see beyond the nose of the plane.

You're almost at the end of the runway now, so quickly pull the stick toward you. Remember, student, when the stick is forward, it makes the plane go down, and when the stick is pulled toward you, the plane goes up. Now the plane is rising off the ground. Up you go! Check your compass to make sure you're going north toward the mountains. Look down below you. The airport is small and far away.

You're going through the mountains now. It looks like you're going into a storm. Be sure to bank the plane so the wings don't tip too much one way. They should be kept level with the body of the plane. It's starting to rain hard now. Reach up to the top of your control panel and press the blue button on the right to start the windshield wipers.

If you look over to the left you'll see the flash of lightning. Don't look too long. Keep your eyes on the altimeter to be sure you stay well above the mountains.

Keep watching for the mountain tops so you can be sure to pass over them. Careful! There's a peak right in your course. Quickly bank the plane or you'll hit it. Whew! That was a close call.

It looks like you're passing through the storm safely. You're almost on the other side of the mountains now, and the landing field is coming up on the right. Pick up your radios and let's make contact with the control tower and let them know you're coming in for a landing. (The teacher as control tower) *Flight NC 211. Cleared for approach to landing. Approach from the southeast.* Now check your seat belts and prepare to circle the landing field until we can come in for a safe landing.

Now let's bring the plane down easy. You have to go slow because the fog is thick and you might miss the field. There it is! You're right on course. Stand by for a landing. Check the air-pressure meter next to the lever control. Now get ready to pull back the brake lever when you touch ground. You're down. That was a good landing. Pull back on the brake lever and let's bring it to a stop. A perfect three-point landing! Congratulations!

Narratives can also be designed for groups. Again, tasks that require input from several persons are useful topics: an operating team, a group of elves in charge of certain tasks in toy making; the expedition team in Thor Heyerdahl's *Kon-Tiki* adventure. Group narratives might also be based on the workings of a car engine or the human heart, with children playing the various parts of each.

In the following example, based on a scene from Washington Irving's "The Legend of the Moor's Legacy" (43), there are parts for four children in each group: Peregil, the Moor, and the two enchanted persons who also play the stone entrance to the cave.

TEACHER: (Two players have their backs to Peregil, forming the cave's entrance. Peregil stands at the entrance of the cave, waiting for the Moor to arrive.)

It is chilly this evening, and Peregil shivers and wraps his cloak a little more tightly around him. As he waits, he thinks about his unhappy lot—being so poor and with so many mouths to feed.

And now he examines for the hundredth time the sandalwood box left by the Moor. Are the Moor's words true? Does the box really hold secrets? He opens it up and carefully takes out the small candle and the fragile piece of paper with the strange Arabic writing on it. He looks at the words, but they mean nothing.

He begins to become impatient for the Moor to arrive. Now a form can be seen through the trees in the distance. Ah, it is the Moor. You greet each other silently, and now you hurry quickly to test the power of the box. Peregil lights the candle and holds it, while the Moor reads the incantation on the scroll. The perfumes from the candle send a sweet odor through the damp air.

Then suddenly there is a distant rumbling like thunder. ("Cave entrance" gives sound effects.) Suddenly the cave entrance opens and reveals a long winding stairway. ("Cave entrance" now becomes two enchanted guards.) You huddle together as you descend the stairs. Shield the candle light, for if it goes out, you will be entombed forever in the cave. As you reach the bottom step you see a large trunk with huge bands of steel encasing it. At each end of the trunk you see two motionless men—enchanted, they are—and their eyes stare straight ahead.

Around the trunk there are many treasures, and you realize that you have indeed found wealth. You slowly and cautiously examine it—pick up a coin, try on a bracelet, examine a precious stone. Yes, it is real. And it is yours. You

> each take as much as your pockets can hold. There is more than enough and you are not the greedy sort.
> You hurry to finish because the candle is small and may burn out. You climb back up the long, steep stairs. You take one more look at the enchanted men, wondering if they saw what you did. They have such a knowing look about them. But you must hurry; there is no time to waste.
> You blow the candle out, and the cave entrance closes. (Guards become the entrance again.) Peregil keeps the paper and the Moor takes the candle. You part, each happier and wealthier—for the moment, at least—than you have ever been in your whole life, and disappear into the shadows of the night.

With experience you will become more flexible in narrating by ad-libbing and expanding or condensing the material according to the children's responses. The experienced leader may even be able to incorporate some of the children's spontaneous ideas into the story as it is being played. It is this kind of give-and-take between the leader and the children that makes the strongest, most meaningful drama experiences.

FOR THE COLLEGE STUDENT

1. Write a 300- to 500-word narrative pantomime on any of the following subjects. Underline the action words. Label the conflict. If appropriate, indicate the leader role you might play.
   a. Select a short folktale or fairy tale and rewrite it as a narrative pantomime. Be sure the story you select does not depend on extensive dialogue to be understandable.
   b. Select a topic from social studies or science or another curricular area appropriate for narrative pantomime.
   c. Use a job or a personal experience you have had that you can describe realistically and in detail.
   d. Choose an inanimate object that can be personified and write a story about it.
   e. Write your story about an inanimate object without personifying it.
   f. Write a story about an insect or animal without giving the subject human characteristics.
   g. Write a story specifically designed for pairs or groups.
2. Narrate your story for your classmates to enact. Discuss together the story's strengths and possible areas for improvement.

BIBLIOGRAPHY OF NARRATIVE PANTOMIMES FOR ADDITIONAL CURRICULAR SUBJECTS

The following symbols are used to indicate the age level the material might be best suited for:

Y   young children in kindergarten, first, and second grades
M   middle-grade children in third and fourth grades
O   older children in fifth and sixth grades

(*Note:* The materials focusing on animal and insect life are often of more interest to children from kindergarten through third grade. Students in fourth through sixth grades generally are more interested in the materials focusing on people. However, you will be the best judge for your own particular class.)

M *All on a Mountain Day,* AILEEN FISHER. Nashville: Thomas Nelson, 1956. This book presents a chapter about each of the wild animals found on a mountainside, from rabbit to bobcat.

Y–M *All Upon a Sidewalk,* JEAN CRAIGHEAD GEORGE. New York: E. P. Dutton, 1974. A yellow ant has an important mission to carry out. (Any of George's writings are superior science lessons and always dramatically written.)

Y–M *All Upon a Stone,* JEAN CRAIGHEAD GEORGE. New York: Thomas Y. Crowell, 1971. A mole cricket searches for and finds his fellow crickets. After a brief meeting, he returns to his solitary life once again. Solo playing is recommended.

Y–M *Amelia Bedelia,* PEGGY PARISH. New York: Harper & Row, 1963. Amelia, a housekeeper, takes all her instructions literally. This popular character has been the subject of many adventures. All are good language lessons, but children must be old enough to understand double meanings to see the humor. It is usually easiest to let everyone be Amelia in solo playing.

M *And Then What Happened, Paul Revere?* JEAN FRITZ. New York: Coward-McCann, 1973. This is another accurate and amusing story of a national hero by one of the most popular history writers for children.

Y *Ants Have Pets,* KATHY DARLING. Champaign, Ill.: Garrard, 1977. A description of the life of Pogo, a farmer ant. It can be played in pairs to include the cricket ant.

Y–M *The Bakers,* JAN ADKINS. New York: Charles Scribner's Sons, 1975. This is a detailed description of bread making.

M–O *Balloon Trip: A Sketchbook,* HUCK SCARRY. Englewood Cliffs, N.J.: Prentice-Hall, 1983. In this book we travel on an extended balloon trip, discovering the many intricacies of this exciting sport.

M *The Barn,* JOHN SCHOENHERR. Boston: Little, Brown, 1968. In an old barn a skunk searches for food; yet to the mother owl, the skunk is food for her babies. Solo playing is probably best.

Y *Bear Mouse,* BERNICE FRESCHET. New York: Charles Scribner's Sons, 1973. A meadow mouse hunts food for her young, escaping a hawk and a bobcat. Solo playing is easiest.

Y *The Bears on Hemlock Mountain,* ALICE DALGLIESH. New York: Charles Scribner's Sons, 1952. Jonathan finds out that there are bears on Hemlock Mountain and discovers a unique way to hide from them in this story based on a Pennsylvania pioneer folktale. Chapter 4 and part of Chapter 8 can be spliced and adapted easily.

M *Beaver Moon,* MISKA MILES. Boston: Little, Brown, 1978. An old beaver is forced out of his lodge and searches for a new home.

O *The Black Pearl,* SCOTT O'DELL. Boston: Houghton Mifflin, 1967. Ramon tells of his adventures with Manta Diablo, a fearsome fish, and of the search for a black pearl in Mexican waters. Many excerpts from this longer novel are useful.

M *The Blind Colt,* GLEN ROUNDS. New York: Holiday House, 1941. A blind colt must learn of the world, its joys and its dangers. This story can be a good lesson in adaption to blindness.

M—O *BMX*, DAVE SPURDENS. New York: Sterling Publishing, 1984. This book presents excellent data and photos (both color and black and white) on bicycle motocross. There are story possibilities in the sections on riding, stunts, proper clothing, and maintenance.

M *Brighty of the Grand Canyon*, MARGUERITE HENRY. Skokie, Ill.: Rand McNally, 1953. The classic story of a burro who spends his winters at the bottom of the canyon, where it is warm, and his summers on the North rim, where it is cool. Many excerpts from this longer book are playable.

O *Call it Courage*, ARMSTRONG SPERRY. New York: Macmillan, 1940. A South Sea Island boy, son of a tribal chief, has many fears of the sea and sets out to conquer them. Numerous solo excerpts from this book are usable.

Y *"Charlie Needs a Cloak,"* TOMIE DE PAOLA. Englewood Cliffs, N.J.: Prentice-Hall, 1982. In this story, a simple narrative pantomime of the process of making a cloak is presented from sheep shearing to final sewing. There is little dramatic tension unless it is played in pairs with the lamb, who sometimes hinders and sometimes helps. Pictures show the lamb's antics, which are also played up in the Weston Woods film of this story. It may be helpful for children to see the film before they play the story.

M—O *Chimney Sweeps*, JAMES CROSS GIBLIN. New York: Thomas Y. Crowell, 1982. A 900-year history of chimney sweeps is presented with illustrations and photographs. Chapter 5, which takes us through a day in the life of a chimney boy in 19th-century London, is perfectly written for narrative pantomime.

Y—M *Cosmo's Restaurant*, HARRIET LANGSAM SOBOL. New York: Macmillan, 1978. A young boy experiences a typical day at a family-owned Italian restaurant. Black-and-white photos add to the information.

Y *Cowboy Small*, LOIS LENSKI. Silver Springs, Md.: Henry Z. Walck, 1977. A little cowboy ropes cattle, cares for his horse, and plays a guitar, among other activities, in his busy day on the ranch.

M *Coyote for a Day*, ROGER CARAS. New York: Windmill Books, 1977. A coyote searches for food and experiences several adventures in this story which begins, "Today you are a coyote. . . ."

O *Coyote in Manhattan*, JEAN CRAIGHEAD GEORGE. New York: Thomas Y. Crowell, 1968. A teenage black girl wants to join a high school group that has voted her out. She finds a caged coyote and sets him free so that the group will change their opinion of her capabilities. The story focuses as much on the coyote and his encounter with the city as it does on the girl.

M—O *C. W. Anderson's Complete Book of Horses and Horsemanship*. New York: Macmillan, 1963. There are many descriptive passages in this book which can be useful for narrative pantomime, but you may prefer to focus on the chapter on riding techniques.

M—O *The Dallas Titans Get Ready for Bed*, KARLA KUSKIN. New York: Harper & Row, 1986. A fictional football team takes off its playing gear and relaxes after a game. Equipment is explained. Good for a quieting activity.

M *A Day in the Life of a Firefighter*, BETSY SMITH. Mahwah, N.J.: Troll Associates, 1981. A firefighter's day is documented with color photographs and text centering on rescuing a young child and putting out a dangerous fire.

O *A Day in the Life of a Forest Ranger*, DAVID PAGE. Mahwah, N.J.: Troll Associates, 1980. A forest ranger goes through a typical day, which involves everything from paperwork to relocation of animals. Photographs are included.

Y—M *A Day in the Life of a Sea Otter*, KAY MCDEARMAN. New York: Dodd, Mead, 1973. A mother sea otter spends her day with her baby searching for food, playing, and escaping dangers. It is easiest to play solo and should be edited to shorten. Black-and-white photographs illustrate.

O *A Day in the Life of a Television News Reporter*, WILLIAM JASPERSOHN. Boston: Little, Brown, 1981. This book, complete with photographs, shows a typical day of a television news reporter in Boston, from an early morning call about a robbery to the evening news broadcast.

Y–M *A Day in the Life of a Veterinarian*, WILLIAM JASPERSOHN. Boston: Little, Brown, 1978. This book documents a vet's many interesting duties, illustrated with black-and-white photos.

O *A Day in the Life of an Emergency Room Nurse*, MARGOT WITTY. Mahwah, N.J.: Troll Associates, 1980. A nurse, through text and photographs, demonstrates her experiences in an emergency room.

Y *A Day of Winter*, BETTY MILES. New York: Alfred A. Knopf, 1961. Numerous sensory experiences with snow are presented in this poetic description.

M *Doctor in the Zoo*, BRUCE BUCHENHOLZ. New York: Viking Penguin, 1974. A fascinating account of the many duties of a zoo doctor is presented with black-and-white photos.

Y–M *A Drop of Water*, SAM ROSENFELD. New York: Irving-on-Hudson, 1970. A drop of water is followed through its many changes in the environment.

Y *Elephants of Africa*, GLADYS CONKLIN. New York: Holiday House, 1972. The adventures of a little elephant within the herd are presented. Solo playing is probably best.

M *Felipé the Bullfighter*, ROBERT YARA. San Diego: Harcourt Brace Jovanovich, 1967. A young boy in Spain tries his hand at fighting a small bull. The beautiful color photographs add to the understanding of the story. Little editing is needed, although it will be more dramatic if the action is condensed into one day's time.

M *The First Travel Guide to the Moon*, RHODA BLUMBERG. New York: Four Winds Press, 1980. A detailed guide covering getting ready, flying to the moon, sports, and the return home. It requires editing to shorten for one playable trip.

M–O *Flying to the Moon and Other Strange Places*, MICHAEL COLLINS. New York: Farrar, Straus & Giroux, 1976. This is a firsthand account of space from one of the early astronauts. Excerpts are usable.

M *Fox and the Fire*, MISKA MILES. Boston: Little, Brown, 1966. A young red fox searches for food and is interrupted by a barn fire.

M–O *Gorilla, Gorilla*, CAROL FENNER. New York: Random House, 1973. This is a poignant description of a gorilla's life in the zoo, with flashbacks to his earlier life in the jungle.

O *Great Survival Adventures*, ROBERT GANNON, ed. New York: Random House, 1973. A collection of nine true stories told by the courageous people who survived their adventures despite great odds. Settings cover the desert to the Yukon, a bailout from a jet fighter to a rowing adventure across the Pacific Ocean. The stories should be edited to shorten them.

M–O *How a House Happens*, JAN ADKINS. New York: Walker, 1972. Steps in the process of building a house are presented, complete with diagrams.

Y *How Animals Sleep*, MILLICENT SELSAM. Scholastic Book Service, 1962. Descriptions of the sleep habits of several animals are given. This experience is also useful for a quieting activity.

Y–M *How to Dig a Hole to the Other Side of the World*, FAITH MCNULTY. New York: Harper & Row, 1979. Detailed instructions are given for taking an imaginary 8,000-mile journey, beginning with a shovel and a soft place to dig to a "no-spaceship" with super-cooling system, fireproof skin, and a drill on its nose.

M–O *i am the running girl*, ARNOLD ADOFF. New York: Harper & Row, 1979. In this story, told in poetic form, Rhonda trains for a running meet.

Y—M *In the Driver's Seat*, RON AND NANCY GOOR. New York: Thomas Y. Crowell, 1982. Through black-and-white photos and text, this book guides us through the steps in driving a front-end loader, combine, blimp, M60 tank, race car, Concorde jet, 18-wheel truck, crane, and train. The "you" wording makes it perfect for narrative pantomime.

M—O *Indian Hunting*, ROBERT (GRAY-WOLF) HOFSINDE. New York: William Morrow, 1962. The author describes Indian weapons, hunting methods, and the ceremonial rites of the hunt. Other books by this native American may also be of interest.

O *Island of the Blue Dolphins*, SCOTT O'DELL. Boston: Houghton Mifflin, 1960. An Indian girl is left alone on an island in the Pacific and manages to survive. There are many episodes to use from this exciting book based on a true story.

O *Julie of the Wolves*, JEAN CRAIGHEAD GEORGE. New York: Harper & Row, 1972. An Eskimo girl must choose between the world of her ancestors and the world of modern white people. Her sensitivity to the wolves and time spent with them comprises much of the story. Many episodes are usable.

O *Kon-Tiki and I*, ERIK HESSELBERG. Englewood Cliffs, N.J.: Prentice-Hall, 1970. This is the account by one of the six explorers in Thor Heyerdahl's expedition that sailed a small raft from Peru to the Polynesian Islands. Excerpts are usable.

Y *The Little Farm*, LOIS LENSKI. Silver Spring, Md.: Henry Z. Walck, 1966 (25). Farmer Small keeps busy throughout the year tending his little farm. There is little conflict, but the progression through the seasons makes this a satisfying story to play.

Y—M *The Little Old Woman Who Used Her Head*, HOPE NEWELL. Nashville: Thomas Nelson, 1935. A little old woman of modest means lives alone on a small farm. The many problems she has and the unconventional ways in which she solves them has delighted children for years. It is good for introducing problem solving, since children will readily see her errors in logic. Sequels are available.

M *Lone Muskrat*, GLEN ROUNDS. New York: Holiday House, 1953. An old muskrat survives a forest fire and makes a new home for himself. His preparations for winter and his encounters with an owl, eagle, and other dangers make a dramatic nature study.

M *Lone Seal Pup*, ARTHUR CATHERALL. New York: E. P. Dutton, 1965. A seal pup loses his mother and must fend for himself.

M—O *The Long Ago Lake*, MARNE WILKINS. New York: Charles Scribner's Sons, 1978. Fascinating data is presented in this book on outdoor life in the Wisconsin north country in the 1930s.

M—O *Lucky Chuck*, BEVERLY CLEARY. New York: William Morrow, 1984. This picture book is about teenage Chuck, who has a job pumping gas and loves his motorcycle. He goes for a ride, following the motor vehicle codes carefully. But then he forgets himself, has an accident, and gets a traffic ticket. The last picture shows Chuck wondering how much gas he will have to pump to pay the fine. It teaches a good safety lesson along with the fun of pretending to ride a motorcycle.

M—O *Lumberjack*, WILLIAM KURELEK. Boston: Houghton Mifflin, 1974. The author describes his personal experiences as a young lumberjack in Canada.

O *The Man Who Was Left for Dead*, JENNY TRIPP. Milwaukee: Raintree Publishers, 1980. The account of the true story of Hugh Glass, who in the early 1800s was badly wounded by a giant grizzly bear. His companions, believing him close to death, leave him alone in the wilderness, but he survives to make a 100-mile journey back to his fort. Chapters 4 and 5 form the basis for an exciting solo pantomime adventure.

Y—M *Maple Harvest: The Story of Maple Sugaring*, ELIZABETH GEMMING. New York: Coward-McCann, 1976. A detailed description of the steps in the process of maple sugaring is presented.

Y—M *The Moon of the Winter Bird*, JEAN GEORGE. New York: Thomas Y. Crowell, 1970. This lengthy story details the dramatic experiences of a sparrow trying to survive Ohio's winter weather.

O *My Side of the Mountain,* JEAN GEORGE. New York: E. P. Dutton, 1959. The various adventures of a young boy who tries his hand at living by himself in the Catskill Mountains provide an excellent nature study.

M–O *Night Dive,* ANN MCGOVERN. New York: Macmillan, 1984. A twelve-year-old girl accompanies her mother, a marine biologist, and other divers on night scuba-diving adventures. Several stories show undersea life, exploring an old shipwreck, as well as the rigors of scuba diving. Color photographs illustrate.

Y–M *Nobody's Cat,* MISKA MILES. Boston: Little, Brown, 1969. The adventures of an alley cat in the city and his struggles are told in a dramatic way.

Y–M *Octopus,* EVELYN SHAW. New York: Harper & Row, 1971. An octopus needs to find a new place to live.

Y–M *The Old Bullfrog,* BERNICE FRESCHET. New York: Charles Scribner's Sons, 1968. On a hot summer day, an old bullfrog sits on a rock looking asleep. The hungry heron edges up, one leg at a time, but at the last minute the wise old bullfrog makes his escape. Although the bullfrog himself does not have a lot of action, he is obviously the center of the conflict. It can be played in pairs or even threes, as there are several other animals. The third player can play the other animals or create sound effects for them.

M *Ox Cart Man,* DONALD HALL. New York: Viking Penguin, 1979. This beautiful picture book depicts day-to-day farm life in nineteenth-century New England. Although more focus is on the father, we see the duties of each member of the household, so it can be played in a group. Although there is no strong conflict, it is a satisfying experience to play because of the completion of the seasons' cycle.

Y–M *Pagoo,* HOLLING C. HOLLING. Boston: Houghton Mifflin, 1957. The growth and adventures of a hermit crab are presented. Many sections of this longer book are suitable for playing.

Y–M *Pete's House,* HARRIET LANGSAM SOBOL. New York: Macmillan, 1978. This text, illustrated with black-and-white photos, details the steps in the building of a young boy's new house.

M–O *The Philharmonic Gets Dressed,* KARLA KUSKIN. New York: Harper & Row, 1982. Over 100 members of an orchestra, including the conductor, are shown getting dressed and ready for a performance in this picture book. You can read each section and let the children choose the clothes they want to put on and the instruments they want to play. Several can be chosen as the conductor. (This part can easily be rewritten to be female.) At the end you can play a short symphonic piece and let the orchestra be conducted. (See Conducting an Orchestra in Chapter 4).

M *The Pine Tree,* GEORGE MAXIM ROSS. New York: E. P. Dutton, 1966. A pine tree struggles for survival. Although this is basically a simple story, it is beautifully written and highly dramatic.

M–O *The Plymouth Thanksgiving,* LEONARD WEISGARD. New York: Doubleday, 1967. The details of the events leading up to the first Thanksgiving are presented simply. There are numerous characters for small groups to play simultaneously or for the entire class to play as one presentation.

Y *Policeman Small,* LOIS LENSKI. Silver Spring, Md.: Henry Z. Walck, 1962 (25). Policeman Small is a traffic policeman on a busy day. Tension is built through his many activities during one day, including a traffic accident. There is more dialogue in this one than in the other Mr. Small stories, but it can be edited. You may also want to try pair or group playing.

M *A Prairie Boy's Summer,* WILLIAM KURELEK. Boston: Houghton Mifflin, 1975. This sequel to *A Prairie Boy's Winter* is equally enchanting.

M *A Prairie Boy's Winter,* WILLIAM KURELEK. Boston: Houghton Mifflin, 1973. This picture book gives separate descriptions of the many rigors and pleasures of living on the Canadian prairie in the 1930s.

O *The Printers,* LEONARD EVERETT FISHER. New York: Franklin Watts, 1965. This is one of a series of over a dozen handsomely illustrated books on colonial craftspersons, including glassmakers, wigmakers, cabinetmakers, and homemakers.

M *Rattlesnakes,* G. EARL CHACE. New York: Dodd, Mead, 1984. A prairie rattlesnake is followed through her life cycle. The story contains good detail with black-and-white photos and may be excerpted from the section where the snake first makes her move into the world through the end of Chapter 3 after she eats her first meal.

Y *Red Legs,* ALICE E. GOUDEY. New York: Charles Scribner's Sons, 1966. This is the story of the most common grasshopper in the United States.

Y–O *Roadrunner,* NAOMI JOHN. New York: E. P. Dutton, 1980. The hurrying desert roadrunner, a comic figure, spends his day running, chasing, and racing with twists, circles, and sudden stops.

O *Robinson Crusoe,* DANIEL DEFOE. New York: Charles Scribner's Sons, 1983. A man is shipwrecked and lives for years on a lonely island. There are many episodes to choose from in this novel.

M–O *Rodeo School,* ED RADLAUER. New York: Franklin Watts, 1976. A detailed narrative account of the training rodeo riders undertake and the techniques they must know.

O *Saint George and the Dragon,* MARGARET HODGES. Boston: Little, Brown, 1984. A retelling, in picture-book format, of a portion of Edmund Spenser's *The Faerie Queene.* George, accompanied by the fair maiden Una, slays the dragon in a three-day fight. The fight scene itself is good for narrative pantomime and can be played in groups of five: Una, George, and three for the dragon (one each for the head, wings, and tail). This is a good story to accompany a study of the Middle Ages in England.

M *Salt Boy,* MARY PERRINE. Boston: Houghton Mifflin, 1968. A young boy rescues a lamb in a storm and gets his wish: to rope a horse. The story is easily edited for solo playing.

M–O *Shackleton's Epic Voyage,* MICHAEL BROWN. New York: Coward-McCann, 1969. The true story of the 800-mile voyage of Captain Shackleton and five men to get help for the rest of his crew stranded on an Antarctic island. It can be played solo or in small groups. The text is simple and short.

O *Shaw's Fortune: The Story of a Colonial Plantation,* EDWARD TUNIS. New York: Collins Publishers, 1966. Data on all facets of plantation life are beautifully and carefully illustrated.

Y–M *Skunk for a Day,* ROGER CARAS. New York: Windmill Books, 1976. Illustrated with black-and-white drawing, this book begins, "Today you are a skunk" and then details the day's events.

Y *The Snail's Spell,* JOAN RYDER. New York: Frederick Warne, 1982. This short experience of pretending to be a snail is perfectly written for a narrative pantomime.

Y–M *The Spider Makes a Web,* JOAN M. LEXAU. New York: Hastings House, 1979. The story of a shamrock spider and how it builds its web is told through text and drawings.

M *Stores,* ALVIN SCHWARTZ. New York: Macmillan, 1970. This book presents much data on the day-to-day operations of forty different stores in one community. Short sections describe the work of each storekeeper or worker and numerous black-and-white photos illustrate the material. Excerpts are usable.

M *Sugaring Time,* KATHRYN LASKY. New York: Macmillan, 1983. Through words and pictures, this book follows a family in Vermont during the maple-sugaring season.

M *Tarantula, the Giant Spider,* GLADYS CONKLIN. New York: Holiday House, 1972. In this explanation, tarantulas are presented as useful insects that need not be feared.

Y–M *Three Days on a River in a Red Canoe*, VERA B. WILLIAMS. New York: Greenwillow Books, 1981. A young boy tells of his camping adventure with his mother, aunt, and cousin. With little editing, this can be played in groups of four with second- and third-graders. Some rewriting is necessary for solo or paired playing.

O *Tiktaliktak*, JAMES HOUSTON. San Diego: Harcourt Brace Jovanovich, 1965. An Eskimo boy is trapped on a rocky island and must make it back to food and safety.

Y–M *Time of Wonder*, ROBERT McCLOSKEY. New York: Viking Penguin, 1957. This is a sensitive description of a summer's experiences in Maine. Detailed information on many aspects of summer life in this part of the country, including a storm, is given.

M–O *The Tipi: A Center of Native American Life*, DAVID AND CHARLOTTE YUE. New York: Alfred A. Knopf, 1984. This book presents excellent data with illustrations on tipis, the sophisticated dwelling of the Great Plains Indians. Story material is possible in the tipi construction and the role of women in the task.

O *To Build a Fire*, JACK LONDON. Mankato, Minn.: Creative Education, 1980. A man in the Yukon, after a brave struggle, loses his battle against the 75-degrees-below-zero temperature. This story can easily be shortened.

Y *The Very Hungry Caterpillar*, ERIC CARLE. New York: Collins Publishers, 1969. A voracious caterpillar prepares for eventual change into a butterfly. This simple nature lesson will delight even the youngest child. Emphasize variety of action in eating the different foods.

M *Vulpes, the Red Fox*, JOHN and JEAN GEORGE. New York: E. P. Dutton, 1948. The descriptive, sensitive story of the life cycle of a fox is presented. Many episodes from this longer book are usable.

Y–M *The Web in the Grass*, BERNICE FRESCHET. Charles Scribner's Sons, 1972. This colorful picture book tells the story of a little spider's dangerous and friendless life.

M *Wharf Rat*, MISKA MILES. Boston: Little, Brown, 1972. This is a realistic portrayal of a rat's survival when threatened by an oil slick near the docks.

Y–M *What Can She Be? A Police Officer*, GLORIA AND ESTHER GOLDREICH. New York: Lothrop, Lee & Shepard Books, 1975. This black-and-white photo picture book tells of the day's work of law-enforcement officers. (Other books in the *What Can She Be?* series include such occupations as farmer, geologist, and film producer.)

Y–M *When Bastine Made Bread*, TRESKA LINDSEY. New York: Macmillan, 1985. In this lovely picture book, six-year-old Bastine spends an entire day baking bread, including such steps as threshing the wheat.

M *The White Palace*, MARY O'NEILL. New York: Thomas Y. Crowell, 1966. This is a beautifully illustrated story of a salmon's life.

Y–M *Who Needs Holes?* SAM AND BERYL EPSTEIN. New York: Hawthorn, 1970. This simple book illustrates some basic science concepts. Some rewriting is needed.

Y–M *Window into an Egg*, GERALDINE LUX FLANAGAN. Reading, Mass.: Addison-Wesley, 1969. A detailed account, with black-and-white photos, of the development of a chicken egg which has had a "window" cut into it. The end section, entitled "Hello, Chick," is recommended for playing.

O *Wolf Run: A Caribou Eskimo Tale*, JAMES HOUSTON. San Diego: Harcourt Brace Jovanovich, 1971. Rather than face certain starvation, a young Eskimo boy sets off to find caribou against almost hopeless odds.

M *The Wounded Wolf*, JEAN CRAIGHEAD GEORGE. New York: Harper & Row, 1978. Roko, a wounded wolf in the Alaskan wilderness, is saved from death by Kiglo, the wolf pack leader. This story based on fascinating research of wolf behavior. Solo playing is probably best.

O *Wrapped for Eternity: The Story of the Egyptian Mummy*, MILDRED PACE. New York: McGraw-

Hill, 1974. This presents fascinating information about a fascinating subject, particularly for older children. For a simpler version, see *Mummies Made in Egypt,* by Aliki Brandenberg (New York: Thomas Y. Crowell, 1979).

Y–M *Your First Airplane Trip,* LAURA ROSS. New York: William Morrow, 1981. This is a useful description of an airplane trip. There is little conflict except for a bit of bumpiness in the ride, but it is a satisfying experience for younger children to play.

SEVEN

Pantomimes for Guessing

In the previous chapters, the pantomimes were designed for the players' self-expression and self-satisfaction. The children often played in unison with no audience observing. While there were opportunities for voluntarily sharing ideas, there was no obligation to do so.

Even so, anyone watching the playing probably would have been able to understand what the children were doing and "saying." In fact, you may have been translating many nonverbal ideas in side-coaching: "I see some happy people," "That's it. Nice and slow," "Oh, you must be tired," and so forth. Pantomime communicates many messages, whether intentional or not.

This chapter covers a variety of pantomime games for guessing. The players have the obligation to communicate; the audience guesses or interprets the ideas based on the players' actions and facial expressions. The challenges and learning experiences thus are shared equally by both pantomimers and guessers.

Children usually find the games highly entertaining as well as challenging, whether they are pantomiming or guessing. You will also find it easy to incorporate numerous curricular topics into these games for additional learning benefits.

GUIDING PANTOMIME PLAYING

Player and Audience

Since pantomimes for guessing require an audience-and-performer arrangement, it is best to avoid having only one child at a time pantomiming for any length of time in front of the rest of the class. Such a procedure places too much pressure on the performer, who may become embarrassed or develop show-off behaviors. And if the rest of the children have to wait their turn too long, they can become bored. Therefore, all of the games presented are designed to involve several children at a time in pantomiming.

You will be encouraging the pantomimers to communicate ideas nonverbally as clearly as possible and the guessers to observe closely and to use analysis and synthesis in translating the messages. But it is important to realize that pantomime is ambiguous, as is all nonverbal communication. This is its fascination; we speculate on it, guess, and test our accuracy constantly. You may need to help the children understand that it may take a little time to figure out what a pantomimer is doing. And a pantomime often looks like something entirely different from what the player is intending.

Shy students may be disappointed or think they have been unsuccessful if their pantomimes are not guessed immediately. They may even say the audience has guessed correctly even if they have not. It often helps to say, "That's a hard one! You have us stumped; I guess you'll have to tell us what your idea was." This helps them feel more comfortable and also reinforces the ambiguity of pantomimes.

Outgoing students may be disappointed, angry, or may think they have been unsuccessful if their pantomimes *are* guessed right away. They often like to confuse an audience so that they can continue performing. They may even say the guess is not correct or accurate enough; they may also change their idea subtly to avoid being guessed. For these students it is helpful to say, "You gave us good, clear details, so we were able to guess it right away." This praises their actions and reinforces the importance of pantomiming good clues.

Limiting Guessing

There is usually no justification for going over three guesses of any one pantomime. This challenges the performers and the guessers to do

To guess a pantomime, you have to watch closely for clues.

their best work. If a pantomime cannot be guessed, the players simply state what they were doing.

If guessing is allowed to continue at length, there can be problems.

One second-grader was performing something extremely elaborate. The directions were to continue pantomiming until the idea was guessed. He kept saying no to each guess, yet he continued pantomiming very intriguing actions. Finally the leader said, "I guess you'll have to tell us what your idea was, Billy." Billy thought for a moment and then answered somewhat sheepishly, "I forgot."

Some children simply do not realize that their full idea cannot always be guessed with total accuracy. They hold out for specific guesses as a kindergartner once did: "You're a lion." "No." "A tiger." "No." "You're a panther." "No, I'm a *lioness with green eyes.*"

Evaluating

As the children pantomime, you can identify, through verbal feedback, the various clues the children are giving:

TEACHER: Sandy, I knew immediately that you were a tiny spring in the clock. You stretched, and then relaxed and jiggled. And each time you did exactly the same movement.

TEACHER: I can tell you have really been studying that book on armor. All five of you were pantomiming so believably I could practically feel the weight of each article of clothing you put on.

It is also helpful to side-coach, speculating out loud on the thinking process in making a guess, perhaps even giving a possible idea or two. Note how this can help the players as well as the guessers:

TEACHER: I wonder what David and Chris are carrying. It must be something that's too big for one person to carry. It looks as if it's heavy, too. What could it be?

Discuss particularly careful pantomimes, pointing out the details that help the audience understand the actions:

TEACHER: What do you suppose Cliff was doing when he moved his hands like this? (Demonstrate.)
CHILD: Taking the cap off a tube of toothpaste.
TEACHER: How did you know it was toothpaste? Couldn't it have been hair cream? Or first-aid cream?
CHILD: No! He squeezed it on his toothbrush and brushed his teeth!
TEACHER: Cliff used a special kind of toothbrush, didn't he? What kind was it?
CHILD: Electric.
TEACHER: How do you know?
CHILD: 'Cause he plugged it in and jiggled.

TEACHER: What was Orlando doing?
CHILD: That's easy. Peeling an onion.
TEACHER: How could you tell?
CHILD: Because he peeled it and cried.
TEACHER: Cliff and Orlando were very careful in their actions. They added details that helped us know what they were doing.

Of course, you should be careful about implying that a child is unsuccessful in pantomiming. Some children will be more successful than others, but it is important to encourage continued work. Discussions should not be allowed to become boring or overly critical. The greatest improvements will come about through practice and through doing, rather than through the extended evaluation of others.

PANTOMIME GAMES

Half and Half

This game is based on a children's game called by various names: New Orleans, Trades, or Lemonade. Divide the class into two groups. They line up and face each other. Traditionally, occupations were acted out for the opposing group to guess. The first group to play walks up to a designated middle line while chanting

TEAM 1:   Here we come.
TEAM 2:   Where you from?
TEAM 1:   New Orleans.
TEAM 2:   What's your trade?
TEAM 1:   Lemonade.
TEAM 2:   Show us if you're not afraid.

Team 1 pantomimes an occupation or trade. Team 2 calls out its guesses, and when the guess is correct, Team 1 must run back to its original place without being tagged by anyone from Team 2. Tagged members, in the traditional game, must join the opposite team. For classroom playing, the chasing and tagging can be eliminated. Or children can hop on one foot for control.

Variations: The game, of course, can be played with topics other than "occupations." The rhyme may also be changed. For example, the following could be used with seasonal activities: "Here we come." "Where you from?" "Kalamazoo." "What do you do?" "Depends on the weather." "Well, give us a clue."

The Sequence Game

For this game, pantomime activities are written or pictured on cards. Since the pantomimes are to be played in sequence, a written cue precedes the pantomime. The cards are distributed at random, with each child receiving a card. (You may also have two or three children to one card.) Each player's pantomime has to be interpreted correctly before the next player knows when to pantomime. Suspense is created in the quiet and careful watching and waiting for one's cue.

The first card might say:

> You begin the game. Pretend to mount a motorcycle. Rev it up and cruise around the room once. Then sit down in your seat.

Another player will have the card that reads:

CUE: Someone pretends to ride a motorcycle around the room.
YOU: Pretend to be a police officer driving in your patrol car. You spot a speeder. Chase the speeder with your siren turned on. Go around the room once and return to your seat.

It is helpful to have the cues and the pantomimes written in different colors. For example, the cue may be in red (stop and look) and the pantomime in green (go ahead). It is also helpful to include directions for standing and sitting. Laminate the cards to make them more durable.

The pantomimes can be unrelated, or they may tell a simple story. The following is an example of a modern Eskimo seal hunt.

YOU: Stand and pretend to put bundles of heavy clothes, sealskin boots, and boxes of food into an umiak in the middle of the circle. Sit.
CUE: Someone pretends to put supplies in a umiak.
YOU: Go to the center of the circle and pretend to step carefully into the umiak. Then sit in the umiak.
CUE: Someone sits down in the umiak.
YOU: Sit down behind the person in the umiak.
CUE: Two people have seated themselves in the umiak.
YOU: Pretend to start the small motor that propels the boat. After a few moments the motor "catches." Sit down as if you are ready to steer the boat.

You should prepare a master sheet with all the pantomimes in their proper sequence, in case the group gets lost. You may even prepare three sets of each game with three master sheets and divide the class into thirds for unison playing. A child from each group can follow the master sheet.

Once children are familiar with sequence games, they can either help transcribe the material on cards or even create their own games. One group of sixth graders worked diligently on a sequence game based on the process of preparing an Egyptian mummy, while another created its version of a Spanish bullfight.

Variations: A sequence game might give practice in learning directions: "Fly south," "Swim east," "Roll a ball northwest," and the like.

Pictures can also be used in place of words. Pictures of animals, of people performing various tasks, or portrayals of different emotions are all

Cue: Someone will motion to you and point to the ship.
You: Pretend to be a patriot sneaking on board the ship to dump the tea. (Sequence Game)

possible. One teacher used pictures of various body parts (for example, head, hand, leg, and ear) her kindergartners were learning. They were simply to move the body part pictured on the lower half of their card after someone performed the cue pictured on the upper half of the card.

Activities which follow a step-by-step sequence work well: performing a task, following a recipe, or tracing the steps a letter goes through being mailed are all fun to do. Similarly, the actions of a simple, familiar story can be made into a sequence game.

Using the alphabet sequence is another possibility. An "A" word (alligator, angry) is followed by a "B" word (bear, bashful) and so forth. You may choose to just let the alphabet itself be the cue to the next pantomime. (See *The Marcel Marceau Alphabet Book,* by George Mendoza [New York: Doubleday, 1970], for an excellent example of this.)

Add-on Pantomimes

Add-ons are played similarly to the sequence game. As before, one player's pantomime is the cue to the next player's pantomime. In this game, however, each child invents an idea to fit the selected topic.

One person begins by pantomiming an idea, while the audience guesses *silently.* The guesser (checked by you) joins the first player and assists. For example, one child may pretend to cook dinner. The second player may decide to set the table, another may make a salad, and so on. The players add on until they run out of ideas or until everyone has contributed.

Variations: Pretend to be various people at an event, adding on to the scene. For example, the Indianapolis 500 pit crew, drivers, fans, owners, flagpersons, and so forth could all take their appropriate places and perform their activities.

Older children might like to add on in pairs. For example, the activity might be "cooking breakfast." One player fries the eggs, while the partner *becomes* the eggs. Other partners for cooks might be oatmeal, bacon, pancakes, toast, and the like.

Try creating objects, with each pantomimer becoming part of the object. For a clock, one player might become the face, another the hands, another the pendulum, and so forth.

Build a Place

In still another variation of the Add-on, children can create a room or location, equipping it with appropriate furnishings or objects. A space is marked off on the floor, with doors or entryways indicated. The players bring one item at a time into the specified area. The goal is to create a complete imaginary environment; therefore, the players must remember where each item is placed so that they do not walk over or through it. Children can furnish a modern living room, a covered wagon, an Egyptian tomb, a science lab, Heidi's grandfather's alpine hut, or a grocery store.

For an added challenge, after children pantomime their new item, they are required to use a previous item in some way. For example, after bringing in test tubes to the scientist's laboratory, the player then lights the Bunsen burner brought in previously.

Variations: Build an entire shelter, following the appropriate procedures. Children may build a log cabin, wigwam, igloo, or modern-day house, constructing walls, roof, and windows in addition to the furnishings.

Even a city, state, or country can be created. Suppose, for example, that the children were to create their state. You might even put masking tape on the floor in the shape of your state. Then the children place the cities in the state by pantomiming actions appropriate to the various locations. One city may be known for a particular sport, another for a type of industry, and another for a certain product. The children may also be required to place the cities appropriately on the map, observing distance relationships.

Books that are useful for this activity would include those by David Macaulay. In *Castle* (Boston: Houghton Mifflin, 1977), for example, he details the construction of a castle in 13th-century Wales. *Underground* (1976) includes all the underground elements of a large city, including sewers, telephone and power lines, cables, pipes, and tunnels. And in *Unbuilding* (1980), he imaginatively reverses the building process by carefully dismantling the Empire State Building, step by step. *Simple Shelters,* by Lee Pennock Huntington (New York: Coward-McCann, 1979), presents simple data and sketches of eighteen various kinds of houses, such as igloos, teepees, stilt houses, and Masai houses. *Skara Brae: The Story of a Prehistoric Village,* by Oliver Dunrea (New York: Holiday House, 1986), outlines the archaeological discovery of a village on an island north of Scotland, showing how stone houses were built and rebuilt.

Count-and-Freeze Pantomimes

Select six or eight volunteers to pantomime simultaneously in front of the rest of the class. They may pantomime individually, in pairs, or in small groups. The children pantomime their ideas while you count to five or ten. (The counting may be as slow or as fast as is needed. If players are having a difficult time, a fast count is more comfortable. If the players are involved and the audience is interested, the counting can be slowed.) Say "Freeze" and then let the audience guess the pantomimes. Players may sit down when they are guessed.

This method is useful when space is limited or when you want only a few children at a time to play. However, it has the largest audience for an extended period. Therefore, the playing and guessing should be kept moving as quickly as possible.

The ideas may be as simple as "something you like to do" or they may be as complex as "connotations of words" (for example, adventure, discovery, sacrifice, freedom, dreams, happiness, invention, or serendipity). Added dimensions to the game might include "Pack something to take on a camping trip; the first letter of your item should be the same as the initial of your first or your last name." Or "Act out an invention; the audience must guess the invention and the inventor."

Pantomime Spelling

Similar to count-and-freeze is spelling out words. Children can spell out a city's name by simultaneously acting out animals whose names begin

A third-grade class acts out and guesses a Count Freeze pantomime game.

In-service teachers spell out T-A-M-P-A using occupations: T-truck driver, A-artist, M-magician, P-pianist, and A-acrobat.

with the appropriate letters. *New York* might be spelled out by seven children pantomiming *n*anny goat, *e*lephant, *w*alrus, *y*ak, *o*rangutan, *r*hinoceros, and *k*angaroo.

The audience can try guessing the words even if they are not sure of each letter. (This is similar to working on a crossword puzzle.) Children can guess in small groups, pooling their guesses and making a group decision.

Count-and-Freeze Charades

As a variation of charades, several children at a time act out words of a title (omitting the articles *a, an,* and *the*). For "Row, Row, Row Your Boat," three people could pantomime rowing, a fourth might point to the audience ("your") and the fifth might mime seasickness.

Syllables of longer names or titles can be acted out by groups also. "Washing-ton," "Indian-apple-us," and "Robin-son Crew-sew" are some possibilities.

Frozen Pictures

For this game, children select a scene, decide what parts they will play, and then freeze into position. Perhaps they freeze into pictures with titles such as "The Night the Ghost Visited," "Pony Express Ride Breaks Record," or "Napoleon Defeated at Waterloo."

Variations: Art masterpieces can be recreated: Seurat's *Sunday Afternoon on the Island of La Grande Jatte,* Daumier's *Accident at the Zoo,* or Picasso's *Guernica.* Statue or museum groupings are also possible.

Frozen picture of Washington crossing the Delaware.

Scenes from favorite stories and books or scenes of historical or current events might be created.

One-liners (see One Liners, Chapter 8) may be added to these frozen pictures to aid the guessing; or the pictures could be set in motion (see Setting Pictures in Motion, Chapter 9).

Intragroup Pantomimes (third grade and up)

This game is a little more complicated and usually too difficult for children under third grade to play. Divide the class into several groups of five or six persons. In each group, three or four members pantomime ideas for two members to guess. The instructions might be "Pantomime all the words you can think of that begin with the letter **r**." Other topics might be rhyming words (**at:** hat, cat, flat, and so on), verbs, household chores, toys, ways we use water, and consonant blends (**st:** stand, street, stop, and so forth).

The three pantomimers do not confer with each other; each thinks of his or her own ideas and enacts as many of them as time permits. The two guessers work as quickly as possible and write down the ideas. If an idea cannot be guessed, the pantomimers *or* the guessers may say "Pass," and the pantomimers go on to another idea.

A time limit of one or two minutes for each topic may be imposed. Afterward the children might discuss the ideas that were "the most humorous," "the most difficult to guess," or "those that appeared on every group's list." Avoid introducing competition by counting the number of words on each list. Or give each group a different topic to work on.

The advantage of this method is that the audience is small and the time limit encourages the children to pantomime quickly. Even the most reticent children will find it difficult not to get caught up in this game, since attention on them will be minimal.

Hint: Caution the children to work quietly so that other groups cannot hear their ideas. This reasoning usually makes more sense to them than just being quiet, and this game can get a little noisy.

ADDITIONAL TOPICS

The following topics may be used with several of the methods discussed in this chapter. Children can choose their own topics; or you may assign them, perhaps giving ideas written on cards.

Who Am I (Are We)? Act out community helpers, storybook or nursery rhyme characters, historical or literary characters, famous scientists, people in current events, and so on.

What Am I (Are We)? Children can pantomime animals, inanimate objects, machinery, toys, plants, and the like.

What Am I (Are We) Doing? This may be as simple as acting out verbs (running, skipping, jumping) or more complete ideas, such as making a cake, driving a car, or milking a cow. Pantomimes may be more challenging and add conflict, such as testing a water bed before purchasing, washing an unwilling dog, or setting up a tent in a windstorm.

What Am I (Are We) Seeing, Hearing, Tasting, Smelling, Touching? Pantomimers react to various sensory stimuli, which may cover such topics as seeing a ghost, listening to loud music, tasting unsweetened lemonade, smelling ammonia fumes, or touching a hot iron.

What's the Weather? Players enact clues for the audience to guess the seasons or the climatic conditions. They may act out seasonal sports or daily chores related to certain times of the year, putting on appropriate clothing for the weather (hot, cold, rainy, windy) or demonstrating various natural disasters.

What Am I (Are We) Feeling? Students act out various emotions. As an additional challenge, limit them to using only certain parts of the body to show emotion (face, hands, feet, or back). You can hold up a sheet to make just the particular body parts visible. Or use expressionless masks (see photo p. 51).

Emotions can also be combined with the "doing" pantomime: show an action and how you feel about doing it (for example, a household chore you do not like to do). Extend the idea by acting out a brief scene showing more than one emotion or a scene in which something happens to change the feeling. For example, "You are happily packing a picnic basket when you suddenly notice that it's raining. Now you can't go on the picnic and you are disappointed."

Where Am I (Are We)? Pantomime being in various locations, such as a zoo, hospital, desert island, haunted house, carnival midway, elevator, and so forth. You may also use particular cities or countries studied.

Let's Get Ready to Go. Pretend to pack supplies for various adventures, such as going on a fishing trip, preparing for a hike, loading a covered wagon, equipping an explorer's ship, preparing for a space launch, and so forth.

Transportation. Players pretend to travel in various ways: on foot or skates, by bicycle, bus, airplane, and so forth. Categories may include modern (electric car, space ship), historical (horse and buggy, high-wheeler bicycle), foreign (ricksha, camel), or fantastic (flying carpet, seven-league boots).

Family or Group Portrait. Members of a family or a group prepare as well as pose for their portrait. It may be a historical family (George Washington's family) or group (the First Continental Congress), a royal family or group, or a literary, animal, cartoon, or television family or group.

Dress Up. Pretend to be certain people dressing in their appropriate clothing for what they are or do: baseball player, ballet dancer, knight, astronaut, desert nomad, or Egyptian priest. Historical and literary characters are good for this game too.

Foods. Pretend to grow, harvest, or prepare and eat familiar and foreign foods: corn on the cob, an ice-cream cone, pizza, a hot dog, lobster, spaghetti, wild rice, coffee beans, peanuts, coconut, and so forth. Students can also do four basic food groups: fruits and vegetables; bread and cereal; dairy products; and meat, fish, and poultry or other protein.

Health and Hygiene. Players can demonstrate various good (or bad) habits, such as brushing and flossing teeth, getting fresh air and exercise, washing clothes, and cleaning house.

Energy and Water Conservation. Students demonstrate various ways to conserve electricity and water at home and school, and in business and industry (for example, turning off unneeded lights, repairing leaky faucets, and turning heat or air-conditioning down).

Occupations. Children can act out various jobs, perhaps pantomiming what they would like to be when they grow up. Consider also community helpers, occupations in Colonial times, occupations in other locations or countries.

Tools. Demonstrate various tools people use to perform certain occupations or tasks: kitchen, carpentry, sewing, household, doctor's, teacher's, and so on. Tools from the past (and in some cases still in use) might include a blacksmith's bellows, a weaver's loom, and a pioneer's butter churn.

Machines. Demonstrate simple tools—such as levers, wedges, and pulleys—as well as more sophisticated machines, such as electrical appliances or construction equipment. Students may demonstrate operating the machinery or becoming the machines. This topic can also include human organs—such as the heart, lungs, or stomach—since they resemble machines.

Sports. Children enact favorite sports or act like favorite athletes. The sports may be categorized into team sports, Olympic events, winter sports, and so forth.

Animals. Different groups of animals may be pantomimed: pets, farm animals, zoo animals, circus animals, mammals, amphibians, or mythical animals.

Biography. Enact a famous or historical person performing a typical activity or acting in a famous event. Students may focus on various categories, such as Famous Women (Sally Ride, Barbara Jordan, Maria Tallchief), Minority Heroes or Heroines (Martin Luther King, Jr., Mary McLeod Bethune, Cesar Chavez), or Famous Scientists (Albert Einstein, Marie Curie, George Washington Carver).

Inventions. Pantomime using or being the invention. The class guesses the inventor as well as the invention (Eli Whitney, cotton gin; Robert Fulton, steam engine; Samuel Morse, telegraph, and so forth).

Musical Instruments. Pantomime the instrument of choice or one from a category, such as orchestral, marching-band, percussion, woodwind, and brass. Asian instruments or those associated with a particular country or culture (Scottish bagpipe) might also be considered.

Safety. Pantomime the dos and don'ts of various activities: use of playground equipment, bicycle riding, water sports, camping activities, household or school activities, or rules for dealing with natural disasters.

First Aid. Demonstrate techniques for treating cuts, insect bites, removing a foreign body from the eye, aiding a choking victim, treating frostbite, giving first aid for burns, and the like.

Festivals and Holidays. Act out various activities associated with holidays in the United States (Fourth of July, Thanksgiving, Memorial Day); celebrations (Christmas, Hanukkah, Halloween, Valentine's Day); other cultures and countries (Chinese New Year, Mexican birthday, French Bastille Day). The audience guesses the custom and the country.

Word Pantomimes. Several games can be played using categories of words or parts of speech. For example, in an opposite game the audience guesses the word that is the opposite of the one pantomimed (hot, cold). This game may also be played with homonyms (weigh, way; the guesser spells both). Other words might be those with long vowel sounds, spelling words, and vocabulary words.

Countries and Customs. Students enact a custom, and the audience guesses both the custom and the country: British afternoon tea; Spanish or Mexican bullfight; Japanese kite-flying contest.

Sign Language. Learn some Indian sign language (see Aline Amon's *Talking Hands—Indian Sign Language.* New York: Doubleday, 1968), finger spelling, American Sign Language (see Mary Beth Sullivan and Linda Bourke's *A Show of Hands.* New York: Harper & Row, Publishers, 1985), or other nonverbal language systems. Use these in place of pantomiming.

PANTOMIME SKITS AND STORIES

As children (from third grade on) become skilled, they may want to do more elaborate pantomimes, individually or in pairs and groups. Some of these may even develop into complete stories. For young children or beginners, you may need to give guidance in choice of material, who plays which part, and other minor assistance.

Encourage plot structure by focusing on the beginning, the middle, and particularly the ending of stories. Remind children that a "story" is being told; it should not ramble on indefinitely and should have an ending.

The focus here is still on pantomime for guessing. However, as they plan their skits some students may see possibilities for dialogue and ask to talk. This is fine; the children will then be creating a verbal skit. (For more verbal skit ideas, see pp. 204–210). Just be sure you also offer experiences that stretch their abilities in communicating without words. Because children's verbal language increases each year, they tend to overlook how much communication can be accomplished nonverbally. Pantomime skits encourage children to pay attention to each other for extended periods of time, a valuable experience in itself.

Evaluating Skits

As children become skilled in pantomime, it should not be necessary to guess each and every detail of a pantomime skit or story. However, evaluation of the overall effectiveness of the communication is still important. Some questions for group discussion might be,

> What was the most understandable moment?
> When did you have difficulty following the story?
> Was it clear who the characters were?
> Were the characters and their feelings believable?
> Was there a satisfying ending?

Ideas for Pantomime Skits

Favorite stories.   Children may act out some of their favorite stories for the class to guess. These might be short stories such as fables or even television shows. You may have some simple costumes and props on hand

The Scarecrow meets Dorothy and Toto. A pantomime drama accompanied by the musical score from MGM's *The Wizard of Oz.*

for the children to use. A story or skit will sometimes evolve from these. For example, a bowl and a spoon may remind children of "Little Miss Muffet" or "The Three Bears." Or a piece of red material may suggest "Little Red Riding Hood." For older students, this activity can "advertise" books to the class and serve as a book report.

Scenario skits. In pairs or groups children can act out skits and stories from instructions or outlines written on cards. The following samples show only some of the many possibilities.

1. Act out a brief pantomime version of "Cinderella."
2. You are having a picnic. After everything is laid out, it begins to rain. You must eat your picnic in the car. (Don't forget to take the picnic items into the car!)
3. Two friends are riding their bicycles. They pass an old house they think is haunted and decide to explore it. While they are exploring, something inside the house frightens them, and they race out of the house and head for home. Decide what the something is that scares them and act out the skit.

Music video. Some years ago there was a television show called *Your Hit Parade.* Each week the top songs (both with lyrics and without) were sung and dramatized in simple fashion. Sometimes it became a real challenge to find new ways to dramatize a song that remained popular for several weeks. Today there is music video, though not all selections are acceptable for children's viewing. Still, you may be able to use some popular songs as material for skits the children can act out to the record's accompaniment. You can share songs from a bygone era also, such as folk songs and folk ballads that tell a story. (See example, pp. 3–4).

Proverbs. Students develop a short skit to illustrate a proverb such as "Make hay while the sun shines," "A stitch in time saves nine," or "A friend in need is a friend indeed."

News story of the week. In groups children illustrate a current news event. Having a newspaper on hand can provide ideas for the skits as well as stimulate interest in reading about them.

Television shows and commercials. Students can act out favorite television shows. Story commercials (those that can be pantomimed and do not require dialogue) may also be enacted. You can relate this to a study of television and the various types of shows: situation comedies, soap operas, variety shows, and so forth. The commercials can relate to a study of advertising techniques, such as using famous personalities for testimony.

You are there. Skits may be based on scenes of scientific or historical significance. Facts about the events might be listed on cards, or the students might be encouraged to do research in preparation. Consider the following: the test drive of the first automobile; the Wright brothers' flight at

Kitty Hawk; the first heart transplant; women's being granted the vote; Madame Curie's discovery of radium; the discovery of King Tut's tomb; Alexander Graham Bell making the first telephone call; and so forth.

The invention. Children act out their version of the discovery of such inventions as laughing gas, suspenders, the rubber band, fire, the mirror, the popcorn machine, fireworks, the wheel, potato chips, snowshoes, or bubble gum. For comparative purposes, refer to *The Invention of Ordinary Things*, by Don L. Wulffson (New York: Lothrop, Lee & Shepard Books, 1981), which tells the story behind the invention of such things as the zipper, breakfast cereal, and the toothbrush.

Charades. This age-old game can be played by older elementary students. Once the game is learned, it is probably best played in small groups so that more students have a chance.

Two teams are formed. One team gives its topic to one of the players from the opposite team to enact for his or her team to guess. A time limit is imposed, though you may wish to deemphasize this feature.

Traditionally, players are given song, play, book, film, or television titles as well as common sayings to act out. Usually the words are acted out one at a time, although they need not be acted out in the order in which they appear in the title. Sometimes only one syllable at a time is acted out. The pantomimers have several aids they can use:

1. They may tell the guessers, "This is a ——— (title or saying). There are ——— — words in it. I'm going to act out the ——— word."
2. The player may say, "This is a short word." The guessers then simply call out as many short words as they can think of until the correct one is called. Words such as *a, an, the,* or various pronouns and prepositions can be handled quickly in this manner.
3. The pantomimer may act out a word that *sounds* like the original word if that would be easier to guess. The word *car,* for example, might be easier to act out and guess than the word *far.*

For additional curricular emphasis, story titles might be from basal readers or popular library books. Sayings might be historical quotes, such as "Walk softly and carry a big stick" (Theodore Roosevelt), "Give me liberty or give me death" (Patrick Henry), or "A house divided cannot stand" (Abraham Lincoln).

Without saying a word. This activity can be played by older or advanced classes. In groups the children prepare a skit to show to the class. However, they must both *plan and rehearse* a familiar story ("The Three Bears," "Little Red Riding Hood," stories in basal readers, and so forth) *totally in pantomime.* Writing notes or mouthing words is not allowed.

To make the game a little easier, first verbally brainstorm some titles and list them on the chalkboard. Then as the groups plan, they choose their story from those listed on the board. Again, they cannot talk, write notes, or mouth words, and are not even allowed to go to the board and point out a title. When all the groups are ready, you too can enter the playing by guiding the sharing of stories with pantomimed instructions, indicating who goes first, leading the audience's applause, and so forth.

This game is a real challenge, but the rewards make it worthwhile. Both you and the children may be amazed to discover how much you can communicate with others without using any words at all. When the stories are shared, do not be surprised if one or two people in a group are acting out a story different from that of everyone else in their group. It demonstrates the difficulty of accurate communication. When the entire activity is ended and talking is allowed, you may need to allow for some moments of chattering as students check out all the pantomiming they were not sure of.

FOR THE COLLEGE STUDENT

1. Play some of the pantomime activities suggested in this chapter. Afterward discuss the special skills required of the pantomimer and the interpreter in acting out and guessing the nonverbal messages. How successful were you in doing each?

2. After playing some of the pantomime games, discuss which pantomime types would be most useful for different grade levels. Also discuss which curricular topics might be particularly suitable for the different types of pantomimes.

3. Create ten pantomime activities, using various curricular topics in each. Vary the types of pantomime games you use.

4. Now select one of the pantomime games you have written and guide your classmates or a group of children in playing it. Consider the various techniques you can use to guide the playing, to help the audience interpret the pantomimes, and to evaluate the playing. Afterward discuss the activity.

5. Create your own type of pantomime, perhaps creating a variation on a type mentioned in this chapter. Teach it to your classmates.

EIGHT

Verbal Activities and Improvisation

In the previous chapters pantomime activities have been emphasized, with verbalizing being encouraged whenever it occurred spontaneously. As you play these activities you will quickly notice that children vary in their readiness to verbalize. Some comfortably express their ideas; others are more reticent in communicating. Therefore, you will need a range of verbal activities to choose from and to correspond to the different skills the children exhibit.

This chapter will give you many selections, ranging from the easier to the more difficult. Although the simple activities can be particularly useful for encouraging shy students to participate, they can also be creatively challenging to the more advanced students. At the same time, challenging activities can sometimes motivate and spark expression in the reticent. Allow for flexibility and experimentation as you familiarize yourself with these activities.

BEGINNING VERBAL ACTIVITIES

Sound Effects

There are many simple verbal activities and games which can help children feel more comfortable with talking. You can begin with just sounds, playing with the voice. Creating sound effects can be an excellent learning experience as well as great fun for all. The voice is a marvelous instrument of sound that has an extremely wide range of possibilities when we take the time to explore it. Without saying a word at all, there can be great flexibility of communication.

Children will enjoy doing this kind of experimenting. And you will soon discover that there are many places in the curriculum for this activity. While students have fun, they will also be learning facts, experimenting with the physics of sound, and creating settings and environments of the mind. Sound effects can be highly dramatic by themselves or when added to more elaborate productions, such as "sound mimes" (pp. 174–75).

Sound effects from literature. There are many excellent stories and poems that focus on sounds. Simply narrate the material (as you did before in narrative pantomime) and pause for the students to make the sounds in the appropriate places, thus exercising the children's listening and interpretive skills.

The list of literature that follows covers a broad range of subjects for you to choose from. For example, the delightful books of Margaret Wise Brown tell stories about a little dog Muffin who, for different reasons in each book, must guess about all the sounds he hears. Many sounds are ordinary, but others are challenging and may require some discussion. What would "butter melting" sound like? Or a grasshopper sneezing? "The Devil's Pocket" has continuing echo sounds, and *Paul Revere's Ride* provides opportunities for an entire drama of sound effects. Children are intrigued by the various sound possibilities and usually have a greater appreciation of the literature after working with it in this fashion.

Tips

1. Some sounds are best made by one student or by just a few, whereas other sounds will require the entire class. Experiment to see what procedure will give the best results.

2. Control the sounds by using an indicator for volume control. Some leaders use an arrow made of wood or cardboard or an oversized pencil. One teacher used a cutout picture of an ear on a stick and simply raised and lowered it to indicate on and off and intensity of volume.

3. It is probably best not to let students operate the volume control—at least not at first.

4. Do not try to do too much at a time. Children may get tired working on a long selection in one sitting.

5. Try tape-recording the selections after they have been rehearsed a few times so that students can hear themselves. It will be easier for them to evaluate their work this way. Consider these like radio dramas, where one's imagination can soar, visualizing entire scenes based on narration and sound effects. Older students will enjoy added information from *The Magic of Sound* by Larry Kettlekamp (New York: William Morrow, 1982). Chapter 4, "Fun with Sound Effects," tells how to make, amplify, and record a variety of sounds.

6. Try adding some musical sounds or other nonvocal sounds for variety. Rhythm-band or Orff instruments have endless possibilities. Experiment also with objects in the classroom that make noise. One fourth-grade class decided the most realistic sound for rain was achieved by running their feet over the little bits of gravel that had accumulated under their desks on a particularly muddy day!

Follow the arrow to know when to make the sound and how loud it should be.

Suggested Literature for Sound Effects

(*Note:* Letters at the beginning of each entry indicate suggested grade levels. Numbers in parentheses refer to numbered anthologies listed in the bibliography at the end of this book.)

Y–M *Bam Zam Boom!* EVE MERRIAM. New York: Walker, 1972. Demolition day brings the excavating and rebuilding of a city apartment house.

Y–M "The Bed," PURA BELPRE (49). The noise of an old-fashioned bed squeaking frightens the little boy and several animals under it in this Puerto Rican folktale.

M–O *Clams Can't Sing,* JAMES STEVENSON. New York: Greenwillow Books, 1980. A simply told but challenging and delightful sound-effect story of two clams who prove to the other animals on the beach that they can contribute to the orchestra concert. This one lets you pull out all your (and the children's) creative stops when it "gets fancy."

Y *Country Noisy Book,* MARGARET WISE BROWN. New York: Harper & Row, 1940. There are farm and countryside animals for Muffin the dog to hear in this classic story.

M–O "The Devil's Pocket," GEORGE MENDOZA (10). Two boys have a mysterious adventure throwing a penny into an old abandoned quarry. Echo effects and exciting tension make this a real "Twilight Zone" kind of story that is good for Halloween.

Y–M *Georgie and the Noisy Ghost,* ROBERT BRIGHT. New York: Doubleday, 1971. Sound effects are important in this story of Captain Hooper's ghost getting a medal for bravery.

Y–M *Good-Night, Owl!* PAT HUTCHINS. New York: Macmillan, 1972. Owl has trouble sleeping because of the sounds made by other animals in the tree. He gets his revenge when it is his turn to be awake.

Y–M *Klippity Klop,* ED EMBERLEY. Boston: Little, Brown, 1974. Prince Krispin and his horse Dumpling go for a ride and meet a dragon in a cave.

Y *Little Toot,* HARDIE GRAMATKY. New York: Putnam Publishing Group, 1967. A little tugboat, who at first only wants to play, experiences accomplishment when he is able to help a stranded ocean liner.

M *The Little Woman Wanted Noise,* VAL TEAL. Skokie, Ill.: Rand McNally, 1943. A woman moves from the city to the country and discovers that she misses the city noises.

M "Louder than the Clap of Thunder," JACK PRELUTSKY (28). A child lists many loud sounds, but says that none is as loud as his father's snoring.

Y *Mr. Brown Can Moo! Can You?* DR. SEUSS. New York: Random House, 1970. Mr. Brown makes all kinds of sounds from a bee buzzing to a hippopotamus chewing gum, and encourages readers to do the same.

Y *Mr. Grumpy's Outing,* JOHN BURNINGHAM. New York: Holt, Rinehart and Winston, 1970. Children and animals join Mr. Grumpy in his boat. They all do what he says not to do, and fall into the water. You can easily add movements to this one.

Y "Night Noises," TONY JOHNSTON (29). Mole and Troll learn that sounds in the night are not made by monsters. Young children will be able to identify with Mole and Troll's fear and will be reassured themselves.

Y *The Noisy Book,* MARGARET WISE BROWN. New York: Harper & Row, 1939. Muffin, a little dog, gets a cinder in his eye and must guess at the many sounds he hears.

Y–M *Noisy Gander,* MISKA MILES. New York: E.P. Dutton, 1978. A young gosling does not understand why his father honks at everything—until a fox enters the barnyard.

Y–M *Noisy Nancy and Nick,* LOU ANN GAEDDERT. New York: Doubleday, 1970. Two children get in trouble for being too noisy.

O *Paul Revere's Ride,* HENRY WADSWORTH LONGFELLOW. New York: Greenwillow Books, 1985. There are opportunities in this famous poem for such sounds as feet climbing wooden stairs, startled pigeons, and horse's hoofs on sand. With extended planning, a shadow drama (with people or puppets or even a combination) could evolve from this.

Y–M *Plink Plink Plink,* BYRD BAYLOR. Boston: Houghton Mifflin, 1971. A young boy hears various sounds at night before he goes to sleep and imagines all the things they could be. For example, a clump bump he imagines to be a pirate clumping on a wooden leg, but it is only branches hitting the door.

Y *Quiet Noisy Book,* MARGARET WISE BROWN. New York: Harper & Row, 1950. The dog Muffin awakes very early and hears the quiet and unusual sounds of a new day, providing material for a challenging listening lesson.

Y–M *Sounds All Around,* JANE BELK MONCURE. Chicago: Children's Press, 1982. In this book we find all kinds of sounds, from the ping of a toaster to fireworks, and are taught some basic concepts about hearing sounds.

M *Too Much Noise,* ANN MCGOVERN. New York: Houghton Mifflin, 1967. An old man tries to find the solution to too much noise in his house.

Y *Winter Noisy Book,* MARGARET WISE BROWN. New York: Harper & Row, 1947. The dog Muffin hears the sounds of winter both indoors and out.

Original Sound-Effects Materials

You can also compose some materials of your own for sound effects. You might even create a group story with the students or encourage them to write their own.

The stories can be based on a number of other materials being studied. For example, stories can be based on the seasons, holidays, or weather sounds. Or a location, such as a supermarket, seaport, zoo, school, or foreign city and the different sounds heard there might be created. You might consider a natural disaster and the preparations and safety precautions surrounding it. An event, such as a space launch, could be created.

Example: The following dramatic incident is based on the surrender of Lee to Grant at Appomattox from information in a social studies text:

Let's imagine it is the afternoon of April 9, 1865.
It's very quiet. . . .
All eyes are looking down the dusty road to the courthouse.
A blue jay calls. . . .
An annoyed squirrel answers back. . . .
In the distance young children shout and begin a game of tag. . . .
The muffled sound of horses is heard . . .
and a gray figure riding a gray horse approaches. . . .
All sounds cease. . . .
Slowly, the gray horse, Traveller, passes the line of waiting Northern soldiers. . . .
He stops at the gate of the McLean house. . . .
General Lee's footsteps on the wooden stairs are clear and brisk. . . .
Now another figure on horseback rides into view. . . .
While the watching men softly sing "Auld Lang Syne" . . .
General Grant disappears into the house . . .
and the battle-weary country waits for peace.

For speech improvement, some teachers of young children have focused stories on sounds many children have difficulty pronouncing, such as "s," "sh," "th," or "r." The sounds can represent specific things, such as "s" the hissing of a snake, "sh" waves on a shore, "th" air escaping from a balloon, and "r" the sound of a car motor. The sounds can be combined in a story about the adventures of a snake who travels by boat, balloon, and car to seek his fortune.

Another variation of sound effects is to select favorite stories and assign certain sounds to each of the characters. Each time the character is mentioned in the story, the sound is made. Consider the characters' looks and personality in order to determine the most appropriate sounds. (For example, Papa Bear's and Baby Bear's growls would be different. Goldilocks' sound might be a tinkling bell or a giggle. Finger cymbals might be the sound for a Princess; a drum might signal the villain; and so forth.) This is a valuable characterization lesson for both drama and for literature study.

Sound Mimes

Older students will enjoy creating sound effects for pantomime dramas and skits, perhaps some of those listed at the end of this chapter. For this activity, one group of children performs the sound effects for the pantomime players. For an even more challenging activity, have the sound effects people create sounds while the pantomimers create appropriate actions and story line. This is a little more elaborate than the sound panto-

Interpretive reading skills are encouraged in verbal sequence games.

mimes on p. 94, since an entire story is being told. Groups might wish to work out their skit and sound effects before presenting them, or they might like to improvise on the spot.

Sequence Games

As in the pantomimes for guessing, sequence games can also be created for verbal activities. The children have an opportunity to talk, but they read the lines written for them rather than having to invent dialogue. Actually, the sequence game is really like performing a short play script. With these materials you can encourage appropriate interpretive reading of the lines, pointing out the opportunities for variety in vocal inflection, pitch, dynamics (loud and soft), timing, pauses, and so forth.

Children will need time to work on sequence games. Often it takes a run-through reading first for the children to familiarize themselves with the material and get into the spirit of it. Usually they ask to repeat the game so that they can switch cards and perfect their delivery. After several playings there is usually an automatic improvement in reading. They also enjoy the challenge of trying to improve their previous reading rate. Once children are familiar with sequence games, they can help transcribe material on cards themselves or even create their own games.

As with the pantomime sequence games, for verbal sequence games the cards are made up with a cue and a line to read (and perhaps a pantomime to perform). (*Note:* It is a good idea to laminate the cards so they will last longer.)

The cards are distributed at random. The first card might say

You begin the game.
Stand and say, "Good morning, ladies and gentlemen. Welcome to the Fourth-Grade TV Personality Show!" (Bow and sit down.)

The next player will have a card that reads:

CUE: "Good morning, ladies and gentlemen. Welcome to the Fourth-Grade TV Personality Show." (Bow and sit.)
YOU: Stand and say, "Brought to you by Multicolored Jelly Beans." (Sit.)

There can be three children with this next card:

CUE: "Brought to you by Multicolored Jelly Beans." (Sit.)
YOU: Stand and cheer and clap. (Sit)

and so forth until a sequence of events or a story is told.

Sequence Games from Literature

There are a number of stories and poems with interesting dialogue or statements in a series that provide excellent material for sequence games. Younger children also enjoy alphabet and number books, as well as simple riddle and joke books. (Because of their built-in sequence, riddle and joke books may not even require written cues.) Older children will also enjoy books with trivia information. They are often motivated to create their own scripts from these books.

Following are some suggestions from literature. In most cases they can be used just as they are written.

(*Note:* Letters in margin at the beginning of each entry indicate suggested grade levels. Numbers in parentheses refer to numbered anthologies listed in the bibliography at the end of this book.)

M *Alexander and the Terrible, Horrible, No Good, Very Bad Day*, JUDITH VIORST. New York: Atheneum, 1972. Everything goes wrong for Alexander one day. He thinks he will go off to Australia until his mother tells him there are bad days there too.

Y–M *Alfred's Alphabet Walk*, VICTORIA CHESS. New York: Greenwillow Books, 1979. Alfred learns the alphabet by going on a walk and seeing, among other things, "a herd of hungry hogs hurrying home."

M–O *Arm in Arm*, REMY CHARLIP. New York: Parents' Magazine Press, 1969. A small treasury of various materials, from jokes to short sayings, presents many possibilities.

Y–M *At Mary Bloom's*, ALIKI. New York: Greenwillow Books, 1976. A little girl's mouse has babies and she wants to tell Mary Bloom all about it. But she worries about the series of events that may happen. Since these events are noises like baby crying and dog barking, you can add sound effects to this story, too.

M–O *Bringing the Rain to Kapiti Plain*, VERNA AARDEMA. New York: Dial Press, 1981. This Nandi tale from Africa tells how a herdsman, Kipat, helped end the drought. It is told in the style of "The House that Jack Built." It can also be done as a shadow drama with many ideas from the beautiful illustrations.

M *Can I Keep Him?* STEVEN KELLOGG. New York: Dial Press, 1971. A boy has a humorous conversation with his mother about having a pet.

M *The Day Jimmy's Boa Ate the Wash*, TRINKA HAKES NOBLE. New York: Dial Press, 1980. A mother questions a child about a classroom field trip to a farm; the child's answers to each question reveal an increasingly chaotic experience.

M *Don't Forget the Bacon*, PAT HUTCHINS. New York: Greenwillow Books, 1976. A grocery list—six farm eggs, a cake for tea, a pound of pears, and don't forget the bacon—turns

Sequence cards based on a poem or story make a game of reading aloud.

into nonsense as a little girl struggles to remember each item. In the end she forgets the bacon!

O *Encyclopedia Brown's Record Book of Weird and Wonderful Facts*, DONALD J. SOBOL. New York: Dell Publishing/Delacorte Press, 1979. The facts and information in this book are frequently tied together so that many parts read like a script. There is ample opportunity for several games from this collection. Students can even create their own skits from this material. (See also *Encyclopedia Brown's Book of Wacky Animals*, 1985, as well as other sequels.)

Y–M *A Flea Story*, LEO LIONNI. New York: Pantheon Books, 1977. Two fleas on a dog decide to go on an adventure. The book consists of the two fleas' dialogue with each other. Try it as a shadow drama.

M *Fortunately*, REMY CHARLIP. New York: Parents' Magazine Press, 1964. For each unfortunate happening, a fortunate one follows.

M *The Green Machine*, POLLY CAMERON. New York: Coward-McCann, 1969. A reckless automobile creates havoc along country gardens. You will probably want to shorten this lengthy story.

M–O "Grey Goose," Traditional (37). This is the story of a gray goose who is too tough to be killed and eaten. Twenty-five lines can be done, one to a card, with the chorus of "Lawd, lawd, lawd" said by everyone after each line. You can also add pantomime for even more fun.

M–O *Hello, Mr. Chips!* ANN BISHOP. New York: E.P. Dutton, 1982. A fun and informative look at the world of computers by way of jokes and riddles.

M–O *Hush Up!* JIM AYLESWORTH. New York: Holt, Rinehart and Winston, 1980. Everyone in Talula County is taking a nap on a hot day until a nasty horsefly lands on mule's nose and creates a domino effect of trouble. It is fun to do the mime with this one also.

M *"I Can't," Said the Ant*, POLLY CAMERON. New York: Coward-McCann, 1961. A broken teapot creates a problem for the various inhabitants of the kitchen to solve. This one is also rather lengthy and will probably need to be shortened.

Y *I Don't Want to Go to School*, ELIZABETH BRAM. New York: William Morrow, 1977. A little girl is reluctant to go to her first day of kindergarten.

Y–M *If You Give a Mouse a Cookie*, LAURE JOFFE NUMEROFF. New York: Harper & Row, 1985. Once you give a mouse a cookie, he will want one thing after another until we are back to the beginning. You can add "And you know what happens if you give a mouse a cookie," and play the story all over again. Try this also as a paired narrative pantomime.

M *Jimmy's Boa Bounces Back*, TRINKA HAKES NOBLE, New York: E.P. Dutton, 1984. This time the boa attends a garden party. This is a sequel to *The Day Jimmy's Boa Ate the Wash*. If you add pantomime to this, you can end with a frozen picture the way the book does.

M–O *Jokes to Tell Your Worst Enemy*, SCOTT CORBETT. New York: E.P. Dutton, 1984. There is much here to choose from—a mixture of jokes, short stories, poems, and so forth. You can mix and match or focus on one subject—such as the sections entitled "History Rewritten Mother's Way" (for example, Paul Revere's mother will not let him go out at night for his famous midnight ride).

M–O *The Judge*, HARVE ZEMACH. New York: Farrar, Straus & Giroux, 1969. This is a comical story of various prisoners warning a judge of a horrible monster coming their way. *Suggestion:* Add "Hear ye! Hear ye! The court is now in session" and "Here comes the Judge" (the latter repeated three times) at the beginning. At the end pantomime the monster (three students linked together) eating the judge with the line "There goes the Judge" repeated three times.

M–O *The Last Cow on the White House Lawn and Other Little-Known Facts about the Presidency*, BARBARA SEULING. New York: Doubleday, 1978. This is a fascinating book of trivial (and not so trivial) information. Let students try their hand at creating their own script for this one.

M–O *"Let's Marry," Said the Cherry*, N.M. BODECKER. New York: Atheneum, 1974. A poem tells, in short, rhymed couplets, the wedding plans for the cherry and the pea.

M *Magic Letter Riddles*, MIKE THALER. New York: Scholastic Book Services, 1974. By adding and subtracting letters in words, you can find the answers to these riddles.

M–O "The Meehoo with an Exactlywatt," SHEL SILVERSTEIN (24). This is a combination of a knock-knock joke and the old Abbott and Costello "Who's on first?" routine—with repetitive possibilities as well.

Y–M *My Mom Travels a Lot*, CAROLINE FELLER BAUER. New York: Frederick Warne, 1981. A little girl lists the good and the bad conditions that result from her mother's travels.

Y–M "One Inch Tall," SHEL SILVERSTEIN (53). What is it like to be one inch tall? This poem, which is also good for math concepts, gives the answer.

M "One Two," SHEL SILVERSTEIN (24). This is a short parody on an old nursery rhyme.

Y *One Was Johnny*, MAURICE SENDAK. New York: Harper & Row, 1962. This forward and backward counting rhyme gives some actions to add for extra fun.

M *The Pain and the Great One*, JUDY BLUME. New York: Dell Yearling Books, 1985. An older sister and younger brother share their jealous feelings about each other.

M–O "Peter Perfect, The Story of a Perfect Boy," BERNARD WABER (30). This is a story comprised of various people's comments about a boy who, we find out at the end, does not exist at all.

M *Pierre: A Cautionary Tale*, MAURICE SENDAK. New York: Harper & Row, 1962. A little boy who always says "I don't care." decides to care when a lion eats him. Try having one person play Pierre (with complete script if needed) to say the "I don't care" lines.

Y–M *The Popcorn Book*, TOMIE DE PAOLA. New York: Holiday House, 1978. Children make popcorn while reading facts about it. Intersperse the popcorn maker's comments with the facts being read, just as the book does.

Y–M *Rain Makes Applesauce*, JULIAN SCHEER. New York: Holiday House, 1964. This is a collection of absurd but delightful statements that are fun to say in as many different ways as possible. The refrain "Oh you're just talking silly talk!" can be said by all on a cue.

M *The Sheriff of Rottenshot,* JACK PRELUTSKY. New York: Greenwillow Books, 1982. Almost all the poems in this collection are useful for sequence games and reading aloud.

M "Sick," SHEL SILVERSTEIN (53). Little Peggy Ann McKay complains of being too ill to go to school—until she discovers it is Saturday.

M *Squeeze a Sneeze,* BILL MORRISON. Boston: Houghton Mifflin, 1977. This is a rhyming game of nonsense sayings, such as "Can you tickle a pickle for a nickel?"

M–O *The Star-Spangled Banana and Other Revolutionary Riddles,* compiled by CHARLES KELLER and RICHARD BAKER. Englewood Cliffs, N.J.: Prentice-Hall, 1974. A collection of puns, word plays, and riddles based on American historical data.

M *Tyrannosaurus Wrecks,* NOELLE STERNE. New York: Thomas Y. Crowell, 1979. This collection of dinosaur riddles is good material for word study.

Y–M *What Do You Do, Dear?* SESYLE JOSLIN. Reading, Mass.: Addison-Wesley, 1961. This is a book of manners for very unusual occasions. The situations are fun to pantomime, too.

Y–M *What Do You Say, Dear?* SESYLE Joslin. Reading, Mass.: Addison-Wesley, 1958. This book gives the obviously socially correct thing to say in very strange situations.

M–O *What If . . .?* JOSEPH LOW. Hartford, Conn.: Connecticut Printers, 1976. Unusual questions receive amusing answers.

M–O "Whatif," SHEL SILVERSTEIN (24). A child speculates on all the horrible things that can happen to a kid. It is amusing, but has undercurrents of seriousness.

O *What's a Frank Frank?: Tasty Homograph Riddles,* GIULIO MAESTRO. New York: Clarion Books, 1984. This collection of homographs (two words spelled the same way but with different meanings) provides material for a fun language-arts lesson.

M *Where in the World Is Henry?* LORNA BALIAN. Nashville: Abingdon Press, 1972. In this question-and-answer game, a mother and child cover an interesting geography lesson ("Where is the city?" "The city is in the state," and so on).

Y–M *Where's My Cheese?* STAN MACK. New York: Random House, 1977. A story about a piece of cheese that travels from one person to another is told in simple dialogue.

Y–M *Who, Said Sue, Said Whoo?* ELLEN RASKIN. New York: Atheneum, 1973. The moral of this story is "Words aren't everything!" Good sound effects accompany this one.

M–O *Yuck!* JAMES STEVENSON. New York: Greenwillow Books, 1984. Two witches cook up potions but say Emma is too young to join them. With the help of her animal friends, she succeeds. Cartoon drawings have dialogue "balloons." You can add pantomime to this one.

Original Sequence Games

After trying some of the preceding materials, you will soon find many of your own sources for sequence games; you may even be inspired to make up your own. Students, too, will want to give it a try. Perhaps small groups of students can prepare games for the rest of the class to play. And the possibilities for incorporating other areas of the curriculum are numerous. Jokes and riddles work nicely. If you use the answers in place of cues, students will be encouraged to think through the answer to the riddles they hear in order to see if their card is the next in the sequence.

You can review famous statements from literature, history, or other sources in a sequence game:

CARD 1: You begin: "I cannot tell a lie."

CARD 2: (Answer) George Washington. "Give me liberty or give me death."

CARD 3:   (Answer) Patrick Henry. "We have not yet begun to fight!" (and so forth)

Or after a study of mythology:

CARD 1:   You begin: "If Athena can weave better than I, let her come and try."
CARD 2:   (Answer) Arachne. "I knew I should have used a superglue instead of wax!"
CARD 3:   (Answer) Icarus. "The only man I'll marry is the one who can outrun me." (and so forth)

The following extended example is from a sixth-grade social studies lesson on exploration in the New World.

1.   You begin the game. Stand and say, "The time is the late 1400s. The place is Europe. Curtain going up!" Sit.
2.   You stand, walk around the circle, and call out, "For sale, for sale, our latest shipment of spices, silks, perfumes, and gems! For sale, directly from the Indies. Come and get it while it lasts!" Return to your seat.
3.   You stand and say (shaking your head sadly), "Too bad we can't have more." Sit.
4.   You jump up and say excitedly, "Ah, but we could if we had a sailing route to the Indies." Sit.
5.   You stand, clap your hands as if you're trying to get someone's attention, and say, "Children—recite today's geography lesson." After two people recite, you sit.
6, 7.   (two cards) You and another person will stand and recite together: "Roses are red, violets are blue. The earth is flat, and that's the truth." Then bow and sit.
8.   You stand and say slowly, "Very interesting." Sit down slowly.
9.   You stand and say, "But not true!" Sit.
10.   You stand and say, "And it doesn't even rhyme." Sit.
11.   You stand and say, "Mama mia, have I got an idea! I'll go west (point one way) to get to the east" (point the other way). (Wait to sit down until someone says, "Noooo!")
12, 13.   (two cards) You stay seated and yell, "Noooo!"
14.   You stand and say, "Everybody knows the earth's flat as a pancake. And if you go too far, horrible sea monsters will get you." Then pretend to be a sea monster, growling and showing claws and teeth. Sit.
15.   You walk slowly around the circle, pretending to be very tired and say, "Poor Columbus left Italy and finally went to Spain—to King Ferdinand and Queen Isabella. They gave him three ships and a crew." Return to your seat.
16.   You stand and rock back and forth on your feet and chant, "Sailing, sailing, over the ocean blue. And when we arrive—if we get there alive—it'll be 1492." Sit.
17.   You stand, look around, put your hand up to your forehead as if you are shading your eyes and shout, "Land ho!" Sit.

18. You stand, pretend to be near death, and gasp out the words, "Thank goodness, I thought we'd never make it." Then stagger and fall down.

19. You stand, pretend to plant a flag in the soil, and say, "I name this island San Salvador and claim it for the king and queen of Spain." Sit.

20, 21. (two cards) You stay seated and cheer, whistle, clap hands, etc. (There will be two of you doing this.)

22. You stand and say, "Columbus and his crew stopped at other islands in the Caribbean Sea also." Sit.

23. You stand and say, "What do you know? We're the first ones to ever take a Caribbean cruise! Think I'll go for a swim." Then pretend to dive into water. Sit.

24. You stand and say in a big, deep voice, "I have named this island Hispaniola, and on it I have built a fort. Guard it well, men! I'm going back home." Then walk around the circle and sit back down.

25, 26. (two cards) You stand, salute, and say, "Aye, aye, sir." Sit. (Two of you will do this.)

27. You stand and say, "Now it's 1513 and I'm Balboa. I have crossed the Isthmus of Panama, and I claim this body of water for Spain. I name it the Pacific Ocean—meaning peaceful (Yawn)—boy, it sure is . . . (then lie down and fall asleep and snore once).

28. You stand, pretend to ride a horse around the circle, and then say, "I'm Cortés. I've spent the last four years conquering Mexico in the name of Spain." Sit.

29. You stand and say, "The year is 1532. Pizarro's the name, and exploring's my game." Then say in a loud whisper, "Listen! I've heard that there's lots of gold and silver down in South America. The king of Spain has agreed to help me get it. What do you say?" After De Soto shakes your hand, you sit.

30. You stand, go over to Pizarro, shake his hand, and say, "The name's De Soto. I think we'd make a good team." Then return to your seat.

31. You stand and march to the center of the circle, and announce in a big voice, "They marched toward the heart of the Inca empire." Then return to your seat.

32. You stand and say in a frightened voice, "Who are these men who steal from us?" Sit.

33. You stand and yell, "Our towns are burning! Run for your lives!" Then pretend to be hit and fall dead.

34. You stand and say, "The emperor will save us!" Then pretend to be hit and fall dead.

35. You stand and raise your hands up as if asking for silence and calm, and say slowly and in a big voice, "I am the emperor. I am God. I have thirty thousand soldiers, and the Spaniards have only a few men. Why is everyone so afraid?" Then fold your arms across your chest and sit down slowly.

36. You stand, cup your hands to your mouth, and call to the emperor, "Hey, Emperor! How about dinner at our place?" Then turn your head and laugh behind your hand. Sit.

37. You stand and announce, "And so the emperor and five thousand unarmed Inca warriors went to a feast. The emperor came in a golden chair carried by slaves. The warriors were killed by the Spaniards." Sit.

38. You stand and shout angrily, "Why do you do this terrible thing?" Sit.

39. You stand and shout, "Gold! We want gold!" Sit.
40. You stand and say, "I will have this room filled with gold if you will let me go free." Remain standing until you hear someone say "What do we do now? Kill him." Then fall dead—but do it in slow motion.
41. You stand and say, "Gold and silver came from all parts of the Inca empire. At first the Spaniards were glad. Then they worried about what to do with the emperor." Sit.
42. You stand and say in a loud whisper, "What do we do now?" Sit.
43. You stand and say very seriously, "Kill him." Sit slowly.
44. You stand and say, "Thus ends a sad chapter in history. Land and wealth gained but at the cost of human suffering. Curtain going down!" (music)

BEGINNING IMPROVISATION

In creative drama, dialogue is usually played *improvisationally*. This means that is is created spontaneously, on the spot, as the students respond to the dramatic situations they are involved in. Improvisation is more natural than the memorization of "canned" speeches, and it is an excellent exercise in learning to "think on one's feet." The spontaneity of improvisation captures everyone's attention—even the players themselves. No one knows exactly what will be said, but you do know that it will evolve from a "real" person rather than from a printed script.

As you work toward the goal of encouraging improvisation of dialogue, you will need increasingly more challenging activities. In this next section the activities will build progressively from simple responses to those requiring more extensive improvisation.

One-Liners

It is often easiest to begin with one-liners, since students need to say or create only one line of speech. Several kinds of activities can serve this purpose.

Familiar One-liners

1. Make a list of familiar one-line statements. Many of these are famous because of *how* they have been said, and children enjoy imitating them.
2. The lines can be placed on cards and distributed as in the sequence game. You may want to identify or paste a picture of the speaker on the card also.
3. You may want to arrange the cards so that they seem to relate to each other. *Examples:* "Who's been sleeping in my bed?" (Papa Bear) "It is I, Big Billy Goat Gruff." "Let's get Mikey!" (Life cereal commercial) "Sit on it!" (the Fonz) "I'll huff and I'll puff and I'll blow your house down!" (the wolf) "COOKIE!" (*Sesame Street's* Cookie Monster) "E. T. phone home." (*E.T.*)

One-liners with Pictures

1. Keep a file of pictures of people or animals in interesting poses or situations, or exhibiting unusual feelings. Pictures should be large enough for everyone to see easily. Large ads from magazines, calendar pictures, and posters work well for this activity.
2. Show pictures to the students and ask them what they think the person might be saying.
3. They pretend to be the person in the picture, saying the statement the way they think the person or animal might say it.

One-liners with Props

1. Interesting props can also stimulate one-liners. The comedian Jonathan Winters (later imitated by Robin Williams) became famous with his ability to create imaginative comments when browsing through an old attic or a trunk of interesting and unusual cast-off clothing (for example, hats, shawls, and spectacles) or other items (for example, a hula hoop, a caulking gun, or a perfume atomizer).
2. Borrowing this technique, students can select a prop, then demonstrate a use for it while saying an appropriate one-liner.
   Example: A folding yardstick can be shaped into several things: (a) a fishing pole, (b) the letter Z, or (c) a triangle. One-liners that can accompany these uses might be
   (a) "Shucks, been here over three hours and haven't had a nibble."
   (b) (holding letter against chest) "Coach, I'm gonna get in there and win the game for old Zorro U."
   (c) (holding triangle around face as a picture frame) "The family doesn't know it, but I can see everything that goes on around here!"

Ad Talks

1. Intriguing lines can be found flipping through magazines. Some interesting examples include: "Amazing!" "I don't believe it." "Yeah, but station wagons are so dull." "Thank you, honey." "How good is the bologna in that sandwich?" "It's better in the Bahamas." "Is your house being watched?"
2. These are placed on cards and then used in a variety of ways such as the following:
   a. Distribute the cards randomly. Students may read them in any order, pretending that they make sense or have some logic. Try using different voices with them also: computer or robot, witch, politician, and so on.
   b. Distribute a number of cards to each player. One person begins, and others choose from their "dialogue packet" and respond. (Whoever stands first gets to say his or her line.) Mixing an equal number of questions and answers can produce interesting results. (Example: "Looking for a new place to go to?" "You never know who you'll meet at an army reserve meeting.")
   c. Distribute alphabetized cards randomly. Then follow the alphabet to find the next statement. ("*Announcing* something you may not want to hear!"

"This case calls for some super detective work!"
(one-liners with props)

"*Be* cool." "*Can* you really manage without money?" "*Decide* for yourself."
"*Exactly!*") This is more fun if children have several cards to choose from.

d. Other kinds of one-liners might be historical slogans such as "54-40 or
Fight!" or "Tippecanoe and Tyler, Too!" Interesting book titles are another possibility. Students can make their own lists and mix and match in
whatever creative ways they wish.

Storytelling

Storytelling is an excellent verbal activity to help students imagine and
create plots. It also encourages the building of details, plot prediction, and
the making of inferences.

Students may build group short stories using the round-robin technique, with volunteers adding another line to the story. If you go around
the circle, you may prefer to let children say "Pass" if they cannot think of
an idea to add. Be prepared to participate yourself and to keep the story
interesting.

When ideas flow freely and students are comfortable with storytelling, you may need to set limits on each one's contribution. Using an egg
timer or a bell can make it into a game. A ball of knotted yarn is another
intriguing way to conduct storytelling. As the "yarn is spun" the ball is
unraveled. When the knot is reached, the ball is passed to another student.

Statements clipped from a variety of sources and placed on cards provide
good material for the "Ad Talks" games.

Older or advanced students will like the idea of being stopped in mid-sentence, which forces the next storyteller to end the thought. This technique also challenges them to listen closer and to mesh their creative thinking with that of another person.

Storytelling with wordless picture books.　One of the easiest ways to begin storytelling is to use wordless picture books which have no text but tell a story in pictures. Children interpret what they see happening in the pictures, using their own words and sometimes even adding dialogue.

Not all wordless picture books tell a story, so choose carefully. You may also need an opaque projector to enlarge the pictures in smaller books.

Some favorite examples follow. (*Note:* Age levels are indicated at the beginning of each entry. Numbers in parentheses refer to numbered anthologies listed in the bibliography at the end of this book.)

M–O *Arthur's Adventures in the Abandoned House,* FERNANDO KRAHN. New York: E.P. Dutton, 1981. Arthur explores an abandoned house and captures some crooks in an ingenious way.

Y–M *The Bear and the Fly,* PAULA WINTER. New York: Crown Publishers, 1976. A bear family has difficulty getting rid of a pesky fly. Humorous violence occurs as the bears swat each other and the fly escapes.

Y–M *Changes, Changes,* PAT HUTCHINS. New York: Macmillan, 1971. A wooden man and woman create needed objects out of miscellaneous wood pieces to solve the many difficulties they run into. Also available on film from Weston Woods.

Y–M *The Chicken's Child,* MARGARET A. HARTELIUS. New York: Doubleday, 1975. A chicken hatches an alligator egg and adopts it as her child. The alligator is chased away by the farmer after eating everything in sight, but redeems himself in the end when he saves the chicken from a fox.

Y *Clementine's Cactus,* EZRA JACK KEATS. New York: Viking Penguin, 1982. A little girl waits patiently for a desert cactus to bloom and is finally rewarded.

M–O *The Damp and Daffy Doings of a Daring Pirate Ship,* GUILLERMO MORDILLO. New York:

Harlan Quist, 1971. Pirates encounter one obstacle after another in seeking treasure. But they are undaunted, and as the book ends, they are building a new ship after their old one sinks.

Y *Deep in the Forest*, BRINTON TURKLE. New York: E.P. Dutton, 1976. Like Goldilocks, a curious bear cub visits a cabin in the woods and finds porridge, chairs, and beds to try. This one is a must for all Three Bears lovers.

M–O *The Gray Lady and the Strawberry Snatcher*, MOLLY BANG. New York: Four Winds Press, 1980. The gray lady runs from a strawberry thief until, in the heart of the forest, he discovers blackberries.

M–O *How Santa Claus Had a Long and Difficult Journey Delivering His Presents*, FERNANDO KRAHN. New York: Dell Publishing/Delacorte Press, 1970. Droll-looking "angels" come to Santa's rescue in this tale.

O *The Inspector*, GEORGE MENDOZA. New York: Doubleday, 1970. An inspector does not notice the dangers surrounding him. His dog attacks each and slowly turns into a monster himself. This one is gory if you are squeamish, but most students will love it.

M–O *Journey to the Moon*, ERICH FUCHS. New York: Dell Publishing/Delacorte Press, 1969. This documents the original eight-day mission to the moon in 1969, indicating what occurred each day. Text is separate from the pictures so that students can check their accuracy.

Y *Lily at the Table*, LINDA HELLER. New York: Macmillan, 1979. Lily has a problem with seven green beans, a chicken leg, and sliced potatoes—until she creates new uses for each of these and more in a fantasy world of food.

O *The Package*, LAURIE ANDERSON. Indianapolis: Bobbs-Merrill, 1971. A package goes from one intriguing person to another. The focus is on characterization and motivation.

Y *Rolling Downhill*, RUTH CARROLL. Silver Spring, Md.: Henry Z. Walck, 1973. A cat who knocks over a sewing basket and becomes entangled in yarn with a dog has quite an adventure with a series of other animals before getting out of her dilemma.

M–O *The Silver Pony*, LYND WARD. Boston: Houghton Mifflin, 1973. A young farm boy is taken on an adventure to various parts of the world and even a journey to the stars before returning to reality and receiving the gift of a real pony. Extensive drawings tell this story.

Y *What Whiskers Did*, RUTH CARROLL. Silver Spring, Md.: Henry Z. Walck, 1965. A poodle puppy has an adventure chasing a rabbit down a hole.

Y–M *Who's Seen the Scissors?* FERNANDO KRAHN. New York: E.P. Dutton, 1975. A tailor has scissors that fly away from him and set off on a cutting adventure through the town.

Y–M *The Wrong Side of the Bed*, EDWARD ARDIZZONE. New York: Doubleday, 1970. A young boy's day goes from bad to worse when he has problems with both family and older children.

Storytelling with Pictures

1. Single pictures (or even a series) of interesting people or animals involved in unusual situations can also stimulate storytelling.

2. At first you may need to start out the story with a rousing or imaginative beginning to get creative juices flowing. (Picture of a man all bandaged up: "This is Melvin Q. Batts. Nothing ever goes right for poor Melvin. One day . . .") You may also need to introduce the conflict and help students focus on the story's conclusion.

3. As a variation, use several pictures with a related theme or setting. After beginning the story with one picture, add other pictures to stimulate the continued storytelling.

Storytelling in Character

Once children are accustomed to creating stories, another dramatic dimension can be added. They can pretend to be characters, with appropriate character voices, gestures, and attitudes, doing the telling.

1. There are many literary sources that show storytellers in action. For example, in the story *Frederick*, by Leo Lionni (New York: Pantheon Books, 1967), the little poet-mouse tells stories to help his friends and relatives forget their hunger. What sort of stories would a little mouse tell to entertain an audience of mice? And how might he sound with his small, squeaking voice? Pa Ingalls entertains his children with short adventures from his past in Laura Ingalls Wilder's series of Little House books.

2. There are also possibilities for storytelling in other areas of the curriculum. Some student teachers were doing a lesson on cowboys in a second grade. They all gathered in one corner on a rug with the lights dimmed, pretending to be around the campfire at night, telling stories about their day's activities. Three children were given the role of "Chuckwagon Charlie," who periodically gave the listeners some "bowls of stew" to eat quietly while the storytellers entertained them. Other examples: Indians of long ago telling myths or stories around a campfire; soldiers relating harrowing escapes in war campaigns; or pioneers telling of hardships as well as happy times in moving West.

3. For yet another variation, select pictures, newspaper articles, or facts from the *Guinness Book of Records* and have students tell the story as if they were the person involved. ("You want to know my recipe for the hottest chili this side of the Rio Grande? Well, it goes something like this. . . .")

More Storytelling Variations

1. "What's Happening Here?" Use interesting and colorful pictures with people or animals involved in unusual situations or even conflicts. The picture may show the middle of the story, but how did the story begin? How will it end? Children may even wish to tell the story from the point of view of one of the characters.

2. "What's the Word?" When students show skill in storytelling, they may wish further challenges. Try telling stories using new vocabulary words, spelling words, foreign words, and so forth.

3. "Math Manipulations." Tell stories using mathematical operations from simple counting ("**One** day, Big Bird decided to take a walk. **Two** monkeys decided to go along. Suddenly **three** friends yelled, 'Help!'") to other calculations, such as multiplication by 2. ("Once there were **two** kings who lived in neighboring countries. They each had **four** daughters. For **six** years everything was fine. The **eight** princesses were good friends, but the kings were jealous of each other.)

4. "Alphabet Story." Tell a story with each sentence beginning with a letter of the alphabet in sequence. ("**A** story about a cat. **B**oy, was he an ornery cat. **C**ats are often ornery, but this one was especially bad.")

5. "What's that Sound?" Tell a story suggested by a series of sounds. (Open a desk drawer, shut a door, and scream.) What story does that suggest? Or start with one sound to begin the story and continue the story suggested by each added sound.

6. "Skeleton Stories." Make up stories using the skeletal framework of props, characters, or settings to stimulate ideas. Motivation will be enhanced if you have the props on hand along with pictures of the characters and settings:
Props: a key, a piece of jewelry, and a telephone
Characters: a pirate, a king, and a clown
Settings: haunted house, castle, courtroom
Experiment with combining the categories, too. There are endless possibilities for this one. They can also be played as Random Skits (p. 206).

Verbal Games

Games in which children pretend to be other characters set in verbal situations are useful for stimulating dialogue. These games are easy to organize and can involve the entire class. The goal is to explore dialogue and to search for information and ideas. General instructions are:

1. Groups of five to eight students take turns being panel members. The rest of the students are audience-questioners.

2. You serve as the moderator-host. In initial attempts and with younger children, you may need to help with the questioning until students become more adept. You may wish to have some questions for students to ask written out on cards.

3. To encourage role playing and help students relax and get into the spirit, props or simple costume pieces may be employed, such as badges, headbands, hats, or other indications of status or role.

Experts

1. Panel members are declared to be experts on a subject. Some examples might be Santa Claus's elves answering questions on how they make certain toys; tooth fairies explaining how children's teeth are collected and used; owners and trainers of fleas for a flea circus; people who knit small socks for birds; or people who have ridden in an alien spaceship. The purpose of giving students expertise is to allow them the security to give their opinions freely. After all, *they* are the experts. Bizarre topics also aid self-confidence, since there is no precedent to follow.

2. Try to give roles to everyone in the class. While the experts talk about their socks for birds, for example, the audience might be people interested in opening their own franchise. Newspaper reporters could question the spaceship riders, and pet owners might be those most interested in pet condominiums.

Juvenile Jury

1. As a variation of an old radio and television show, this game features a panel of children who give advice on particular problems.

2. The audience poses certain questions or situations, such as "My little brother always wants to play with my toys and I don't want him to." Such problems can sometimes be more easily solved by peers than by adults trying to impose rules. Children frequently repeat advice they have heard from adults, but it sounds more acceptable when a peer gives it.

3. Advisers will love wearing simple robes (like judges or professors).

Trinkets such as these can stimulate ideas for the Experts game: knitters of miniature leg warmers for birds; inventors of homes for insects; designers of hats for fairies; barbers who specialize in the troll trade.

To Tell the Truth

1. As a variation of another television show, a panel of three (or more) children pose as a particular famous person who may be living (current events), historical (social studies), or fictional (literature). Children might also play inanimate objects, such as a particular food, means of transportation, invention, and so forth.
2. All the panel members must research the character, but one is designated the true character and must give accurate answers to the best of his or her ability. Other panel members are allowed to give inaccurate answers.
3. The audience poses questions to determine who the character is. Questions may be limited to twenty, or a time period may be imposed.

What's My Line?

1. This game, based on a classic television show, can be useful for a unit in career education. It features a panel who have an occupation which the audience tries to guess within twenty questions. Panel members all have the same occupation and take turns answering the questions. Only yes or no answers are allowed; an occasional maybe is permitted.
2. A questioner may continue to question the panel until receiving a no answer.
3. As a variation use occupations of the future (flight attendant on a space ship) or occupations of the past (town crier, court jester, stagecoach driver).

Liars' Club

1. This television game show operates on the premise that the panelists know the true use of a particular object. Actually, only one panelist has been told what the object is; the others must create believable explanations.

2. For the classroom, instead of a panel, volunteers may present their explanations. No one is told the actual use of the object until the game is over. In the spirit of fun rather than competition, a vote might be taken on the most believable explanation before the object's true identity and use are told.

3. Objects for discussion may be antiques or unusual or new products on the market. Some suggestions are an eyelash curler, rug beater, Chinese yo-yo, braille stencil, knitting stitch holder, candle snuffer, vegetable steamer, and staple remover. Some students may know what some of the objects are already. They may either give the real explanation or still choose to make up a plausible one.

4. For other curricular emphasis, children might pretend to be archaeologists trying to identify how the object was used by a particular culture they have been studying. Or they may be museum directors who must determine the true identity of an object in order to label it appropriately for a museum display.

Variation: "Language Liar's Club" can be played by guessing definitions of words. A panel offers their definitions, with only one person knowing the correct one. Suggested words are épée, turgid, neologist, brouhaha, sacrosanct, lugubrious, oleaginous.

I've Got a Secret

1. Again, borrowing from television's past, this game can easily be adapted for classroom use. Several on a panel share a secret for the audience to guess.

2. Panel may answer only yes or no. Limit to twenty questions.

Examples:

Category: Fictional character from Mother Goose. "This secret involves something this person did while dressed in a certain way." (Wee Willie Winkie—ran through town in his nightgown)
Category: Historical character. "This secret involves a message this person delivered. What was the message?" ("One if by land and two if by sea," Paul Revere) Or "This secret involves something this person had that was made of wood." (George Washington's false teeth)

Character Panel Discussion I

1. This activity has many variations. Panel members are given roles to play, or they may establish their own, usually with varying viewpoints.

2. The audience, who play either themselves or a character role, question the panelists. (If audience members play a role, they should identify themselves before asking their questions.)

3. The goal of the game is to seek information and ideas. Final decisions are not necessary. The following suggestions are only some of the many possibilities:

a. A panel of characters in a given story may be questioned by the audience as to their actions and motivations for behaviors not detailed in the stories. This gives all the children the chance to probe characters' lives and personalities further. For example, the panel might all be Goldilocks. The audience ask whatever questions they wish: "Did you like being in the bears'

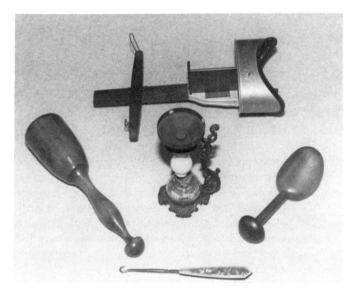

Props for "Liar's Club" (clockwise): stereoscope, darning egg, button hook, wooden potato masher, and (center) antique vaporizer.

house?" "Did your mother spank you when you got home?" "What were you doing in the woods all by yourself?" Or Sleeping Beauty might be questioned about what it was like to be asleep for so long: "Were you glad when the prince woke you up? Is he the prince you would have chosen?" The thirteenth fairy might be asked, "Why were you so upset about not being invited to the christening?" "Why did you wish the princess to be killed—and by a spinning wheel?"

b. The panel may be comprised of several of the main characters in a story such as *A Wrinkle in Time* (130). Questions might be asked of the children about their adventures. Or you might choose to focus on Mrs. Who, Mrs. Which, and Mrs. Whatsit.

c. Panel members may be characters who have a common trait or behavior. Perhaps they are characters who have interesting or troubling adventures like Tom Sawyer, Harriet the Spy, Pippi Longstocking, or Henry Huggins. Consider also mythological characters, presidents, inventors, or explorers, and the questions that might be asked of them (for example, presidents who held office during wartime: "What was your biggest concern about the war during your administration?" "If you had it to do over, what would you do differently?").

d. Discussions could also take the form of a guessing game. Assign roles or identities to the panelists in secret. They answer questions anonymously for a given time period. By the kind of answers they give and the way they speak and conduct themselves, the audience guesses who they are.

IMPROVISING EXTENDED DIALOGUE

Thus far, all the verbal activities have been fairly simple. Most of the dialogue interaction has mainly involved limited verbalizing, storytelling, and posing questions and giving answers in the verbal games. There are many other dialogue situations you can set up for children to improvise dialogue at length. Older and advanced children will even be able to develop stories and skits in groups. This section will cover some of the materials and methods you can use in helping children improvise extended dialogue.

Sources for Dialogue Materials

There are many sources for dialogue materials. Some may come from literature, such as the verbal guessing game between Rumpelstiltskin and the queen when she reveals his secret name, or Toad's fast talk in *Wind in the Willows* (126) as he tries to get himself out of trouble spots. Some literature totally revolves around dialogue scenes. For example, in the story *Not This Bear!* by Bernice Myers (New York: Four Winds Press, 1967), a little boy in a furry coat and hat has to convince a family of bears—who are sure he is one of their relatives—that he is a boy and not a bear. A poem like "Univac to Univac" (42) suggests that computers, when they are alone with each other, gossip about humans' limitations.

Dialogue scenes may also be based on a variety of curricular topics and improvised out of the imagination and resourcefulness of the leader and the children. For example, scenes of buying and selling (social studies emphasis) can be added to *Caps for Sale* (p. 120) or *The Elves and the Shoemaker* (p. 267). The Thanksgiving season prompted one group of second graders to be desperate turkeys trying to talk hungry Pilgrims with muskets out of eating them for dinner! Imagine the dialogue scene that may have taken place when Governor John Winthrop had to convince the doubting people of Massachusetts that the water in the New World was pure enough to drink. Consider also the discussions and arguments that precede many policy decisions of governments and other legislative bodies. Or in science there are the many inventors and discoverers who have had to explain, and sometimes persuade others of, their viewpoints in order to get financial assistance or acceptance of their ideas. Virtually every area of the curriculum has topics that can be explored through dialogue activities.

The Leader's Role in Facilitating Dialogue

Improvised dialogue is often most easily generated and most dramatic when there are problems to be solved or when conflict is present. Problems require discussion; conflict encourages further explanation of different sides of an issue. Therefore, you will usually get more participation and deeper involvement from students if you focus on topics where problems and conflict exist.

Some children can improvise dialogue readily and with little difficulty. They may be verbally sophisticated, or they may have progressed to a point where they are ready to experiment with improvisation. Some children need a great deal of help and guidance. Your own participation in the scenes may be crucial to success in dialogue work.

The leader as moderator/mediator. As in the verbal games on pp. 188–91, you can facilitate in improvisation by playing a moderating or mediating role. This role is a neutral one which encourages players to consider relevant questions in examining their situations or solving their problems. At times, the mediating role is a specific character.

It is not always necessary to bring a discussion or debate to a final close. The airing of views is initially the most important goal. To this end, it is important to let students interchange roles frequently to permit them to see the various sides of an issue. To achieve this, you can replay and recast scenes many times. You can even stop a scene in the middle and let new players enter and continue.

When a conflict is resolved or a compromise is reached, the discussion is usually ended. This sometimes happens unexpectedly. If tension is high and you feel no conclusion is being reached, you may want to let the class take a "straw vote" to give children the opportunity to indicate their feelings of the moment. If you or the students want to conclude or settle upon some decision, it is helpful to present this goal in your instructions: "Try to find an answer to your problem." Although not all students will be able to do it, problem solving will be a challenge worth adding. A unique and unexpected compromise often comes out of these discussions, and that can be a great source of satisfaction for everyone.

Simple Debate: Method I

1. Divide the class in half, and present each with an opposite viewpoint to uphold. You can easily play this at the desks, which simplifies organization.
2. You play the moderator or mediator.
   With this format you can use a number of situations. Some suggestions follow.
   a. *opposites game:* One side makes all the positive statements they can think of, while the other half responds with negative ones. Ideas can be called out by volunteers on either side of the room alternately. The statements may be made in response to each other or simply presented randomly. For example:

Yes.	No.
It's a beautiful day.	There's rain in the forecast.
Ice cream.	Spinach.
Vacation.	Schoolwork.
I love to watch television.	The set's broken.

   b. *literature example:* In Roald Dahl's *Charlie and the Chocolate Factory* (69), Willy Wonka has difficulties with several children. One little girl, Violet, swells up like a blueberry and turns purple after disobeying orders not to chew the experimental gum. The Oompa-Loompas, or factory workers, have to take her away to the juicing room. Willy, the owner of the factory, is upset with Violet for disobeying his rules, but he would like to have her problem solved, too.

   Although Violet really has no choices given to her in the book, you can use the situation for a simple debate with half the class being Oompa-Loompas trying to convince the other half of the class, who play Violet, that being juiced is her only option. Violet argues for other solutions.

You, playing Willy, can call on those who have ideas to express. You may also pose questions to each side, if this assistance seems helpful. ("What will happen to Violet in the juicing room?" "What sorts of machines and equipment do you have in there?" "Violet, why did you disobey the orders?" "Has this ever happened to you before?")

  c. *social studies example:* A similar arbitration scene might be played between the Pilgrims and the crew of the *Mayflower*, based on information in Wilma Hays's book (71). Captain Jones wants to help the Pilgrims get settled before leaving them to fend for themselves in a new country. But he is also worried about his crew. They are anxious to get home because it is December and the sailing will be difficult. Each day the crew members become more hostile. Both the crew and the captain had wanted to be home for Christmas, but now it is impossible.

  One half of the class plays the Pilgrims; the other half plays the ship's crew. You can play Captain Jones and moderate the two sides of the argument, encouraging a discussion of the various reasons for going or for staying.

Simple Debate: Method II

1. Present an idea to the class for the scene. (You can use the preceding examples, but here is a new one: A creature on the moon who wants to accompany a reluctant astronaut back to earth in the spaceship.)

2. (optional step; useful if children need assistance) Brainstorm with the students some of the different reasons the space creature would give for wanting to go to earth. Then brainstorm some of the reasons the astronaut would give for not being able to take the moon creature.

3. (optional step; useful if children need assistance) Now pair the students and let them rehearse or try out the scene briefly—at their desks—all talking at the same time. (It can be a little noisy, but you will survive.) Switch roles and repeat.

4. Let the students share their ideas as follows:

  a. Select several volunteers for sharing. You might have five pairs in front of the class. (If children are shy, you can have two astronauts talking with two moon creatures, thus making conversational groups of four.)

  b. Give each pair (or group) a number. The pair (group) may talk when you call out their number.

  c. Call numbers randomly and give each pair (group) a few moments to share.

There are several advantages to this procedure for sharing. First of all, a number of students are allowed the opportunity to share, so they do not have to wait long to get a turn. Second, you are in control of the sharing. If some students have little to say, you simply call another number to relieve the pressure on them. Some students, if they cannot think of something to say, may begin to giggle with embarrassment or possibly start to fight. By being able simply to call another number, you can bail them out. (You can call their numbers again after they have had a little break to collect their thoughts.) This procedure also makes it easy to cut off those who would go on forever if you let them.

Extra challenge. Highly verbal students will enjoy this additional challenge: they must pick up the thread of the previous pair's (or group's) conversation and continue it. This forces them to listen carefully to the rationale of other players and develop it further.

Character Panel Discussion II

This format, suggested in simpler form on pp. 190–91, can be used as a structure for presenting different viewpoints. Again, these are easy to set up, since the students can remain in their seats. The following are some possibilities for you to consider:

A. 1. You (or a competent student) pretend to host a television talk show or a public forum.
   2. All the panelists (four to six students) are the various stepmothers from folktales and fairy tales who feel they have been given a "bum rap." They tell their side of the story and try to convince the audience they are not as bad as they have been portrayed.
   3. The "audience" questions the details of their stories. (You can also use this with other characters and personages in literature or history: villains, witches, traitors, and so forth.)

B. 1. Again, you host or moderate a talk show or forum. Choose a character usually assumed to be a villain, and see how he or she might be looked at in a new light. For example, in "Little Red Riding Hood," is it possible that the wolf might be a sympathetic character?
   2. Panelists could be his supportive mother, an employer, or a Boy Scout leader who speak on his behalf and answer questions the audience poses. To keep the tension, an equal number of panelists should speak on behalf of Little Red Riding Hood and her grandmother.
   3. The audience ask questions of either "side."
   Note: It is usually easier and more fun to do this one without having the original characters present. They tend to become protective about the usual interpretation of their character and get in the way of the group's being able to talk about them in new and different ways.

C. Historical events may also be played in this format.
   1. A panel of members of the Virginia Company might try to convince the audience to settle in the New World.
   2. The audience knows about the hardships and failures of the earlier colonies, however, and is reluctant.

D. 1. You may also assign characters and viewpoints to the panel and the audience.
   2. Write instructions and pertinent data for each character on note cards and distribute them. If the class does not know who is receiving what instructions, the scene can be even more realistic.

Example: "A Town Debate"

a. A town meeting is called; you might play the mayor.
b. Two panelists present the side of those who want a new factory built. One might be the president of the company, and the other a local contractor who

will do the building. Both emphasize the number of jobs that will open up in the community, which has an unemployment problem.

c. The other two panelists might represent environmentalists. One has data about the company's past record of waste-disposal abuse, and another believes the plant location will pose unsolvable problems.

d. Members of the audience are the citizens of the community. Some are unemployed and hope for new jobs. Some work for the construction company which will do the building, and they want to be loyal to the company. Some are concerned because they live next to the plant site. The remainder are not sure how they feel about the issue.

The leader playing a major character role in a scene.   Another way to assist children with dialogue is to play a role yourself. The kind of dialogue you initiate should be modified according to each child's readiness to talk. *Narrow questions* need only limited responses. They may require a yes or no answer ("Do you like your job?"), a short reply ("When do you think the rest of your crew will return?"), or a choice between alternatives ("Is that easy or difficult to do?"). Because these questions can be answered easily, the child is under minimum pressure.

Broad questions call for more reflective thinking. They ask for reasons, opinions, value judgments, and so forth. For example: "How do you feel about your job?" "What kind of working conditions would you prefer to have?" "Why have you chosen to stay behind when others have journeyed on ahead?" Verbal children prefer the challenges of broad questions, but more reticent children can feel threatened by too many of them too soon.

The following example demonstrates the leader's use of narrow questions while playing a scene based on the story *Caps for Sale*, by Esphyr Slobodkina (p. 120). The children have been grouped in threes. They have been asked to think of villagers they might be and of the different reasons they might have for not wanting to buy a hat from the peddler. Notice how they give limited responses and the leader has to carry the scene. Narrow questions are used to continue the playing so that the children can still feel successful.

LEADER: Good morning. Isn't this a fine morning? (the three children giggle and only one responds)
CHILD 1:   Yes.
LEADER: What are you doing on this beautiful day?
CHILD 1:   Cleaning.
LEADER: Ah, well now, I have just the hat for you. It's the latest in dusting caps. Just the thing to wear when you're cleaning. Won't you buy one? (more giggling.)
CHILD 1:   No.
LEADER: Aw, shucks. Do you mind telling me why?
CHILD 1:   (pauses and then whispers) I don't know.
LEADER: Would you like to look at any other hats I have here?
CHILD 1:   No. (the other two shake their heads)

LEADER: Well, thank you very much for your time. I guess I'll have to try
         someplace else. Goodbye.
ALL: Bye.

In the next example, the leader is able to pose more challenging
questions to the children. The children, in groups, have created with their
bodies the star-making machines in Dr. Seuss's story "The Sneetches" (41).
The leader approaches each group, pretending to be a Sneetch who is
afraid to enter the machine. The children, as owners of the machines, will
lose a customer if they cannot convince him of the machine's safety. Notice
how they are quick to respond and have creative approaches to the problems posed.

LEADER: Mr. McBean, I sure would like to have a star, but I'm afraid to go in
          that machine. It looks awfully complicated. How can I be sure it won't
          hurt me?
CHILD 1: Well, you needn't be afraid. Look, I'll go in first, and you can see that
          I'm okay when I come out. (Child goes through the machine.) See, not
          a scratch!
LEADER: Well, look at that. All right, I think I'll try your machine. (This is done
          and the leader goes to another group.) I'm afraid of the dark, Mr.
          McBean, so I don't think I'd like to go inside that machine of yours. It
          looks awfully dark in there.
CHILD 2: Naw, not really. Once you get inside, the stars make it all shiny and
          bright enough to see.
LEADER: Well, that makes me feel a lot better. I guess I wouldn't be scared
          then. (He tries this machine.)

There are times when children do not immediately answer a question
the leader poses. They may lack knowledge and understanding of the
topic, or they may simply need time to think. After allowing sufficient time,
you can reword the question or continue the dialogue as if the unanswered
question were not important to the conversation. The goal is to help children feel successful enough to continue engaging in dialogue activities.

The leader and children as the same character together.   You can sometimes cast children in a role with you. This technique can be used with both
reticent and verbal children. For the reticent, they can identify with the
role whether they verbalize or not. For the verbal children, you can encourage them to ask questions, make comments, and respond to each other. Yet
you still remain on hand to step in and present your own ideas in role if
they are needed.

Leading discussion in character role.   Another technique you can use—
one that involves you considerably more than the previous techniques—is
to start a discussion with children as a character. The character may be an

invented one or a character from literature or history. For example, you might make an opening statement such as,

> "Let me introduce myself to you. I'm sure you've heard of me. I'm the Old Woman Who Lived in a Shoe. I've been told you might have some ideas of how to take care of all the children I have. I could sure use some help."

With this opening, the stage is set for a dramatic discussion. The children will have many ideas about how they think children should be cared for. You can listen to all their ideas, reminding them that you are old ("Take them to the zoo on weekends? I'm not sure I'd have the energy.") have only a shoe for a home ("Do you have any idea what it's like living in a shoe with all those children? If we just had a little more space.") and on a limited income ("Broth without bread wasn't punishment, you know; it was all we had to eat that day"). Your responses encourage the children's thinking, make them stretch for ideas, and motivate them to find answers to an intriguing problem. Your responses also develop your character, making you a real person with a real problem, worthy of their attention.

Curricular topics can also be pursued in this manner. For example, suppose you have been studying about the Westward movement in social studies. After reviewing some of the information, you might make an opening statement such as,

> "Now that we have decided to move by wagon train out West, we'd better get our things organized and ready."

You, in the role you have established as a member of the party, can now ask further questions about what people are taking with them, who will be leading the wagon train and what qualifications the person has, what route they intend to take, and so forth.

Children generally have ready answers, drawn from their knowledge of the subject, in this case perhaps supplemented by television and films. If you find that the children—or even you, for that matter—lack some needed information, you can stop the drama (just as children do in their pretend play) and, as yourselves, discuss the information needed to continue the playing. For example, you may feel the need to know what kind of food, medical supplies, or weapons were used on wagon trains. You may even wish to take time to research the questions and return to the drama another day with your new-found knowledge.

Discussions of this nature do not really have a preconceived beginning, middle, and end; they evolve. You, as the leader, have a responsibility to keep the interest and motivation level high, but you may drop one thread of development and switch to another whenever you think it is desirable. ("Ah, now, finding a quiet place for all those children to do their schoolwork *is* a real problem. Do you have any ideas for that?" "He thinks we need to find out just how serious and committed everyone is about making this journey.") Or, you can stop the discussion and simply ask the children if they wish to continue. You may find out that they have other ideas they want to explore or other characters they want to play. This break also gives you thinking time to prepare your next move.

During the discussion, you constantly assess the group's progression with the topic. Be flexible enough to keep the discussion focused on the children's needs and interests. At the same time, you bear the responsibility of keeping the group organized and on task. You also want the children to have an awareness of the deeper concerns the topics offer. (Ex: How can life be made a little easier for a single parent with many children and little money? What kind of person would it take to be a pioneer starting life over in a strange, new place? What kind of organizational rules were needed for a wagon train—a mobile community—to get along together?)

Roles the leader can play in discussion.   In the discussion format, there are various types of roles you can choose to play. All are designed to keep the discussion flowing.

1. You may be a *person seeking information:* "What are some inexpensive, nourishing meals I can serve that children will like? They're such picky eaters." "I was told there is a wagon train here that I could join. Tell me about your plans so I can decide whether to go with you."

2. You may be a *person presenting information for the group to consider:* "I'm the only survivor of a wagon train that met with ill fate. There are many dangers that lie ahead for you. I hope you have considered what you will do should you meet them. How have you prepared for _____?" (Present several problems for the children to discuss.)

3. You may be a *person requesting a decision.* In this case you may let the group discuss the problem by themselves. "The road ahead is blocked. You can take the northern route which will go through rough lands and swollen streams. Or you can take the southern route which goes through hostile Indian territory. Which way will you go?" Then give a reason to absent yourself from the group. "I'm weary from my long ride and must rest a while, but I'll return soon to hear your decision."

4. You may be a *person who is in need of help:* "I have just ridden here from another wagon train. We were attacked by a band of robbers and have lost half our party. Others are wounded and need medical attention. Can you help us with fresh supplies?"

5. You may also be a person who is *second in command.* Since you have been sent to give orders for someone else, you cannot be responsible for the demands being made. "All I know is the wagon master asked that each of you leave one of your possessions here to lighten our load. I'm to collect them." "You can refuse if you like, but what will I tell the wagon master?"

Risks in leading improvised discussions.   Because you cannot always predict the direction these discussions will take, there is some risk involved. Some of the more troublesome difficulties you can run into are:

1. Children may turn against the character you are playing. Be careful of choosing a villainous or negative character until you feel skilled enough to handle it. You may try a potentially negative character if the person is in a weakened

state—such as a witch who has lost her power, a ghost who would like to find a friend, or a general who is weary of war.

2. Children may be eager to engage in physical action or fighting rather than discussing.
3. Children may not take the topic seriously.
4. Your discussion questions run dry.

Aids the leader can use to lessen risks.

1. At first, try an idea for a limited time period. A good time to try out these discussions is a few minutes before the end of the period, before lunch, or before the end of the day. Then, if there is any difficulty, you have a logical stopping point. The break period will give you time to collect your thoughts and decide how, or if, you want to continue with the discussion.

2. Stop the drama and discuss any difficulties openly. Any time you are uncomfortable with what is happening, you can just stop. You can say (in your own voice), "Let's sit down and discuss what happened." You can even ask the children, "What do you think our problem is?" or "I think that our drama might be going off in a difficult direction. What do you think we should do?" This also gives everyone a chance to take a breath and collect themselves before continuing. Furthermore, just knowing that you can stop any time you want or need to is a stress reliever that can give you the courage to let things go on a bit longer just to see what will happen. The children may just be able to find their own way out of a difficulty as easily as if you had intervened yourself.

3. Switch to a related drama exercise or activity. If ideas are not forthcoming or if the discussion appears to be getting out of hand, simply stop and switch to another type of drama exercise or activity related to the topic. Many of the activities already covered in this text can be useful. For example:

Solo Narrative Pantomime "Let me tell you what my day is like living in a shoe with all those kids. You pantomime as I describe it."

Solo Verbal Activity "Let's go around the circle; each of you describe an inexpensive toy you like to play with that maybe I'd be able to get for my children." "Each person tell about one possession you have brought with you that has great meaning for you."

Frozen Pictures "Let's give ourselves courage by creating a picture of one thing in our new life out West that we are looking forward to."

Count and Freeze Pantomime "Demonstrate a game I could teach my children to play that would keep them entertained."

Build a Place Pantomime "Create a covered wagon, loading it with appropriate supplies."

Paired Verbal Activity "In pairs, one of you will be a prospective wagon master interviewing for this job. The other will be the person responsible for your hiring."

4. Switch to a related curricular activity such as writing, drawing a picture, or researching further information. "Draw a picture of the kind of shoe you think would make the best house." "Write out the recipe for your favorite, inexpensive dish."

In the Westward example, children might develop more specific characters for themselves. Have on hand a collection of photographs from magazines or other sources. Children choose one they wish to identify with and give the person a name, a history, and personal reasons why they have decided to move West. These character profiles can be shared with the class. Students might write a diary entry about how the journey is progressing thus far; or they may write a letter to a relative left behind. For a research activity, children might discover what kinds of wagons were used by wagon trains. They can draw a picture of the one they think their group should take. They might also draw a map of the route the wagon train will be taking.

Obviously, these discussions and related activities can extend over a period of time. By investing time in developing the topics, the depth of playing and the commitment to them increases. Therefore, you need not be concerned that you get things finished off each drama period with all the loose ends tied up. In fact, it is often best to leave the session on a high note, with an exciting "to be continued" feeling. The group may then return for the next session eagerly anticipating the next development.

CREATING AND PLAYING SKITS

Children, generally third-graders and older, eventually will be ready to create their own skits in small groups to share with the rest of the class. At first they will probably reenact stories that are fairly familiar to them, such as folktales or shows they have seen on television. Some youngsters who have seen the famous MGM *Wizard of Oz* film several times, for example, can reenact many scenes verbatim. However, skits can also be created in a number of ways and with a number of kinds of stimuli.

Planning an Ending

The skits will often be short, rather episodic, and without a completed ending—particularly at first. This usually happens because the group has not been able to reach an agreement on the story line. (Remember, group decision making is not an easy task.) Another reason may be that as they are actually playing the skit, new thoughts occur to them and they begin improvising and ad-libbing additional ideas, without anyone knowing what is going to happen next. If their skits have strong conflict, then arguments, shouting, or even a physical fight may be all they can think of to do. (And they sometimes cannot even bring *that* to a close!) A third reason is that they simply do not realize the importance of deciding on an ending. They keep on playing, even though some of them are becoming embarrassed and even panicked if they see no way out of their dilemma.

Pressing them to decide on an ending for their skits thus becomes a major task for you. The author once instructed some children to be sure to plan an ending for their scene and then asked if they knew why. One child's answer was, "So we'll all know when to quit." That says it pretty well, and is an explanation worth sharing with children.

In spite of your precautions there still may be times when students reach a dead end. You then have several options.

1. You may walk up to them privately and quietly ask, as a reminder, "Do you have an ending?"
2. If an ending is not forthcoming, you may be able to narrate them out of the difficulty. *Example:* Some students had developed skits based on returning an item to a store's complaint department. One group could not settle its argument, so the leader narrated: "And so the complaint manager and the irate customer never got a chance to find out who would win the argument, for a bell sounded the closing of the department store. And to the strains of the Muzak playing 'We Wish You a Merry Christmas,' they all went home."
3. It may even be possible to step into the scene as a mediating character and negotiate. In the above scene, for example, the leader might have stepped in as the store manager to help work out an agreement between the two. It may even be that a member of the audience can see a mediating character they can play to help their classmates out.

The Audience for Skits

As before, you may have to encourage sensitive audience behavior. Some students are not unduly critical of each other and in fact may identify with, and be supportive of, each other. But there are those who will become impatient with their classmates. They think *they* would know what to say or do in the same situation, so they may call out instructions: "Maybelle, tell him you don't want to go!" "Psst, George, give him a shove!" Just a quiet reminder to anxious audience members will sometimes suffice; at other times you may need to explain that prompting from the audience interrupts the players' thinking and bothers them more than it helps them.

Evaluation

Students sometimes say, "We need to rehearse more" or "We don't like what we're doing." This self-evaluation says they feel that something is lacking in their work. In this case the best remedy may be to allow them to keep improvising together and working on their ideas rather than subject them to outside evaluation.

When they do share their work and are ready to evaluate, focus first on self-evaluation with such questions as

What did you like about the (your) scene?
What moments were the most enjoyable for you? Why?
If you could do it over again, what would you want to change? Why?
How successful do you think the ending was to the (your) scene? Why?

When students have developed a great deal of confidence in their ability to create skits, you may want the audience members to give their evaluations. Positive evaluation is paramount, so your wording of discussion questions should reflect this:

What did you *like* about the scene?
What were the things said by certain characters that were *especially believable?*
What lines of dialogue were *especially typical* of the characters?
During what moments did people *help each other?*

Your own positive feedback will be important, especially if some students insist on being overly critical of classmates. Or if the scene could benefit from additional challenges, you may need to suggest these. However, continued playing and experiences in skit-making also can result in more involving and believable dramatization.

EXAMPLE FROM "TAPER TOM"

The following is an account of a third grade's enacting of a scene from a story called "Taper Tom" or "The Princess Who Couldn't Laugh" (43). Another variation is "The Golden Goose" (56). It exemplifies many of the techniques suggested in this chapter.

The leader created a scene in which numerous contestants offer their ideas for making the princess laugh. She played the part of the princess to help carry the conversations as well as aid in the organization of the various entertainments the contestants were presenting.

In the role of the princess, she ordered that the contestants announce themselves to the audience and bow upon entering and leaving the courtroom: "State your name, my good man (or woman), and bow before the court."

In their discussion before playing, the children had suggested a variety of antics to make the princess laugh. But when they enacted their ideas, they were all variations on the theme of pratfalls. The ideas were accepted by the leader, but for the second playing she suggested that they think of new ideas, omitting any falls.

For the replaying, the children suggested adding a panel of princesses, some servants, and a guard. Since the leader felt her participation might still be needed for organization, she created the authority role of queen.

During this playing the children's ideas for making the princess laugh included tickling feet (without touching), telling jokes, flipping pancakes, playing in a musical band, dancing, and acrobatics. The queen had little to do as the children duplicated much of what she had established in her previous role as princess. They carried on their conversations easily, and the "princesses" were particularly adept at keeping the entertainment progressing from one act to another: "Servants, give this man some money for his show; but we're still not laughing! Next!"

The leader's intervention was necessary, however, when one of the band musicians pretended to drink liquor. At first the leader ignored the drinking, but when other children began to imitate it, she took on the "queen" role and calmly and quietly told them there would be "no drinking on the job." They obeyed, and the scene proceeded smoothly.

SKIT IDEAS

Familiar stories. An easy beginning for group skits are reenactments of familiar material, such as favorite television shows, television commercials, and other material students have seen numerous times. After brainstorming for topics as a class, students divide into groups to plan their dramas.

Silent movies. Students can create skits from old silent movies or films shown with the sound turned off. Check the school media center for films and filmstrips of wordless picture books that may be used for this purpose.

Comics and wordless picture books. Select cartoon strips from the Sunday paper or comic books with enough action that the basic plot of the situation is understandable. Block out the dialogue and have students create the story in their own words. Or select wordless picture books that

"Just keep saying, 'There's no place like home.'"

have several characters interacting. Students make up the dialogue that would accompany.

Talking pictures.   Select pictures which show several people (or even animals or objects) in a problem situation. Students select the picture they want to work with and develop a skit around it. They may open the playing with a frozen picture and then present their solution. Or they may want to begin the scene prior to the picture.

Proverbs and sayings.   Students develop skits to illustrate proverbs. What stories do the following suggest? Two heads are better than one; All that glitters is not gold; A fool and his money are soon parted. Consider proverbs and sayings from various cultures.

Skits from ad talks.   Using the ad-talk cards explained on pp. 183–84, you can randomly distribute perhaps five to each group. Students are to create a skit, using as much dialogue as they wish, but incorporating their statements somewhere. As the skit is played, it is fun to hold up the card for the audience to see when the statement is given. It is an intriguing challenge and often amazing to note how seemingly unrelated statements can be incorporated into a logical story line. You might even let some groups use the same cards and see what variations result.

News story of the week.   Students recreate their version of a news event. Having newspapers at hand can provide ideas for the skits as well as stimulate interest in reading further about them.

Stories from advertisements.   Newspaper ads can stimulate the imagination to speculate on the story behind them. Items that are for sale or messages in the "Personals" section might pose possibilities. For example, "House for sale. Furnishings included. Vacating immediately. Best offer" might make one think of a story like *The Amityville Horror.* Or "Lose 10 pounds a week! Success guaranteed or your money cheerfully refunded." What really happens when someone is not successful?

Opening lines.   Skits can be based on opening lines, such as the following:

1. It seemed a perfect day for the event. Crowds were gathered for the momentous, historic occasion. One person in the crowd, however, seemed out of place.
2. Silently and without warning it came on them like a thief in the night. Not until the following morning were they aware of what had happened.

Famous last words.   Create skits that begin or end with intriguing lines like the following:

"I have an idea that will revolutionize the world!"
"You never listen to anything I say."
"I told you we should have called the police."
"I know exactly what I'm doing."
"See if I ever invite you to a party again."

Commercials. Create commercials not usually seen on television:

1. Sell yourselves as a group: What skills, abilities, or personalities do you have that can be salable? Who would you like to have hire you? What will you charge? Are your services guaranteed?
2. Recycle products: Create a commercial for things that might otherwise be thrown away (one large oversized glove, used bubble gum, a cracked mirror, one old tennis shoe).
3. Sell products from the past: How might a guillotine, a suit of armor, a covered wagon, or a spinning wheel have been marketed in their day? Or create commercials for products of the future, such as lifelike robots, solar-powered cars, personal space ships, or wristwatch television sets.

(Note: You can relate this to a study of persuasive advertising techniques, such as the bandwagon approach, testimony, and appeal to status.)

Solve the problem. What ways can students think of to deal with the following situations?

1. Two television announcers try to fill in the time before a delayed space launch, but they have already said almost everything they can think of.
2. A persistent salesperson tries to sell a product in order to meet a daily quota.
3. Two people who speak different languages try to communicate with each other. A third is a translator. (Use nonsense language or repeat words like "applesauce" to simulate a foreign language.)
4. A person gets on a crowded bus with a briefcase that is ticking.
5. Two people are arguing. A third tries to enter as a peacemaker, even though she does not know what the argument is about.

Random skits.

1. Prepare sets of cards with settings, props, and characters. Use pictures if you can.
2. Groups select one (or more) card from each set.
3. Plan a skit using the cards selected.
4. Shuffle the cards for an infinite variety of combinations.

settings: elevator, Island of No Return, museum at midnight, abandoned mine shaft, lost and found department, information desk, haunted house, tower with revolving restaurant, hijacked airplane.

characters: spy, detective, genie in a bottle, Frankenstein's monster, Superman or Superwoman, ghost, good fairy, Snoopy, statue that comes to life.

Fourth-graders act out their version of a television commercial for cough medicine.

props: treasure map, magic wand, flying carpet, poison apple, cape to make you invisible, sneezing powder, singing harp, seven-league boots, old jalopy, air balloon with a slow leak.

Role-playing situations.   Once students have had some experience with dialogue scenes and other creative drama activities, it will be easier to do the role playing suggested in many social studies texts. Students can dramatize various ways of handling personal and social problems. Sometimes the dramatizations show unacceptable behaviors, but usually the consequences of those behaviors are shown in the skit or are discussed afterwards. Searching for the most appropriate solutions becomes the goal. *Examples:*

1.   Children have the habit of crossing an elderly couple's lawn. They angrily confront the children one day. What happens?
2.   A group of children are throwing hard-packed snowballs at passing cars and shatter a windshield. The car stops, and the driver starts shouting at the group. What happens next?
3.   A group of friends are bored and are looking for something to do. A couple of them suggest shoplifting for the fun of it. The others are not so sure. What does the group finally decide to do?
4.   A group of friends are playing. Two children, new to the neighborhood, enter the scene and ask to play. Some of the children do not want to include the newcomers. How does the scene end?

Prop stories.

1.   Keep a selection of interesting props, bits of costume, pieces of material, and the like.

What skit can be created based on this bag of props?

2. Brainstorm some ideas for a couple of them: "Who might have owned this jewel box?" "What does this key unlock?" "Where is the treasure chest buried?"
3. Select three or four for each group to base a skit on.
4. After the stories are planned, students may add other props and costumes to the skits. *Example:* a scarf, candlestick, pocket watch, and mallet might suggest this story: A woman (wearing the scarf) and her husband (carrying the pocket watch) are hit with a blunt object and robbed. The only clue is the candlestick, which was dropped by the thief. The thief, who was the butler in disguise, is apprehended when his fingerprints are found on the candlestick. He is brought to trial, with the mallet serving as the judge's gavel.

Dialogue scenes from literature.   Poems and stories often involve interesting dialogue encounters one can build on. Some suggestions are listed below. (The following symbols are used to indicate the age level they might be best suited for: Y—kindergarten, first, and second grades; M—third and fourth grades; O—fifth and sixth grades.)

M–O "Barter," SARA TEASDALE (1). "Life has loveliness to sell . . ." What would Life as a salesperson have to sell? What would Life say trying to convince someone to buy? What would you trade for Life's loveliness?

M–O "A Cave Beast Greets a Visitor," JACK PRELUTSKY (28). A cave beast responds to questions; he is the only one who talks. Who is talking to him and why? What else might the person ask?

Y–M "Doorbells," RACHEL FIELD (4, 43). Who is at the door, and what do they want? How does the homeowner receive them? You might play the homeowner first.

M–O *The King's Fountain,* LLOYD ALEXANDER. New York: E.P. Dutton, 1971. A king wants to build a fountain without understanding that it would cut off the water supply to the people. A poor man tries to find someone to persuade the king to reconsider. Each has his excuse, and the poor man is left to speak to the king himself.

M–O "Ma! Don't Throw That Shirt Out," JACK PRELUTSKY (28). A kid argues with Mom to keep his favorite shirt, even though it is falling apart.

M "Mean Song," EVE MERRIAM (46). Mean things are said in nonsense words. Who is the speaker, and why are they so angry? What does the other person say?

M "Overheard on a Saltmarsh," HAROLD MONRO (37). A goblin and a nymph argue over some green glass beads. What reasons do they have for wanting them? Of what value are they?

M–O "Phizzog," CARL SANDBURG (4). Create a dialogue scene in which you receive your newly made face and you want to exchange it. To whom would you speak? What bargain would you strike?

M–O "Southbound on the Freeway," MAY SWENSON (37). A visitor from "Orbitville" mistakes cars for Earth creatures, and gives an interesting description of them. To whom is he reporting?

M–O "Summons," ROBERT FRANCIS (37). A person asks to be summoned if something important arises. What would be something important to summon a person to? How will the summoned person react?

Y–M *The Tiger in the Teapot*, BETTY YURDIN. New York: Holt Owlet, 1968. A family tries to entice the tiger out of the teapot before teatime. Little sister succeeds.

M "The Tiger, the Brahman, and the Jackal," FLORA ANNIE STEEL (4). A Brahman enlists the aid of a clever jackal to help him outwit a tiger who wants to eat him.

O "A Travelled Narrative," CHARLES M. SKINNER (56). Ichabod, a "shiftless fellow," tries to sneak out of the general store with butter hidden under his hat. The other customers try to detain him with conversation so the butter will melt and give him away.

O "Two Friends," DAVID IGNATOW (42). It seems that two friends who pass each other and talk hurriedly really do not listen to each other's comments.

M "The Zax," DR. SEUSS (41). Two Zax meet and neither will give way for the other—ever. Why?

Dialogue guessing games. Verbal students will like the challenge of this game.

a. Students work out a scene on their own, without identifying the characters in it.

b. You stop the scene periodically so that the audience can guess from the clues who the speakers might be. Here are two examples:

Example A: "I don't want you coming around here again!"
"But what harm did I do?"
"Harm? What about the food you ate and the furniture you broke?"
"Well, the food wasn't my idea of terrific—and the furniture wasn't very well made anyway!"

Goldilocks and Papa Bear

Example B: "I know you can do it; I have a lot of faith in you."
"Well, I've sewn a lot of things, but this is a real challenge."
"Here's the design we have in mind."
"Ah, but five points are just as easy to make as six. . . ."

George Washington and Betsy Ross

Add-on scenes.   Similar to the add-on pantomimes in Chapter 7, an interesting and challenging way to play dialogue scenes is to begin with one or two players setting up a situation. It is generally easier if there is a problem situation that others can try to solve. Then as the playing progresses, characters invented on the spot can enter the scene.

As an example, one group of sixth-graders began a situation with a person being stuck in a revolving door of a department store. Various characters added on to the situation with their ideas: a floorwalker who tried to keep things under control; sympathetic clerks with various ideas for calming the customer who began to panic; a harried mother with a child who refused to leave the store without going through the revolving door; and so on. These scenes may have no ending but can be stopped when everyone has run out of ideas or simply by saying "Freeze" at any point and then discussing what has taken place. (*Note:* It is a good idea to quickly and privately check on each child's idea for the scene *before* they play it in order to weed out any inappropriate ones.)

FOR THE COLLEGE STUDENT

1. Collect stories and poems suitable for sound-effects activities.
2. Create your own sound-effect story. Base it on a curricular topic.
3. Practice telling or reading a story while using the arrow control.
4. Adapt a story for a sequence game.
5. Write a sequence game; base it on a curricular topic.
6. Collect interesting pictures, props, and one-liners useful for stimulating verbalization.
7. Try round-robin storytelling with your classmates, using some of the techniques mentioned in this chapter.
8. Lead your classmates in one of the verbal games. Play the role of moderator or mediator.
9. Create your own verbal game or adapt some of the ones presented in this chapter.
10. In groups, brainstorm for ideas for discussions, dialogue scenes, and skits based on literature or on other curricular topics. Keep a file of these materials.
11. Select or create a dialogue scene and play it with a group of your classmates. Take turns being the initiator and practice asking narrow and broad questions.
12. Try leading a discussion in a character role with your classmates. Afterwards, consider the various turns the discussion might have taken. What alternatives might you use?
13. Select one of the skit ideas presented in this chapter and plan it out with some classmates. Share your skits with the rest of the class.

NINE

Encouraging Creative Work

Many children are able to create ideas easily and freely. They are self-confident and give original responses to the ideas and questions the leader poses. Others need stimulation and encouragement to develop into creative thinkers. This chapter will present some ways to encourage children's creative work in drama. The basis for the activities will be movement, with opportunities for dialogue following the pantomime. We will begin with some fairly simple creative pantomime activities and techniques to guide their playing. In the second half of the chapter, some methods for creative story building will be presented.

SIMPLE CREATIVE PANTOMIME ACTIVITIES

Creative pantomimes may be played solo or in pairs or groups and may come from a variety of topics. Following are some examples:

1. *exploratory movement:* "Squeeze into the smallest (or roundest, hardest, fastest) thing you can be. What are you?"
2. *literature:* "Let's pretend you are a gingerbread boy and have just come to life in the oven. The door is still closed and you're waiting to get out. I'll be the old woman who baked you, and when I open the door, you jump out and do one thing you think the gingerbread boy would do in his first moment of life *before* he runs away. . . ."
3. *the study of shapes:* "This time, pretend you're using something that is in the shape of a circle; maybe you'll ride a bicycle, eat a doughnut, or swing a lasso."
4. *the interpretation of a musical selection—pantomime solo:* "Now that we've heard Paul Simon's song, 'Feelin' Groovy,' let's act out as many ideas as we can. What

"Be as small as you can be. . . . What are you?"

are some of the things you do when you're feeling groovy? I'll play the song again and whenever I say 'Now,' you change what you're doing and try something else. . . ."

Similar activities may be played in pairs and groups:

1. *being shadows in pairs:* "Decide between you who will be the shadow and who will be the person the shadow is following and imitating. You'll have to decide who the person is and what he or she does during a day's activities."
2. *being robots in groups:* "After you divide into groups, you'll need to decide what sorts of jobs your robots are working on: are they painting a house or working in a restaurant? Then once you've decided on the job, you'll need to plan all the things your robots do."

FURTHER AIDS FOR GUIDING CREATIVE WORK

One needs an accepting, nonjudgmental environment to feel free to create. All the following techniques are useful in helping children feel as comfortable as possible in their work.

1. Brainstorm some ideas verbally before playing. ("What kinds of community helpers are there?") Or brainstorm by simply playing. ("I'll count to five, and you see if you can act out five different community helpers.")
2. Keep the playing brief at first, and let as many children as possible play in unison so that there is little or no audience watching. This technique lets children work privately and for their own satisfaction and self-evaluation, without the pressure of being judged by others.
3. If you need to check on what the children are doing, keep the ideas private. As they play, you can ask them to freeze while you come around and talk to them individually. Your responses need only accept the idea: "Ah, that's

interesting." "Oh." "Um, hum." "Really?" and so forth. No judgments of good or bad need be made.

4. Side-coaching.

   a. As the children play, remind them of the different ideas they mentioned in discussion, note some of the ideas you see being played, or suggest other possibilities for them to consider.

   b. Use recorded music to stimulate students' thinking as well as to provide a background to fill in any awkward silences.

5. When the playing is ended, you can comment on what some of the ideas were without identifying the players. ("I saw some people putting insulation in the attic, chopping wood for a wood-burning stove, turning off lights—all kinds of ways to save energy.") This technique shows acceptance of the students' ideas and lets the rest of the class learn what the various ideas were.

6. As children become confident in creating, they will want to share their ideas with each other. Those who wish may do so, either by telling what they did or by demonstrating their ideas, sometimes even for audience guessing.

CONTROL TECHNIQUES IN CREATIVE PANTOMIME WORK

Leaders are sometimes afraid to let students be creative in their playing for fear they will get out of control. Providing a definite structure or framework for creative work can keep the class organized and lessen your anxiety.

1. At first select topics with a built-in control. Children are usually more motivated to play quietly if they are secret agents doing undercover work, museum statues which come to life when all is dim and quiet, or elves secretly doing good deeds or slyly making mischief.

Leader listens appreciatively to child's pantomime idea.

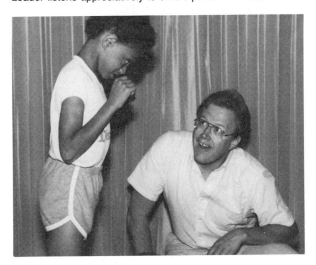

2. Always be definite about when the children should start and stop their pan-tomiming. Following are some suggestions:
   a. You may simply say "Begin. . . . Freeze."
   b. You may count, saying for example, "Think of three things you can do as I count to 3. . . . 1, 2, 3."
   c. "When the record begins, you may move; when it stops, you freeze."
   d. For more extended playing, you may be more inventive and say, for example (mysteriously): "When the lights go off, that will be the signal that Halloween night is here. And all you little hobgoblins will come out from your hiding places (desks) to dance your own little dance (solo at the side of the desk) in the moonlight. But when the clock strikes five o'clock (hammer on a small gong), you must return to your hiding places again where no human eye can see you."
   e. Children's inventiveness and length of playing time needed will vary with each individual. Therefore, you may wish to tell the children that they are to sit down when they have finished their pantomime and wait quietly for others to finish. This technique may seem strange at first, but you and the children will soon become accustomed to it and will find it helpful for many activities.

Mechanical Movement

Mechanical movement is another technique one can use for con-trolled creative work. You can be the operator who manages the "on" and "off" switches.

> *suggested characters:* robots, windup or mechanical toys, music boxes (use a recording of Frank Mills's "Music Box Dancer"). For group work, create machines (both real and imaginary), such as household appliances and indoor and outdoor machinery of all sizes. For imaginary machinery, students might invent "a homework machine," "a machine to wake you up *and* get you out of bed in the morning," or "a dream machine." Other mechanical group work might include clocks with characters that move as the hour strikes (Leroy Anderson's "Syncopated Clock"), a mechanical circus, or a merry-go-round (Aaron Copland's "Circus Music" from *The Red Pony*).

You can have the children simply try out the movements. Or you can create together story line situations for the dramatization. For example:

1. Last year's toys in Santa Claus's workshop help Santa finish making all the new toys. Their batteries run down, and they slowly come to a stop. You might recharge them, one by one, so that they can continue their work and return to the shelf before Santa awakens.
2. Robots are going on a picnic. It rains, and the robots all "rust" and are "frozen." You can oil them up, one by one, so that they can return home.

You may also choose to create machines from literature. Consider such stories as the following:

"The Doughnuts," ROBERT McCLOSKEY (87). A doughnut machine goes haywire and cannot stop making doughnuts. Children will probably mention "the part that squeezes out the

Students work out their ideas for creating the various parts of a machine.

dough," "the flipper to turn the doughnuts over," "the paddle that keeps pushing the doughnuts along," and "the chute where they come out."

Mr. Murphy's Marvelous Invention, EILEEN CHRISTELOW. New York: Clarion Books, 1983. Mr. Murphy, a pig inventor, creates a unique housekeeping machine for his wife, but it cannot do anything right.

"The Sneetches," DR. SEUSS (41). Children can create both the "Star-On" and "Star-Off" machine. What parts do you need in this fanciful machine that can put stars on and take them off Sneetches' bellies?

"Setting Pictures in Motion" or "Coming to Life"

For still another technique, students create a picture that is frozen but then comes to life on cue, and then returns to a still picture once again. For example:

"When the music begins, your idea of "slithy toves" will come to life and "gyre and gimble in the wabe." When the music stops, the still picture of the Jabberwocky's home will return" (4, 57).

"In this short poem, 'The Shopgirls' (34), we are told that when the shopgirls leave the stores and the working day is over, certain things in the store come to life. What might some of these things be and how would they move? What do they do all night? What position might they freeze into at daybreak?"

"This picture shows five people in an accident of some sort. In your groups decide how the situation might have begun and what happened to lead up to this moment. Think of another still picture to begin with, then act out the moments leading up to this picture and freeze into it."

Another way to set a picture in motion in a dramatic way is to do it in sequence. Each child is assigned a number. When you call "All the ones," they move, then twos add on to the ones and so on. You can even reverse this counting so the picture returns to its frozen position once again. For example:

"For your 'rumpus' (Maurice Sendak's *Where the Wild Things Are*), you will all be frozen as a 'wild thing.' This group will be ones, this twos, and this threes. I'll play the music, and when I call your number you can move. When I call another number, you must be frozen again."

"Now that we've studied early railroad building in the United States, we can create our own railroad crew. Divide into groups of five. In each group you'll decide who will be those who lay the ties or 'sleepers,' the 'shakers' who hold the spikes, those who hammer, those who carry the water, and the supervisor. When you've worked that out, I'll give numbers to each."

CREATING FIGHTS AND BATTLES: STAGE COMBAT

Fight scenes are described in many stories and in other curricular materials. These are always exciting to play, but it would obviously be foolhardy to let a group of children enact a fight scene without some previous preparation. Students need to learn how to "stage" fights, as, they are in fact handled in movies, in the theatre, and on television.

Fighting is of interest to many children. They are usually intrigued and impressed with the fact that the realistic fights they see in dramas are really artful pretense and organized with great care. They like to learn, the way actors and stunt people do, how to throw a punch without making actual physical contact with the partner. They also like the challenge of pretending to receive a blow in a convincing manner.

Throughout all stage combat work it is wise to focus on the challenge of skill development: "Anyone can shove and push people around and even hit them. But it takes skill and concentration to make pretend fighting look real so that no one gets hurt." When students are capable of working out combat ideas in cooperation with each other and rehearsing "staging" techniques, they are often greatly pleased. It takes far more skill than an ordinary playground brawl, and is certainly more satisfying for all.

The following procedure is recommended for teaching this kind of lesson:

1. First children work alone, imagining the partner. They must practice and perfect their skill in stopping the blow at the precise moment before contact. The point of contact they aim at may be imagined or may be a wall, their desk, or the palm of one hand. As was described in "Setting Pictures in Motion" (this chapter), you call the blows. You might pretend to be the one receiving the punches and give appropriate verbal response: "One. (pause) Ugghh! Two. (pause) Ooh, you got me there." (and so on).

2. They next pretend to receive the blow. Again, the partner is imagined. As well as calling the blows, you might tell them where the punches will be: 1,

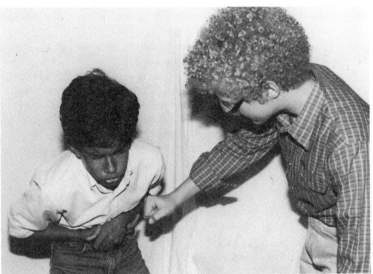

Pretending to hit; pretending to be hit. Learning to master the pretense of fighting.

stomach; 2, chin; 3, left shoulder. Now you might pretend to be the one giving the blows and say: "One. Take that! Two. And that! Three. That'll teach ya, ya ornery varmint!"

3. Now they can work in pairs, but again you count. They may decide on five punches. Go slowly, perhaps even freezing after each count to make sure all rules are being followed.

4. Speed up *only* when they exhibit appropriate skill and sensitivity to each other. If you see any problems at all, stop immediately!

When children have shown real skill and care in their work, they may be allowed to try some scenes of fights from different sources: social studies, science, or literature. The fights may be between people or animals. Along with these dramas there might be valuable discussions on historic weapons or animal armor.

Selected Stories with Fight Scenes

Y–M *The Elephant's Child,* RUDYARD KIPLING. New York: Walker, 1970. After the elephant's child gets his trunk, he goes home and spanks all his relatives (various animals) the way they used to spank him. How can children show both spanking scenes in pairs? Before playing you might discuss the different ways the various animal relatives (giraffe, ostrich, hippopotamus, baboon) would spank.

M–O *The King's Stilts,* DR. SEUSS. New York: Random House, 1939. The Nizzards (large birds) and the Cats have a battle. The story says that "the fur flew fast but the feathers flew faster. It took only ten minutes."

M *The Knight and the Dragon,* TOMIE DE PAOLA. New York: Putnam Publishing Group, 1980. A knight and a dragon fight each other unsuccessfully in this picture book with very little text.

Y *Millions of Cats,* WANDA GÁG. New York: Coward-McCann, 1938. The cats all "bit and scratched and clawed each other" and finally ate each other up. How can they show this in pairs?

M "The Murgle and the Munn," JACK PRELUTSKY (28). This is a fight for pairs. The two make a decision to meet again, since the fight was so much fun.

O "Robin Hood's Merry Adventure with the Miller," HOWARD PYLE (43). Robin Hood and his men plan to play a joke on the miller, but their plan backfires. The fight begins with the miller opening his bag as he pretends to search for money, continuing with the blows he gives the flour-covered men, and ending when Robin gives three blasts on his horn.

CREATING PANTOMIME STORIES

Many children are capable of creating stories on their own that they can enact with little assistance from a leader. Others, however, may be dependent on a leader to give them ideas to work with and guidance through creating plot outlines. This section will cover some of the ways you can help students create and play stories of their own.

In the process of plot building you will be giving a framework for students to develop a story that is meaningful and satisfying to them. The stories are action based and played out in pantomime. In addition you will learn how to extend the story by adding verbal experiences after the pantomiming.

Steps in the Process of Creative Plot Building:
Overview

1. Present an intriguing idea that can be played in pantomime. The playing may be solo, in pairs, or in groups. You may play a role yourself.
2. Guide the students through a series of approximately five discussion questions to assist them in planning their own stories. The questions help them

create a beginning, a middle, and an end to their stories as well as a conflict and a resolution.

3. Side-coach the unison playing of the stories. (Sometimes half the class plays for the other half, and then players and audience switch.)
4. Follow-up discussion may be with the leader in character role. Other verbal activities are also possible.
5. Replay (optional).

Now let us look at each step a little closer.

Choosing an Idea

The topics for a creative story, whether fact or fiction, can come from a number of sources as you tap your own imagination.

literature: "The little boy in *Harold and the Purple Crayon* (Crockett Johnson [New York: Harper & Row, Publishers, 1955]) has such interesting adventures with his magic crayon. Let's pretend that you have a crayon like his and you're going to draw an adventure you'd like to have. . . ."

social studies: "Let's suppose that you are members of a conservation crew working with wildlife in Africa. It's your job to catch the wild animals and tag them so that you can learn more about them. . . ." (pair or group playing)

science: "As the world-famous team of Dr. Pinna and Dr. Lobe, the ear experts, you will need to use your secret invention to make yourself small enough to travel in your patient's ear to find the source of the problem. . . ." (pair playing)

music: "Listen to this music called 'Neptune' from *The Planet Suite* by Holst. Imagine yourself a space explorer and this music is what seems to be coming from a new planet you're about to land on. What kind of place do you think the planet will be?"

Discussing Ideas

Discussion questions essentially focus on character, setting, plan of action, conflict, and resolution. In other words the children need to plan who they are, what they are going to do, what problems they might have, how they will solve them, and how the story will end. The specific wording of these questions, however, will depend on the topic and on the leader's objectives in using the material.

Discussion outline. The discussion format usually involves five questions, although you can combine several short or related questions into one. Generally the *first* question introduces the idea; the *second* and *third* questions build the adventure; by the *fourth* question, the conflict is introduced; and with the *fifth* question, the story is brought to a close.

With individual playing, the children plan their ideas in a large group discussion. With pair and group stories, however, the children will have to discuss their ideas together. It is also possible for many ideas to be played individually first and then as pair and group work in replayings. The following are three examples of discussion outlines:

In a creative story, children make up and act out their own plots.

Individual Playing

TEACHER: Now that we've read about *Harold and the Purple Crayon*, it might be fun to go on our own magical adventure. Let's suppose you have a crayon like Harold's that will draw anything you want.

1. Where would you like to go on your adventure?
2. How will you get there? Do you need to take any supplies with you?
3. What are some of the things you'd like to see and do? What unusual things might happen to you?
4. Harold's trips are not without some problems. What kinds of problems could happen to you on this adventure?
5. But with a magical crayon Harold usually figures a way out of any problems and gets back home safely. How do you think you could solve your problems, and how will you return home?

Paired Playing

TEACHER: It's Halloween. You and a friend have decided to visit a haunted house. At least you think it's haunted.

1. What might be some of your reasons for going?
2. You're going at night and it's a bit chilly. What things will you need to take with you? What route will you take?
3. How will you go about investigating the house? What are some things you want to check? What do you think you might find?

4. What problems might you run into in a haunted house? At least there will be the two of you to face them together; maybe you'll even be able to help each other out. What do you think could happen?

5. Anyone who visits a haunted house is probably confident enough to survive anything. Let's suppose your venture turns out all right. Bring back a souvenir, though, to prove you were really there. We'll find out what your souvenir is after you return.

Small Group Playing

TEACHER: Let's suppose that it's Boston, 1773, and you are the group of people called the Sons of Liberty, who object to the high tax on tea. You disguise yourselves as Indians, board a tea freighter at night, and throw the tea overboard.

1. Now, what are your plans for disguising and arming yourself for tonight? Your disguise should be good enough to fool the British.

2. Next you need to plan your strategy for getting down to the harbor and out onto the ship without being spotted. How will you do that?

3. Once you get to the harbor and get on board the ship, how will you take it over and get to the tea? How will you take care of the crew?

4. It's always good to be prepared for problems. What sort of problems do you anticipate, and how will you solve them?

5. After the mission is completed, you'd better lay low—maybe even go into hiding. How will you do that?

The Leader's Role

Some ideas you select can be enhanced by your playing a role in the drama. In the drama about the Boston Tea Party, for example, you might be an older patriot who says:

> "My friends, I'm afraid my age and infirmities prevent me from joining you this night. This 'tea party' you're planning should make quite a surprise for the British. I'm glad I have this shop for you to meet in. You should be safe here."

Or in Palmer Brown's poem "The Spangled Pandemonium" (4, 36) you might be the mayor of the town who is concerned for everyone's safety with this animal on the loose. Perhaps you have called in the children as expert "spangled pandemonium" catchers and say to them:

> "As the mayor of this town, I want you to know we're all counting on you. Our fair city has never had a crisis like this before. But I've been assured by the people who have hired you before that you're the ones for this job."

Hints on Wording Questions

1. Keep questions limited to five, or the discussion may last too long.

2. Remember that the questions follow the story line format. There must be a

beginning, a middle, and an end to the stories, with a conflict and a resolution.

3. The questions should help the children think of *action* they are going to pantomime. Avoid situations where characters interact, particularly with dialogue, or the children may have nothing to pantomime.

4. Keep the questions following the chronological order of the story, moving it forward. Do not back up and change the direction of a story or ask questions that are not directly related to it.

5. Ask questions that are open-ended and encourage embellishment of ideas. If a question can be answered with just a yes or no, it will build minimal plot.

6. Ask intriguing questions that will draw the students into the idea:

   a. Give the children importance. You might open a discussion, for example, by saying that Paul Bunyan has the flu and has called on them for help feeding the hungry lumberjack camp. Children might become expert goblin catchers, called upon by the person in Rose Fyleman's poem "The Goblin" (4) to rid his home of this noisy creature. Or the President might send them on an important mission back into history to discover needed answers to pressing problems.

   b. Add tension to the questions to build interest. In the Halloween adventure outlined earlier, for example, there is the suggestion that the house may be haunted. Or those who go on adventures with the Half-Pint Jinni (82) must always be sure to double their wishes, since he can grant only half ones. Or perhaps there is the pressure of time: a job must be finished by midnight, or a magic spell will wear off.

7. It is helpful to word the questions tentatively so that the students can change their story as they hear more ideas discussed. "What *do you suppose* you'll do next?" for example, leaves the way open for flexibility.

Do not try to get answers from everyone on every question. Discussion should continue only as long as it is motivating the students and the ideas are flowing. Most students will want to get to the playing as soon as possible.

The importance of the class-wide discussion is for the evolving of numerous ideas, the cross-fertilization of thinking, and the expanding and elaborating of creativity. Students may hear ideas that will mesh with theirs; or they may hear an idea they like better than their own. You too may even be inspired with new ideas. Discussions are most valuable when this kind of creative process is taking place.

Discussions also help you see the ideas the children have so that you can better organize the playing. If fierce combat is suggested, for example, you may decide to preview some fighting or carefully control space so that the story can be played safely and successfully. Discussions also help you interpret what you see the children playing. Because a child mentions that her balloon ship will develop a leak, you can understand why she is swirling and sinking during the playing.

As students gain skill in this kind of story building, they may not always need a lot of discussion time. You may be able to give the entire outline of your discussion questions and let them plan it all in one gulp. It is not unusual for some students to give you their entire story after you ask the first question. They may be several steps ahead of you!

PLAYING AND SIDE-COACHING

Preview Playing

You may want to have children preview part of their ideas before playing their entire story. For example, how will they get into their armor before going off on their adventure as a knight? Or before a story on skydiving, you may want children to check out the procedures and maneuvers a diver goes through to have a safe and stable fall with both arms and legs apart. Such maneuvers must be automatic for the skydiver; preview playing would thus simulate actual conditions.

Instructions for Playing

At first, students may create brief stories of perhaps only 30 seconds to a minute in length; gradually, with a topic that interests them, they should increase their playing time to three minutes and possibly even longer. Since not all students' stories will last for the same length of time, it is best to instruct them to sit down when they have finished their story and quietly watch others.

Even though students are making up their own beginnings and endings for their stories, you should give signals for both. Your signals will add more to the playing if you make them as imaginative as possible:

> "When you hear the clanging of pots, you'll know the cook's signaling you cowboys for the new day of driving cattle on the open range. You'll know the day is ending when you hear the soft strums of the guitar by the campfire."

If you play a role, your instructions can take on special meanings. For example, you might pretend to be a supervisor of child laborers in a sweat shop in the early 1900s who begins the playing by ordering:

> "All right, you ragamuffins, get to work! And make no mistakes! There'll be no pay for the sloppy and lazy. Get started, and be quick about it!"

Or in an adventure about Miles Standish and a party making the first trip to the shore of the new land, you might play one of the Pilgrim fathers who stays behind on the *Mayflower:*

> "Goodman Standish and friends, be at rest about those of us who would remain on board ship. We will be safe. But, good brothers, be vigilant. The shore looks peaceful, but dangers would lurk. Do not tarry."

When most of the students have ended their playing, you can narrate or side-coach an ending for those still playing if it looks as if they need help in finishing. (Some can go on forever if you let them!) It is also wise to narrate or side-coach an ending if you see the playing deteriorating at any time.

Side-coaching Hints

1. As before, music will play an important part in encouraging the students' ideas and providing a background for their dramas.

2. Since students have created their own stories to play, they should not need more than just a few reminders of the various stages of their plot—the beginning, the action, the problems they may be encountering, and the solutions they may have. Many will be too engrossed in their playing to pay much attention to side-coaching.

3. Side-coaching is usually needed more for individual playing than for pair and group playing. When students work with each other in these stories, they rely more on their classmates than on you for assistance.

4. You can also lend to the drama in your side-coaching by playing a character role. In the following example, students are creating stories about race-car driving. They are in groups that include the drivers and their pit crews. You can lend authenticity and drama in the role of the official announcer of the race:

> "It's a great day for the races, all you fans out there! The cars are lined up for the beginning of this day-long race. The excitement here is high; the atmosphere is tense. The engines are roaring, and the race is about to begin. At the wave of the flag, each team is on its own. Good luck! . . . And they're off! What will be the outcome of this race is anybody's guess. . . ."

Other techniques are also possible. In the earlier example of the Pilgrim father, you might pretend to write in a diary and express your thoughts aloud as side-coaching:

> "On this day we have made the decision to explore this new land. We know not what dangers lie ahead. Several of our party have been sent to explore, and we can only hope and pray that all will be well with them. . . ."

5. It is usually best to word the side-coaching tentatively, since the students' ideas are all different and you really do not know all the details of each story. Also, the students are not moving through the various stages of their stories at the same speed.

> "It *seems as if some* people have already left on their mission. . . ."
> "I *wonder if anyone* has run into a problem yet. . . ."
> "You're all such clever detectives, I'm sure you'll all be able to *find the clues you need* to solve the case. . . ."

6. Do not interject any new idea in the side-coaching. If you call out ideas such as "Look out for that shark!" or "Suddenly you discover gold!" you will only confuse the playing. These ideas are appropriate to narrative pantomime but would be interruptions in these original stories.

DISCUSSION OR DIALOGUE FOLLOW-UP WITH THE LEADER IN A CHARACTER ROLE

When the playing has ended, many students will want to tell you what happened in their stories, elaborating on the ideas they mentioned earlier. There may be times when you will ask them to write their experiences in story, diary, or newspaper-article format; or you might have them draw a picture or just discuss what happened.

However, you will not want to miss the opportunity to extend the story or plot idea through character dialogue. If you play a character role, you have the chance to explore so many more ideas and concepts with the students.

Ideally in your questions you want to extend the story and build on the students' creativeness. It is often helpful to use props, pictures, costume, or anything else that will stimulate ideas. In the following example, the creative story has been based on Mary Ann Hoberman's poem, "The Folk Who Live in Backward Town" (32, 36). The children's stories have centered on a day in the life of one of these people, who "take their walks across the ceiling" and "only eat the apple peeling," among other unusual behaviors. The leader plans to play the role of a visitor to the land, and the questions which have been planned are as follows:

1. I'm afraid I'll have a problem during my visit, and I always like to be prepared. What are some things I should be especially careful about?" (The leader is prepared for the fact that some children may give their responses in backward sentences.)
2. "I understand you've had a recent campaign to find a slogan for your town. What were some of the suggested slogans?"
3. "Say, here's a sign I just found over there. I can't read it, and I wonder what it's for. Can anyone tell me?" (The sign could spell DANGER backwards and perhaps could be held upside down. The children have to read it and then explain its importance.)
4. "I have a gift here (hold imaginary box) from the mayor of my town to the mayor of yours. Where's the mayor? (Someone will probably volunteer.) I don't know what it is, Your Honor, so I guess you'll have to open it to find out. I hope it's something you can use." (The child opens the gift and tells what it is. If this proves popular, there can be more gifts and more mayors, or council members, or other dignitaries.)
5. "I'd like to take back some photos of your town to show my friends and neighbors. Have we got some people who wouldn't mind having their picture taken? I like action shots, so you'll need to be doing something. Who'd like to be first? (This can be done in groups like the frozen pictures; see p. 161.)

Opinions, evaluations, descriptions, or other categories of verbalization also can be explored. You may even introduce new problems to be solved. The following examples are from a variety of topics:

1. Newspaper or television reporter talking to the survivor of a plane crash: "The rescue team said they had no trouble finding you. You were a big help to them. What exactly was it that you did to help them find your location?"

2. Head elf to apprentice elves who have done good deeds: "I have to write your good deed down in this record book and then evaluate its importance on a scale of one to five, with five being the highest. What was your deed, and how important would you say it was?" (The children's ratings can be negotiated.)

3. Government official to secret agent: "There's one expenditure here in your report that I can't quite figure out. It's listed as 'miscellaneous,' but the amount you've given is $1,035.74. You'll have to justify that, I'm afraid."

4. Dr. Timepiece talking to children who have just gone through a time machine to another period of history: "I'm trying to perfect my machine. What improvements would you suggest?"

5. Wizard whose lost wand the children have found: "You deserve a reward for your efforts. What would you like—within the power of my wand—to have as your prize?" (Any outlandish request can be labeled "outside the power of my wand.")

6. Royal monarch to an early discoverer: "This is the only map we have of the territory you have just explored. On the basis of your explorations, what changes will need to be made?"

Dialogue with Verbal Children

It is generally best to ask questions of the group as a whole and then call on volunteers. If students are highly verbal, you need to move quickly from one student to another. Another alternative is to pair or group the children for discussion. A spokesperson can report the answer.

Highly verbal students will sometimes be interested in joining you as questioner. You might then give them a general role as "my assistants," "my colleagues," or similar titles.

If students have played their dramas in small groups, they may see even more opportunities to create dialogue. And if the majority of the class is highly verbal, you will want to utilize other verbal activities, such as panels of experts (p. 188) or even verbal skits (discussed at the end of Chapter 8).

Dialogue with Reticent Students

If the creative story has been intriguing and the questions are captivating, often even the shyest person will want to become involved. However, it is a good idea to be prepared with simple questions that can be answered yes or no for students who find it difficult to speak up in a classroom ("Did you have an exciting adventure?" "Did you find what you were looking for?" "Were you scared?" and so forth). Even nodding or shaking the head in answer to a question can be a big undertaking for some children.

As another precaution it is helpful for you to have an "out"—a reason you can give in case a child appears ready to speak and then freezes up at the last moment. For example, as a "newspaper reporter" you might say to an inventor, "I can understand your not wanting to talk to me; this invention of yours is probably top-secret stuff."

Replaying and Sharing (Optional)

Once the students have tried an idea they like, they may ask to play it again. They may have new ideas. Some may want to include ideas they have heard from others. Or they may want to work with a partner after playing solo. They may also desire to share their ideas by playing them for the rest of the class.

Before sharing or replaying, you can take the opportunity to have them evaluate their work by asking what they might like to change or what they particularly liked about their previous playing.

SAMPLE LESSON PLAN: THE BORROWERS
(lower elementary)

Objectives

1. Experience a creative-movement and creative verbal experience based on literature.
2. Create a story with a beginning, a middle, an end, a conflict, and a resolution.
3. Deal with the concept of size relationships: small borrowers in normal-sized home.
4. Imagine problems that could be encountered in a given situation and create appropriate solutions for those problems.
5. Have opportunities to respond to character questioning related to experience.

Preparation and Materials

   A.   Space: area in center of room with desks around edge of room
   B.   Supplies

1. Small objects, such as small metal pillbox, fancy beaded ballpoint pen, small decorative mirror. One prop for final discussion: small pair of child's plastic craft scissors, for example
2. Record player; recording of "Arabian Dance" from Tschaikovsky's *Nutcracker Suite*
3. Copy of Mary Norton's book *The Borrowers* (66)
4. Pictures from the text (enlarged, if possible)

   C.   Length of session: 45 minutes (approximately)

Motivation

Recall the book if they already know it or simply tell them briefly about the tiny people who live under the floorboards of a person's house. When the people in the house are asleep at night, the little people search for and "borrow" small objects from the house to furnish their own miniature home. Show illustrations so that children can see objects such as postage stamps, thimbles, and pins being used in the Borrower's house in unique ways.

Discussion Questions

1. "Suppose you were a Borrower, and you needed to redecorate your home. Look at these objects and tell me what you think you might be able to use them for." (Children's answers might include such ideas as: the pillbox as a baby bed, the pen as a decorative column for the porch, or the mirror as a skating rink for the children.)

2. "Suppose that tonight's the night for the borrowing trip. You're going to get these objects—or perhaps something else. What equipment will you need to take with you on your trip?" (You could use string and safety pins to hook various objects with and to climb up the drapes. You could use a wagon from a dollhouse to carry things in. Better have cotton to stuff in the dog's ears so he won't hear us and start barking.)

3. "What other things will you be looking for tonight?" (I need a new picture for the wall. My rug is worn out and I want to get a handkerchief for a new one. I want a swimming pool, and there's a soup bowl in the china cabinet that would be perfect.)

4. "Borrowing is a dangerous business. Homily, you know, always worries about her husband, Pod, when he goes on one of these missions. And Arrietty had to wait a long time before she was old enough to go with him.

A Borrower assists her "injured" partner in a creative story.

What's so dangerous about borrowing, and what particular problems do you think you might run into?" (Household pets could hurt you. If you got near a bathtub filled with water and fell in, you might drown. If anyone sees you, you'll have to move out and go to another house because they'll be after you for sure.)

5. "How will you be able to avoid these problems and get home safely with all your new furnishings?" (I have a map of the house with all the danger points marked. I'm just gathering the stuff together tonight and will make another trip tomorrow to carry it back; I always wear dark clothes so it's harder to see me.)

Directions for Playing

"I can see you have all your ideas worked out, so we'll get ready for the mission. I'll dim the lights so it will be more like nighttime. Now, you have all your gear ready, so you'll just be resting and waiting for the household to go to bed. When you hear the clock strike one o'clock, you'll know you can be sure everyone's asleep. Remember that you must be as silent as possible or you might wake someone up, and you know what that will mean. You know the household awakens at five o'clock, so when you hear the clock strike five, you'd better scurry back home. When you have reached back home, just sit down quietly in your playing space and wait for others to finish."

"We will need to do this in two shifts—so shift one will work from one o'clock until three o'clock; shift two will work from three o'clock until five o'clock." (Designate who is in which shift.)

Side-coaching. (Start the record player.) "It's very quiet now and almost one o'clock. . . . Everyone's gone to bed. . . . (Strike a metal platter for the clock.) It's time! . . . Quietly you begin your adventure. . . . I believe some people are checking their equipment for one last time. . . . Some have already started out. . . . I hope you'll be able to see well enough. . . . It's so dark this time of night. . . . There are so many dangers out there, too. . . . Oh, oh, I think someone may have had some difficulty. . . . All we can do is hope they'll be okay. . . . Borrowers are used to living by the skin of their teeth, so I guess they'll do all right. . . . Ah, it looks as if some have been successful and have all the things they came for. Good. . . . Some appear to be heading home (over half the children are now seated). . . . Oh dear, it seems to be very close to three o'clock and time for the second shift to take over. . . . I hope everyone is nearly finished or they'll run out of time. . . . (Strike the "clock" three times.) Three o'clock and everyone who's left needs to hurry home. And it's been such a tiring night, you all fall exhausted into bed." (Fade out the record.)

"Now, while the first shift rests, the second shift will begin their work." (Repeat the playing as above.)

(Turn up the lights.) "Well, that was an exciting adventure. Let's hear about what happened to you. What was the scariest part for you?" (Discuss.)

The Leader in a Character Role

"Now, let's suppose I'm a Borrower from another house and I've come to visit you. I've never been borrowing before, and my parents sent me here to talk to you so I could learn. They told me you're the most famous Borrowers and you know all the ins and outs of this business. Will you help me with some questions?"

1. "How did you get to be so good at borrowing?"
2. "What was the closest call you ever had in borrowing?"
3. "Can you tell or show me what you're most proud of having borrowed? What's the nicest or best thing you have?"
4. "What's the most important thing I should know about borrowing? Do you have any secret tricks you could tell me about?"
5. "My parents told me you're planning to have a garage sale soon. What things are you planning to get rid of? Why?"
6. "I found this on your doorstep." (Show scissors or other small object.) "I wasn't sure if you lost it or if you have it out there for a reason. What is it used for?"

(Other roles for highly verbal children who can join you as questioner: "Some friends of mine who are ready to start borrowing." "Out" for reticent children: "Excuse me, I should have remembered that it isn't always safe to talk; someone could overhear us and then your life would be in danger.") "Thanks for talking to me. I have to go home now. I know you've had a very busy night, so I'll let you get a little sleep. 'Bye."

Quieting activity.   (as leader) "And so the Borrowers put away their things, fluff up their pillows on their beds, lay down their heads, and quietly go to sleep." (Play restful music such as "Aquarium" from Saint-Saëns's *Carnival of the Animals*.)

SAMPLE LESSON PLAN: ROBOTS (upper elementary)

Objectives

1. Experience creative mechanical movement and creative verbal experience based on topic of robots.
2. Gain practice in creating a story with a beginning, a middle, and an end.
3. Deal with the concept of a mechanical robot's possibilities for work.
4. Imagine problems that could be encountered in mechanical devices and create appropriate solutions.
5. Provide opportunities to respond to character questioning related to the experience.
6. Provide opportunity to become more familiar with computer concepts such as programming, GIGO (garbage in/garbage out), and user friendly.

Preparation and Materials

1. Space: area in center of room with desks around edge of room.
2. Supplies: ad statement cards; small nondescript piece of machinery
3. Equipment: record player
4. Books: catalogue advertising of a personal robot, or use one of the robots discussed in *Robots in Fact and Fiction* by Melvin Beyer (New York: Franklin Watts, 1980)
5. Music: use any "mechanical-sounding" musical recording plus some quieting music
6. Visual aids: pictures of robots

Warmup. Introduce the advertisement for a personal robot that rolls on rubber wheels, has a stationary tray-type arm, a manual grasping hand to carry objects, flashing eyes, and a tape-recorded voice.

1. Do a warmup activity being robots doing calisthenics or aerobic dancing to music. (Give the opportunity to move as the robot would move, translating calisthenics designed for the human body over to a robot's body.) Divide students into two groups, taking turns with brief exercise activity. Try interpreting how a robot would do toe touches, jumping jacks, knee bends, and so on.
2. Do ad talks (see p. 183) using a robot or a mechanical voice.

Discussion Questions

1. "Suppose you were a robot. What type of job might you do? Where do you work?" (Children's answers might include: in an office doing odd jobs, in a house doing simple housework tasks or belonging to a kid like me who has him as a servant.)
2. "What are all the things you have to do in a day's time? What's your typical day like?" (Deliver mail, run copy machine, get coffee; dust, empty wastebaskets, run a vacuum cleaner; it follows me around to carry my books, brings me breakfast in bed, does my paper route.)
3. "Suppose today, as you're in the middle of all your work, something goes wrong. What might that be? And what happens to you and all your work?" (I could start doing things all wrong and pour coffee in the mailbox and run lots of blank paper; I'm cleaning because a lot of company's coming, and I'm trying to mop and spill the bucket of water and short all my circuits and go haywire; I throw the papers on the porches, but I got programmed wrong and the papers start breaking windows and knocking stuff around.)
4. "Oh dear. Well, we'd better get things back to normal again. What could happen to stop all this damage and make things right again?" (I have to be sent out for repairs and get straightened out and finish the day; someone comes and blows me dry with a hair dryer and I still have to be fixed but at least I stop messing things up; some people tackle me and punch in the right code so I can do it right.)
5. "Now I'd like to know what robots do when they've finished a hard day's work. What would you do to relax?" (I watch TV in the lounge; I have my own room so I go there and listen to records; I like to play chess with myself and see if I can trick myself.)

Directions for Playing

"I think we're ready to give this a try. Since there isn't enough space for everyone this first time, we'll take half of you for the first playing and half for the second. I'll play some mechanical-sounding music for you to pantomime to. Get in your places. And be sure you stay in your own space, especially since you said so many things would go wrong. I'll let you know when you're switched on. When you finish your story, just freeze where you are." (Record starts.)

Side-coaching (as needed). "Robots, get ready for a new day. You're switched on—now. . . . Oh, boy, a robot's day never seems to end. . . . It's work work work all the time. . . . You've sure been thoroughly programmed . . . so many jobs are being done . . . I hope the people who own you are aware of the complete job you're doing for them. . . . Ah, and today is that special day when you're to do your special job . . . it's so very important that everything goes right . . . everybody's counting on you. . . . Oh dear, I think I see some things looking not quite right. . . . Is it possible? . . . Oh, I hope someone can save you from making such as mess of things. . . . Whew, good, I think some robots must have been helped . . . they seem to be getting back to normal—or at least they've been stopped from doing any more damage. . . . Some are completely done in I see . . . and now almost all robots are finished. . . . We'll shut off the last few as the music ends." (Fade music out.)

The second group of players enact their stories.

Follow-up Discussion

"Now that you robots are back to normal again, I'd like to check with you on some things. Allow me to introduce myself. My name is McGillicutty, and I'm a marketing analyst. I've heard about you robots, and I want to talk directly to you about your capabilities so I'll know how to market you in this country.

Questions. (Students can be encouraged to use the "computer-sounding" voice used earlier in the ad-talk activity.)

1. "Just how user friendly are you? Is it possible to make you even more user friendly than you are? And if so, how might we do that?"
2. "Which of your parts need replacing most frequently? What is the cost for that?"
3. "I've heard it said that some of your early customers had complaints. For example, some said you didn't work fast enough; you were too noisy; and one even claimed you talked too much. Would you care to respond to any one or all of those complaints?"
4. "Oh by the way, here's a small piece of machinery I found on the floor. I think it might be a part of one of you. Who claims it?"
5. "I understand you are the first model of personal robot and that there are others in design and manufacturing right now. How are the new models different from you, and are the differences significant?"
6. "One final question—and this is strictly personal and off the record. You can level with me. As a robot, do you ever have a desire to become even more human than you are now? Why or why not?"

(Other roles for verbal children: Instead of questioning in the leader role, you could set up a panel of robots who are questioned by the class playing prospective buyers. If they all like talking as robots, you might want to set up paired conversations with robots interviewing other robots for jobs. "Out" for reticent children: "I'm terribly sorry. Your manufacturer probably considers that classified information.")

"Thanks for talking with me. I have to go write my report. I know you've had a busy day, so I'll let you relax now."

Quieting activity. "Robots, please return to your packing cases. We need to have you sent out for servicing and overhauling after your experience today. You're all inside? Good. I'm shutting off all your power now." (Play restful music for a few moments.)

FOR THE COLLEGE STUDENT

1. Outline lesson plans for two separate creative stories. One is to be based on fiction or fantasy; the other on fact. One should be for individual playing; the other, for pair or group. Refer to the sample outlines on p. 220–21 and to the preceding sample lesson plans.

   a. *introductory materials:* Write out objectives, preparation and materials, and motivation.

   b. *discussion:* Form five carefully worded discussion questions to help the children get a story line for their ideas. For each question, give three possible answers (speculative on your part) which three children might give you. When you have finished this section, check the five answers you have received from each child to see if each has a completed story line. If not, examine the questions again for possible problems.

   c. *organization of playing:* Indicate whether any, and what kind of, preview playing is necessary. Give the directions for children to get organized. Give directions for beginning and ending the playing. Specify if you are in a character role.

   d. *side-coaching:* Write out in exact wording some side-coaching comments appropriate to the story idea. If you are side-coaching in a role, specify your character.

   e. *final discussion in character role:* Explain your character for the final discussion. In words as your character would say them, write out five open-ended questions appropriate to the story and your character. Or suggest other verbal activities that would be appropriate for a follow-up playing of the idea. What roles could be given to highly verbal children who might join you? Include an "out" for the reticent child.

2. Lead your classmates in one of your lesson plans. Discuss afterward the effectiveness of the plan. What were the strengths? How might it be improved?

3. Keep a file of materials that would be appropriate for creative stories. Be sure to include both fictional and factual ideas. In addition to literature and textbook information, you might also want to consider newspaper clippings, pictures, music, slides, films, props, and costumes.

TEN

Story Dramatization

A number of stories and various ways of dramatizing them have been presented throughout this text. The stories used for narrative pantomime focused on action, whereas the stories used for verbal activities and improvisation focused on dialogue. But there are also many stories, some simple and some more complex, which have both action and dialogue. In this chapter, we will examine some additional ways of approaching story dramatization.

Traditionally in creative drama, the term *story dramatization* refers to the process of creating an informal play from a story, improvisationally and with the leader's guidance. The procedure generally includes

1. sharing a story or other piece of literature with a group of students;
2. planning the characters, scenes, and events;
3. playing;
4. evaluating; and
5. replaying.

After much interchanging of roles and experimenting with ideas, the story-play can be "set" similar to a rehearsed play. The playing and experimenting may take place during one class period or may extend over several days' or even weeks' time. The process, however, is the improvisational method. No script is memorized. No one student is cast permanently in or "owns" any one role. And the play is the result of the group's work, facilitated by the leader.

Within this general framework, there can still be many ways to dramatize any given story. Two specific approaches, circle story dramatization and segmented story dramatization, will be presented. Several sample lesson plans are also included. You and your students will eventually decide for yourselves what methods you want to use with the stories you choose to dramatize.

SOME PRELIMINARY CONSIDERATIONS

Selecting the Story

Several considerations should be made in selecting a story for dramatization. First, the story should be of good *literary quality*. (There is a bibliography at the end of this chapter to get you started.) The story should also be one that appeals to you as well as to the children.

Second, there should be plenty of interesting *action* in the story that can be played without elaborate staging. Next, the *dialogue* should be interesting, but not so difficult that the children become frustrated in their attempts to improvise from it.

Finally, the *characters* should be believable. There should also be enough characters (or the possibility of adding characters) to permit a significant number of children, if not the entire class, to be involved in the playing.

Presenting the Story

Stories may be presented in a variety of ways. They may be read or told in your own words. Picture books are usually shared visually with the children, particularly if the illustrations help in seeing action and characterization. There may even be times when you will want to share audio recordings or filmed versions of a story.

Most experts would agree that folktales should be shared orally whenever possible, as they were originally told rather than read or recorded. Besides, oral telling allows you to maintain eye contact with the audience, helping you judge how the children are reacting to it.

Whatever method you use, you must focus on helping the children understand the action of the story and the interaction of the characters so that they can re-create it and expand upon it.

Dialogue

An important part of the presentation of the story is the dialogue. Children usually listen carefully to the dialogue in the stories that are read or told to them, repeating it in their playings and improvising upon it.

Sometimes the addition of dialogue to the storytelling helps the children see verbalizing possibilities. It is particularly helpful to change indirect dialogue to direct dialogue. For example, a line might read:

> As the young man went down the road he met an old woodcutter. He asked the old man if he knew the way to town. The old man told him to follow his nose.

By adding direct dialogue in the telling, this passage could be changed to:

> As the young man went down the road, he met an old woodcutter. "Excuse me, sir," he asked, "I wonder if you could tell me the way to town?"
> The old man answered, "Follow your nose, follow your nose. You can get to almost anywhere you want if you just follow your nose!"

If the dialogue is too complicated, it should be simplified. Otherwise children might be frustrated trying to remember it. Even if you encourage them to "tell it in your own words," they may feel compelled to recreate the original wording and experience failure in the attempt. For example, in telling the story *Bartholomew and the Oobleck,* you can omit the magicians' lengthy poetic chant and simply say, "While they mixed the oobleck, they said their magical chants."

Casting the Story

Because you will be playing the story several times, and because you will want each playing to build on the previous one, it is important to establish a solid beginning. The following suggestions should help.

1. Cast the most competent students for the first playing in order to establish an appropriate model for the rest of the class to build on. Shy or slower students can benefit from seeing the story enacted by others before they undertake it themselves.
2. Double and even triple casting (two or three students playing one character) will also be useful. This technique will allow more students the opportunity to play the story and will provide the security needed for improvising freely. It is helpful to remember: "What one can't think of to say, the other one usually can." Students with special needs (visually or hearing impaired, physically or mentally handicapped, for example) can also benefit from the assistance of their classmates, particularly in moving about the room.
3. You may need to assist with the main role, particularly in first playings with younger children and even with some of the most competent older students. This technique allows you to "walk the students through the story," mapping out the playing areas as you go along. If you are also using the technique of double and triple casting, you can easily and unobtrusively "tag along" and still be available to help as needed.

Aids for Organization

The main concern with story dramatization will generally be "How will I keep things organized?" It is a legitimate concern, but with some careful planning, many problems and difficulties can be alleviated.

Following are a number of organizational suggestions for you to con-

"I'll show you I'm not afraid," says the Captain of the Guard. (triple-casting of one character)

sider. They are designed to help you remember the story line you are playing and to avoid having students all moving and talking at the same time. The techniques usually evolve quite logically as you work with the stories. In time you will find the techniques that work best for you and your students, as well as for the stories that will become your particular favorites.

1. Briefly review the plot of the story before you start to play it. As it is reviewed, write a simple outline on the chalkboard or on a chart.
2. Organize space carefully. You will usually want to have the major scenes take place in the middle of the playing circle or in the front of the classroom. However, other areas of the room, such as the corners, will be useful for additional scenes. It is particularly helpful to place the scenes around the room, sequencing them in the same order that they appear in the story.
    You will need to think this organization through ahead of time. It may be helpful to map it out on the chalkboard for everyone's reference. Later as you feel more comfortable and flexible and as the children gain experience, you will want to consult them for their ideas on mapping out the scenes. Create specific locations using classroom furnishings. For example, a teacher's chair can become "the king's throne," or a teacher's desk might become "a banquet table."
3. Use the students' desks or tables whenever possible. These can be "homes" for the citizens of the town, "stores" for shopkeepers, or "horses" for the king's army. Try also to keep at least some students at their desks (or seated on a rug) until "their scene" is ready to be played. During these "sitting-out" periods, you can refer to the students as the "audience" so they will not feel

While part of the class acts the story, the rest wait for their cue at the desks.

left out or neglected. They may also be able to assist with some sound or lighting effects when they are not involved in the actual playing of the story.

4. Look for the natural controls within the story. The characters may take a nap or rest. Sometimes they are in an immobile position due to enchantment (as in "Sleeping Beauty") or other reasons. Often they "return to their homes," or desks. Capitalize upon these moments to give legitimate quiet periods. You may even find that you can add such moments to your story if they do not already exist.

5. Designate characters in some way so that you—and they—can remember who is playing which part. An easy method is to make headbands with pictures of characters on them (see photo p. 268). Simple costuming with hats, props, and pieces of fabric is also useful but may take more time. You may wish to add these after initial playings and when you are sure the children want to continue playing the story. Separating and grouping the students in various parts of the classroom, as well as using the name tags and costumes, will help you (and them) see the layout of the story and remember the characters.

Organization through Narration and Character Role

Two additional techniques (both of which have been discussed in previous sections) will be indispensable to you in dramatizing a story. They are *narration* and *playing a character role*. Narration will help you guide the dramatization from outside the story. If you play a character role in the story, you can guide the playing from within. And you can use both techniques interchangeably in the same story dramatization.

Ways to guide using narration. Following are some of the various ways your narration can assist in story dramatization. It can

1. open the story:
   "Once upon a time there was . . ."
2. guide the story if it lags or if the children forget the sequence of events:
   "And then the bear started off down the road. . . ."
3. control the action if problems arise:
   "Finally the people decided to stop arguing and do something about the situation. . . ."
4. add pantomime ideas if the children need suggestions:
   "The rabbit looked at himself in the mirror and admired his new clothes."
5. provide transitions for scenes, indicating passage of time or change of environment:
   "The next morning the old lady went out to the smokehouse. . . ."
6. close the story:
   ". . . and he never went looking for trouble again."

Guiding by playing a character role.

What Role Do I Play?

1. You can play the main role, either by yourself or with perhaps one or two students. This technique can be useful with shy students or those who need considerable assistance. Even when students are experienced in story dramatization, you may be able to help revitalize a story by playing a character role yourself. Once you "carry" the children through a story by playing a role, the children will usually be ready to take over by the second or third replaying.
2. You may choose to play a secondary role, such as a king's prime minister or a friend to the central character. If these roles do not already exist in the story itself, they can usually be easily added. This gives you the opportunity to be available if help is needed.
3. You may step into a scene in a spontaneously invented role to assist if students have forgotten the sequence of events or to reactivate the students' involvement if the playing is becoming too mechanical or superficial.

By playing a character role you can:

1. carry the dialogue, initiating the interactions:
   "I believe I've lost my way. Can you give me directions to get to the nearest town?" Or if playing a role with students, "We've got some things to sell. Let us show you some of them."
2. give directions and assistance in character to help the story along:
   "Well, I don't believe these people can help us at all. Over there's someone else who may be able to."
   "I don't know about you, but I'm getting hungry. Maybe there's a place around here where we can get something to eat."
3. control the action and discipline:

Leader can assist students in dialogue by playing a character role.

> "As the king's prime minister, I must remind you that you cannot go into the throne room until you are quiet. And you must bow to the king before you speak. Are you ready?"

4. reactivate involvement, offering new situations for students to react to and new challenges for them to solve:

> "This letter just arrived, and it's addressed to you. I'm sure everyone here would like you to read it aloud."

> "Say, excuse me, but do you have a peddler's license? I'm the inspector here in this town, and we don't allow door-to-door peddling unless someone has a license. I'll have to ask to see yours."

Evaluation

Evaluation of the dramatization should be made after each playing. The emphasis should focus on the positive elements that can be observed in order to ensure that they will be repeated in subsequent replayings.

You need to consider such questions as "Would someone who had not heard the story told be able to follow it from our presentation?" "When was the story most understandable?" "In what parts of the story was the action clear?" "What parts of the dramatization were most interesting (or exciting, sad, or other predominant emotion)?" or "When were the characters most believable?

When the evaluation is made, it is best to use the characters' names rather than the children's names. This practice can be encouraged when children comment on their own playing or when speaking about the contributions of others.

TEACHER: The *king* really seemed to care about his subjects.
CHILD: The *soldiers* all talked at the same time. I think they should wait for each other.
CHILD: I spoke the *captain's* orders in a gruff voice, but I tried to show that he was a kind person by smiling just a little.

Replaying the Story

As the children evaluate, additional ideas are often suggested. These changes and new ideas can also be incorporated into replayings. You and the class together may also think of ways to include sound effects, lighting, music, or other additions the children can operate for themselves. These changes and additions should grow out of group creative process, facilitated rather than imposed by you.

You may wish to consider alternative procedures in replayings after the children have become familiar with the story. For example, middle and older grade children, particularly, may want to divide into smaller groups, each presenting their own rendition of a replaying. Some become fascinated with the narrator role and ask to play that part. Some may see ways to produce and present the story as a puppet play on their own. Whatever additional creative challenges are seen by you or by the children can more easily evolve when undertaken after the initial playing has taken place.

Now let us look at one method of playing simple stories.

CIRCLE STORY DRAMATIZATION

Many simple stories can be dramatized easily and quickly. In one method of playing these stories, *circle story dramatization,* the emphasis is on the easiest and most orderly manner to involve all the students in playing the action or basic story line. In a sense, this method is more like organizing a game, since little emphasis is given to characterization, emotion, and sensory awareness. For young children, who want to play as many parts as they can and to act out all the action and excitement immediately, this method is particularly suitable. Even for many older groups this technique will be desirable, especially if the students are eager to see quick results in their efforts at making a play.

With circle story dramatization you visualize a story being dramatized in a circle. The circle may be seats in a circle, students sitting in a circle on a carpeted area, or a circle around the outer aisles of the room. Even the most active students understand and sense an orderliness about a circle and will usually be cooperative. You and they will also quickly learn the procedure and will be able to adapt it yourselves to other stories.

Generally stories that fit this method best have one or two main characters and an indefinite number of one other character type. The characters are often stereotypical, with little variation in personality. For example, in "The Conjure Wives" (see the bibliography at the end of this chapter), there is a voice and perhaps a leader or main witch, but all the rest of the characters are witches. Their main characteristic is greediness.

Other stories that fit this method particularly well have one or two main characters and a series of different characters who are introduced gradually. The dialogue is simple and usually repetitive. Such stories are often called cumulative. "Henny Penny" is a classic example of this type. Some stories have cumulative scenes within them. Dr. Seuss' *Bartholomew and the Oobleck,* for example, becomes cumulative when Bartholomew goes off in search of a solution to the oobleck problem.

In playing circle stories, you, with perhaps one or two other students, can play the main part initially. This gives you the opportunity to move the story along, to initiate dialogue, and to role model the playing. You can even alternate between being a narrator and playing your role. The rest of the children will sit in a circle arrangement and become the other characters when they appear in the story.

Following are lesson plans for three circle stories, with some added hints on playing them. Feel free to add your own touches and additions to the suggested instructions and to adapt the methods to similar and favorite stories of your own.

SAMPLE LESSON PLANS FOR CIRCLE STORY DRAMATIZATION

"WHY THE BEAR IS STUMPY TAILED"

"Why the Bear is Stumpy Tailed" in *Popular Tales from the Norse* by Peter Christian Asbjørnsen and Jørgen Moe, translated by Sir George Webbe Dasent. New York: Putnam Publishing Group, 1908. See also (4). The same story frequently appears in legends of the North American Indians. See, for example, "How the Long-Tailed Bear Lost His Tail," in *The Long-Tailed Bear and Other Indian Legends,* Natalia M. Belting. Indianapolis: Bobbs-Merrill, 1961.

Synopsis

A bear is told by a sly fox that he can catch fish if he will just put his tail down in the water and wait for the fish to bite. Since it is wintertime, the bear cuts a hole in the ice and begins to fish. He waits patiently, but in the meantime the water freezes over. When he gets up, he discovers his tail is caught fast. As he struggles to free himself, he pulls off his tail. And that is why bears have short tails today instead of long ones.

1. Casting
    a. You may play the bear along with perhaps one or two other children.
    b. Double- or triple-cast the part of the fox.

c. The rest of the children sit in a circle and form the pond the bear fishes in. They can hold hands rigidly and take on a "frozen look" as the ice freezes.

d. Additional characters may be created. One group of second graders suggested that skaters could be skating on the pond as the bear arrives. They also wanted trees, a setting sun, and snowflakes falling as night approached. The trees and falling snowflakes can be played either by the same circle of children forming the pond or by additional children. The sun may be played by two children joining arms in a large circle which moves through (over) the pond in an arcing path to indicate rising and setting. Perhaps as many as six skaters can be included.

2. Action

a. The bear and the fox meet. You can narrate, "Once upon a time a fox had a string of fish he had just caught and met a bear who eyed those fish very hungrily."

b. The bear goes off to fish, and the fox returns to his home. "So the bear decides he will try catching fish the way the fox said he did. The fox returns to his home, and the bear goes off toward the pond. He feels very hungry and can hardly wait to catch a long string of fish."

c. "The ice skaters are skating on the pond as the bear arrives. The bear watches them skate for a while (here you can play a Strauss waltz). . . . Then the skaters skate slowly to their homes (seats in the circle)."

d. "The bear settles himself down on the ice and waits for the fish to begin to bite. His coat is thick and heavy, and he feels snug and warm, even though his tail is in the icy water. He looks around at all the sights. The bear sits there all afternoon. The sun passes over the pond and sets slowly. The wind blows the trees (the trees move), and it gets colder. Snowflakes begin to fall gently to the ground. (Snowflakes fall.) The cold wind freezes the pond into a solid mass of ice. (The pond becomes rigid.) And the ice freezes tightly around the bear's tail."

e. "Now the bear decides it is time to go home. But when he gets up, his tail sticks, and he must pull and pull until finally he gets loose—but his tail pops off. Oh dear, poor bear. And that is why, to this day, bears have short tails instead of long ones."

3. Dialogue

a. The bears and foxes talk briefly to each other about the fish and how they were caught. The foxes usually remember to tell the bears how the fishing is done.

b. No other dialogue is required, though children may suggest other ideas. The bears might want to talk to each other as they fish, for example. Or they might have a few words to say to the skaters. Encourage whatever ideas the children have.

Note: See additional ideas for this story discussed on pp. 253–55.

"THE CAT AND THE PARROT,"
SARA CONE BRYANT (3, 39)

After the children are familiar with the story, the leader can play a minor role . . .

Selected Variations

FAT CAT, JACK KENT. New York: Parent's Magazine Press, 1971. This is a modern illustrated version with the same plot but different characters humorously portrayed.

The Greedy Fat Old Man, PAUL GALDONE. New York: Clarion Books, 1983. Called an American tale, a fat old man replaces the cat and different characters are eaten.

"Sody Sallyraytus," RICHARD CHASE, in *Grandfather Tales* (17). This is an Appalachian version of the story. A bear eats up various family members who go to the store to get baking soda (sody sallyraytus) to make biscuits. The family's pet squirrel outwits the bear. (Several students can be the bear and encircle, holding hands, the family members when they are eaten. Several students might also form the bridge and react to all it sees happening.) This version's subtle humor makes it more appropriate for middle- and older-grade students to play.

Synopsis:

A parrot is the dinner guest of a cat. A meager meal is served, but the parrot returns the invitation and serves a feast. The greedy cat eats everything, including his host, and casually sets out for home. On the way he meets, one by one, an old woman; an old man with a cart and a donkey; a wedding procession, including a newly married prince, his wife, soldiers, and many elephants walking two by two. The cat tells everyone he meets to get out of his way. When they refuse he eats them: "Slip! slop! gobble!" He finally eats two land crabs who pinch a hole in his stomach, and everyone escapes. The cat is left to sew up his coat.

    1.   Casting
        a.   You play the cat with one or two other children. Two children can play the parrot.

. . . or let the children take over by themselves. ("Cat and the Parrot")

    b.   Cast the other characters that are met and organize them in a circle or around the room in the order they appear in the story.

2. Action

    a.   It is easiest to begin the playing when the cat visits the parrot's house and eats up the parrot.

    b.   To designate that they have been eaten, characters can line up behind the cat and continue the journey. Here it is fun to play a follow-the-leader game. Of course, all the "eaten" characters must imitate the movements of the cat, since they are all one entity. The cat might experience a bit of queasiness and slow the movements down as the stomach gets fuller. The cat might decide to skip, to climb a hill laboriously, or to walk across a swinging bridge or a log very carefully. In a first playing, it is best to stay in a circle formation as much as possible. In subsequent playings, the follow-the-leader scene can move about the room.

    c.   After the cat falls asleep under a tree, the children escape from the stomach and tiptoe back to their seats, or "homes," one by one. Here you may assume a narrator's voice and direct this part if needed. ("The first ones out of the stomach were the land crabs, then the soldiers," and so on.) Then, as the cat, you wake up and finish off the story by sewing up the hole in your coat, much to the character's dismay and the children's delight.

3. Dialogue

    a.   The dialogue is repetitive. The cat tells everyone to get out of the way or they will be eaten up. Some of the characters will protest, but of course the cat eats them anyway.

    b.   You might let all the children say "Slip! slop! gobble!" as a chant each time someone is eaten.

CIRCLE STORY DRAMATIZATION AS PART OF A LONGER LESSON PLAN

There may be times when you will want to make a circle story part of a more extended lesson plan. One such lesson plan based on the story *Bartholomew and the Oobleck* is presented here for your use. (Note: This story is also on pp. 255–58 as an example of the segmented story dramatization method so that you can compare it with circle story dramatization.)

BARTHOLOMEW AND THE OOBLECK, DR. SEUSS (New York: Random House, 1949)

Synopsis

King Derwin of Didd complains to his page boy, Bartholomew, that he is bored with the weather. The problem is turned over to the magicians, who suggest that "oobleck" would be a good solution, though they have never made it before. As the oobleck begins to fall the following morning, the King is delighted and declares a holiday. But the joyousness is short-lived when it is discovered that the oobleck is green, sticky, and falling in greater abundance hourly. Only the king's magic words "I'm sorry" stop the oobleck and restore sanity to the kingdom once again.

Introduction

Option A: Begin with a discussion of sticky substances: "What is the stickiest thing you can think of?" "Did you ever get stuck in something really sticky?" Children might share experiences of times they got gum stuck in their hair, walked on hot, sticky tar, or ate sticky candy.

Option B: Discuss things children may have wished for that did not turn out as well as they thought. Children might share experiences of times they got toys, articles of clothing, or food products that were not as good as had been advertised or a trip they took that turned out less than satisfactory.

Warm-up

Option A: "Let's pretend that you have something on your desks, a little substance of some sort, and you try to brush it away. Whoops, it sticks to your hand. No problem, just brush it away with both hands. Uh oh, your hands stick together. Try to pull them apart. Now what can you do?" Here you might want to let the children suggest some ways to get their hands unstuck, try them, and see what might work. Children might hold one arm around their heads or neck and pull mightily; some might step on a hand; some might blow warm air on their hands to soften the substance. You can also narrate a few more tries, getting the children more stuck to other parts of their body until they are totally stuck to themselves. Then wave your "wand of unstickiness" and set them free. Or if they get unstuck themselves, you can congratulate them on their cleverness.

Option B: Do a count-and-freeze pantomime of acting out a wish that turns bad. This can be done with several children individually or with small groups acting out one child's experience.

Presenting the Story

Read or tell the story *Bartholomew and the Oobleck.* (It is preferable to tell it, showing the pictures; by telling, you can simplify some parts and emphasize others.)

Playing the Story

1. Casting
   a. You can play Bartholomew with perhaps one or two other students. Use a boy and a girl.)
   b. Three to five students can play the magicians.
   c. Three students can play the bell ringer, three more the trumpet blower, and another three the captain of the guard.
   d. Two can play the king, or if you prefer, you can have a king and a prime minister or a king and queen.
   e. The rest of the students can be divided into townspeople and people in the palace. The book's illustrations show various occupations in the kingdom, and mention is made specifically of musicians, the laundress, and a cook in the palace. Students will feel more special if you give them specific jobs or have them choose an occupation. They will be acting out their routine tasks when they become stuck in the oobleck.
2. Action
   a. Before starting the story, place the students around the room in the circular pattern. The throne room is at the front of the classroom. On the king's right (as he sits on his throne) are the magicians in the corner as if "offstage." On the king's left are the three bell ringers. In the back corners of the room are the three trumpet blowers and the three captains of the guard. Seated at the back desks are the people of the kingdom, and at the front desks are the people of the palace.
   b. In the opening scene the king complains about how boring the weather is. You can narrate a brief opening, such as "Once upon a time, in the kingdom of Didd, there lived King Derwin who was bored with the weather. One day he was overheard complaining to his pages." Here the king usually picks up the cue and begins complaining. Or as Bartholomew, you can open the scene by saying to the king, "Your majesty, isn't it a beautiful day today? Just look at that sun. . . ."
   c. If the king does not remember to call the magicians, you (as Bartholomew) can suggest it. The pages can also legitimately escort them to the palace with the admonition to be sure to bow before speaking to the king. The dialogue here is simple enough, but if needed, you can tell the magicians what it is the king wants. The magicians can be escorted back to their workplace.

d. Here you can narrate how the magicians work late into the night; if they need help thinking of actions to perform, you can side-coach or narrate how they take down bottles from the shelves, pour and stir the different ingredients, whisper magic chants, and so on. Narrate or side-coach that everyone in the kingdom goes to sleep, including the king and Bartholomew. Finally, the magicians too are finished with their task and go to sleep.

e. Continue narrating: "The following morning, the king got up early and looked out the window and was delighted with what he saw. But Bartholomew woke up, looked out the window, and wasn't sure how to react. Small green specks dotted the sky. It was the oobleck. The king called for Bartholomew and declared a holiday." Now you can join the Bartholomews and either exchange some brief dialogue with the king or make your way over to the bell ringers to declare a holiday.

f. The bell ringers will not be able to ring the bell because of the oobleck, and now you realize that there is no cause for a holiday. Instead you must warn the people of the kingdom.

g. Move to the trumpet blowers and the captains of the guard. Students usually remember what to do and say as the characters in *f* and *g*. Your job as Bartholomew is just to ask for help and be surprised when oobleck gets in the way. Standard lines such as "Oh dear, what's the matter?" or "Uhh, I don't think I'd do that if I were you" will probably come naturally to you as the students play their parts.

h. Now, as Bartholomew talking to the other Bartholomews, you can suggest, "We'd better get back to the palace." As you go through the back desks in the classroom, comment on the various people in the kingdom, the jobs they're doing, and how they are stuck in oobleck. You can even stop and talk briefly to a few: "What happened to you?" "How long have you been stuck like this?"

Trumpet blowers try to get the "oobleck" out of their instruments.

i. As you approach the front desks, you can do the same with the people in the palace.

j. As you go to the throne room (the front of the classroom) the king (and partner) will also be stuck. Here there is an exchange of a little bit of dialogue. You can talk about how bad things are in the kingdom; the king tries to think of some magic words; you shame the king into saying he's sorry. (If the king has trouble here, you can narrate "And if you listened closely, you could hear the king say softly, 'I'm sorry.'"

k. Narrate an ending such as, "And no one knows why, but as soon as those magic words were spoken, the oobleck began to melt until it finally disappeared altogether. And then there *was* cause to celebrate. The bells rang, the trumpets blew, and the guards marched, and everyone cheered ("Hip, hip, hooray!") in honor of the day the oobleck came *and left*." Lead the class in applause for themselves and return them to their seats.

3. Dialogue

   a. The king complains about the weather, calls for magicians, declares a holiday, and says "I'm sorry."

   b. The magicians usually have no trouble remembering to suggest oobleck and the fact that they have never made it before.

   c. The bell ringers, the trumpet blowers, and the captains of the guard usually have no trouble remembering their difficulties with the oobleck if you have emphasized them in the storytelling.

   d. The dialogue with people of the kingdom and the people in the palace is optional.

Evaluation

Have a brief discussion of what they liked best. Check for any trouble spots in organization or plot line, dialogue, and so forth.

Replaying

Since this story will take some time, you will probably not replay it the same day. Be sure to remind them that parts will be exchanged in another playing.

Quieting Activity

Bring all the children back to their seats. Have them stand at the side of their desks and instruct them to melt into their seats for the quieting activity. Then narrate a brief paragraph about a piece of oobleck melting slowly. "As the king said those magic words, 'I'm sorry,' no one knows why, but the oobleck started to melt. Just like snow on a warm, sunny winter day, the oobleck got smaller and smaller until it disappeared completely, bit by bit. And, now, as I count to three you will finish melting into your desks." (Here you might play a quieting musical selection.)

SEGMENTED STORY DRAMATIZATION

A second method of story dramatization is *segmented story dramatization*. For segmented story dramatization, a story or even an entire book becomes a stimulus for creating numerous separate (or segmented) drama activities. Technically speaking, any piece of literature or idea can be handled with this method.

An Explanation of Segmented Story Dramatization

The method has evolved from two basic sources. First, as is commonly done in the rehearsal of a play, the script is worked on part by part. Segmenting a story simply breaks it down into more workable rehearsal units. And many of the activities used in segmented story dramatization are similar to the ones that have already been covered in preceding chapters. Circle story dramatization allows the class to experience the plot of a story; segmented story dramatization gives children more opportunity to play a variety of characters in a variety of situations.

The second source for segmented story dramatization comes from improvisational theatre techniques that encourage exploration of characters and situations. As is true with improvisation, many of the activities in segmented story dramatization (see the sample lessons beginning on page 253) extend beyond the original story line and may introduce new characters or new situations. For example, in "The Emperor's New Clothes" there is a solo verbal activity which asks the emperor's mother (an invented character never mentioned in the original story) how her son became so interested in clothes and whether he has always acted the way he does now. Such an activity encourages children to explore the many possible dimensions of the story characters and the motivations for their behavior. A student, pretending to be the emperor's mother, for example, may answer that the royal family once fell on hard times and the emperor, as a child, really had only one change of clothing. Now he seems to be trying to make up for his earlier deprivation. Another student might explain that her son has always enjoyed clothes. In fact, as a baby he cried to have his diapers changed even when they did not need to be; and as a toddler he would cry if his romper outfits were not changed each hour.

Creating Segmented Activities

In segmented story dramatization, both pantomime and verbal activities are developed. Each of these categories is then divided into solo and then pair and group activities. The number of activities you develop will depend on your own inventiveness as well as on the children's interests and abilities.

Once the list of activities is created, you simply select ones which would be most meaningful for your group to try out. Since you will often develop more activities than would be played in one session, you can pick and choose from the list of activities, as you would from a menu. Each story will thus provide several lessons, should you and the students care to try all the activities.

The Wording of Segmented Activities

There are some considerations you should note in the wording of the various activities in the sample lessons. Generally they are worded simply and briefly and can be stated as instructions in their present form. You may, however, need to add side-coaching instructions or other elaborations as you see the children's response to them. Some procedural steps of this nature are indicated in the first sample lesson.

Even with the brief wordings, you should note carefully the special features which help make the activities as intriguing as possible as well as the words which keep the class organized and controlled. The importance of these features cannot be overemphasized and are often crucial to the success the children will have in playing the activities. As one example, there is frequent use of the words "carefully," "special," and "urgent," which lend importance to the activity so that students become more involved in them. The roles suggested are often those of experts.

There are also control features mentioned earlier in Chapter 9. The students may be asked to play while the leader counts, as the music plays, or while the drum beats or the tambourine rattles, and so forth. In dialogue activities, there are often conflicts to solve, an important technique mentioned throughout Chapter 8 that encourages dialogue flow.

Use with Younger and Older Children

Younger children, who are more interested in seeing things in "wholes," will not be interested in extensive use of segmented activities. They will, however, enjoy the additional challenges of a few of these activities, particularly when they are repeating stories they have played several times. Several such activities can then be added to a circle story dramatization as it is being replayed. And as they show interest and abilities in playing these activities, you can add them to the first playing of new circle stories. In the first sample lesson plan beginning on page 253, there are some procedural suggestions for using these activities with younger children.

Older students are able to bring many creative ideas to these activities. They find them challenging and react to them as they might to new games to play and new puzzles to solve. Especially as they become more experienced, you will be able to give older students an activity and let them work it out on their own. They will even have ideas of their own to suggest for activities.

PLAYING SEGMENTED ACTIVITIES

Playing Solo Activities

It is generally best to begin with some solo activities, both pantomime and verbal, at the desk. These solo activities serve as a good warm-up to the pair and group activities. For pantomime solo activities, the students all play simultaneously. These are usually brief scenes that often benefit from the addition of musical background or side-coaching.

The verbal solos are usually short responses of a sentence or two. For these you can call on as many volunteers as you wish. Some children will be able to deliver quite a lengthy speech, however, so you may need to limit some of the responses. If there are more volunteers than you have time for, try pairing the students and let them share their ideas with each other. You may also play the part yourself and let the students question you.

You may choose to play a character role in the verbal solos, pretending to be a newspaper interviewer or other information seeker, to give the students a person to respond to. As you play, you may find yourself asking additional interview questions which will give further challenge to the students. As the children see these interviews being modeled, they will probably want to play the role of the interviewer themselves. In that case a solo activity can easily become a paired activity. Likewise, paired activities can be developed further into group scenes.

Playing Pair and Group Activities

Next you can move to the pair and group pantomimes and finally to the pair and group dialogue scenes. For these, divide the class into pairs or small groups and let them try their hand at some of the activities. Let each pair or group share its ideas and interpretations with the rest of the class. As an alternative procedure you may assign different activities to each pair or group. However, most classes will probably want to play all the activities eventually, especially if the activities are intriguing and creatively challenging.

For the pair and group verbal activities you can let students rehearse a bit and then share the scenes, as in the method described on page 194. Some children may even want to try their hand at playing these scenes spontaneously, without rehearsing first, for the challenge of "thinking on their feet." Do not push for this, however, as there are always some children who will not enjoy this pressure. To end the lesson you can return to one of the desk activities for a quieting experience.

Putting It All Together

Students often get so interested in the creative challenge these activities pose that they do not worry if all the characters and situations can be incorporated into a completed dramatization. Sometimes they do not even consider "putting the story together" as a necessary step. The deeper exploration into the various aspects of the story is often satisfying by itself. But it is also true that you have really rehearsed the story in bits and pieces after playing the various activities. So it is then easy to select the ones you and the students like best, arrange them chronologically, and use them as a basis for creating your own improvised play from beginning to end. Either way you choose, you are bound to have much fun and many learning experiences.

"WHY THE BEAR IS STUMPY TAILED" 2

(*Note:* This story is suitable for young children. See page 242 for the story synopsis and for the circle story method of playing this same story. Only a few activities are presented for this story, but they are elaborated upon with procedures that are often necessary in encouraging improvisational ideas from younger children. Note that these procedures parallel those covered in Chapter 8.)

Pantomime Solo

1. "Pretend you are the bear, cutting a hole in the ice and then settling down to catch the fish. What will you do to pass the time while you wait for the fish to bite?"

Sample Procedure for #1

TEACHER: What do you think the bear takes with him in order to fish? How does he cut the hole in the ice?

CHILD 1: The pond is covered with snow, and the bear has to shovel it away before he can cut the hole.

T: So you're going to take a shovel.

C 2: The bear cuts a hole with his sharp claws.

T: Can you show us how you would do that? (The child demonstrates.)

C 3: He has an ice cutter and a tiny ice house and a small heater.

T: Ummm, sounds like a well-equipped bear. You've all got good ideas. Now, tell me, when that bear had to sit there for such a long time, he must have gotten tired. I wonder what he did to pass the time? What would you do if you were that bear?

C 4: I think he gets cold and wraps his muffler around his ears and twiddles his thumbs. Then he hums a song about the summertime to himself.

T: The song is to help him feel warmer?

C 4: Yes, but I don't think it really works. (The teacher laughs.)

C 2: He reads a book.

> T: Any particular book?
>
> C 2: No, just a book.
>
> T: I see, just anything to take his mind off how cold he's getting.
>
> C 5: He keeps looking for someone to come and talk to him, but no one comes. So he just counts all the trees he can see.
>
> T: Ah, like counting sheep before you go to sleep at night. You have so many good ideas. We haven't heard them all, but you seem ready to play them. Stay at your desk, and while I play the music, you pretend to be the bear when he goes to the pond, cuts a hole in the ice, and then fishes with his tail. (As the playing begins, you may side-coach and remind the children of the ideas they have given.)

2. "The story doesn't tell us, but I wonder what the bear is doing before he ever meets the fox. Think of three things you think a bear might do, and as I count to three, you act them out." (Children's ideas might include the following: he's combing his beautiful tail; he's looking for food; he's sleeping because it's wintertime and he loves to sleep.)

3. "Suppose you are the fox. Let's see what you would be doing before you meet the bear with your string of fish." (He's planning all the ways he's going to trick the bear and writing all the ideas down in a notebook; he's buying the fish at a fishmarket; he's ice fishing but he's doing it with a real fishing pole.)

4. "Be one of the skaters who come to skate on the ice. You have a lot of fancy moves to show off to anyone who might be watching. As I play the music, try out some of your fanciest skating."

5. "When the wind blows and it gets colder, the trees sway their branches and snowflakes fall gently. Let's have this half of the class be the trees; this half the snowflakes. Follow the sound arrow to make the sounds of the wind."

Verbal Solo Sample Procedures

1. "You are the bear and I'll be the fox. What would you say to me when you see me with a long string of fish? Remember how you like fish." (Hold up a string of fish and lick chops as you admire them. Call on volunteers for their responses.)

> CHILD: Those are good-looking fish. Where'd you get them?
>
> C 2: I want some fish like that. I'm hungry.
>
> C 3: Hello, Fox. Where'd you get those fish? I'll buy some from you.
>
> (and so forth)

2. Teacher: Good. Now let's pretend I'm the bear and you're the fox. What would you say to me? (as the bear) Hey, Fox, where'd you get those fish?

> C 4: Uh, well, see, you cut a hole in the ice and put your tail in it. They'll bite and you'll get some.
>
> T: No kidding! (to another child) Say, where'd you get your fish?

C 5:   Same place he did. (indicates C 4)
T: By golly, I guess it must be true. (calls on another child) What about your fish? Where'd they come from?
C 6:   It's real easy. You just cut a hole in the ice.
T: And I put my tail in?
C 6:   Yeah. Way down deep.
T: I just have to ask one more fox. This is really a strange story. How did you get your fish?
C 7:   You put your tail in the water, but you have to wait a long time. But it's really fun to do. And these fish are delicious.
T: Yes indeed, I'll bet they are.

(*Note:* If you want to encourage more dialogue, you can pretend to be unconvinced and say "Aw, I don't believe that. You just made up that story." Then the foxes will have to work a little harder to convince the bear of their fishing method.)

Now that the children have played the scene with you, you can have them pair up and share their short conversational scenes, a few pairs at a time.

Verbal in Pairs and Groups

1. "Suppose that the bear suddenly realizes that he is stuck in the ice and that he has been tricked by the fox. But he doesn't want to admit what has happened because he's embarrassed. Think of someone who comes by the pond, sees the bear, has a reason to ask the bear to leave and tries to coax him away. Because he doesn't want them to see he's stuck, he has to give a reason why he can't leave." (Children's ideas might include the following: his mother wants him to come home to supper, but he says he isn't hungry; a friend asks him to play, but he says he would rather ice-fish; a little squirrel asks why he doesn't chase him the way he usually does and the bear says he's getting too old for that. Play in pairs or as a group scene.)
2. "A tail salesperson has heard about the bear's loss of his tail and comes to sell him a new one. What kinds will he offer from his sample case, and which one will the bear finally decide to buy?" (Play in pairs.)

BARTHOLOMEW AND THE OOBLECK 2

(*Note:* See page 246 for the story synopsis and for the circle story method of playing this same story.)

Pantomime Solo

1. "You are Bartholomew blowing the whistle that only the magicians can hear." (Take it from its special hanging place, blow some of the dust off it, now blow, and so on.)
2. "You are the bell ringer trying to ring the bell that is stuck in oobleck; now

be the trumpet blower trying to play your horn even though a large blob of oobleck just fell into it; and finally be the vain captain of the guard combing your moustache very carefully."

3. "You are a small drop of oobleck. As I count to ten, grow slowly into one big blob and begin to ooze out of your desk. When I reach ten, become a frozen blob of oobleck."

4. "You are a villager with an occupation of your choice. As the oobleck starts to fall, you try to continue your work in spite of great difficulty. As the music comes to an end, you will become completely frozen."

5. "Be Bartholomew investigating the first piece of oobleck to fall down from the sky. Use all your senses (sight, touch, taste, smell, hearing) in examining it."

6. "Be the king seeing the first drops of oobleck falling; now be Bartholomew seeing the oobleck fall. How did your reactions differ?"

Verbal Solo

1. "You are Bartholomew. Explain to us what it is like working for King Derwin. What do you like the most about your job? What do you like the least?"

2. "You are King Derwin of Didd. Why is it so important to you to have a change in the weather? What else bores you?"

3. "You are King Derwin's mother or father. He seems to be bored with many things. What was he like as a child growing up?"

4. "You are one of the magicians. Explain the positive qualities of oobleck now that you have mixed some up in your cauldron."

5. "You are the captain of the guard tasting and eating the oobleck. Your mouth gets stuck, but you still try to say one very important sentence. What is it?"

6. "You are a weather forecaster for the kingdom of Didd. You do not know the story of the oobleck, but you notice that the weather patterns appear to be different tonight. Give your report."

"You are the Captain of the Guard tasting and then eating the oobleck. Your mouth gets stuck, but you still try to say one very important sentence. What is it?"

Pantomime in Pairs and Groups

1. "In pairs, one of you will mirror the captain getting ready for work in the morning, combing his hair, his moustache, shaving, and so forth." Switch roles.
2. *count-and-freeze pantomime of the various occupations of the towns-people:* "As I count to ten, you will perform your duties and slowly become stuck. We will guess what job you are doing."
3. *build-a-place pantomime:* "Create the palace of King Derwin of Didd. Remember that he is often bored, so there are probably a lot of things in the palace for his amusement."
4. "Create frozen pictures of the various scenes you think might have happened when all the people became stuck in oobleck."

Verbal in Pairs and Groups

1. "The magicians have a discussion over what kind of weather to make. In addition to oobleck, they find that there are some other possibilities in their book of magic that sound even more interesting. Let's hear some of that discussion in groups of five."
2. "Suppose the king has called on the magicians to help with another problem he has. And suppose the results are as disastrous as the oobleck incident. In groups of five enact in a brief skit what the king's other problem is and what happens this time."
3. "In a private place late one evening, two factions of the kingdom of Didd meet to discuss the possible dethronement of King Derwin. One faction believes the king has not exercised good judgment on a number of occasions; the other feels that the King has many good qualities. Let us hear some of that debate." Divide the class into two groups. You play a mediating role, perhaps as Bartholomew or a Prime Minister.
4. "The children and the adults of the kingdom of Didd are not in agreement about the oobleck. The children have found it to be fun and interesting, while the adults find it intolerable. What arguments does each side have?" (You might like to use the first simple debate method on p. 193 for this activity.)
5. Play the experts panel with oobleck exterminators being questioned by townspeople and members of the court about the details of their work.
6. "The town council is meeting in open session to brainstorm ways to get rid of the large supply of oobleck that will not melt. How many ways can they think of to handle the problem?" Several small groups can work on this activity simultaneously.
7. "The wise men of the kingdom of Didd have been given the task of exploring new ways to make use of the large supply of oobleck that will not melt. How many uses for oobleck can they think of?" Again, small groups may brainstorm ideas simultaneously and report their ideas.
8. "The magicians have been ordered to appear before a higher court of magicians because of their role in the disastrous oobleck incident. What are their reasons for doing what they did? The higher court will vote whether to judge them innocent of wrongdoing or to revoke their magician's license."
9. "Suppose the castle minstrels create a ballad of the oobleck story. In

small groups, create your own ballad to sing for the neighboring kingdom." Use "Greensleeves" melody, "Scarborough Fair," or other ballad
tune children may be familiar with.

THE EMPEROR'S NEW CLOTHES, HANS CHRISTIAN ANDERSEN

Sources

The Emperor's New Clothes, translated and illustrated by Erik Blegvad. New York: Doubleday, 1974. Small ink drawings, alternating black and white pictures with full
color ones.

The Emperor's New Clothes, illustrated by Monika Laimgruber. Reading, Mass.: Addison-Wesley, 1973. This book received the *New York Times* choice of Best
Illustrated Children's Book of the Year.

The Emperor's New Clothes, JACK AND IRENE DELANO. New York: Random House, 1971.
The Delanos explain that the folktale did not originate with Andersen. Their illustrations present a Puerto Rican setting.

Synopsis

A vain emperor who is particularly fond of his wardrobe is visited by two
rogues posing as weavers. They claim to be able to weave fabric invisible to
those unworthy of the office they hold. Of course, everyone pretends to see the
imaginary fabric in order not to lose their jobs. A parade is held to show off the
emperor's new clothes, but only when a small child innocently calls out "But
the King has nothing on!" do the people finally realize the swindle and their
own gullibility.

Pantomime (solo at desks)

1. "You are the emperor who loves clothes, and you are posing for your
   latest portrait. How will you pose to show off all the new garments you're
   wearing? As I count to five, pose in five different positions that will show
   the garments to best advantage."

2. "You are the emperor, proudly walking in the procession, listening to all
   the appreciative comments of the admiring crowd. Then you hear the
   voice of the child saying you have no clothes on. You freeze. How will
   you look? I'll play processional music. After you've paraded a few moments (in place), I'll say the child's line and stop the music. That will be
   your cue to freeze."

3. "The rogues wove their cloth at night by candlelight. Be one of the
   candles slowly melting and then burning out as daybreak approaches."
   (This may serve as a quieting activity.)

4. "Suppose that when the emperor doesn't get his way, he throws a temper tantrum. Demonstrate one of his temper tantrums—silently and in
   slow motion as I count to ten."

5. "The emperor returns to his palace after the procession. Think of how he
   must feel, and then think of three things he might do. As I count to three,

pantomime each of your three ideas." (This can also be done as a count-and-freeze pantomime; see page 160).

Verbal (solo at desks)

1. "Suppose you are the emperor's son or daughter. What birthday present are you getting for your dad this year? How do you know he'll like it?"
2. "Suppose you're the emperor's mother or father. How did your son get so interested in clothes? Has he always been like this?"
3. "You're the parade marshal who is planning the procession. Who will be in it, what will be the parade route, and what will be the order of people in the procession?"
4. "You are one of the rogues, giving your description of the fabric you have woven. You might include comments on the lovely patterns, the careful attention to detail, the unusual color combinations, and so forth. Give us your sales pitch."

Pantomime for Pairs and Groups

1. "You are the two swindlers setting up your loom. You're unpacking it and setting it up carefully for this special job. The court is watching you, so look professional."
2. "In groups of eight to ten, create and become the special loom on which the marvelous fabric is to be woven."
3. "You are the swindlers putting on a good show of how diligently and carefully you work at weaving, cutting out, and sewing these garments. As the music plays, put on your best performance."
4. "You are the rogues when you are certain that no one is watching you work. What will you do to pass the time and to entertain yourself, locked up in the workroom?"
5. (*groups of six*) "The emperor is being dressed for the great procession by the two rogues. Mirror this activity."
6. "In groups of ten create a frozen picture of the procession. Decide who each of you is, and we'll see if the rest of us can guess."
7. "The band is rehearsing for the procession. A conductor leads as you each play a different instrument." Use groups of six: one conductor and five band members. (March music such as Elgar's "Pomp and Circumstance" might be used.)

Verbal in Pairs and Groups

1. (*groups of three*) "The emperor has learned his lesson about listening to clothes swindlers. But today new swindlers come to town. What will they try to sell to the emperor? Will it have unusual qualities as the special cloth did? Remember that the emperor may be harder to convince this time."
2. (*groups of three*) "You are the old minister visiting the rogues. When you cannot see the material, you make up excuses. What are they? You'd like to leave but the rogues keep showing you more things for you to admire. How will you finally get away from them?"
3. (*pairs*) "You are an official who is to visit the weavers and see how the work is coming along. You don't trust them and you don't really believe

A sturdily constructed three-fold screen of a castle provides scenery for many folktales.

their story, but you don't want to say so to the emperor. What else will you use as your excuse to him to get out of going on this mission?"

4. "Suppose you are the emperor's wife (or brother) who is given a meager supply of funds for clothing. You'd like a new outfit and you're trying to get money from the minister of finance, who claims no more money is available. Show him your pitiful wardrobe as evidence that you need a bigger clothes allowance. What other arguments can you give to make your case?"

5. "You are the citizens of the kingdom where the emperor spends huge sums on clothing. There are a number of community projects that need tending to. You go as a committee to the emperor to present your case on behalf of the kingdom. The emperor and his advisors reluctantly decide to fund one of the projects. Let's play the scene and find out how the emperor decides which project will be funded."

6. *(groups of three)* "The rogues have received an order of knighthood to wear in their buttonholes and the title of Gentlemen Weavers. Now that they have left the kingdom, they would like to sell this prize. They bargain with a used goods merchant for the best price they can get for this medal."

7. *(pairs)* "The emperor has spent the entire kingdom's treasury on clothes for himself. Now he must go to the bank for a loan. He must try to convince the bank president that he will be a good credit risk. The bank president is a shrewd operator."

8. *(groups of five)* "The kingdom's garment workers are exhausted from trying to keep up with all the new clothes orders the emperor demands. We hear them complaining as they work. The scene ends when they decide to go on strike."

9. "You are a clothing designer who has just designed a new outfit for the emperor to wear. It is the most unusual design the emperor has ever

seen. Convince the emperor to order this outfit from you, even though the emperor is not sure it's suited to him."

10. "The emperor holds a press conference some time after the incident with the rogues. Reporters still have questions about what happened, but they must be diplomatic in asking them so as not to embarrass or anger the emperor. The emperor may enlist the aid of his minister or other officials in answering the questions." Set this up as a character panel discussion (p. 195).

THE PHANTOM TOLLBOOTH, NORTON JUSTER (New York: Random House, 1961)

Synopsis

Milo, a boy who is bored with school and with life, finds a mysterious package in his room. He opens it to find a tollbooth, a small electric car, and a curious map. Joined by a watchdog named Tock and a boastful Humbug, Milo travels to many lands and adventures. They are even able to restore the princess of Rhyme and Reason to the Kingdom of Wisdom and to reunite King Azaz of Dictionopolis and Mathemagician, his brother and the ruler of Digitopolis. In the process, Milo learns that there are a great many things that are exciting in life if one just takes the time to see and experience them.
(*Note:* The book emphasizes a great deal of play on words and mathematical references that require some sophistication to understand. A feature-length live and animated film version was made by Chuck Jones for Universal in 1969.)

Pantomime Solo

1. "Be the watchdog Tock carefully winding yourself with your left hind leg."
2. "Pretend that you are picking off your initials from the letter tree and eating them. Use your face to show what they taste like. Are they sweet, sour, bitter, salty, mushy, hard, sticky, or cold?" Afterwards students might explain their reasons for their interpretations.
3. Read the section in chapter 11 where the awful DYNNE appears out of the bottle. Notice that it begins small and gets larger, growing hands and feet and a large frowning mouth. At the end it drinks what is in the bottle in three gulps. Have half the class create their individual versions of DYNNE growing while the other half creates the sound effects to go with it. Use the sound arrow. It may be helpful to practice the pantomime and sound effects separately first and then put the two together.
4. "The awful DYNNE expresses its emotions to extremes. As I count three, be the DYNNE (1) collapsing in a fit of hysterics, (2) sulking in the corner, and (3) sobbing uncontrollably. But each emotion is to be done in slow motion and without any sound."
5. "You are Milo almost ready to say the word "but." Instead you hold it in your mouth to drop it into the cannon as the ammunition that will break

open the sounds for Silent Valley. While I count to five, pantomime how you think this might have looked."

6. "You are Canby. Be as tall as can be, short as can be; generous as can be, selfish as can be; strong as can be, weak as can be; graceful as can be, clumsy as can be; fast as can be, slow as can be; and happy as can be, sad as can be." Add other actions the students suggest.

7. "You are the Dodecahedron with twelve sides or faces all showing different emotions. As I count to six let's see half of those faces one by one."

Verbal Solo

1. "Be Milo sighing a deep sigh of boredom so great 'that a house sparrow singing nearby stopped and rushed home to be with his family.'"

2. "Milo is bored in spite of all the things he owns that he can play with. Tell us, Milo, what are some of the things you have and why don't you enjoy playing with them?"

3. "The Whether Man in Dictionopolis welcomes Milo but speaks very fast and repeats everything several times. Pretend you're this person and let us hear some of your welcoming remarks to Milo and Tock."

4. "The Lethargarians in The Doldrums have several strange laws and a daily schedule they follow. Be one of the Lethargarians, speaking the way you think they might sound, explaining some of the ways you live." If a child falters, he or she can easily be excused because Lethargarians seem to find everything a tremendous effort: "I'm so sorry to have troubled you. Perhaps you'll feel better after a rest." or "I see that's it's two o'clock and time for your early afternoon nap."

5. "Be the watchdog Tock who goes ticktick all day, explaining the sad story of your name, becoming increasingly sad as you speak, until you are sobbing. I know it's painful for you to tell this story, so perhaps several of you could take turns." (This activity is storytelling in character, using the round-robin technique.)

6. "Be one of the merchants in the Word Market. What are you selling and what is your sales pitch?"

7. "Suppose we are all people who have landed on the Island of Conclusions. Let's talk about what conclusions we jumped to to get here. What ideas do you have for getting away from here? Who wishes to speak first?"

8. "You are Milo, and the little man in Silent Valley has just handed you the letters and messages from the people to the Soundkeeper. Would you read one of the letters for us, please?"

9. After Milo's word was shot from the cannon and released the Soundkeeper's vaults, all the sounds of history rushed forth. Reread this paragraph in chapter 13, and have each student think of one sound or saying (like a one-liner) they think would have been released. Then wave the sound arrow over the class slowly from one side to another. As the arrow passes over them, the students say their sound or statement. You might want to try this a second time, letting the students continue to make their sound or repeat their saying, building in intensity and then settling back down as the sounds disappear over the hill and all returns to normal.

10. "At the end of the story the Humbug says he has arranged a lecture tour. Pretend you are the Humbug giving a small lecture. To whom will you speak and what will be your topic?" This activity is fun to do as a pantomime, since the Humbug is such a blustery fellow, or as a short speech delivered spontaneously, or as a prepared speech students take time to develop. Perhaps you will want to give students individual choices in these possibilities.

Pantomime in Pairs and Groups

1. *count and freeze in groups of five to eight:* "There are many strange and unusual people Milo meets on his journey. Select one, think of something he or she might do, and act it out while the rest of us guess who the person is."

2. *count and freeze:* "Suppose the Terrible Trivium captured you. What never-ending task will he have you do? Demonstrate your task while the rest of us guess what it is."

3. "In groups of five create a frozen picture of one of the scenes in the book for the rest of us to guess." Some possibilities are Milo assembling the Tollbooth with some children being the booth itself; Tock flying with Rhyme, Reason, Milo, and Humbug after the Castle in the Air is destroyed; scenes from the celebration carnival at the end, and so forth.

4. *conducting an orchestra* (p. 96): Create the colorful symphony with all the imaginary instruments. Play a rainbow, a sunset, a storm, or any other scene you and the students decide upon. Even though the music is seen and not heard in the story, it might be helpful to play a selection from Grofé's *Grand Canyon Suite* or Respighi's *Pines of Rome* in the background. See if the entire class can be involved in this one. You or a student might be Chroma the Conductor. Another playing could be with Milo as conductor, losing control and causing a week's time to be played. Chopin's "Minute Waltz" might be useful for this second playing.

5. Have the whole class create the main street of the city of Reality. Remember that there are crowds of people rushing along with their heads down or driving in cars and trucks, seeming to know where they are going and what they are doing, even though there are no buildings. Use the procedure explained on p. 91, starting with just a few children, making sure they can move about without touching each other and carefully adding a few people at a time until the entire class is participating. Music will help; play a fast record or something at a fast speed. Khachaturian's "Sabre Dance" is one possibility. Since this scene will change when Rhyme and Reason are returned, you might play it twice, with a "before" and an "after." The "after" scene will be much slower, of course, with people seeing and reacting to the world around them, which should "reappear" as they react to it in pantomime.

6. Divide students into groups of five or six: "In each group you are the people of Silent Valley creating a pantomime skit to explain to Milo in your own way what happened to your community to bring on the absence of sound." (See "Without Saying a Word," p. 168.)

7. *build a place:* "Create Mathemagician's workshop, including some of the items mentioned in chapter 15 as well as other ideas you may have."

Verbal in Pairs and Groups

1. *one-liners:* "You are the people in the marketplace when the fight between Humbug and Spelling Bee upsets all the word stalls and everyone's speech becomes scrambled. What might you say?"
2. "Let's have a panel of five who are King Azaz's advisors. Remember that
   you each give short answers, saying the same thing in slightly different
   ways, as we ask some simple questions of you. We'll rotate who answers
   first each time." Some questions might be "Do you feel important working for King Azaz?" "What's the best advice you've ever given to the
   king?" and "What is the most important word in the English language?"
3. *language liars club.(See p. 190.)* A panel of word experts guess the
   definitions of words. Use some words mentioned in the book, such as
   "quagmire," "flabbergast," and "upholstery." You may provide cards to
   the experts with suggested definitions, only one of which is the correct
   one. The audience can vote on which expert gives the correct definition
   in their estimation. Afterwards clarify which definitions are accurate.
4. Have a simple debate between two sides: people who grow down and
   people who grow up. Individuals on each side give the advantages they
   see for their condition. You can play Milo in order to moderate the
   debate.
5. *storytelling in character:* All children pretend to be the Spelling Bee,
   creating a story using spelling words. Use round-robin storytelling, with
   each child adding on a sentence incorporating one spelling word. For
   example: "Once upon a time there was a king who lived in a castle (c-a-
   s-t-l-e)."
6. There are a number of interesting sounds in chapter 11 that could be
   created. You might divide the class into small groups and assign them
   each a sound to create. For example: "a blindfolded octopus unwrap-
   ping a cellophane-covered bathtub"; "a square-wheeled steam roller
   riding over a street full of hard-boiled eggs"; "a handful of fingernails
   being scratched across a mile-long blackboard"; "a fast-moving freight
   train being derailed into a mountain of custard." Students could make up
   their own ideas to add to this list. You may wish to make an entire project
   of this chapter, working on many sounds individually and then reading it
   as a radio drama with sounds, tape recording it or performing it live as a
   separate playlet.
7. "In pairs, one of you will be Milo, Tock, or Humbug being interviewed by
   the Senses Taker. Remember that our heroes are anxious to escape
   from the demons that protect Ignorance, but the Senses Taker has an
   unending list of questions that have to be recorded in five different
   places." You may wish to use the procedure of shared dialogue described on p. 194.
8. *paired dialogue:* "Select two people in the story and create a conversation between them. The rest of us will try to guess who you are by what
   you say and how you say it. The people may or may not have met each
   other in the book, so the conversation can be invented." For example:
   Faintly Macabre does not speak with Officer Shrift in the book, but they
   could have an imaginary conversation together for this activity. Again,
   you may wish to use the procedure of shared dialogue described on p.
   194.

FOR THE COLLEGE STUDENT

1. Select a story suitable for circle story dramatization. (Refer to the following story bibliography or select your own.) Plan out the dramatization using the samples given in this chapter. Present the story to your classmates or to a group of children and lead them in the dramatization. Afterwards, discuss the effectiveness of the activity with your classmates. What changes or alternative procedures might be used with the story?
2. Select a story or a book for segmented story dramatization. (Refer to the following story bibliography or the list of books in the Appendix, or select your own.) Proceed as above, playing a representative sampling of the activities you design.

STORY BIBLIOGRAPHY

The materials are arranged in alphabetical order according to title. The numbers in parentheses refer to the numbered anthologies at the end of the book. The following symbols are used to indicate the age level they might be best suited for:

Y   young children in kindergarten, first, and second grades

M   middle-grade children in third and fourth grades

O   older children in fifth and sixth grades

Y "The Adventure of Three Little Rabbits," author untraceable (43). Little rabbits get stuck in some spilled syrup and almost become rabbit stew. You can use two or three little old men and women and the rest rabbits in a circle story dramatization. This is a good story for spring or for a science lesson about how syrup softens and melts when heated.

O "All Summer in a Day," RAY BRADBURY (26). Children on Venus anxiously wait for the sun, which shines for only one hour every seven years. Margot, a newcomer from earth, remembers the sun and is resented by some of her classmates. Minutes before the sun appears, they lock her in a closet and forget about her during their sun-filled hour outside.

M–O "Anansi and the Fish Country," PHILIP SHERLOCK (2). Anansi tries to trick fish by pretending to be a doctor. With the circle story method of dramatization, the many fish can sit in a circle to play their part.

M *Anatole and the Cat*, EVE TITUS. New York: McGraw-Hill, 1957. A clever mouse outwits the cat who hampers his work as a cheese taster in Duval's cheese factory in France. Other Anatole stories may also be of interest.

M *Angus and the Mona Lisa*, JACQUELINE COOPER. New York: Lothrop, Lee, & Shepard Books, 1981. Angus, a cat of French ancestry, takes a trip to Paris, and with the help of Antoinette, a cat who works for Interpol, prevents two thugs—Pigeon and Turtle Dove—from stealing the Mona Lisa from the Louvre. French vocabulary and references to places in France offer a language and geography lesson in addition to an exciting mystery.

Y *Are You My Mother?* P.D. EASTMAN. New York: Random House,1960. A baby bird hatches and goes off in search of its mother. But since he does not know what she looks like, he mistakes other animals—and even a steam shovel—for her. This easy-to-read book with limited vocabulary is a natural choice for circle story dramatization.

Y *Ask Mr. Bear*, MARJORIE FLACK. New York: Macmillan, 1932. It is Danny's mother's birthday and he does not know what to give her. The hen, the goose, the goat, the sheep, and the cow suggest gifts they are most familiar with. Danny decides to ask Mr. Bear and returns home to give his mother a big bear hug. Using double- and triple-casting, the animals can be grouped in a circle.

M–O *The Bremen Town Musicians*, PAUL GALDONE. New York: McGraw-Hill, 1968. See also (3, 4, 39, 43). In this Grimm Brothers' tale the owners of a donkey, dog, cat, and rooster consider them too old to be kept anymore. So the animals go off to seek their fortune elsewhere. On the way they find a band of robbers and wealth to keep them secure the rest of their days. Can be set up as a circle story. Compare with "Jack and the Robbers" in this bibliography.

O "The Case of the Sensational Scent," ROBERT MCCLOSKEY (87). Robbers, a suitcase with $2,000, a skunk, and aftershave lotion create an unusual detective adventure for Homer Price.

M–O "Clever Manka," PARKER FILLMORE (4). In this Czech folktale, a young woman proves her intelligence on more than one occasion.

O *The Clown of God*, THOMAS ANTHONY DEPAOLA. New York: Harcourt Brace Jovanovich, 1978. A once-famous juggler gives his final performance before the statue of Mary and the Child. This story is best for mature groups.

Y–M *The Cock, the Mouse, and the Little Red Hen*, LORINDA BRYAN CAULEY. New York: Putnam Publishing Group, 1982. This is a retelling of the story of the Little Red Hen who does all the work. In this version she saves the cock and the mouse from being the fox family's dinner. It has easy dialogue and beautiful illustrations. The mouse and the cock do lots of "grumbling," which can be mimed, or children can create dialogue for it.

M "The Conjure Wives," FRANCES WICKES (43). Selfish witches are turned into owls in this story that is perfect for Halloween. There may be one head witch and one voice (two children can play this if one speaks and the other does the knocking). The rest of the children are the witches who learn that greediness does not go unpunished.

Y–M *The Country Bunny and the Little Gold Shoes*, DUBOSE HEYWARD. Boston: Houghton Mifflin, 1937. This is an old favorite that has been reissued. A little country girl bunny proves that she can grow up to be an Easter Bunny. It can be played as a circle story, particularly for the scenes with the 21 little bunnies. Because it is a longer story, you will probably need more than one session to play it.

M *The Cuckoo's Reward*, DAISY KOUZEL and EARL THOLLANDER. New York: Doubleday, 1977. A cuckoo helps save the grain from fire in this Mexican folktale. In Spanish, the story is *El Premio del Cuco*, also by Doubleday, 1977.

O *The Devil's Bridge*, CHARLES SCRIBNER, JR. New York: Charles Scribner's Sons, 1978. The Devil promises a French town that he will build them a bridge for the price of a human soul.

M–O "The Doughnuts," ROBERT MCCLOSKEY (4, 39). Homer Price, an enterprising boy, has an adventure with a doughnut machine that just will not quit making doughnuts.

Y–M *Drakestail*, JAN WAHL. New York: Greenwillow Books, 1978. In this traditional French folktale, a very clever duck, with the help of some unusual friends, outwits a greedy ruler and becomes king. See also (3). Try this as a circle story.

O *Duffy and the Devil*, HARVE ZEMACH. New York: Farrar, Straus & Giroux, 1973. A devilish imp, in the manner of Rumplestiltskin, helps Duffy, a servant girl, with her chores. She so impresses Squire Tovel that he marries her. In the 1800s in Cornwall, England, this humorous tale was often performed by actors (mummers) who went from door to door at Christmas time.

M *The Elephant's Child,* RUDYARD KIPLING. New York: Walker, 1970. The elephant's child, who has "'satiable curtiosity," finds out some answers to his questions but gets a long nose doing it in this mythical explanation of the elephant's trunk. After he discovers all the advantages of having a long nose, his relatives decide they want one too. See also (4, 22).

Y *The Elves and the Shoemaker,* FREYA LITTLEDALE. New York: Four Winds Press, 1975. See also (3, 4, 39, 43). The age-old Grimm Brothers' tale of the poor shoemaker who was aided by kindly elves. See also *The Shoemaker and the Elves* in this bibliography.

O *Everyone Knows What a Dragon Looks Like,* JAY WILLIAMS. New York, Four Winds Press, 1976. Only the road sweeper believes the old man who claims to be a dragon and offers to save the city from the Wild Horsemen of the North. For the boy's sake, the dragon comes to the rescue. This story has a Chinese setting and demonstrates that things are not always what they seem.

M *The Fence,* JAN BALET. New York: Dell Publishing/Delacorte Press, 1969. A poor family in Mexico is taken to court by a rich family because the former sniffed the delicious aromas from the kitchen of the rich family's house. The judge outwits the rich family with a sentence that is given in accordance with their own logic.

O *Finzel the Farsighted,* PAUL FLEISHMAN. New York: E.P. Dutton, 1983. Finzel is a fortune teller who can see into the future with great accuracy, but is nearsighted in dealing with the present. Nevertheless, he cleverly outwits a thief who robs him.

Y–M *Gillespie and the Guards,* BENJAMIN ELKIN. New York: Viking Penguin, 1956. Three brothers with powerful eyes become guards of the kingdom. The king offers a reward to anyone who can get past them. Gillespie, a young boy, tricks the guards when they overlook the obvious.

Y *The Gingerbread Boy,* PAUL GALDONE. New York: Seabury Press, 1975. See also (4). This is the classic story of the little cookie that runs away from all who chase him, until he meets a fox. It works nicely as a circle story. The running can be limited by having each group of chasers stop to rest; they can still all say the chant of the gingerbread man. See also *Journey Cake, Ho!* in this bibliography. There are many other variations to this story: see for example "Johnny-cake," an English version in (13); "The Pancake," a Norwegian tale in (4) and (39); "The Wee Bannock," a Scottish version in (14).

O *The Golem: A Jewish Legend,* BEVERLY McDERMOTT. Philadelphia: J.B. Lippincott, 1976. A rabbi in Prague creates a clay figure to help suppress an uprising against the Jewish community.

M–O *Granny and the Desperadoes,* PEGGY PARISH. New York: Macmillan, 1970. Granny captures some escaped criminals and forces them to do her many farm chores before she turns them over to the sheriff. They return to jail most willingly after working for her. There are only a few characters, but children love to add neighbors and farm animals.

Y–M *Hansel and Gretel,* ELIZABETH D. CRAWFORD. New York: William Morrow, 1980. See also (3, 4, 39). This is the classic Grimm fairy tale of two children left alone in the woods to encounter a witch. See also the version by Rika Lesser (New York: Dodd, Mead, 1984).

O *Harald and the Giant Knight,* DONALD CARRICK. New York: Clarion Books, 1982. In medieval times, a group of knights decide to use Harald's father's farm for their training ground. But, Father cannot plant and will not have food or money to pay his rent to the baron. Harald, who once admired the knights, comes up with the plan to scare them away by weaving a huge reed knight.

Y *Henny Penny,* PAUL GALDONE. New York: Seabury Press, 1968. See also (3, 4, 39). The old tale of the hen who thinks the sky is falling when an acorn drops on her head. A panic ensues in the barnyard. A circle story is possible for this one. Although the story seems complicated with all the names, children usually catch on quickly and love repeating them.

Paper headbands for *The Gingerbread Man.*

H *Horton Hatches the Egg,* DR. SEUSS. New York: Random House, 1940. Horton, the elephant who hatches an egg for the lazy Maizie bird in spite of numerous odds, is eventually rewarded for his faithfulness.

M "How Jahdu Took Care of Trouble," VIRGINIA HAMILTON (50). In this trickster tale, Jahdu outwits Trouble and frees everyone from the huge barrel they have been caught in. Those who are in the barrel can sit in the circle for a circle story dramatization.

O "How Pa Learned to Grow Hot Peppers," ELLIS CREDLE (45). Pa is too easygoing to raise peppers with zip in them, so the family has to find a way to get him fired up.

M "How the Animals Got Their Fur Coats," HILDA MARY HOOKE (48). All the animals get lovely new coats except the moose, who gets the leftovers. Charming characters appear in this Canadian Indian legend.

M "How the Birds Got Their Colors," HILDA MARY HOOKE (48). In this delightfully funny Canadian Indian legend, all the birds get colorful feathers except the sapsucker.

M "How the Little Owl's Name Was Changed," CHARLES E. GILLHAM (5). Brave Little Owl takes fire away from evil men in this Alaskan Eskimo folktale.

M *How the Sun Made a Promise and Kept It,* MARGERY BERNSTEIN. New York: Charles Scribner's Sons, 1974. In this retelling of a Canadian myth, the sun is captured and the animals take on the task of freeing it.

M–O "Jack and the Robbers," RICHARD C. CHASE (21). This is an Appalachian version of "The Musicians of Bremen."

M *Jim and the Beanstalk,* RAYMOND BRIGGS. Reading, Mass.: Addison-Wesley, 1970. In this new version of an old tale, the Giant wants a set of false teeth, a pair of glasses, and a red wig. Children might like to make up their own new version of an old tale after experiencing this one.

O *Joco and the Fishbone,* WILLIAM WIESNER. New York: Viking Penguin, 1966. Joco the hunchback chokes on a fishbone and everyone tries to get rid of the body. Joco eventually coughs up the bone. This is a retelling of a tale from *The Arabian Nights* that also compares with "Old Dry Frye" in this bibliography.

Y *Journey Cake Ho!* RUTH SAWYER. New York: Viking Penguin, 1953. The journey cake escapes Johnny as well as a variety of animals in this Appalachian retelling of the old favorite "The Gingerbread Man."

M–O *Kassim's Shoes,* HAROLD BERSON. New York: Crown Publishers, 1977. Kassim finally agrees to throw out his old shoes but then has trouble getting rid of them because everyone keeps returning them.

M *King Midas and the Golden Touch,* AL PERKINS. New York: Random House, 1969. This is a retelling of the Greek mythological tale of the king who loved gold too much. See also "The Golden Touch" (3, 4, 39, 43).

Y–M *King Rooster, Queen Hen,* ANITA LOBEL. New York: William Morrow, 1975. Rooster and Hen decide to become king and queen and gain their servants along the way in this Danish folktale. An encounter with a fox changes everyone's mind. This can be played as a circle story as long as you carefully plan the animals' escape from the fox.

O *The King's Stilts,* DR. SEUSS. New York: Random House, 1939. When the king's stilts are stolen by the evil Lord Droon, he becomes too depressed to protect the kingdom from its main enemy: large birds called Nizzards. Eric, the pageboy, comes to the rescue. Since there are many Nizzards and cats, students seated in a circle can play both these parts.

M–O "The King's Tower," HAROLD COURLANDER (38). In this Latin American tale, a foolish king desires to reach the moon and commands a carpenter to build a tower for this purpose. The tower is built of stacked boxes and is not quite tall enough to reach the moon. The king climbs to the top and commands that the box on the bottom be brought up to the top to make the tower the exact height needed. Of course, the inevitable happens. See also "Tower to the Moon" in this bibliography.

M–O *Legend of the Bluebonnet,* TOMIE DE PAOLA. New York: Putnam Publishing Group, 1983. A Comanche Indian tribe, in the midst of famine, is saved by the sacrifice of a young girl's warrior doll. The Great Spirits show their forgiveness of the tribe's selfishness by sending small blue flowers to cover the ground. And in this land now known as Texas, the bluebonnet blooms each spring as a reminder of the young girl's sacrifice for her people.

O "The Legend of the Moor's Legacy," WASHINGTON IRVING (43). A humble water carrier inherits a secret passport to a cave of riches. See narrated scene p. 143–44.

Y–M *The Little Engine That Could,* retold by WATTY PIPER. New York: Platt & Munk, 1954. A little engine is able to take the stalled, larger train over the mountain to deliver Christmas toys. The journey of the train can take place around a circle or around the classroom. The theme is twofold: perseverance pays off, and even smaller persons can help the larger and more powerful.

Y *The Little Rabbit Who Wanted Red Wings,* CAROLYN BAILEY. New York: Platt & Munk, 1978. A charmingly illustrated picture-book version of an old tale of a little rabbit who discovers that what we wish for may not always be the best for us.

Y *Little Toot,* HARDIE GRAMATKY. New York: Putnam Publishing Group, 1939, 1967. Little Toot is a tugboat who would rather play than work. He is challenged to prove himself and does so by rescuing a stranded ocean liner. Much of this story can be narrated, but children also like to play the other tugboats and add dialogue. At least one playing should be solo narrative pantomime (shortened, if you like) so that everyone can have a chance to be this popular character. If played in a circle, the children can be the ocean.

Y–M *Loudmouse,* RICHARD WILBUR. New York: Macmillan, 1968. A little mouse with a very loud voice turns out to be an effective burglar alarm.

M *Lyle, Lyle, Crocodile,* BERNARD WABER. Boston: Houghton Mifflin, 1965. A crocodile who is more human than animal has remarkable adventures. Other *Lyle* stories may be of interest.

Y–M *Madeline,* LUDWIG BEMELMANS. New York: Viking Penguin, 1939, 1977. Madeline lives in a Paris convent with eleven other little girls. After she is rushed to the hospital for an appendectomy, she becomes the envy of her friends. It can be played as a circle story. Characters include Miss Clavel, Madeline (both of which can be double-cast), Dr. Cohn, and all the other children in the convent. You will want an ambulance driver, traffic police, and other secondary characters in this story.

M *The Magician Who Lost His Magic,* DAVID MCKEE. New York: Abelard-Schuman, 1970. Melric loses his magic after misusing it by helping people do things they should do for themselves. He gets the magic back just in time to save the day for the king.

M–O *Many Moons,* JAMES THURBER. New York: Viking Penguin, 1943. Princess Lenore is ill from eating too many raspberry tarts but can be cured, she says, if she can have the moon. The court jester finds a solution.

Y–M *Mike Mulligan and His Steam Shovel,* VIRGINIA LEE BURTON. Boston: Houghton Mifflin, 1939. See also (4). Mike Mulligan's unique solution to collecting the money for digging the basement of the town hall with his steam shovel, Mary Anne, makes an old story remain ever popular.

Y *Millions of Cats,* WANDA GAG. New York: Coward-McCann, 1938. See also (39). A little old man discovers many more cats ("hundreds of cats, thousands of cats, millions and billions and trillions of cats") than he expected to. This can be played as a circle story. Make sure the clawing is "pretend," perhaps with an imaginary partner. To signify they have been eaten, the cats can, on a signal from you, go behind their desks or sit on the floor in front of their chairs.

Y–M *The Mitten,* ALVIN TRESSELT. New York: Lothrop, Lee & Shepard, 1964. A little boy's lost mitten becomes a haven for several animals until a Bear tries to enter. For a circle story dramatization, the circle can resemble a mitten's shape. Compare with the next story.

Y *Mushroom in the Rain,* MIRRA GINSBURG. New York: Macmillan, 1974. A mushroom expands when numerous animals seek shelter under it. Everyone is able to fit because a mushroom grows larger in the rain. Perfect for circle story dramatization. Compare with the preceding story.

O *The Nightingale,* trans. Eva Le Gallienne. New York: Harper & Row, 1965. This is the Hans Christian Andersen tale of the emperor of China who orders the nightingale to stay in court and sing his beautiful song. When he receives a gift of a mechanical singing bird, he forgets the nightingale. When the depressed emperor is near death, the nightingale returns to save his spirit. The beauty of nature is extolled.

M *No Help At All,* BETTY BAKER. New York: Greenwillow Books, 1978. This humorous Mayan Indian legend is about West Chac, the rain god of the West, who helps a young boy one day and then asks for his help in return. But everything the boy does is "no help at all," except by accident.

O *The Nose Tree,* WARWICK HUTTON. New York: Atheneum, 1981. Three poor soldiers each receive a special gift from a little man. When a princess/witch tricks the men of their gifts, the little man again comes to their aid to outwit her.

Y–M *Not This Bear!* BERNICE MYERS. New York: Four Winds Press, 1967. A little boy in a furry hat and coat is mistaken for a bear by a bear family. He has to convince them that he is not one of them. Be sure to double- or even triple-cast the little boy.

M–O *Of Cobblers and Kings,* AURE SHELDON. New York: Parent's Magazine Press, 1978. Because of his common sense, a cobbler rises from one important position to another until he becomes grand chancellor. Then he notices that the people of the kingdom have no shoes.

O "Old Dry Frye," RICHARD CHASE (17). An old preacher accidentally dies and everyone tries to get rid of the body, afraid they will be accused of his murder. This Appalachian folktale is derived from one that goes back to *The Arabian Nights*. Compare it with *Joco and the Fishbone* in this bibliography.

M–O "Old One Eye," RICHARD CHASE (17, 52). In this Appalachian story, an old lady unwittingly frightens robbers who plan to steal her money. It is fun to add a general store scene in the beginning where the robbers hear about the old lady's riches. (*Note:* Excellent music for these last two tales can be found on an album by Richard Chase entitled "Instrumental Music of the Southern Appalachians" [Tradition Records, TLP 1007].)

O *Petronella*, JAY WILLIAMS. New York: Parent's Magazine Press, 1973. A princess rescues a prince in this turnabout tale.

Y–M *Petunia*, ROGER DUVOSIN. New York: Alfred A. Knopf, 1950. Petunia, a goose, thinks she has knowledge because she owns a book, even though she cannot read. Children will delight in knowing what Petunia does not—that "firecrackers" does not spell "cake."

M–O *The Pied Piper of Hamelin*, TONY ROSS. New York: Lothrop, Lee & Shepard Books, 1977. An illustrated story version of Robert Browning's poem of the piper who rids the town of rats but who gets his revenge when the town refuses to pay.

O "A Portrait Which Suited Everyone and Pleased No One," M.A. JAGENDORF (43). Tyll Ulenspiegel is commissioned to paint the court portrait, but each member wants a flattering picture of himself. This is one of the many tales about this legendary German prankster.

M–O *Princess Rosetta and the Popcorn Man*, retold by ELLIN GREENE. New York: Lothrop, Lee & Shepard Books, 1971. When Princess Rosetta of Romalia is stolen by a neighboring kingdom, only the popcorn man's solution works.

Y–M "The Princess Who Could Not Cry," ROSE FYLEMAN (43). When not even the wisest men in the kingdom have an answer, a peasant girl solves the princess's problem with an onion.

O *Punch and the Magic Fish*, EMANUELE LUZZATI. New York: Pantheon Books, 1972. In a dream, Punch experiences the old tale of "The Fisherman and His Wife" with Punch and Judy and some modern touches. There are five children and a cat in addition to the fish and several minor characters.

O *The Rabbi and the Twenty-Nine Witches: A Talmudic Legend*, MARILYN HIRSH. New York: Holiday House, 1976. A rabbi notices that troublesome witches do not appear on rainy days. When he tricks them out into the rain, they shrink into nothing.

M *The Reluctant Dragon*, KENNETH GRAHAME. New York: Holiday House, 1953. A peaceable dragon is not interested in fighting a knight.

O "Rip Van Winkle," WASHINGTON IRVING (43). The American tale of a man who falls asleep for twenty years to return to a world that has forgotten him. Compare with "Urashima Taro and the Princess of the Sea" in this bibliography.

O "Robin Hood's Merry Adventure with the Miller," HOWARD PYLE (43). Robin Hood and the miller fight for the right of way on a log.

M *Rum Pum Pum*, MAGGIE DUFF. New York: Macmillan, 1978. In this retelling of a folktale from India, a blackbird seeks revenge on the king who has stolen his wife. In his quest, he is helped by Cat, Stick, River, and Ants, who also have reason to confront the king. They join him by jumping into his ear and each, in turn, helps outwit the king. Compare this story with *Drakestail* in this bibliography.

Y *Runaway Marie Louise*, NATALIE SAVAGE CARLSON. New York: Charles Scribner's Sons, 1977. A little mongoose runs away when her mama spanks her for being naughty. For various reasons none of the other animals will take her in. She goes to a witch toad who wisely sends her back home, where Marie Louise learns that you can still be loved even if you are punished. This story is easy to play as a circle story.

Y–M *The Saggy Baggy Elephant*, K. JACKSON AND B. JACKSON. Racine, Wis.: Western Publishing, 1947, 1974. A little elephant is teased by a parrot for his loose skin. Sooki, as the little elephant calls itself, does not know what animal it is until a herd of elephants (may be played by children in a circle) welcomes it as one of their own. An elephant parade (accompanied by Henri Mancini's "Baby Elephant Walk") can end this story or an "elephant hop" (instead of bunny hop) for the 1, 2, 3, kick dance the elephants do.

O "Saltin' the Pudding," B.A. BOTKIN (56). In this old American folktale, Ma does not have time to salt the pudding. So without checking with each other, everyone else in the family adds his or her pinch.

Y *The Shoemaker and the Elves*, CYNTHIA AND WILLIAM BIRRER. New York: Lothrop, Lee & Shepard Books, 1983. This age-old Grimm's story tells of the poor shoemaker who is aided by kindly elves. Another popular version is illustrated by Adrienne Adams (New York: Charles Scribner's Sons, 1960). See also *The Elves and the Shoemaker* in this bibliography.

M–O *Six Companions Find Fortune*, KATYA SHEPPARD. New York: Doubleday, 1969. A retired soldier finds a strong man, a hunter, a blower, a runner, and a frost maker to help him win a race. The king does not give the promised reward and tries to get rid of them in various ways. But each plan is foiled by the specific skills of each man.

O *The Sorcerer's Scrapbook*, MICHAEL BERENSTAIN. New York: Random House, 1981. A wizard, a sorcery-school dropout, tells his story of how he came to help a duke capture a unicorn. Told in a humorous way, the story gives some of the lore and myths of medieval times.

M *Sparrow Socks*, GEORGE SELDEN. New York: Harper & Row, 1965. In Scotland, a family's sock business falls off until the son makes socks for sparrows. All who see the socks decide they want a pair just like them, and business is soon booming again.

O *The Squire's Bride*, P.C. ASBJÖRNSEN. New York: Atheneum, 1975. See also (43). An old squire decides to marry a young woman who has other ideas. She fools the squire's servants into dressing a donkey for the wedding.

M–O *The Stone in the Road*, STEPHEN SESKIN. New York: Van Nostrand Reinhold, 1968. Efforts to find gold under a huge stone present this story's conflict. It has a medieval setting. See also "Stone in the Road" (43).

M–O *Stone Soup*, MARCIA BROWN. New York: Charles Scribner's Sons, 1947. Three soldiers return from the war and stop in a village for food. The villagers are tired of feeding soldiers, and they hide all their food. The soldiers teach them how to make soup out of stones, with a few vegetables and meat added for flavor. Can be played as a circle story.

M–O *A Story—A Story*, GAIL E. HALEY. New York: Antheneum, 1970. The African tale of how all stories came to be Anansi's, the spider man. Anansi must capture and give to the sky god a leopard, hornets, and a dancing fairy whom men never see.

M–O *Striding Slippers*, MIRRA GINSBURG. New York: Macmillan, 1978. A shepherd makes magical striding slippers to help him in his work, but those who steal them seem not to be able to control them. Students will love pretending that their shoes are walking where they themselves do not want to go.

Y *The Strongest One of All*, MIRRA GINSBURG. New York: Greenwillow Books, 1977. In this retelling of a popular old tale, a lamb is the main character. The simple text makes it easy for young children to play as a circle story.

M "Taper Tom," GUDRUN THORNE-THOMSEN (43). Tom, a magic goose, and a string of people stuck to it make a sad princess laugh. See also "The Golden Goose" (56).

Y *The Three Billy Goats Gruff*, MARCIA BROWN. San Diego: Harcourt Brace Jovanovich, 1957. This version of the age-old story of the goats who outwit the troll under the bridge is considered one of the best.

Y "The Three Little Pigs." Several editions. This is the story of two foolish pigs and one smart pig who outwit a greedy wolf.

O *Three Strong Women*, CLAUS STAMM. New York: Viking Penguin, 1962. In this Japanese tall tale, a wrestler meets his match with a strong family of women who train him to become a champion.

Y "Ticky-Picky-Boom-Boom," PHILIP SHERLOCK (2). Tiger is chased by yams from Anansi's fields and tries to find hiding places with his friends. This African folktale has an enjoyable repetitive chant that everyone will want to say. As a circle story, children can do their chasing around the circle, or you may choose to have them simply tap their hands on their thighs in rhythm.

M–O "Tower to the Moon," SHIRLEE P. NEWMAN (16). This story is very much the same as "The King's Tower," listed in this bibliography.

Y–M *Two Hundred Rabbits*, LONZO ANDERSON and ADRIENNE ADAMS. New York: Viking Penguin, 1968. A rabbit watches, and tells the story of, a young boy who wishes to entertain the king for the castle festival. A rabbit parade solves the boy's problem. Most of the children can play the forest animals and the rabbits. Use march music for the parade or perhaps teach the children the bunny hop.

M *Tye May and the Magic Brush*, MOLLY BANG. New York: Greenwillow Books, 1981. This is a retelling of a Chinese fairy tale in which a young girl has a magic paintbrush she uses to help the poor. A greedy king tries to get it from her, but she outwits him. Another version, *Liang and the Magic Paintbrush*, by Demi (New York: Holt, Rinehart and Winston, 1980), has a boy as the hero.

M "The Ugly Duckling," HANS CHRISTIAN ANDERSEN (4, 39). The sensitive story of a "duckling" who is rejected by all other animals until he happily discovers that he is actually a swan.

M–O "Urashima Taro and the Princess of the Sea," YOSHIKO UCHIDA (4, 11). Urashima is enticed to live in the sea and spends much more time there than he at first imagines. When he returns home, he finds how much time has elapsed. This Japanese folktale compares with "Rip Van Winkle." See narrated example p. 118–19.

M–O *The Vinananee and the Tree Toad: A Liberian Tale*, VERNA AARDEMA. New York: Frederick Warne, 1983. A little tree toad is able to capture the bothersome Vinananee.

M–O *The Wave*, MARGARET HODGES. Boston: Houghton Mifflin, 1964. In this Japanese story there is a small earthquake, and Grandfather knows a tidal wave will follow. The villagers are unaware of the danger, and Grandfather decides to burn his rice fields to warn them.

M–O *When Noodlehead Went to the Fair*, KATHRYN HITTE. New York: Parent's Magazine Press, 1968. This old tale is told in the classic fashion of Noodlehead's adventure, which begins with a carrot and ends with the capture of two robbers. Plan out carefully the running at the end, using techniques explained at the top of p. 216.

M *When the Drum Sang*, ANNE ROCKWELL. New York: Parent's Magazine Press, 1970. In this African folktale, a little girl who sings beautiful songs is kidnapped by a man who hides her in a drum and forces her to sing. Her parents discover her and must trick the man to release her from the drum.

O *When the Porcupine Moved In*, CORA ANNETT. New York: Franklin Watts, 1971. Porcupine moves in with Rabbit. He demands his own way, even when Rabbit's wishes differ. Porcupine's talkative relatives even move in. Finally Rabbit uses reverse psychology and outwits Porcupine. It has wonderful characters and plenty of opportunity for dialogue and presents a good lesson in solving interpersonal conflicts.

Y *Where Can an Elephant Hide?* DAVID MCPHAIL. New York: Doubleday, 1979. The elephant Morris wants to be able to hide like the other animals. But their methods of camouflage

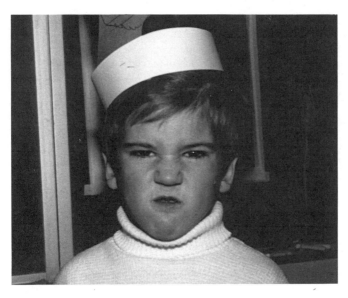

A "Wild Thing" gets ready to roar.

do not work for him. He finally finds a place to hide—and just in time to escape the hunters. It is a good science lesson in animal camouflage.

Y *Where the Wild Things Are,* MAURICE SENDAK. New York: Harper & Row, 1963. Max is sent to his room for punishment and imagines that he goes off to a land inhabited by Wild Things. This can be played as a circle story with the children in the circle becoming the trees that grow in Max's bedroom, the ocean Max sails, and the Wild Things that Max tames. See p. 216 for a technique to handle the "rumpus" scene.

O "The Wise Old Woman," YOSHIKO UCHIDA (40). In a Japanese village a cruel lord banishes anyone over age 71 from his village. A young farmer disobeys and hides his mother, who later saves the village with her wisdom. An excellent lesson in ageism.

O *The Woodcutter's Duck,* KRYSTYNA TURSKA. New York: Macmillan, 1972. Bartek outwits the army commander who wants the young man's pet duck in this Polish folktale.

O "The Youth Who Wanted to Shiver," ERIC CARLE (12). A young man wonders what shivering is and goes through some harrowing experiences in order to find out. But only when he is doused with minnows and cold water in his warm bed does he understand!

ELEVEN

Planning Drama Lessons and Units

Throughout this text, you have been given many ideas for drama activities and even some lesson plans. The activities have progressed from the simpler to the more complex. As you have seen, almost any of the single activities can be incorporated into classroom teaching at any time and with various curricular subjects. Lesson plans for some of the longer activities can range from 15 or 20 minutes to 45 minutes. Sometimes it has been recommended that a lesson plan cover two or more class periods.

But various situations exist for drama teaching. You may have the luxury of being able to teach drama lessons that last for a full hour. There may also be times when you will want to create an extended drama lesson or unit around a topic or theme. You may want to extend this lesson over several days' time, spending perhaps 20 or 30 minutes each day on an activity. In these cases, you will want to design a plan that is more than just a series of activities. This chapter is designed to help you in sequential lesson planning.

CONSIDERING GOALS

Some leaders may be in teaching situations where creative drama is taught as a theatre art. A major emphasis will then be on drama goals. Perhaps the children need encouragement in verbal communication and so verbal games or dialogue scenes are a priority. Or perhaps the children have had a number of experiences with narrative pantomimes and you want them to try pantomimes for guessing.

Even with an emphasis on drama goals, the classroom teacher is usually expected to combine drama with other areas of the curriculum. For this reason lessons often have a curricular-related theme or topic—such as Pilgrim life, westward movement, seasons, or current events—which ties the activities together. The specific learning objectives you want children to cover in these curricular topics will also be considered.

If personal development goals are part of your concern, they must also be taken into consideration as you plan the lesson. Perhaps the children need assistance in listening to one another, and you decide to use pantomime activities as a way of focusing their attention on each other. Perhaps you want them to work in small groups to develop socialization skills and cooperative behaviors.

SELECTING AND SEQUENCING THE ACTIVITIES

For beginning teachers, the recommended approach is to brainstorm a list of possible activities you could use for a given lesson or unit. Cover as wide a range as possible, including simple activities, narrative pantomime, pantomimes for guessing, verbal activities, story dramatization, and so forth. Then select the most appropriate ones and sequence them.

For an hour's lesson, generally three to five activities should be planned. Backup material or alternatives to the activities should also be included. Being overprepared will give you more flexibility as you see the group's response to the lesson.

The lesson should be built just as the structure of a story or a play takes shape. The first activity may be considered a warmup. For the specialist who teaches only drama, this activity may be crucial in developing rapport with the group. Warmup material should not be too difficult for the children to do and should put everyone in a relaxed mood, ready to work together. If you are working with a class that is already "high" at the beginning of the period, it might be appropriate to use warmup material that will expend their excess energy and calm them down. In this case it should also be highly structured and highly controlled. One activity should be used as the core of the lesson; this is generally the most challenging activity. Then the lesson should begin to taper off and end with a quieting activity.

As the activities progress they should become more challenging. To analyze levels of difficulty, consider again the chart on p. 26. For example, you might choose to do a pantomime game from the many listed in Chapter 7. According to variable 3 on the chart, pantomimes are easy activities compared with verbal. But they are also advanced, according to variable 5, since they require an audience of guessers. At the same time, it would probably be easier for students to perform a pantomime of their favorite sport in a count-and-freeze pantomime (p. 160) than it would be to participate in creating a group frozen picture (p. 161) of a current event. The former relies on the students' individual and personal interest (variable 4: solo playing) and something they are familiar with (variable 8: informational content), whereas the latter requires group decision making (variable 4: pair and group work) and a knowledge of current events (variable 8: higher data content). Although each activity is a pantomime for guessing, other variables affect the level of difficulty. You need not adhere slavishly to a thorough analysis of each activity you choose to do, but an overall consideration of the variables will help you sequence your activities so that students will experience maximum success.

You also need to determine (perhaps even as the lesson is progressing) just how much time and effort should be put into a given activity. It may take more than one playing to achieve the depth of involvement desired. At the same time, if the children are not responding to the material and you cannot see a way of combating the problem, then the activity may simply need to be dropped.

Remember that activities can be handled as run-throughs. Other times, you will want to challenge the children with further concentration. In the latter case the material will need to be broken down into smaller, more workable units.

Whenever an activity is repeated, a new challenge should be added. Otherwise there is the danger that the activity will "plateau" and begin to get stale. Ultimately, an activity with numerous repetitions and no new challenges simply becomes boring.

The end of the drama lesson should have a relaxing and calming effect on the group. The children should have a chance to think about the experience they have just had and to absorb it. Particularly if the class is to move on to seatwork after the drama lesson, a quieting activity is almost mandatory.

SAMPLE LESSON PLANS

Following are two sample lesson ideas for two different grade levels. They are presented as one approach to lesson planning. There are five activities in each, with alternative suggestions for some.

It is not intended that all the material necessarily be covered in a one-hour session. Rather, the plans provide the leader with flexibility and the opportunity to make decisions according to the group's responses during the playing. The lessons may also be used over a span of several days, spending perhaps twenty minutes each day on an activity. Time will also vary according to how familiar students already are with the information.

WINTER (SNOW)

Grade Level: K to 3

Objectives

1. Gain an understanding of the winter season and the various activities connected with it.

---

2. Experience creative movement in enacting winter activities.
3. Communicate and interpret nonverbal messages through pantomimes for guessing.
4. Dramatize a folktale with opportunities for pantomime and verbal interaction.
5. Experience characterization of selfish and generous qualities in the trees and the helplessness of the wounded bird.

Preparation and Materials

1. Copy of *The Snowy Day,* by Ezra Jack Keats (New York: Viking Penguin, 1962)
2. Copy of the folktale "Why the Evergreen Trees Keep Their Leaves in Winter" by Florence Holbrook (43)
3. (optional) Pictures of people engaged in various wintertime activities
4. (optional) Paper headbands for characters in the story dramatization of the folktale

Motivation and Warm-up Activity: *The Snowy Day* (play at desk or other limited area)

1. Open session with comments about winter and snow appropriate to the experiences of the children.
2. Read and show pictures from the book, a narrative pantomime story about a small boy who has his first memorable experience in the snow.
3. Narrate or side-coach the story, which includes dressing for snowy weather, building a snowman, making a snow angel, and being a mountain climber. The ending is the return indoors, taking off outdoor clothing, going to bed, and dreaming of a wonderful day in the snow. (*Suggestion:* End the playing with Peter in bed so that the children are seated. Omit playing the book's ending of going outdoors again on the following day.)

Half and Half Pantomime: Snow Activities (pantomimers in front of the class; guessers at their desks)

1. Discuss with children snow or winter activities not included in *The Snowy Day.* Show pictures of people engaged in winter activities such as ice skating, skiing, and feeding birds. Children add their own ideas to the discussion.
2. Divide class in half. One group performs a winter activity for the other group to guess. Depending on the maturity of the children, you may tell them what to pantomime or let them decide. Or have activities written on a few cards and let them draw one card.
3. Switch groups perhaps three times.

Story Sharing: "Why the Evergreen Trees Keep their Leaves in Winter" (at desks or in the story corner)

1. Tell or read this folktale of a little bird with a broken wing who cannot fly south with the other birds as winter approaches. When it seeks shelter in the trees, it is rejected as being too small and unimportant. Only the evergreens offer help. When the wind blows in the winter and causes all

the trees to lose their leaves, the frost king tells it to spare the leaves of the evergreen trees because of their kindness to the little bird.

2. End with a brief discussion of their reactions to the story and the various characters.

Story Dramatization

1. Review the story if you read it on a previous day.

2. Act out the sensory and emotion pantomimes and some of the brief verbal interaction from the story at desks or in a circle.

   a. Children are the various birds flying south for the winter. You briefly side-coach and narrate a few words about the various kinds of birds, the flapping of wings for the birds' takeoff, soaring to higher altitudes, and circling around one more time to encourage the little bird to join them or to say good-bye.

   b. (Continue side-coaching.) "Now you're the little bird with a broken wing trying to fly, sadly watching your friends leave. You feel the cold and puff out your feathers to protect yourself from the wind."

   c. "Now you are the trees—the birch, the oak, or the willow—standing proudly, feeling very important. You don't like strangers. Uh-oh, it looks as if someone's coming."

   d. Children continue to play the trees. You play the little bird (either by yourself or with a couple of children you choose quickly) and approach some of the trees and ask for permission to make a home in their branches. Some children will forget that they are the trees who say no to the little bird. (They may feel sorry for the bird, especially if you are convincing.) If this is the case, you can say "Oh, you must be one of the friendly evergreen trees."

   e. Now you can narrate or side-coach the trees briefly through the

The birds fly south for winter.

The wounded bird asks the maple trees for shelter.

experience of having the cold and wind touch their leaves, making them shake loose and fall a few at a time. You can play the wind yourself, coming near them and touching a few trees at a time ("This row" or "This table"). This is a nice control feature, as the trees must wait until you give them a signal. (*Note:* Little children may literally fall to signify the leaves falling. Be prepared to side-coach a slow motion fall should this be the case.)

f. "Now you are the friendly evergreen trees who are much kinder to the little bird. They offer their branches, protection from the north wind, and even berries to eat. And here comes the little bird with the broken wing." Again, you (by yourself or with two more children you select quickly) play the bird and interact briefly with a few of the trees.

g. To end these warm-ups, you can briefly narrate the ending of the story: "And so, the little bird was protected by the friendly evergreens and the frost king rewarded them. And that is why to this day evergreen trees keep their leaves in winter."

3. If the children want to continue, you may wish to put the story together as a small playlet. You may decide to play the wounded bird with the children in order to help with the dialogue. Or if the children are verbal and feel confident, you may only need to narrate a little from the sidelines.

Cast (in order of appearance)

wounded bird	played by two children (You may choose to play with them.)
birds	played by three children
unfriendly trees	groups of two or three each for an oak, a birch, and a willow
wind	two children
wind sound effects	played by the same three children who were the birds
frost king	two children

Discussion and Evaluation

Questions such as the following might be asked:

1. "Was the story clear?"
2. "Could we see a difference in the two kinds of trees—the selfish and the generous?"
3. "How many different tree shapes, or kinds of trees, did we see?"
4. "How could we tell the bird was wounded?"

Replaying of the Story, Switching Parts

Other Additions for Future Playing

If the children enjoy playing the story and repeat it several times, you might wish to encourage them to consider additions such as the following:

1. a scene showing how the bird's wing was wounded
2. a scene between the birds when the wounded bird's problem is discovered
3. a scene at the end, showing the return of the birds in the spring who discover the young bird well again

Quieting activity: *melting snow statue* (may be played at desks or in larger areas). Children are snow statues melting in the warm sun: "Your right arm melts the fastest and starts to slide down you round body. Now your left arm starts to slip. The sun gets higher in the sky and starts to melt your head. Your face starts to run, and your head begins to roll off. Then your shoulders begin to slump and your back begins to curve. You're only about half as tall as you once were. The sun is getting warmer, and now you're beginning to melt faster. You sink into a large lump. Now the lump starts to spread out until you are just a puddle of water."

If children are in larger areas of space, after a moment of relaxation you (as the frost king) may touch the children, one by one, as a signal to return to their seats.

ABRAHAM LINCOLN

Grade Level: 4 to 6

Objectives

1. Gain an understanding of some of the events in the life of an important American historical figure, recalling information previously studied.
2. Experience pantomiming and interpreting pantomime of occupations of Lincoln's time.
3. Enact dialogue situations appropriate to circumstances of Lincoln's presidency.

4. Dramatize in groups an interpretation of an episode in Lincoln's life demonstrating personal characteristic of honesty.

Preparation and Materials

1. Copies of Abraham Lincoln biographies. Suggestions:

   Abraham Lincoln, INGRI D'AULAIRE and EDGAR PARIN. New York: Double-day, 1939.

   Abraham Lincoln, Friend of the People, CLARA INGRAM JUDSON. Chicago: Follett, 1950.

   . . . If You Grew Up with Abraham Lincoln, ANN McGOVERN. New York: Four Winds Press, 1966.

2. Copy of the poem "Nancy Hanks," by Rosemary Carr and Stephen Vincent Benét (4, 57)

3. Picture of the Lincoln Memorial in Washington, D.C., or other Lincoln statues

4. (optional) Other pictures of Lincoln which might motivate or illustrate points in the lesson

Warm-up Activity: "Nancy Hanks" (Play at desks)

1. Read the poem by Rosemary Carr and Stephen Vincent Benét. It is written as if Nancy Hanks, Abe Lincoln's mother, is speaking. It suggests that she comes back to today's world and wonders how her son made out.

2. Then you, perhaps joined by some other students, can play the role of Nancy (or Tom, Lincoln's father) and ask questions of the rest of the class, who are to convince you that Abe did, indeed, "get on." If students are verbal, you may let them handle the dialogue alone while you play a moderator. Nancy should pretend to find it difficult to believe all the information about Lincoln. Her objections might be "But when I died, Abe and his pa were barely making it in that log cabin in Indiana. How could he have become a president?" "But we were so poor, Abe couldn't even go to school more than just a few days. Where'd he learn to read and write?" Other points of information she might ask: "What happened to Tom, Abe's father?" "What did Abe look like when he grew up?" "Do you have a picture of him?" and so on.

Count-and-Freeze Pantomimes: Jobs Lincoln held (Use front of classroom.)

1. Review, if needed, the various jobs held by Lincoln during his lifetime (rail splitter, postmaster, carpenter, peddler, surveyor, sawmiller, lawyer, storekeeper, farmer, riverboat driver, and president).

2. Several students at a time will act out one of these occupations for guessing.

   Option A: Do a build-a-place pantomime of Lincoln's log cabin in Indiana or a general store where Lincoln worked. Refer to texts above for data and illustrations.

   Option B: In groups, create frozen pictures of famous scenes in Lincoln's life.

Group Scenes: "Honest Abe"

1. Review or read to the class some of the stories or legends about how Lincoln got the nickname "Honest Abe." There are several stories, including his walking six miles to return six pennies to a woman who overpaid him for some cloth and the amount of time he spent working to pay off a library book he inadvertently damaged.
2. Students may reenact one of these scenes, showing their version of what they think might have happened. Or students might create a new story, based on data they know about Lincoln and the time period in which he lived, to demonstrate how someone might come to be known as a particularly honest person.
3. Groups of approximately five students each discuss and plan a scene. Share scenes in front of the classroom. Scenes may be in pantomime or may include dialogue.

Dialogue Scene: The Open Door Policy

1. Review or read about Abraham Lincoln's belief that everyone should have a right to talk to the President. There were always crowds of people to see him, and he made every effort to see as many as possible.
2. Discuss: What kinds of people would come to see the President, and what reasons would they have? How would Lincoln be able to talk to so many people?
3. Students decide who they are and what their reason for seeing the President might be. If students work in pairs and groups, more will have a chance to participate. Alternative plan: Have person's (or group's) role and reason for visit written on cards for students to select.
4. Set the scene in the White House (the front of the classroom) and the waiting room (students' desks). You may want to set a time limit on each person's visit. Some interviews may also have to be "postponed" to a later date if your allotted time ends before children have a chance to play their ideas.
5. You may need to play Lincoln at first to guide the playing. The drama can be enhanced if you introduce others into the scene—"Let me get Mrs. Lincoln, who will want to meet you, since you've come all the way from Illinois . . ." or "Here's my son Tad who's just about your age . . ."—and draw volunteers from the "audience." You will need to find ways to end each visit tactfully, diplomatically, and appropriately.
6. If, or when, you turn over Lincoln's role to a student, you can play a presidential aide and be on hand to assist when needed. In this role you can monitor the "crowd" and introduce those who are waiting to see the President. In this role, you can also introduce additional people into the scene: for example, a photographer who wants to get a picture of the many people who come to see the President. (This may be done as frozen pictures.) *Note:* You may need to help students with information about cameras of the period.
7. Eventually students will take the presidential aide role themselves. Then you may choose to introduce other kinds of tension or problems by entering a scene as, for example, the secretary of state, who says Lincoln is late for a Cabinet meeting. The secretary might also be upset over Lincoln's spending so much time with people, which should encourage the student playing Lincoln, as well as others, to defend this policy.

Quieting Activity: Lincoln statue (Play at desks)

1. Show class a picture of the Lincoln Memorial or other Lincoln statue.
2. On a count of 10, the students slowly transform from themselves into the statue.

   Option: Class could slowly become a statue of Lincoln at any stage of his life in an important moment. As the students are frozen, you could quietly comment on the various positions the students are in and possibly identify some of the scenes.

EVALUATION IN CREATIVE DRAMA

In teaching creative drama in the elementary grades, we provide opportunities for children to participate in dramatic games, pantomime, verbal games, storytelling, story dramatization, or any one of the myriad of activities covered in this book. It is important, however, to assess children's progress along the way. Only then will you know the successes of your program and be able to plan the direction of subsequent lessons.

The most widely-used method of evaluation in creative drama is class discussion, similar to those suggested throughout this text. If videotape equipment is available, you may want to use it periodically to help children evaluate themselves and to assist you in observing the children more carefully. However, you may also be required to make a more formal written evaluation. The next section will consider this topic.

Cautions in Evaluating

Although it cannot be argued that teachers must check students' progress in all educational ventures, there are some cautions you should be reminded of. First of all, many educational goals are difficult to pinpoint, let alone define. Drama is no exception. Often in the process of explorative learning, undefined goals emerge and are achieved unexpectedly. Ironically, those serendipitous goals or objectives may turn out to be even more significant than any of your predefined ones.

In addition if you design a drama activity around, or limit it to, only one or two skills or objectives, you may overlook the larger goals of instruction, the chance to explore drama experiences that emerge spontaneously, or even the opportunity to just play with ideas in a creative way. Furthermore, as is the case with many educational goals, many drama goals will be beyond precise measurement. In the attempt to measure a skill in a precise way, you could lose sight of other possible outcomes.

Being alert to these potential problems can save you considerable time and frustration. The mark of a creative and effective teacher is one who lets the children and their needs define the direction of the lessons rather than the other way around. You should also be alert to the learnings the children make *when they happen* rather than looking for them *only* when you schedule yourself to do so.

Teacher Evaluation

Every teaching situation is different and will probably require a little different format. The following checklist is presented as a *sample* only. It is not intended that all items are needed for any one activity or lesson. Nor is the list complete for all activities, since it does not include specific curricular objectives. For example, if you have studied pioneer log cabins and the students play Build a Place, constructing a cabin in pantomime, you will probably expect that students will include furniture and household goods appropriate for the setting and the time period. You may then wish to include that objective in that day's evaluation. Finally, many of the goals will also need special consideration or adaptation depending on individual children's needs, such as the gifted, those with handicaps, or those with other individual differences.

Since you will be involved with the children during the drama lessons, it will be necessary for you to evaluate them at a later time, preferably as soon after a lesson has been taught as possible. A periodic assessment is usually as effective as keeping a daily record and should enable you to see students' growth and progression more readily.

You may choose simply to *check* the items you see a child demonstrating favorably and record a *minus* for those that are not favorably performed. What is not applicable may simply be left blank. Or you may choose to use a rating scale (for example: 1 poor, 2 fair, 3 good, and 4 superior) for each item, marking only those that are applicable.

By placing all the students' names lengthwise along the top of the paper, you should easily be able to make your report on one sheet. Another option is to focus on only a few students at a time in any one assessment. This should be less overwhelming than trying to evaluate every student after each lesson.

DRAMA SKILLS AND BEHAVIORS CHECKLIST

Date: Lesson Title: Students' Names

BODY MOVEMENT AND PANTOMIME SKILLS

 demonstrates coordination and control
 reacts with appropriate sensory awareness
 uses appropriate gestures/facial expression
 communicates ideas and concepts through pantomime
 "reads" others' nonverbal communication
  with acceptable accuracy

VERBAL EXPRESSION

 speaks clearly and distinctly
 uses vocal variety and inflection
 improvises dialogue appropriately

CONCENTRATION

---

follows directions; focuses on tasks
sustains involvement in playing

IMAGINATION

contributes original ideas
reacts spontaneously

EVALUATION AND CRITICAL ANALYSIS

makes constructive contributions
incorporates suggested improvements
into playing

SOCIAL AWARENESS AND COOPERATION

contributes to group effort
listens/observes with appreciation

Children's Self Evaluation

In addition to the teacher's evaluation instrument, it is important that the children's self-evaluation, as individuals and as a group, be encouraged. Aesthetic judgments are developed as they are given voice. Children need opportunities to make and defend their points of view with each other. And since not even so-called educated critics of the arts would agree with each other, children may not either. Neither should group consensus be considered the final word in the matter. Lone defenders of a viewpoint are often proved more accurate or insightful at a later date.

Likewise it is also true that tastes change and develop. Over a period of time, we all change our minds and directions about what appeals to us and what bores us. We may adopt the popular style of the day and then later reject it with as much energy as we first embraced it. Children too need opportunities to experiment with varying artistic ideas before they can come to any conclusions about their judgments.

For self evaluation, young children may be questioned orally in a brief conference. However, it is also possible to have older students write a periodic self-evaluation. Students may

1. circle "usually," "some of the time," or "hardly ever" for each item.
2. write out their answers, perhaps even indicating "why" or "why not"

Questions might be similar to these:

1. Do I participate and contribute to the activities?
2. Do I stay focused and concentrate when I am playing?
3. Am I a good observer or audience member for my classmates?
4. Do I participate and contribute to group planning?
5. Am I careful to consider my classmates' feelings?
6. Do I offer original ideas?

These evaluation formats should not result in using creative drama as a routine drill. Rather, drama experiences should be enriching to the entire curriculum and enjoyable for all.

FOR THE COLLEGE STUDENT

1. Select a curricular theme or topic. Brainstorm with a group of your classmates the many drama activities the theme suggests. Working together or individually, select five activities from your list for a drama lesson, sequencing them appropriately. Use the sample lesson plans as a model.
2. Design and teach a lesson plan to your classmates or to a group of children. What changes did you make in the lesson plan as a result of the group's responses? Analyze afterward your successes and ways you could improve.
3. Discuss with your classmates various ways of evaluation one might use in creative drama. Refer to evaluation methods used in other curricular subjects. Which ones might serve as useful models for creative drama?
4. Construct your own evaluation checklist
   a. for a general use in creative drama
   b. for a specific lesson plan
   Use the evaluation checklist after working with your classmates or with a group of children. Discuss and compare your ideas with your classmates.

Story and Poetry Anthologies and Books for Dramatization

Throughout the text, numbers in parentheses have referred to these correspondingly numbered anthologies and children's novels.

(1) *All the Silver Pennies*, BLANCHE JENNINGS THOMPSON. New York: Macmillan, 1967.

(2) *Anansi, the Spider Man*, PHILIP M. SHERLOCK. New York: Thomas Y. Crowell, 1954.

(3) *Anthology of Children's Literature*, 5th ed., EDNA JOHNSON, EVELYN R. SICKELS, FRANCES C. SAYERS, and CAROLYN HOROVITZ. Boston: Houghton Mifflin, 1977.

(4) *The Arbuthnot Anthology of Children's Literature*, 4th ed., MAY HILL ARBUTHNOT, rev. by Zena Sutherland. Glenview, Ill.: Scott, Foresman, 1976.

(5) *Beyond the Clapping Mountains*, CHARLES E. GILLHAM. New York: Macmillan, 1964.

(6) *Catch a Little Rhyme*, EVE MERRIAM. New York: Atheneum, 1966.

(7) *Catch Me a Wind*, PATRICIA HUBBELL. New York: Atheneum, 1968.

(8) *Children's Literature for Dramatization: An Anthology*, GERALDINE BRAIN SIKS. New York: Harper & Row, 1964.

(9) *Cinnamon Seed*, JOHN T. MOORE. Boston: Houghton Mifflin, 1967.

(10) *The Crack in the Wall and Other Terribly Weird Tales*, GEORGE MENDOZA. New York: Dial Press, 1968.

(11) *The Dancing Kettle and Other Japanese Folk Tales*, YOSHIKO UCHIDA. New York: Harcourt Brace Jovanovich, 1949.

(12) *Eric Carle's Story Book: Seven Tales by the Brothers Grimm*. New York: Franklin Watts, 1976.

(13) *Favorite Fairy Tales Told in England*, VIRGINIA HAVILAND. Boston: Little, Brown, 1959.

(14) *Favorite Fairy Tales Told in Scotland*, VIRGINIA HAVILAND. Boston: Little, Brown, 1963.

(15) *Fire on the Mountain and Other Ethiopian Stories*, HAROLD COURLANDER and WOLF LESLAU. New York: Holt, Rinehart and Winston, 1959.

(16) *Folk Tales of Latin America*, ed. Shirlee P. Newman. Indianapolis, Ind.: Bobbs-Merrill, 1962.

(17) *Grandfather Tales*, RICHARD CHASE. Boston: Houghton Mifflin 1948.

(18) *Gwot! Horribly Funny Hairticklers,* GEORGE MENDOZA. New York: Harper & Row, 1967.

(19) *The Hat-Shaking Dance and Other Tales from the Gold Coast,* HAROLD COURLANDER and ALBERT KOFI PREMPEH. San Diego: Harcourt Brace Jovanovich, 1957.

(20) *The Hare and the Bear and Other Stories,* YASUE MAIYAGAWA. New York: Parents' Magazine Press, 1971.

(21) *Jack Tales,* RICHARD C. CHASE. Boston: Houghton Mifflin, 1943.

(22) *Just So Stories,* RUDYARD KIPLING. New York: Rand McNally, 1982.

(23) *Let's Marry Said the Cherry,* N.M. BODEKER. New York: Atheneum, 1974.

(24) *A Light in the Attic,* SHEL SILVERSTEIN. New York: Harper & Row, 1981.

(25) *Lois Lenski's Big Big Book of Mr. Small,* LOIS LENSKI. New York: Derrydale Books, 1985.

(26) *Medicine for Melancholy,* RAY BRADBURY. New York: Doubleday, 1959.

(27) *Mouse Tales,* ARNOLD LOBEL. New York: Harper & Row, 1972.

(28) *The New Kid on the Block,* JACK PRELUTSKY. New York: Greenwillow Books, 1984.

(29) *Night Noises and Other Mole and Troll Stories,* TONY JOHNSTON. New York: Putnam Publishing Group, 1977.

(30) *Nobody is Perfick,* BERNARD WABER. Boston: Houghton Mifflin 1971.

(31) *Now We Are Six,* A.A. MILNE. New York: E.P. Dutton & Co., 1927.

(32) *Oh, What Nonsense!* selected by William Cole. New York: Viking Penguin, 1966.

(33) *Once the Hodja,* ALICE GEER KELSEY. New York: Longman, 1943.

(34) *On City Streets,* ed. Nancy Larrick. New York: M. Evans & Co., 1968.

(35) *Piping Down the Valleys Wild,* ed. Nancy Larrick. New York: Dell Publishing, 1968.

(36) *The Random House Book of Poetry for Children,* selected by Jack Prelutsky. New York: Random House, 1983.

(37) *Reflections on a Gift of Watermelon Pickle,* ed. Stephen Dunning, Edward Lueders, and Hugh Smith. Glenview, Ill.: Scott, Foresman, 1966.

(38) *Ride with the Sun,* ed. Harold Courlander. New York: McGraw-Hill, 1955.

(39) *The Riverside Anthology of Children's Literature,* 6th ed., ed. Judith Saltman. Boston: Houghton Mifflin, 1985.

(40) *The Sea of Gold and Other Tales from Japan,* YOSHIKO UCHIDA. New York: Charles Scribner's Sons, 1965.

(41) *The Sneetches and Other Stories,* DR. SEUSS. New York: Random House, 1961.

(42) *Some Haystacks Don't Even Have Any Needle,* compiled by Stephen Dunning, Edward Lueders, and Hugh Smith. Glenview, Ill.: Scott, Foresman, 1969.

(43) *Stories to Dramatize,* ed. WINIFRED WARD. New Orleans: Anchorage Press, 1981.

(44) *Tales from the Cheyennes,* GRACE JACKSON PENNEY. Boston: Houghton Mifflin, 1953.

(45) *Tall Tales from the High Hills,* ELLIS CREDLE. Camden, N.J.: Thomas Nelson, 1957.

(46) *There Is No Rhyme for Silver,* EVE MERRIAM. New York: Atheneum, 1962.

(47) *The Thing at the Foot of the Bed and Other Scary Tales,* MARIA LEACH. New York: World Publishing, 1959.

(48) *Thunder in the Mountains: Legends of Canada,* HILDA MARY HOOKE. Don Mills, Ont.: Oxford University Press, 1947.

(49) *The Tiger and the Rabbit and Other Tales,* PURA BELPRE. Philadelphia: J.B. Lippincott, 1965.

(50) *The Time-Ago Tales of Jahdu,* VIRGINIA HAMILTON. New York: Macmillan, 1969.

(51) *Time for Poetry,* rev. ed., MAY HILL ARBUTHNOT. Glenview, Ill.: Scott, Foresman, 1959.

(52) *Twenty Tellable Tales,* MARGARET READ MACDONALD. Bronx, N.Y.: H.W. Wilson, 1986.

(53) *Where the Sidewalk Ends,* SHEL SILVERSTEIN. New York: Harper & Row, 1974.

(54) *The Wicked Tricks of Tyl Uilenspiegel,* JAY WILLIAMS. New York: Four Winds Press, 1978.

(55) *Windsong*, CARL SANDBURG. New York: Harcourt Brace Jovanovich, 1960.

(56) *World Tales for Creative Dramatics and Storytelling*, BURDETTE S. FITZGERALD. Englewood Cliffs, N.J.: Prentice-Hall, 1962.

(57) *The World Treasury of Children's Literature*, book 3, ed. Clifton Fadiman. Boston: Little, Brown, 1985.

(58) *Yertle the Turtle and Other Stories*, DR. SEUSS. New York: Random House, 1958.

BOOKS FOR DRAMATIZATION

The following longer books are highly recommended for extended dramatization work. They are only a representative sampling of the fine literature available for today's children. Some are older classics that remain as viable today as they were when first printed. Others have been selected for their historical and geographical settings, relationship to other areas of the curriculum, social themes, and their variety of heroes and heroines.

The books are listed alphabetically according to title. Suggested grade levels are indicated in the left-hand margin.

(59) M–O *Alice's Adventures in Wonderland*, LEWIS CARROLL. New York: Macmillan, 1960. The classical stories of Alice's adventures after tumbling down a rabbit hole into a land of unusual inhabitants and circumstances.

(60) M *All Alone*, CLAIRE HUCHET BISHOP. New York: Viking Penguin, 1953. Two boys who are in charge of the herds in the French Alps violate the rule of constant vigil.

(61) O *Amos Fortune, Free Man*, ELIZABETH YATES. New York: E.P. Dutton, 1950. The true biography of a slave who struggles for and eventually gains his freedom.

(62) M–O *. . . And Now, Miguel*, JOSEPH KRUMGOLD. New York: Thomas Y. Crowell, 1953. The story of a sheepherding family in New Mexico is presented.

(63) Y–M *A Bear Called Paddington*, MICHAEL BOND. Boston: Houghton Mifflin, 1958. A charming humanlike bear arrives in London and is adopted by a family. Life becomes full of adventures that border on the disastrous. Sequels are also available.

(64) M–O *Ben and Me*, ROBERT LAWSON. Boston: Little, Brown, 1939. The ever-popular and amusing story of how a mouse helped Benjamin Franklin with his many inventions and achievements.

(65) M–O *The Black Cauldron*, LLOYD ALEXANDER. New York: Holt, Rinehart and Winston, 1965. Taran and his friends must find and destroy the evil Black Cauldron.

(66) M *The Borrowers*, MARY NORTON. San Diego: Harcourt Brace Jovanovich, 1953. Life is full of adventures for the little people who live under the floorboards of the house and borrow small objects to furnish their home. Sequels are also available.

(67) M–O *By the Great Horn Spoon!* SID FLEISCHMAN. Boston: Little, Brown, 1963. A young boy and his aunt's butler stow away on a ship headed for California gold in this humorous, historical fiction adventure.

(68) M *Carolina's Courage*, ELIZABETH YATES. New York: E.P. Dutton, 1964. Carolina, a pioneer girl on a wagon train, is able to assist in the advance through Indian territory.

(69) M *Charlie and the Chocolate Factory*, revised edition, ROALD DAHL. New York: Alfred A. Knopf, 1973. A young boy wins the opportunity to tour a famous and unusual candy factory owned by the equally famous and unusual Willy Wonka.

(70) Y–M *Charlotte's Web*, E.B. WHITE. New York: Harper & Row, 1952. Wilbur the pig, with

the help of his barnyard friends and most particularly Charlotte the spider, develops into a most unique pig.

(71) Y–M *Christmas on the Mayflower*, WILMA P. HAYS. New York: Coward-McCann, 1956. A dramatic conflict is presented when the crew of the *Mayflower* wants to return to England before the safety of the Pilgrims in a new land is assured.

(72) Y–M *The Courage of Sarah Noble*, ALICE DALGLIESH. New York: Charles Scribner's Sons, 1954. The true story of a little girl who bravely accompanies her father into the Connecticut territory in the early 1700s.

(73) O *Danny the Champion of the World*, ROALD DAHL. New York: Alfred A. Knopf, 1975. Danny and his father, a widower, manage a filling station and live in a nearby caravan in England. Their love and respect for each other is a strong theme throughout the book along with a marvelous adventure of poaching pheasants, which eventually involves many villagers.

(74) Y–M *The Drinking Gourd*, F.N. MONJO. New York: Harper & Row, 1969. A New England boy learns of the Underground Railroad in the 1850s.

(75) M–O *Ellen Tebbits*, BEVERLY CLEARY. New York: William Morrow, 1951, 1979. Life never seems to be simple for young Ellen, who experiences misunderstanding along with her many other adventures. Ellen is a typical American child of the more innocent days of the 1940s, but her experiences are as popular with children today as they ever were.

(76) M–O *Fantastic Mr. Fox*, ROALD DAHL. New York: Alfred A. Knopf, 1970. Mr. Fox and his family, along with other burrowing animals, outwit three farmers who are out to destroy him once and for all in this suspenseful, fast-moving tale full of humorous characters.

(77) O *The Forgotten Door*, ALEXANDER KEY. Philadelphia: Westminster Press, 1965. In this intriguing science-fiction story, Jon, a boy from another world, falls through a forgotten door into this world. Because he is different, both he and the family who befriend him must deal with the fears and prejudices of the less tolerant citizens of the community.

(78) M–O *From the Mixed-Up Files of Mrs. Basil E. Frankweiler*, ELAINE L. KONIGSBERG. New York: Atheneum, 1967. In this modern mystery adventure Claudia and her brother run away to live for a week in New York City's Metropolitan Museum of Art and make an exciting discovery about a particular statue.

(79) O *The Great Brain*, JOHN D. FITZGERALD. New York: Dial Press, 1967. This popular autobiographical account of the author's brother, a lovable schemer, has its setting in the late 1800s in Utah. The sequels are equally appealing.

(80) M *The Great Cheese Conspiracy*, JEAN VAN LEEUWEN. New York: Random House, 1969. A gang of mice, who have learned about burglaries from old gangster movies, decide to rob a cheese store.

(81) M *The Great Quillow*, JAMES THURBER. San Diego: Harcourt Brace Jovanovich, 1944. Quillow outwits a giant and saves his town.

(82) M *The Half-Pint Jinni*, MAURICE DOLBIER. New York: Random House, 1948. There are humorous and exciting adventures in store for those who know a small genie who can grant only half a wish.

(83) M *Harriet the Spy*, LOUISE FITZHUGH. New York: Harper & Row, 1964. To counteract the loneliness caused by affluent and indifferent parents, Harriet keeps a notebook on her observations of people.

(84) M–O *Henry Huggins*, BEVERLY CLEARY. New York: William Morrow, 1950, 1978. The ever-popular antics of a young boy and his dog Ribsy are presented with humor and warmth. It is now available in Spanish, with translation by Argentina Palacios, (William Morrow, 1983).

(85) M–O *Henry Reed, Inc.*, KEITH ROBERTSON. New York: Viking Penguin, 1968. A humorous story of an enterprising boy and his friend Midge that provides delight to older elementary readers.

(86) O *The High King*, LLOYD ALEXANDER. New York: Holt, Rinehart and Winston, 1968. This last of a five-book chronicle about Prydain, an imaginary realm, can stand independently of the others in the series. Taran, an assistant pig keeper, gathers forces to defeat Arwan, the ruler of the Land of Dead. Although not easy reading, this book is recognized as a classic in combining fantasy within a historic time period.

(87) M–O *Homer Price*, ROBERT McCLOSKEY. New York: Viking Penguin, 1943, 1971. A young boy in a small midwestern town manages to capture robbers with the help of his pet skunk and to solve a problem of too many doughnuts among other adventures.

(88) M–O *How to Eat Fried Worms*, THOMAS ROCKWELL. New York: Franklin Watts, 1973. Billy Forrester makes a bet that he can eat 15 worms in 15 days for $50. The plot centers on the many schemes the other bettor uses to keep Billy from being successful.

(89) M *James and the Giant Peach*, ROALD DAHL. New York: Alfred A. Knopf, 1961. Inside a magic peach, James finds many insect friends, and together they have a fantastic journey across the Atlantic from England to New York.

(90) M *John Billington*, CLYDE ROBERT BULLA. New York: Thomas Y. Crowell, 1956. This is an historical fiction account of a young boy who was one of the passengers on the *Mayflower.*

(91) O *Johnny Tremain*, ESTHER FORBES. Boston: Houghton Mifflin, 1943. Johnny, a young silver apprentice in Boston, struggles to maturity during the 1770s in this classical book of historical fiction.

(92) O *King Arthur and His Knights, The Story of*, HOWARD PYLE. New York: Charles Scribner's Sons, 1954. The legendary king of England and the many tales of his equally legendary knights are presented.

(93) M–O The Little House series, LAURA INGALLS WILDER. New York: Harper & Row. These several books document the classical and true stories of an American pioneer family in various midwestern locations. They also inspired a long-running and popular television series.

(94) M *Mary Jemison: Seneca Captive*, JEANNE LE MONNIER GARDNER. San Diego: Harcourt Brace Jovanovich, 1966. The exciting biography of a courageous white girl who was captured and adopted by Indians in the late 1700s.

(95) O *Mrs. Frisby and the Rats of NIMH*, ROBERT C. O'BRIEN. New York: Atheneum, 1971. Laboratory rats from the National Institute of Mental Health seek to make a better world for themselves.

(96) M *Mr. Popper's Penguins*, RICHARD and FLORENCE ATWATER. Boston: Little, Brown, 1938. Still a favorite after many years, this story tells of Mr. Popper who, after writing of his interest in South Pole expeditions, receives a gift of a penguin from Admiral Drake. With a zoo's gift of a mate for the penguin, they increase to twelve. The Poppers train and take the penguins on the theatrical circuit in order to make enough money to care for them.

(97) Y–M *The Mouse and the Motorcycle*, BEVERLY CLEARY. New York: William Morrow, 1965. A mouse named Ralph has interesting adventures with a toy motorcycle. Sequels of Ralph's adventures are also available.

(98) O *My Brother Sam Is Dead*, CHRISTOPHER and JAMES COLLIER. New York: Four Winds Press, 1974. An American family in Connecticut during the Revolutionary War are on opposing sides—the Tories versus the Patriots. Events before, during, and after the war change their attitudes.

(99) M–O *Old Yeller*, FRED GIPSON. New York: Harper & Row, 1956. Set in the 1860s in

Texas, this story focuses on the comic and heroic behaviors of a mangy dog who strays into a boy's life.

(100) M–O *The Peterkin Papers*, LUCRETIA HALE. Boston: Houghton Mifflin, 1924. This collection of classical, nonsensical stories of a family and their absurd problems remains as popular today as it was a hundred years ago when it first appeared.

(101) M *Peter Pan*, SIR JAMES BARRIE. New York: Charles Scribner's Sons, 1950. The classic story of a boy who does not want to grow up.

(102) O *The Phantom Tollbooth*, NORTON JUSTER. New York: Random House, 1961. Milo has many adventures in a fantastical land. He tries to be the mediator between two kings who are having a dispute over the importance of mathematics compared with language.

(103) M–O *Pinocchio, The Adventures of*, C. COLLODI. New York: Lothrop, Lee & Shepard Books, 1983. The 100th-anniversary edition of this famous puppet who longs to be a real boy.

(104) M–O *Pippi Longstocking*, ASTRID LINDGREN. New York: Viking Penguin, 1950. Pippi, a superhuman girl whose widowed father is off at sea, lives by herself and is independent. Her style of living and her adventures are unorthodox and appealing to children who must follow other rules.

(105) O *The Pushcart War*, JEAN MERRILL. Reading, Mass.: Addison-Wesley, 1964. In a humorous spoof on the traffic problems in New York City, pushcart vendors, who are being overrun by the Mighty Mammoths (truck drivers), start a war with peashooters.

(106) Y–M *Rabbit Hill*, ROBERT LAWSON. New York: Viking Penguin, 1944. The small animals are concerned about the "new folks" who are moving into the empty house.

(107) O *Robin Hood, The Merry Adventures of*, HOWARD PYLE. New York: Charles Scribner's Sons, 1946. The legendary accounts of the outlaw-hero of England are presented.

(108) M *The Robot and Rebecca*, JANE YOLEN. New York: Alfred A. Knopf, 1980. In the year 2121, Rebecca Jason receives a robot for her ninth birthday. With its help, she is able to solve a mystery involving twin children and alien creatures.

(109) M *Sam, Bangs and Moonshine*, EVALINE NESS. New York: Holt, Rinehart and Winston, 1966. Sam, a fisherman's daughter, makes up fanciful stories. Trouble begins when she tells her friend about her mermaid mother.

(110) M *Sarah Whitcher's Story*, ELIZABETH YATES. New York: E.P. Dutton, 1971. Based on a true account, this story is of a pioneer girl in New Hampshire who becomes lost in the woods for four days.

(111) O *The Secret Soldier: The Story of Deborah Sampson*, ANN McGOVERN. New York: Scholastic Book Services, 1975. A true story of a young woman who disguised herself as a young man and fought in the Revolutionary War is recounted by a well-known historical writer.

(112) O *Shadow of a Bull*, MAIA WOJCIECHOWSKA. New York: Atheneum, 1964. Everyone expects Manolo to be a great Spanish bullfighter like his father, but he makes his own choice in the end.

(113) M *Something Queer Is Going On*, ELIZABETH LEVY. New York: Dell Publishing/Delacorte Press, 1973. Fletcher, the basset hound, has been kidnapped, say Jill and Gwen. Their search for him leads them to a dog commercial for television in this slim volume that can be handled almost like a short story.

(114) Y–M *Squaps, the Moonling*, URSINA ZIEGLER. New York: Atheneum, 1969. A shy moonling hangs on the suit of an astronaut and is taken back to earth. He can only say "squaps," he likes the rain, and he can float when there is a full moon. This story will be particularly enjoyable to E.T. lovers.

(115) Y–M *Sumi's Prize*, YOSHIKO UCHIDA. New York: Charles Scribner's Sons, 1964. Sumi, a little Japanese girl, is the only girl to enter a kite-flying contest.

(116) M *Tales of a Fourth Grade Nothing*, JUDY BLUME. New York: E.P. Dutton, 1972. Peter is convinced his life is worth nothing with a little brother like Fudge who does everything wrong, including eating Peter's pet turtle.

(117) M–O *This Time, Tempe Wick?* PATRICIA GAUCH. New York: Coward-McCann, 1974. A true story about a girl named Tempe Wick who lived in New Jersey during the Revolutionary War. Forgotten and disillusioned Pennsylvania soldiers try to rob Tempe of her horse so that they can return home, but she outwits them in a clever way.

(118) Y–M *Thy Friend, Obadiah*, BRINTON TURKLE. New York: Viking Penguin, 1972. A young early-American Quaker boy tries to reject a friendly and persistent seagull.

(119) M–O *Tom Sawyer, The Adventures of*, SAMUEL CLEMENS (Mark Twain). Many editions. The American classic of a Missouri boy's adventures on the Mississippi River in the 1800s.

(120) O *Treasure Island*, ROBERT LOUIS STEVENSON. New York: Charles Scribner's Sons, 1981 (reissued). Young Jim Hawkins and the villainous but appealing rogue Long John Silver sail to a tropic isle and become involved in a climactic battle for treasure.

(121) O *Tuck Everlasting*, NATALIE BABBIT. New York: Farrar, Straus & Giroux, 1975. The Tuck family discover they are incapable of dying after drinking from a spring in a strange forest. Twelve-year-old Winnie Foster, who has run away from home, meets Jesse Tuck and falls in love. She plans to reunite with him at age seventeen, but learns she must decide between mortality and immortality.

(122) O *Twenty and Ten*, CLAIRE HUCHET BISHOP. New York: Viking Penguin, 1953. When Nazi soldiers come to a mountain retreat in search of 10 Jewish children, 20 fifth-grade French children become involved in hiding them in a cave in this adventure based on a true story.

(123) M *Venture for Freedom*, RUBY ZAGOREN. New York: Dell Publishing, 1969. The son of an African king, Venture, was sold into slavery in America in the 1700s. This account is based on his autobiography.

(124) M–O *The Wheel on the School*, MEINDERT DEJONG. New York: Harper & Row, 1964. The children of Shora, a little fishing village in the Netherlands, involve the whole town in their project to get the storks to return.

(125) M–O *While the Horses Galloped to London*, MABEL WATTS. New York: Parents' Magazine Press, 1973. On his carriage ride to London, Sherman guards a cooking pot which he uses to outwit the outlaw, Rough Roger.

(126) M–O *Wind in the Willows*, KENNETH GRAHAME. New York: Charles Scribner's Sons, 1935. The charming adventures of Mole, Rat, Badger, and Toad never grow old. Toad is assisted by his friends in conquering his craze for motorcars and in gaining back his family estate from the Wild Wood animals who take it over when Toad is imprisoned for driving violations. (See also the more recent edition with illustrations by Michael Hague. New York: Holt, Rinehart and Winston, 1980.)

(127) Y–M *Winnie-the-Pooh*, A.A. MILNE. New York: E.P. Dutton, 1954. Winnie, a stuffed bear, and his animal friends have many delightful days. See also *The House at Pooh Corners* for more adventures.

(128) O *The Witch of Blackbird Pond*, ELIZABETH GEORGE SPEARE. Boston: Houghton Mifflin, 1958. After leaving her home in Barbados, Kit Tyler feels out of place in a Puritan community in Connecticut. Her spirited personality arouses suspicion, and she finds herself accused of witchcraft.

(129) O *The Wonderful Wizard of Oz*, FRANK L. BAUM. New York: Macmillan, 1962 (reprint). A Kansas cyclone carries Dorothy and her dog Toto to the Land of Oz where she makes friends with a scarecrow, a tin man, and a lion.

(130) M–O *A Wrinkle in Time*, MADELINE L'ENGLE. New York: Farrar, Straus & Giroux, 1962.

Children search for their father who has been in outer space for over a year on a classified mission. Traveling through time they land on the planet Camazotz, which is under the rule of a black force, IT, where their father is a prisoner. Sequels are *A Wind in the Door* and *A Swiftly Tilting Planet.*

Index